New Forest

The Forging of a Landscape

Hadrian Cook

WIND*gather*
PRESS

Windgather Press is an imprint of Oxbow Books

Published in the United Kingdom in 2018 by
OXBOW BOOKS
The Old Music Hall, 106–108 Cowley Road, Oxford, OX4 1JE

and in the United States by
OXBOW BOOKS
1950 Lawrence Road, Havertown, PA 19083

Paperback Edition: ISBN 978-1-911188-19-3
Digital Edition: ISBN 978-1-911188-20-9 (epub)

A CIP record for this book is available from the British Library

For a complete list of Windgather titles, please contact:

United Kingdom
Oxbow Books
Telephone (01865) 241249
Fax (01865) 794449
Email: oxbow@oxbowbooks.com
www.oxbowbooks.com

United States of America
Oxbow Books
Telephone (800) 791-9354
Fax (610) 853-9146
Email: queries@casemateacademic.com
www.casemateacademic.com/oxbow

Oxbow Books is part of the Casemate group

Front cover image: Sunbeams through early morning mist (istock.com/RichardALock)
Back cover image: Wetland and restored river section near to Brockenhurst (photo: author)

Contents

List of Illustrations

Preface

As a postgraduate student in education I was once invited to contemplate whether 'some areas have more geography than others'. This deliberately absurd proposition is nigh impossible to answer, for everywhere on Earth has its geographical description and relationship with other places. So, aside from complexity, what can be 'more or less' about that? And it should always be recalled that most places on land have been altered by humans to some degree.

One *possible* answer to the question posed is implicitly political: *we value some areas more than we do others.* Certain areas are undeniably sought out by the educator, scientist, scholar, artist or tour guide more than others. The English landscape we see today is the outcome of political processes which underpin raw economic development, incorporating both national policy and local conflicts in the utilisation and distribution of natural resources; landscape is the outcome of human intervention in nature.

Alongside the Norfolk Broads and South Downs, the New Forest is one of Britain's first 'lowland' national parks. The establishment of the New Forest National Park (not without controversy) was contested mostly on the basis that there have been clear and (sometimes) effective forms of legislative provision and governance over 900 years. Protecting a cherished area from the ravages of the modern world is quite another matter, for it was to be demonstrated within a decade of National Park establishment that central government perhaps cannot be wholly trusted with heritage forested areas.

As the newly established New Forest National Park Authority (NFNPA) set about conserving this amazing historic landscape, in January 2011 we read of proposals from the Coalition Government for a 'Sale of Forests'. In what amounted to a plan to privatise Forestry Commission land, petitions were signed, MPs contacted and a perfect storm of a media furore created. Historically, even Oliver Cromwell (the Lord Protector of the Commonwealth of England, Scotland and Ireland) did not follow through plans to sell off the royal hunting forests in the 1650s. Since then, the New Forest and Forest of Dean specifically have not been dis-afforested (that is, deprived of its royal hunting forest status by statute). These important areas remained in Crown hands, eventually with the Forestry Commission acting as Crown agents.

Could the New Forest be privatised? Could it be handed over to a voluntary sector concern? In reply to the plans nationally, the Woodland Trust retorted that it had insufficient funds, while the National Trust appeared more positive. Had some policy maker not understood the term 'forest', for it was originally a Norman legal definition by no means synonymous with 'tree cover'? Were the extensive heathlands to be privatised as well? Would the resources of public institutions still be required?

In a media maelstrom that both reflected and provoked a pitched battle between stakeholders and Government, newspapers as different in outlook as the *Sunday Telegraph*, the *Independent* and the *Guardian* were up in arms over privatisation plans. The *Guardian* could comment that it may be 'David Cameron's Poll Tax'. Perhaps echoing Mr Cromwell, even the late Mrs Thatcher had never presumed to privatise the assets of Mrs Windsor. In the Crown Estate there exists a quasi-state corporation that, in practice, deputises to the Forestry Commission. These assets are positioned between an investment on behalf of the Crown and an old-style nationalised industry.

Middle England, with its concern for countryside access and conservation, rose to a man or a woman. The *Independent* could announce on its front page (17 February 2011) that the Government had retreated and, by the end of that month, the privatisation of national forests was, to all intents and purposes, dead in the water, leaving ministers of the Crown looking somewhat foolish. The nation was seriously perturbed over access to this most cherished of areas.

Faced with adversity, the British can never resist an enquiry. *The Independent Panel on Forestry* (2012) was chaired by the Bishop of Liverpool to keep it clear of Government.[1] To those who study sustainable development, the report presses the right buttons, linking issues of carbon capture and storage, amenity, conservation, the rise of a 'green economy' and so-on. Also and interestingly well away from any 'bonfire of the quangos' (least there be a forest fire) the panel proposed a Forest Services organisation:

> 'We believe there is a continuing role for the public forest estate in England, and that the public forest estate should be managed by a new public forest management organisation evolved from Forest Enterprise England, which currently sits within the Forestry Commission. The organisation will have a new statutory purpose to sustain and build the social, natural and economic value of the estate for the long term, for the benefit of the nation.'

The official governmental response was remarkably positive. The idea of a new, public forest organisation was accepted, the principle of public ownership accepted, public access re-affirmed, new woodland areas will be planned and there will be emphasis on the economic sustainability of the forest estate, including the development of new markets for products.[2]

Yet the media was hit again in the winter of 2013/2014 at the turn of the New Year. *The Times* exploded with reports that ancient woodlands might potentially be sacrificed to house building, road building and the like.[3] Owen Patterson – among other things a history graduate and then Secretary of State for the Department for Environment, Food and Rural Affairs – proposed 'biodiversity offsetting' that would create 'mature habitats' replacing those destroyed by development. Once more there is nought for our comfort and it takes time to establish an ancient wood! *The Times* (correctly) made the connection between 'last links to the Ice Age' and ecosystem services provided by ancient woods within the English landscape. The Woodland Trust likewise registered its concern as well as providing a list of ancient woodlands under threat.[4] At the time or writing, succeeding Conservative governments have gone quiet on woods and forests; one might hope this is because we, as a nation, value forests more than any government might imagine? Brexit concerns may partly explain this, yet worrying signs persist[5] and there remains a determination to sell off 'government land' to raise revenue.

We do cherish the right to enjoy English forests, be we young or old, able-bodied, disabled, sporting or otherwise, campers, twitchers, botanists, historians, archaeologists, horse riders, dog walkers or anyone else. Suggestions that such pleasures are under threat affront British notions of the Great Outdoors. And perhaps for the first time in ages, the Forestry Commission came to be valued in the public mind for what it does, notably in providing access to forests. Otherwise and despite efforts to enhance 'localism', we are forced to question who really asked the forest dweller, the conservation professional, the historic holders of offices such as verderers or agisters or anybody else? What role might a National Park Authority have in privatisation of function?

The Diamond Jubilee (2012) reminded us of the lingering presence of monarchy. Whatever one thinks of that institution, real power has clearly moved from being 'absolute' in Norman times (the royal hunting forest was but a token of the constitutional position enjoyed by William I and his successors) to something puzzling called a 'constitutional monarchy'. 'Monarch' after all, means 'one ruler' and that institution still seeks to wrap itself in symbolic and quasi-mystical power where once hunting was a part of the mystique.

The status, function and power of the Crown shifted from despotic 'top-down' government in the Norman period, towards attempts to embody the British State. Medieval hunting forests became a part of the Crown Estates and because the New Forest was never legally dis-afforested; Crown interests persisted, as private sale of the land was not possible. In a complicated and fascinating story, we see the abdication of profit once due to the Crown to state institutions, the rise of non-economic values in landscape, a realisation of 'conservation' and finally a framework for sustainable development realised in the National Park who are now custodians of a national treasure.

This volume is humbly offered in order to tell the story for a substantial area of frankly rather economically poor land that has emerged as a largely open access national treasure embodied in a national park. The twists and turns of governance arrangements, or management priorities and practices are truly astonishing and, for complexity, outstrips most other tracts of land.

Hadrian Cook
Salisbury
Mayday 2017

Acknowledgements

Many have kindly assisted me with this volume, some with comments on the draft, some with valuable information, often with both. I am particularly indebted to these individuals: Dr G. Peter Buckley (of the former Wye College, University of London), Dr John Chandler, Clive Chatters (Hampshire and Isle of Wight Wildlife Trust), Richard Clements (University of the West of England), Andrew J. Lawson (formerly Wessex Archaeology), Dr Mark Page (Victoria County History), Peter Roberts (New Forest Association), Dr Kathy Stearne (formerly of Natural England). Library services of the Christopher Tower Reference Library in Lyndhurst, Wiltshire Council and Kingston University have supplied much documentary information. All reasonable attempts have been made to obtain necessary reproduction permissions for illustrations.

Glossary of Historic Terms[6]

Afforest (legal), place an area under forest law and administration; the creation of a forest by stipulated procedures ('sylviculture', modern spelling 'silviculture') establish a tree crop on an area which has not carried wood for some time

Agist, admit cattle to forest for a given period or to take in cattle to graze at a certain rate, hence 'agistment'

Agistator, *agister*, *agistor*, official responsible for receiving payments for agistment; officer responsible for supervising, charging for and enrolling commoners' cattle grazing and pannage

Agisting, taking in of commoners' cattle by agisters on payment by the week, month or other period

Agistment, herbage of a forest or the right to it; grazing dues or income from agisting; grazing of unenclosed woods and waste within a forest; common of herbage and the money received for it. The *Charter of the Forest* allowed every free man to agist his own woods and hedges in a forest with his own beasts at any time, under view of the verderers, unless they abutted the king's woods, which must be agisted first

Amercement, financial penalty for an offence imposed by a court

Assart, area of clearance in woodland or waste; cultivated forest land from which trees have been grubbed up; the act of clearing; grub up trees and underwood of forest land to convert to arable or pasture. If licensed, may be inclosed only with small ditches and hedges, to allow passage of deer

Attach, arrest or place under control of court

Attachment Court, also known as Verderers', Woodmote, Wardmote or Forty-day courts. Meetings of verderers every 42 days in each bailiwick to receive and enrol the attachments by foresters, woodwards and other officers of those accused of offending against vert and venison contrary to Forest Law. Although established to protect vert, courts of attachment frequently came to take pledges for the appearance of poachers and other culprits against venison

Axebearer, forest officer

Bailiff, agent of lord of manor, landholder's steward, originally king's representative in a district

Bailiwick, administrative subdivision of a forest; district (of a forest) under a separate jurisdiction

Beadle, an officer going throughout the forest, like unto the Sheriff's special bailiff to make proclamation and levy distress ordered by forest courts

Beasts of the chase, animals allowed to be hunted in a chase: red deer (hart, hind), fallow deer (buck, doe), roe deer until reign of Edward III (buck, doe), fox, marten

Beasts of the forest, animals having 'privilege within the forest': red deer (hart, hind), roe deer until reign of Edward III (buck, doe), hare, boar and beasts and fowls of warren

Beasts of venery, literally, beasts that were hunted, synonymous with 'beasts of the forest' and venison

Beasts/fowls of warren, animal allowed to be hunted in a warren: roe deer (buck, doe), hare, coney

Birds of warren, also 'fowls of warren', birds allowed to be hunted in a warren, q.v.: pheasant and partridge

Black coal, charcoal

Bole, main stem of a tree below where branching begins

Boscage, money paid for windfall wood

Bowbearer, forest official, originally an office held by serjeanty

Brash, remove side branches from a tree, or material so removed

Breast height, standard height for measuring the girth of a standing tree, usually 4 ft 3 ins (1.3 m) above ground level

Browse, *Browsewood*, cropped shoots and small branches of trees to feed deer, cattle, *etc.*

Brush, brushwood small growth cleared before planting trees

Buck, male of fallow (or roe) deer, especially in its sixth or later year, hare, rabbit, goat *etc.*

Buck leap or *Freeboard*, strip of land outside the whole boundary of a deer park, stretching 5–7 m from the pale. Also known as 'buck's leap', term sometimes confused with the term 'deer leap'

Cant, unit to *subdivide* coppices into working units; an area of variable extent on which coppice is cut, or grows at an even age

Charcoal, charred wood used as fuel, made in woodland by burning rough wood cut into lengths of two to three feet, stacked for drying for several months, then piled into a pit of about 15 ft (4.6 m) in diameter for burning which normally took about 24 hours to dry but much longer for green wood

Chase, act or process of hunting; a doublet of 'catch'

Chase, exclusive hunting reserve of landholder in which s/he had rights to hunt deer and boar, *i.e.* a private forest; hunting ground without officers and courts where forest laws, such as for the lawing of mastiffs, did not apply; the equivalent of a park without a fence. Some chases, in royal and private hands, did have courts and officers

Cheminage, payment for passing through a forest during Fence Month (q.v.); specifically charged on carts and pack animals. The *Charter of the Forest* (1217) limited the collection of cheminage to foresters in fee paying farms for their bailiwicks, and forbade its collection from people carrying material on their backs. Compare 'thistletake'

Chief Forester, a 'keeper'

Collier, charcoal maker

Common, area of land within a manor where its tenants or those of other manors had the right to graze livestock; right of occupiers of ancient forest tenements (all others being purprestures), of neighbouring townships by ancient custom, and of other persons given license, to graze forest herbage

Common of estovers, the right to gather fuel wood, sometimes 'by hook or by crook'

Common of herbage, may exist for sheep by prescription or grant, but without surcharge (it is not an automatic forest or chase common right)

Common of pasture, the right to graze waste; could be limited to customary tenants or occupants of dwellings built before a certain date, restricted to certain times of year, limited to certain sorts of animals, or subject to the custom of levancy (the number of beasts a person could put out to common pasture) and couchancy (lying down of animals). See *Agist*

Common of marl, the right to dig clay, chalk, sand or other mineral materials

Common of mast, or pannage – the right to graze swine on beech mast and acorns in autumn

Common of turbary, the right to dig turf for fuel

Compartment area, of variable extent forming a unit for forest management

Coney, rabbit (also 'conigree, cunnigrey, cunny', and 'coniger') nourished in warrens and burrows

Conifer, tree belonging to the family *Coniferae*, usually evergreen with cones, needle-shaped leaves, and producing wood known commercially as 'softwood'

Constable, officer, peace-officer, from Latin *comes stabuli*, 'Count of the Stable', a dignitary of the Roman empire transferred to the Frankish courts. Later office-holders so-called included custodians of castles, often entrusted with the supervision of nearby forests

Coppice, (i) small wood consisting of underwood and small trees grown for the purpose of periodic cutting, (ii) to cut back trees to their base so they will shoot again, (iii) an area of wood so treated. Rotation is typically 8–25 years

Coppice with standards, coppice woodland in which some trees are allowed to grow to full height for timber, usually on multiples of the coppice rotation

Coroner, officer of the crown, originally elected within a county, honor, manor, liberty or borough, but with the consent of the crown; duties included 'keeping the Pleas of the Crown' (holding inquests into local matters in which the king had a financial interest)

County Woodward, Crown officer responsible for supervision of royal woods in an individual county

Court Baron, manorial court which enforced payment and services due to the lord

Court Leet, manorial court which dealt with the administration of the communal agriculture, keeping law and order, and the customs of the manor

Covert, wood with thickets and closed canopy, often used to shelter game

Crown, institutional power and authority of the monarch, as in 'Crown lands', modern power is vested in and represented by, the government

Crown of tree, the upper branches and foliage

Customary (i) written collection of traditional rules and laws of the manor, (ii) description of tenants holding by accepted custom in a particular manor

Deadwood(s), kiln faggots, lowest grade woodland material such as dead coppice, brambles

Deer (fallow), beast of the chase; species of deer 'nourished in parks'; accounted the most noble game after the stag, *i.e.* red deer, as opposed to fallow bucks

Deer (red), beast of venery, that is, of the forest

Deer (roe), beast of the warren, chases out other deer

Deforest, clear or strip forests of woodland (to be distinguished from 'disafforest', q.v.)

Demesne, land possessed or occupied by the owner himself – later land not held of owner by free tenants; ancient demesne – property belonging to the king from time of the Norman Conquest manorial land which the lord held for himself, untenanted

Dis-afforest, free forest land from the operation of forest law (to be distinguished from 'deforest', q.v.); remove an area of land from the constraints of Forest Law; release land from forest law

Enclosure, the act and process of enclosing areas of land previously part of the open woods or fields, including forests and commons. See *Inclosure*

Encoppice, inclosing of a wood or coppice after the cutting of underwood so that the young spring may shoot; enclose an area of cut coppice to protect young shoots from browsing

Encroachment, illegal occupation of property or land

Estover, necessity allowed by law, especially wood which a tenant may take from the king or landlord for repairs of his property; tenants' right to take wood for repair of buildings, hedges, carts, *etc.*; right to take wood from common land for fuel and other purposes. See *Common of Estovers*

Farm, legal rent for land or property, deriving from Latin *firma*, a fixed money rent

Fee, hereditable right to estate or office of profit, technically held on condition of feudal homages; possession of land for a fixed annual service or payment (*e.g.* forester-in-fee)

Fence month, from'defence month', *i.e.* the period when a forest must be closed and undisturbed to allow fawning (when female deer bore young), fixed by the *Charter of the Forest* (1217) as from St Edmund's Day (9 June), 15 days before Midsummer (Feast of John Baptist's Nativity), to 15 days after (St Cyril's Day), during which no swine, sheep, goats or commonable beasts were allowed in a forest, or persons off the highways, and forest officers kept watch and ward night and day in their own bailiwicks. The modern New Forest Fence month[7] is 20 June–20 July, when fawns are born. In customary practice, these were never strictly enforced but after the *Deer Removal Act* (1851), the Crown began to enforce the removal during these periods

Forest (legal), hunting preserve of the king or lord-marcher, subject to forest law but not necessarily woodland; originally an area of land in which only the owner had the right to hunt deer and boar. Special laws were applied in this area which was outside the jurisdiction of common law

Forest (semantic), a wood, a wooded tract of land

Forest eyre, highest forest court, established by Henry II, held by itinerant forest justices, under the authority of two Chief Justices of the Forest, one for north and one for south of the river Trent, after 1238. Attendance was required of all forest officers, who must bring their rolls of record from Attachment and Swanimote courts. Appeal against judgement at an eyre could only be made to the court of king's bench, to which cases concerning illustrious offenders were also usually removed

Forester, keeper; officer appointed by letters patent under oath to preserve vert and venison within a forest and walk his bailiwick daily, attach offenders and present them at courts of attachment, Swanimote and eyre, and to lead regarders on their inspection of a forest

Grove, (historic) collection of timber trees only, (modern usage) small wood, stand of trees

Gypsy, traditional term applied to Romany nomads or travellers. Their traditional livelihoods included the making and selling of low-value forest products such as simple furniture and brooms, and the trading of horses, frequently reared in forests and sold at fairs on forest peripheries

Groom keeper, under or deputy forester

Groundsel, large timber, usually for the foundation of a timber building

Heyning, see Winter Heyning

Hono(u)r, collection of estates held by a single (typically noble) lord, not necessarily grouped geographically, with its own structure of courts, ministers, and administration

Hurdle, woven panel of wattle, used as temporary fencing; usually of willow or hazel, cut in winter and woven in summer

Inclosure, two modes of inclosure (see *Enclosure*), were allowed in forests: of felled woods by large temporary hedges and ditches to protect regrowth against grazing deer and cattle, and of licensed assarts by permanent hedges and ditches small enough to allow the passage of deer. See also *Assart*, *Purpresture*

Justice in eyre, chief or king's, see *Forest eyre*

Justice seat, supreme forest court; meeting, and meeting-place, of forest eyre; the sitting of a forest eyre, or place where it occurred

Keeper, generic term for supervisory forest officer, both superior (*e.g.* the warden of a forest) and local, who was usually the officer responsible for guarding vert and venison and presenting offenders, attached to a particular bailiwick

Knee, or *knee-piece*, a curved piece of wood used in the construction of the framework of ships, normally from the large trunk

Lawn or *laund*, enclosed pasture within forest, originally to provide grazing and hay for deer, or open grassy space in woodland where deer would naturally congregate

Leap, or *deer leap* or *salter*, construction allowing deer access across a pale into a deer park, so built to prevent them from leaving the park

Levant and couchant, definition of the number of beasts a person could put out to common pasture as being what could be supported 'standing and lying' on his own land over winter; measure of common rights consisting originally of the number of commonable animals permitted on a tenement

Ley, land, often open-field strips, temporarily under grass; area of arable land temporarily converted to grass in order to provide stock with sufficient food

Liberty, also known as 'franchise', the exemption by royal decree from general provisions or regulations, whether judicial, commercial, or ecclesiastical, by which powers could be exercised and appointments made locally (within manors) by lords, burgesses, clerics, or corporations, or regionally (within honors); exemption might also be claimed as prescriptive, that is existing from time *immemorial*; see also *Palatine*

Lodge, place where hunter or hunting party may take lodging and/or refreshment; place of habitation for keeper; (v) resting up of a buck

Man(n)er, mainour, maynour, necessary condition of arrest for a forest offence under 25 Edw 3 ch. 12: 'a man was said to be taken with the manner: for venison, when he had wounded a wild beast, and was found with a hound drawing after him to recover it; when he was found at a stand ready to shoot at a deer, or with greyhounds on a leash ready to slip; when he had killed a beast, and was found carrying it away; when he was found in a forest is a suspicious manner, and was bloody; and for vert, when he was found cutting or carrying it away'

Manor, (originally) a territorial unit of land held by an overlord, later in the Middle Ages it had the much looser meaning of any economic unit of land which could consist of all demesne land without tenants

Manorial court, lords of manors had the right to hold courts (see also *Court baron* and *Court leet*) presided over by their steward; the records were kept in manor(ial) court rolls

Mast, fruit of beech, oak and other forest trees used as food for swine; fruits of oak and beech used for fattening swine, typically in autumn, fruits of beech, oak and sweet chestnut used for fattening pigs, either collected for them or fed from the ground

Nutting, custom of gathering nuts on Holy Rood Day, the Feast of the Exaltation of the Holy Cross, 14 September, first day of the open season for the hunting of hart and buck

Officer, strictly speaking, the necessary judicial personnel of forest courts, *i.e.* verderers, foresters, regarders, agisters and woodwards, but supplemented by ministerial functionaries such as wardens, axebearers, bowbearers and rangers and their deputies

Outlaw, person declared to be outside the protection of the law; person committing an offence in a forest where he did not live could not be tried in the courts of that forest, but was outlawed at the instigation of its swanimote, making his goods and chattels forfeit and removing the protection of the law from him

Palatine or *palatinate*, originally pertaining to a palace, thus 'such as have any special office or function in a sovereign prince's palace'; descriptive of a noble (in England a duke, earl, or bishop) having (quasi-)sovereign, princely powers and status, and hence of the area over which those powers obtained

Pale, originally associated with a deer-proof fence, but can refer to the whole boundary of a deer park – ditch, bank and fence

Pannage, pasturage of swine (also right of, payment for): acorns, beech-mast, *etc.*, as food for swine; right to graze pigs in woodland, usually chargeable; feeding swine in the woods in autumn; payment for so doing; money received by agisters for the feeding of commoners' pigs on acorns and mast; the acorn and mast itself, or the profit from it. Agisting swine must be ringed. Private woods in a forest were subject to the same restrictions as agistment. According to the *Charter of the Forest* (1217), pannage was by permission of the forest justices, at 1 or 2 pence per pig

Park, (1) enclosed area in a forest where deer may be collected (entering via 'leaps', q.v.) and 'parked' for protection and maintenance; (2) enclosed area outside a forest in which rights of hunting are enjoyed by a lord, often treated to landscaping in the seventeenth and later centuries; area surrounded by a rail, pale or hedge within which beasts of the forest belonged to the franchisee. Commoners with rights to herbage and pannage could take only that which was surplus to the needs of the game in winter and summer; if there were no such surplus, 'he that hath the herbage and *pannage* cannot put any beasts in the park'

Parker, forest official in charge of a park

Purpresture (noun, royal forests), unlicensed inclosure (on previously unenclosed land) or building, especially a new house within the forest or common land; enclosure of or encroachment upon land; erection of buildings or other encroachments in or into a forest. See *Assart*, *purpresture* (law), *waste*

Perambulation, established boundaries of forests and parishes (the latter being annually walked) walked and then written account of the boundaries of manors, parishes and forests; many private (and some royal) forests did not have perambulations

Plantation, crop of artificially sown or planted trees; enclosure containing trees deliberately planted, unlikely to renew themselves once clear-felled, this could allow natural regeneration without ground preparation and careful replanting

Pollard, (verb) to cut back a tree to within a few metres (3–4 m) of ground level; (noun) a tree so treated; method of producing light timber in woodland pasture. Trees were cut at a height out of reach of the browsing of livestock to produce a pillar-like trunk where new growth emerged from the crown and the cycle of cutting would be anything from ten to twenty years depending on the tree species. Pollards were used in deer parks to produce a leafy fodder

Powderwood, wood used for manufacture of gunpowder charcoal, usually alder and alder buckthorn

Preservator, an officer appointed to protect Crown wood and timber

Purlieu, area adjoining forests which had been added to them by Henry II or one of his sons, Richard and John, and then disafforested by Henry III. Where, as in areas disafforested before 1184 (Henry II's Assize of the Forest) it was an offence under that legislation to obstruct the king's deer. Land disafforested by Edward I was still subject to certain restrictions on hunting. Also land afforested (in the legal sense) and subsequently disafforested; land put out of forests, and therefore no longer subject to regards, by perambulation under the *Charter of the Forest* (1217). However, the king retained possession of deer, which must be allowed to return to forests by the owners of woods, under the control of a ranger who presented offenders at swanimote courts

Purpresture (law), wrongful encroachment upon another's property; especially any encroachment upon, or inclosure of, that which should be common or public, as highways, rivers, harbors, forts, *etc.*[8] (see *perpresture* in context of royal forests, above)

Ranger, forest officer responsible for returning straying deer from purlieus back within the forest pale, though not all forests had them

Reeve, initially an official elected by villagers (frequently unwillingly) to act as an intermediary between them and the lord of the manor; he looked after the husbandry, maintenance of the ditches, banks and hedges, and the ploughs

Regard, inspection of a forest by regarders with foresters and woodwards, presented to the swanimote court next before and preparatory to an eyre

Regarder, officer responsible for making triennial inspections of forests to discover trespasses. A ministerial rather than judicial officer appointed by royal letters patent under oath, twelve per forest, to hold a regard and enrol all offences discovered for presentation through a swanimote to an eyre. Duties specified in the *Charter of the Forest* (1217)

Robora, a medieval term for pollard

Royal prerogative, sovereign's right to reserve to himself things 'of the most excellency, that are upon the earth', such as gold, silver and game, irrespective of possession of the land in or on which they are found

Sergeant, tenant who holds his property or land in return for service(s) (generally other than military)

Silviculture or historic *sylviculture*, the practice and art of cultivating and managing trees and woodland. The term can be regarded as a forerunner to the modern usage of 'forestry'

Slang, strip of land (used as a measure of coppice)

Several, close or inclosed field

Shaw, a small wood or spinney, especially one growing along the edge of a field

Sheriff, *shire reeve*, the executive officer acting in a county on behalf of the king or earl

Spinney, a small *wood* that was not necessarily a coppice; could be planted artificially, or managed as high forest

Squat or *squatter*, encroach on land, usually common land for the purpose of habitation, and the person so doing; such encroachments were often accepted by the manorial lord as a source of revenue, especially where associated with industry and could grow into settlements

Standard, standell, standil, standle or *standrell*, tree which stands alone or above the underwood; a large tree grown in a coppice crop; tree selected to remain standing after the rest of the stand has been felled; selected tree allowed to grow to full size in a coppice

Steward, lawyer who directed officers on court procedures

Surveyors-general (of Crown lands, and of woods, forests, *etc.*), chief officers within the Crown's Offices of Lands and of Woods

Swanimote, also *swainmote*; court of freeholders to inquire into all offences against vert, and venison (in purlieus as well as forests); local forest court responsible for judicial and administrative regulation of the forest; also known as swainmote; in which verderers acted as judges, and presentments were made by foresters and other officers

Tenant at will, tenant established as a reward with a revocable tenure

Tenant in chief, person who held land directly from the king, often the owner of a large number of manors, in which case he might choose to sub-let, 'enfeof', to under tenants

Tithe, legal obligation (by the eighth century) to give one-tenth of all the produce of land to the work of God, the great tithes of corn and hay and the small tithes of livestock, wool and non-cereal crops generally going to support the parish priest but sometimes to an absentee rector or religious house with rectorial rights. After the Reformation, tithes often went to lay persons or corporations such as university colleges

Transhumance, the seasonal movement of livestock to summer pastures, often upland which could also be forest

Turbary, common right to dig peat for fuel from manorial waste

Underwood, small trees and shrubs growing beneath taller timber trees; low cover generally consisting of holly, hazel, willow, alder, and thorn; wood standing or cut, produce of coppice or pollarded trees

Underkeeper, walker; person appointed under oath by a forester to look after deer and vert on his behalf

Venison, originally all beasts of the chase, effectively red deer, fallow deer, roe deer, and wild boar; game animals; any hunted beast; every beast of the forest, protected by forest law

Verderer or *verderor*, judicial oficer of royal forests; official with overall responsibility for the care of both the vert and the venison in a forest; judicial officer appointed under oath by sheriff through royal writ

Vermin (of the chase), bird or animal deemed disruptive of other species (of larder and/or sport) and for that reason hunted; conflation of some beasts of chase and warren comprising foxes, martins, wild cats, polecats and squirrels

Vert, habitat for deer; trees and underwoods; green hue, green hugh: all vegetation in a forest

Vicinage, the right to graze common waste abutting commoners' own if it were not fenced off, and of forest deer to do the same

Walk, district of the forest under the oversight of a keeper

Walker, official responsible for a forest walk; see *Underkeeper*

Ward, administrative division in a forest

Warden, Lord warden, chief ministerial officer of a forest, appointed by the sovereign; chief warden; primary ministerial officer of a forest, also responsible for releasing any person unlawfully imprisoned by foresters or verderers pending appearance in attachment, swanimote or eyre court, paying treble damages through the sheriff for failure to do so, and the amercement of non-attenders at swanimotes

Warren, (legal) one of the three lesser hunting franchises, together with chase and park; a piece of ground preserved for hunting beasts of warren 'a warren of conies, also a certain, or limited, fishing in a river'. Topographically, a coney warren ('coneyburrow') within a forest, chase or park, or standing independently

Warrener, official responsible for a warren; master of the warren

Waste, (verb) unlicensed felling of underwood, wood or trees; destroy without licence trees or underwood, even if stumps are left to spring again, or pasture in a forest; the 'outrageous' forest offence of destroying trees; distinguished from an assart by the visibility of five other standing tree stumps from any particular one. Noun; unclaimed land, damage or destruction of trees; area of land within a manor where its tenants or those of other manors had the right to graze livestock

Wattle, cleft sticks used to make hurdles, usually of hazel, but sometimes willow, which might be used in the round

White wood, broadleaved species (not oak) for charcoal burning

Wildwood, 'virgin forest'

Winter Heyning, the season when there is exception from the liberty of commoning in some forests. In the modern New Forest it is 22 Nov–4 May,[9] a period when commonable stock could not be depastured, so they do not compete with deer for the browse. See *Fence Month*

Wood, area occupied by trees; product of cultivated trees; every wood in a forest provided shelter for venison; group of trees which do not touch each other (as distinct from 'covert')

Wood bank, boundary bank surrounding (or sub-dividing) a wood, with an external ditch

Woodward, officer appointed for the management and sale of Crown wood and timber; gamekeeper in private forest woods swearing fealty to the king's game; official, a reeve, responsible for preventing trespass or theft in a forest; forester, man in charge of, or caring for woods; keeper of a forest wood, who must present any offenders against vert; according to the *Charter of the Forest* (1217), failure by a private woodward in a forest to report a dead deer found in his wood led to forfeiture of the wood to the king

Notes

1. The Independent Panel on Forestry (2012) http://www.defra.gov.uk/forestrypanel/files/Independent-Panel-on-Forestry-Final-Report1.pdf.
2. Government forestry and woodlands policy statement (2013). Defra. https://www.gov.uk/government/uploads/system/uploads/attachment_data/file/181809/pb13871-forestry-policy-statement.pdf.pdf.
3. The *Times* 4 January 2014 'Ancient woods face axe in drive for homes'.
4. https://www.gov.uk/biodiversity-offsetting, The *Times*. *Ibid*.
5. *The Guardian Environment Blog* 17 Feb 2015 'Privatisation of UK woodlands is happening by the backdoor', Mark Avery.
6. This is a glossary intended for use in connection with historical rather than modern terms associated with the New Forest. It is simplified and mostly derived from information from *Forests and Chases in England and Wales*, *c*.1000 to *c*.1850, St John's College, Oxford and available at http://info.sjc.ox.ac.uk/forests/glossary.htm. See this reference for more detail and also the etymology of terms.
7. http://www.newforest.hampshire.org.uk/history4.html.
8. http://www.thefreedictionary.com/Purpresture.
9. http://www.newforest.hampshire.org.uk/history4.html.

CHAPTER 1

A New Book on the New Forest

Into the forest

Some time ago, John Manwood could write:

> 'A forest is a certain territory of woody grounds and fruitful pastures, privileged for wild beasts and fowls of the forest, chase, and warren, to rest and abide there in the safe protection of the King for his delight and pleasure; which territory of ground so privileged is meered [has boundary] and bounded with un-removable marks, meers and boundaries either known by matter of record or by prescription and also replenished with beasts of venery or chase and with great coverts of vert for the succour of the said beasts there so reside…'[1]

By no means all covered by trees, a (legally defined) medieval forest was a mix of woodland, heath, pasture and scrub whose management was devoted to hunting by the king and those he favoured.[2] There were also forest dwellers, people who were of lower social rank, whose economic interests lay elsewhere. Furthermore there is nothing in this late sixteenth century passage concerning commercial forestry as may be understood in a modern sense (previously and more attractively termed 'silviculture') or about public enjoyment, conservation of landscape value and certainly nothing that even borders on the romantic. For Manwood, after all, was a lawyer.

Back in the mythical realms, it is also noted that hunting of both boar and deer was important in Celtic societies, evidenced by the boar *Twrch Trwyth* that appears in the Welsh epic *The Mabinogion*. He gave chase across the west of Britain and, like boar, deer (stags in particular) had mythic status among Celtic peoples.[3] Herne the Hunter, a ghostly figure and likely a thinly disguised horned deity of uncertain pagan origins (Germanic, Celtic or both) is usually linked with Windsor Great Park. Tales of hunting and folklore in ancient forests indicate, at least, cultural links with antiquity.

As an identifiable wooded entity, what we know as the New Forest has a history dating back millennia, but the significant legal event was the creation of the royal forest, possibly about 1079 by William I, 'the Conqueror' (who reigned 1066–1087). His son, William II 'the Rufus' (reigned 1087–1100), was killed (or assassinated, it is unclear) while out hunting there in 1100. The Normans had furthermore imposed a governance system *where there was already an established manorial system* from the late Saxon period.

It was Domesday Book (1086) that caused the area first to be referred to as the New Forest (*Nova Foresta*).[4] The term 'forest', as already noted originally a legal term, defined the laws of a defined area set apart from the common laws

FIGURE 1.1. The 'vert': a typical New Forest Scene.

PHOTO: AUTHOR

of England. And it was then felt appropriate to describe it as 'new', perhaps because of the new legal status it was to receive. This new status permitted the Crown to exact its (often arbitrary) rule in a fashion that, even to the Normans, would not have been possible where the manorial system operated alone. The open spaces in the New Forest, dominated by heath, sometimes gorse scrub, sometimes bog, remain because tree plantation has been controlled, and only permitted within the 'inclosures'. Technically, these actually form 'exclosures' for large grazing animals whose grazing maintains the open areas where turf was also removed for domestic burning. Heaths have a history of their own, linked to peat cutting and burning, while the rabbit-grazed lawns appear as golf greens in a landscape rugged by lowland British standards.

The Sovereign remains the legal owner of the Crown Estate which is in effect under Treasury regulation. Medieval monarchs inevitably made choices that would affect ordinary folk. Individual kings' (and some queens') desires and priorities affected royal forests. In management of the royal forests, we see the whim of individual rulers offering them as dower, selling of produce and taking an interest or otherwise in the venison, and a dwindling involvement in their management as the 'vert' (forest vegetation, Fig. 1.1) until wider state interests would replace the whims of the royal household. However, it is all too easy to become pre-occupied with the actions of the rich and powerful; ordinary people struggled to make a living from poor quality land in a highly regulated environment.

Overall, human actions have made an indelible mark on the land cover and land use patterns within the Forest. The social, economic and political influences are no less interesting. We have a first glimpse of the nature of the most powerful of the forest laws in the Assizes of Henry II (1166),[5] the monarch who seems to have presided over forest law at its maximum development and imposition in order to protect the king's interests in hunting.[6] The Assize of the Forests, held at Woodstock, is dealt with in Chapter 5, and was apparently most savage indeed.

'Bad' King John granted away part of the forest to the Cistercians in 1204 demonstrating that there evidently remained a call on relatively better quality land in the formation of Beaulieu Abbey in 1204. There was thus created an agricultural estate in the south of the forest. Interestingly, their abbey was to be dissolved by that even more popular royal despot, Henry VIII (reigned 1509–1547). Well before Henry, reform was perhaps inevitable.

Legal reforms and management changes

Into a world infamous for alleged despotic rulers and like the more famous *Magna Carta* of 1215, the *Carta de Foresta* (*Charter of the Forest*) of 1217[7] actually limited the expansion of aristocratic interests and went further to ensure the 'rights' of ordinary people against feudal overlords. The charter can therefore be seen as part of the long democratisation process in England as well as providing us with an early glimpse of forest governance in which *Nova Foresta* was a significant player. Given time, aristocratic interest in hunting waned yet what remained – or even grew – was the economic imperative of maintaining crown revenues.

As a result, we see efforts to reform silvicultural management. Coppicing, everywhere else in Britain today celebrated by conservationists and landscape historians, apparently was to fail as a system of economic return. It was the later construction and naval interests that benefitted from far-sighted re-afforestation in the seventeenth century that supplied shipyards at Buckler's Hard. Governance, however, was to present problems for centuries and confusion was intertwined with genuine efforts to make this large tract of marginal land viable.

From Tudor times onwards, there was clear governmental interest (as distinct from crown interest) in the New Forest. The creation of new officials outside the royal forest hierarchy, and this time at the behest of the Exchequer, would be problematic, for these acted to improve, later maximise, revenue from the forest while the ancient officers with sinecures, were still in place. A *Divisum Imperium* (divided jurisdiction) thus arose in the mid-sixteenth century. It arose from the creation of the post of Surveyor General of Woods, Forests, Parks and Chases and his deputy surveyors by central government. It might have been seen that the old (Norman) governance system remained in parallel and this would be the case until the abolition of the post of Lord Warden in the nineteenth century. Legal and governmental reform would lead to a *de facto* recession of crown interests with the abdication of responsibilities to the Office of Woods.

More unfortunately, and well into the eighteenth century, there was corruption caused by incompetence and greedy forest officials, yet the national interest in sorting these problems resulted from a desire for efficient production of timber for the navy. Consequently legal changes in the nineteenth century within the forest were draconian. Then, in the immediate post-First World War period, the newly formed Forestry Commission (1919) replaced the Office of Woods and took charge of commercial forestry, a situation that pertains to the present. Throughout all this time, commoners' rights to graze and use resources of timber and turf continued so as to create an interesting arena for conflict in resource management.

The New Forest as it stands is 'typical' of many royal hunting forests established by the Normans. It is also atypical because it has survived relatively intact, unlike (for example) the nearby Forest of Bere.[8] This is likewise situated on an area of poor soil, is relatively close to the New Forest and it also supplied timber to the navy. The New Forest we experience today remains an outcome of changing political objectives combating economic interests and more nebulous cultural values that have shaped and preserved its landscape.

Previous accounts

William I's officials apparently saw the New Forest as of sufficient merit to produce its own section in the Domesday Survey of 1086. In a masterful account of the royal forests of Northamptonshire (Rockingham, Whittlewood and Salcy forests) between 1558 and 1714, P. A. J. Pettit succeeded in synthesising economy, law, geography, history, land use and other facets of royal forests.[9] Interest specifically in the New Forest is documented by many accounts written from very differing perspectives and meaning that a study of the literary accounts gave insight into the values of the writer and his time.

John Wise's *The New Forest, its History and Scenery*, was first published in 1883 and prone to Victorian sentiment.[10] Brian Vesey-Fitzgerald's anecdotal and journalistic 1966 *Portrait of the New Forest*[11] contains some interesting material on post-medieval writers. Inevitably, stereotypes also forge an area's identity in the popular mind, and the trickle of publications on the forest continued.

Following a serious outbreak of office clearing during the author's time on the academic staff of Wye College, University of London a colleague presented him with E. M. Yates's (1985) monograph on the medieval landscape of the forest.[12] This occasional paper from the Geography Department of King's College London contains insights into historical geography that, one fears, may have been otherwise forgotten. There are also many quality research papers, notably those published in the *Proceedings of the Hampshire Field Club and Archaeological Society* (*Hampshire Studies*) relating to many aspects of the archaeology, ecology and documentary history of the forest. For integrated historical ecology, there is no upstaging the late Colin Tubbs's book *The New Forest*, published in 2001.[13]

For a beautiful modern illustrated introduction, we have Clive Chatters' and Mike Read's book on the New Forest National Park.[14] In 2010 Adrian Newton edited an informative volume *Biodiversity in the New Forest* that, among other things, reminds us of this conservation resource in southern England, that is presented in an accessible and themed fashion.[15] Stephen Ings's title, *Shot for a White-Faced Deer*,[16] refers to an earlier book[17] recalling an accident when an unfortunate woman was allegedly killed, mistaken for a deer. The title gives clear indication of a lingering economic relationship with forest deer and manages to invoke earlier, brutal times. For those of more literary inclinations, there is a fine introduction to writers' impressions of the forest in Ian McKay's edited volume, *A New Forest Reader*.[18] Alternatively, for transcriptions of historic documents together with commentaries of the period covered by each volume, there is the New Forest record series edited by either Richard Reeves or Peter Roberts.[19]

Within the perambulation of the New Forest are 145 square miles (37,555 hectares), including private estates, residential and farming land, 'open forest' and 'inclosures' (otherwise described as woodland enclosures).[20] The forest's size as a parcel of land, its small area in private ownership and the unusual category of 'inclosures' confirm that it is an unusual area. By implication, the overwhelming majority belongs to the Crown, and there remains relatively little opportunity for agriculture, as understood in the usual sense. Inclosures have been deliberately planted, generally since the seventeenth century. The definition of an 'ancient woodland' adopted by most authorities for England and Wales is defined as dating from before AD 1600; ostensibly because plantation forestry only developed after this time and in any case maps were not sufficiently detailed to distinguish between type of woodland.[21] In many respects this is arbitrary and, as will be later shown, it is unlikely that plantation was completely absent during the medieval period.

So, why do we need another book on the forest? One answer is that events have overtaken earlier accounts, and there is a need to 'defragment' interest in the area, producing what is humbly offered as a fresh and integrated look at history, conservation policy, changing economy and governance. These are written in the light of modern political and conservation imperatives while contemplating what remains as an optimistic, but uncertain future.

Characteristics of the New Forest

Perceptions have not always sat easily with modern ideas about environmental management or with contemporary world views. While modern values arose from Victorian romanticism (and to be fair it certainly was a driver for conservation), between 1882 and 1889 interests in landscape and amenity caused the introduction of around 300 ornamental trees or 'exotics' to the forest.[22] This reflects something other than a will to conserve what is, or indeed might have been present under different (yet native) conditions. In deference to perceived earlier beliefs mentioned above, within the cultural matrix of aesthetic enjoyment, biological conservation and economic productivity, the high priestess white witch Sybil Leek (described as 'an inspiration to other witches') introduced a witchcraft theme to Burley by starting a forest coven.[23]

All was not as intriguing and there was real resentment elsewhere. Following the Second World War, a period of frustration and friction (arising between the Forestry Commission and conservation interests) had included eschewing a New Forest National Park in the 1940s. Rising 'conservation ethos,' a continuing interest in countryside access and a realisation that all UK National Parks no longer belonged in 'upland' areas finally led to the National Park establishment in 2005.

Since 1949, the establishment of National Parks has been the means by which England, Wales and later Scotland chose to identify and manage cherished areas.[24] Ironically, the New Forest was to experience potentially negative developments arising from different legislation in the same year; as we have seen, it was to be 56 years before the New Forest achieved this status. Even if detractors from the National Park complained that the historic governance in 2005 was more than adequate (asking why another layer of bureaucracy is needed?), we can at least celebrate its recognition – for at last the New Forest has a single voice to speak for its interests.

While elites pleasured, planned, planted or plotted, so poorer members of society felt the need to guard common rights while marginalised people squatted or lived a nomadic life. Today urban dwellers of southern England demand access to the countryside. A consensus had emerged whereby the New Forest is an area recognised for its beauty, ecology, intrinsic landscape value and recreational provision. Despite agricultural activity on its southern side, much of the area occupies lamentably poor soil and this observation is essential to understanding the forest's development. The subsequent landscape mosaic arises from historic systems of land holding, the hunting pleasures of elites, the development of silviculture and latterly culture, recreation and conservation, within a predominantly medieval landscape. Yet the historic stereotype is an oversimplification, for even if kings no longer hunt there, economic interests on the Crown lands co-exist with historic rights to graze alongside modern recreation.

Counterintuitively, a former chair of the New Forest National Park Authority informed the author that we are dealing with a functionally urban economy (Chapter 9).[25] This is not the rural England we might expect. To the casual visitor scrutinising deer or ponies safely grazing, or wondering at the Ancient and Ornamental Woods, a realisation that facets of the modern forest economy are more like urban areas than anything else would come as a surprise.

It is useful to conceptualise any account of the New Forest around five interwoven concepts. These are: *economically marginal land*, *resource conflict*, *boundaries*, *governance* and the resulting *changing management objectives*. Many royal hunting forests were clearly located on poor soils and difficult topographies that had limited potential for agricultural development.[26]

1. Economically marginal land

The history of the New Forest may be seen as an exercise charting the utilisation and development of *economically marginal land*. With an abundance of soils that are developed on sands, gravels, acidic peat or nutrient poor clays with drainage problems, it would be found problematic to sustain, in the long term, agriculture as understood in conventional farming and horticulture and particularly as there are better soils within striking distance. Where agriculture became established in the middle ages, it was on areas of less problematic soil. Otherwise, land not in agriculture certainly does not mean it is abandoned nor bereft of human activity. Whether it was the royal forest, or else later interest in silviculture or modern forestry, the mosaic of heathlands, wetlands, lawns and trees including extensive tracts of woodland or modern forestry, means it had to be controlled and put to use in one way or another. Beyond the direct pleasure of kings, these generally had economic purpose.

The truth is that the New Forest would have looked very different left to nature's own devices; it would scrub over and eventually mature secondary woodland would dominate. This not only would represent a loss of economic potential, but would also present opportunity for refuge by 'marginal' social groups such as outlaws or squatters who may be perceived by some to threaten social order. In practice, Romany people lived in the forest for much of the post-medieval period until their effective expulsion in the twentieth century.

2. *Resource conflict*

Resource conflict occurs wherever there is competition for a natural resource between different groups of people. From the eleventh century, the New Forest manifested crown interests. It was ideal for woodland and grazing was ideally managed with deer in mind. Common people were actually required to manage and administer the area under the forest laws, but their interests in gathering fuel, grazing and planting crops could be at variance with crown interests, something realised through the management of the underwood; coppice was failing economically and managerially in the late medieval period (Chapter 4), yet coppice products remained important to local economic needs.

Later, from the seventeenth century, state interests in timber came to an uneasy accommodation with those who otherwise made a living within the perambulation of the New Forest. Small-scale industrialisation furthermore appears in various guises, notably a ceramic industry in Roman times, gravel extraction, and development associated with shipbuilding at Buckler's Hard in the eighteenth century. Today, we may view visitor pressure as an 'industry', with attendant resource conflict that potentially threatens conservation interests.

3. *Boundaries*

Boundaries are both *external* and seen as the perambulations (set at various times) defining the forest edge, yet there are also clear *internal* boundaries that separate different land covers, ownerships or common land from forest land. A modern land use planner might set a boundary according to supposed 'land capability'; that is a property presumed to describe the potential for forestry or agriculture derived from soil type, drainage, topography and other site characteristics and from climate. Actually, practical experience of soil and land management resulted in broadly defined historic boundaries resulting from agronomic considerations where they are not otherwise the result of land holding. Royal hunting forest legal definitions, eighteenth-century resource surveys (such as Drivers' map, though not published until 1814)[27] and Acts of Parliament in the nineteenth century all produced different external boundaries for the New Forest before the National Park. There are also common rights within the forest and there are a number of 'adjacent commons' around it (Chapter 8). To clarify:

> 'Contrary to a widespread belief, however, all common land is private property. It belongs to someone, whether an individual or a corporation, and has done so from time immemorial. The owner of the common land is the lord of the manor within which the common lies, or his legal descendant and representative today. The common lands of England and Wales are therefore not public property, despite their name, nor have they ever been during the past thousand years'.[28]

So that within the perambulation 'ownership' was originally that of the Crown, outside ownership is by some other agency, manors in historic times and large nearby estates today, others include the National Trust, parish, town and Hampshire County Council.[29]

The term 'perambulation' still maintains its currency and today it refers to the New Forest Act 1964 and encompasses crown land (managed by the Forestry Commission), privately owned land and manorial wastes ('commons') that are subject to common rights, as well as privately owned and enclosed land (Figs 1.2 and 1.3).

In the 1990s and early 2000s there was some dispute regarding imposition of the Park; as part of this, interests concerned about the western boundary sought to include much of the floodplain of the Hampshire Avon in the National Park in the hope of preventing the expansion of gravel extraction.

At different times the poor pressurised the commons, producing squatter encroachments and also abortive efforts to develop farmland. Hence boundaries become a real issue for the economically marginalised. Interesting developments in land parcelling and land-use occurred around the peripheries of the New Forest although 'internal' boundaries are manifest not only in land cover parcelling, but also in terms of 'frontiers' of cultivation. This periodically occurred during times of population pressure (tending to increase cropland and grazing pressure) or afforestation, as economic conditions dictated. Land under pressure of population tends to be pressed into more intensive uses until its limitations become apparent. The detail of boundary form is an outcome not only of soil and site characteristics, but also of land holding, land use and simple demographics.

FIGURE 1.2. The New Forest 1964 perambulation.

THE FORESTRY COMMISSION 2004, GOVERNMENT OPEN LICENCE

4. *Governance*

Then, *governance* is the regulatory process by which land resource conflict, land holding matters and subsequent conservation interests might be achieved. Variously, the lost forest laws of (it is sometimes presumed) 1079, the Assizes of Henry II (1166), the *Charter of the Forest* (1217), the *Orders and Rules of the New Forest* (1537) and numerous subsequent laws concerned with timber, deer management and subsequently the National Park not only legislate but also seek to provide an administrative structure appropriate to the time. This 'top down' approach may be contrasted with the operation of manorial and other local courts and commoners' rights that provided an element of 'localism' in forest

management. Even if manorial courts are not generally seen as enlightened institutions from the point of view of the poor, at least they had local rather than national reference. Most recently, the accommodation required to bring the National Park together with the historic forest officers, the verderers, has proved an interesting subject for governance analysis because of uncertainty of roles versus newly defined statutory duties.[30]

FIGURE 1.3. The Map of Percival Lewis, 1811 (http://www.fromoldbooks.org/Lewis-LawsOfTheNewForest/).

5. *Changing management objectives*

Over time, *changing management objectives* have greatly influenced the form of the New Forest. Ignoring, for the present, earlier periods, there has been concern to protect both venison (Fig. 1.4) and vert for hunting. There were changes in the roles of forest officials, the rise of timber production for local and national markets, the rise of the landscape and conservation ethics and finally a convergence of management paradigms. Governance issues considered state controlled timber production, commoners' interests, attempts at the cultivation of crops, visitor pressures and the rise of a whole new economy of conservation and recreation – only partly measurable in monetary terms.

FIGURE 1.4. The venison: a New Forest red deer.

iStock.com/ KIT_LEONG

Such complexity can be played out because, effectively, much of the area not under freehold or commoners' rights remained as crown lands, albeit long managed by state agencies such as the Forestry Commission or the NFNPA. Such a status might have saved it as *de facto* public sector owned land. Hence, the New Forest may be viewed as largely one state-backed enterprise – at the very least from the seventeenth century.

An approach

Only when historians became cognisant of economic principles during the first half of the twentieth century was the sub-discipline of economic history truly born. One pioneer was Sir Michael Postan, who looked at medieval society using economic descriptions[31] yet to some it deviated from pure historical narrative. Then at the end of the century, a new departure reflected the obvious: that politics and history have always been inextricably linked. In the 1990s green history was born. This relates the environmental history, beloved of palaeo-environmentalists and landscape historians, to a political dimension, although it should be clear that green history remains an academic discipline separate from the consciously campaigning 'green movement'.

It is environmental historians such as John Sheail who developed our notions of environmental history from a more or less political standpoint,[32] seeking (among other things) to explain the motives of those who are commonly referred to as 'stakeholders'. The approach taken here likewise mixes descriptions of political and economic dimensions in describing the New Forest landscape. Like economic history, green history has instrumental value, for green history can inform the sustainable development debate.[33] In short, it may be asked: 'Have we been this way before?' or 'What happened when we tried that last time?' As we strive to achieve that most nebulous of attributes, 'sustainability', there arise major challenges for the New Forest National Park Authority (NFNPA) or its partnership organisations. Today, visitor pressure should be added to considerations of the management of basic natural resources available within the area, for those living off the forest land itself would never be rich, something we surmise was first experienced in prehistory!

Political scientists tell us that 'governance' is about steering rather than top-down command and control;[34] it is about 'how things are done' and can result in complicated analysis of political, including regulatory, processes. Further analysis generally looks at key socio-economic factors such as social inclusion, stakeholder interests, markets, hierarchies, networks and communities. Without being over-analytical, we now have a framework with which to address historical environmental management, and potentially its relationship with contemporary societies and economy. The New Forest, after all, takes our understanding in 900 years from management under something like absolute monarchy (the Normans) to effectively state land with more-or-less open access. The political reaction when *de facto* 'public forest' ownership may have been challenged (identified in the Preface of this book) is a reflection of the value placed in England's forests when, during recession, the dominant neo-liberal economic paradigm is under question. We have seen how most detractors from forest sales are identifiably middle class, leaving an interesting conundrum for future commentators on the countryside access debate. Historically it was the poor who mostly lost out or who felt threatened by past forest governance.

The New Forest is instructive because within one area, many insights may be gained into natural resource exploitation. These range from Mesolithic and Neolithic hunters, through the development of 'agricultural' landscapes from the Neolithic into the Bronze Age. The Romans brought some industrial development, while the pastimes of Norman kings developed the landscape for hunting. Later it served national strategic interests, providing timber for shipbuilding until iron battleships took to the seas. By the nineteenth century elements of historic and aesthetic romanticism evident in writing about the forest would to lead to modern values of landscape amenity and conservation. The forest provided for bombing practice and airfields during World War II. Aesthetic it may be, but it is created as a working landscape influenced by political and economic interests backed by social and legal forces.

The aim of this book is to scrutinise the trials and tribulations of an area that includes some otherwise economically marginal land. Four critical themes are identified that bring together the complexity and perhaps explain why another book on the New Forest has been produced. These are:

- The shaping of the natural environment into human prehistory
- Human intervention through natural resource management
- The governance and management of the forest over time, stressing pressures on resources and attempts at exclusion of certain social groups.
- Policies and designations to conserve the New Forest

Following this scene setting chapter, Chapter 2 is concerned with linking the present Forest, its land cover and ecology with the historical narrative, Chapter 3 then describes what is known about the area from prehistory to the Norman Conquest. Chapter 4 describes aspects of the medieval Forest, Chapter 5 the governance arrangements that emerged at that time. Chapter 6 is concerned with the drastic changes into the post-medieval period in terms of the shift towards timber production, Chapter 7 with the long and painful decline of the medieval Forest arrangements to the extensive reforms of the nineteenth century. Chapter 8 covers the rather difficult twentieth century, especially the conflict between softwood production and conservation and finally and Chapter 9 describes the rise of the modern conservation ethos into the present century.

This volume is therefore aimed to reflect a complicated narrative around the evolution caused by changing management and economic objectives reflecting governance arrangements at different times. Once the domain of kings, it is today in effect open-access largely state land. It is aimed at the interested general reader, students of environmental history and indeed anybody who has enjoyed the glades and heathlands of the New Forest. How did it all start?

Summary

If the New Forest is atypical of rural England as a whole, it is arguably an extreme version of its own kind: a surviving royal forest and an arena in which to see certain political development, including the changing nature and power of the Crown, of conservation *vs.* production issues and latterly public interest and participation. Today 'statism' plays a role in both its *de facto* state ownership, management and guaranteeing both the preservation of the landscape and Forest stakeholders within the National Park. The latter has furthermore had to accommodate a (seriously reformed) historic governance system of 'verderers', 'agistors' and their associated judicial system.[35]

John Manwood (see the top of this chapter) was writing at the end of an era. Whether intended in a legal sense, or in a modern literal sense, we like the New Forest because the landscape either includes a mosaic of heathlands, wetlands, lawns and trees, or else it presents extensive tracts of woodland or forestry of one kind or another. Yet, it is all too easy to see the forest as a deeply conservative place. Certainly its land use options and style of landscape have changed less than the productive agriculture landscapes and urban areas that surround it. The New Forest has evolved a way of sustaining landscape and livelihood, yet it entered the twenty-first century as a core part of the array of planning and conservation designations. The remaining chapters will explore these ideas.

Notes

1. Manwood J. (1598) *A Treatise and Discourse of the Laws of the Forest*, 143 (modernised spelling).
2. Forestry Commission (2008) *A History of the Crown Lands*. http://www.forestry.gov.uk/pdf/eng-new-forest-b2-history.pdf/$FILE/eng-new-forest-b2-history.pdf.
3. Introduction to Britain's Lost Wildwood. http://www.south-coast-central.co.uk/wildwood.htm.
4. The Medieval Forest. http://www.newforestnpa.gov.uk. data/assets/pdf_file/0008/26648/history1-forweb.pdf. New Forest National Park.
5. Assizes of Clarendon (n.d.) F.
6. J. Bond (1994) Forests, chases, warrens and parks in medieval Wessex. In M. Ashton and C. Lewis (eds), *The Medieval Landscape of Wessex*, 115–58. Oxbow Monograph 6, Oxbow books, Oxford.
7. *The Charter of the Forest of King Henry III*. http://info.sjc.ox.ac.uk/forests/Carta.htm.
8. E. Preston and S. Wallis (2006) *The Forest of Bere*. Devon Books, Halsgrove, Wellington; Bond 1994. *op. cit.*
9. P. A. J. Pettit (1968) *The Royal Forests of Northamptonshire: A Study of their Economy 1558–1714*, xv. Northampton Record Society, Northumberland Press, Gateshead.
10. J. Wise (1883) *The New Forest, its History and Scenery*. Southeran, London.
11. B. S. Vesey-Fitzgerald (1966) *Portrait of the New Forest*. Robert Hale, London.
12. E. M. Yates (1985) *The Landscape of the New Forest in Medieval Times*. Dept of Geography, King's College London.
13. C. R. Tubbs (2001) *New Forest, the History, Ecology and Conservation*. New Forest Ninth Centenary Trust, Fordingbridge.
14. C. Chatters and M. Read (2006) *The New Forest National Park*. Halscrow, Tiverton.
15. A. Newton (ed.) (2010) *Biodiversity in the New Forest*. Pisces Publications, Newbury.
16. S. Ings (2010) *Shot for a White-faced Deer*. Hobnob Press, Salisbury.
17. R. C. De Crespigny and H. G. Hutchinson (1899) *The New Forest, its Traditions, Inhabitants and Customs*. John Murray, London.
18. I. McKay (ed.) (2010) *A New Forest Reader: A Companion Guide to the New Forest, its History and Landscape*. Hatchet Green, Southampton.
19. http://www.newforestcentre.org.uk/new-forest-record-series acc. sept 2017.
20. The New Forest undated. http://www.newforest.hampshire.org.uk/today3.html.
21. G. P. Buckley pers. comm. (2013).
22. Forestry Commission (2008) *op. cit.* in note 2.
23. http://www.bbc.co.uk/southampton/features/newforest/witches.shtml.
24. *The National Parks and access to the Countryside Act* 1949. http://www.legislation.gov.uk/ukpga/Geo6/12-13-14/97.
25. Clive Chatters pers. comm. (2010).
26. J. Bond (1994) *op. cit.* in note 6, 120; G. Bathe (2013) Of Commoners and Kings. In: Rotherham, I. (ed.) *Cultural Severance and the Environment. Environmental History* vol 2. Springer, Dordrecht, 177–190, DOI https://doi.org/10.1007/978-94-007-6159-9_12.
27. The New Forest 2007. http://www.newforest.hampshire.org.uk/historic_maps/maps_intro.html.
28. W. G. Hoskins and L. D. Stamp (1963) *The Common Lands of England and Wales*, 4. New Naturalist, Collins, London.
29. New Forest Association (n.d.) *A History of the New Forest and its Adjacent Commons*. New Forest Association, Fordingbridge.

30. A. Passmore (2004) New Forest Notes http://www.newforest.hampshire.org.uk/forest_notes/notes_nov04.pdf.
31. M. M. Postan (1972) *The Medieval Economy and Society*. Penguin Books, London.
32. For example see J. Sheail (2002) *An Environmental History of the Twentieth Century*. Palgrave, London.
33. For example see H. F. Cook (2008) A tale of two catchments: water management and quality in the Wandle and Tillingbourne, 1600 to 1990. *Southern History* 2008, 78–103.
34. H. Cook and A. Inman (2012) The voluntary sector and conservation for England: achievements, expanding roles and uncertain future. *Journal of Environmental Management* 112, 170–77.
35. The Forestry Commission (2012) Verderers and Agisters. http://www.forestry.gov.uk/forestry/INFD-6A4KQ7.

CHAPTER 2

Under the Greenwood Tree

'To dwellers in a wood, almost every species of tree has its voice as well as its feature.'
Thomas Hardy[1]

'I talk to the trees ... that's why they put me away' Spike Milligan[2]

Landscape ecology, function and value

An elected member once asked an ecologist on the staff of his county council if the ecologist knew how many trees there were in that particular county, and if he did, was this sufficient to supply the oxygen demands of the population? There is no known record of the ecologist's reply, nor if this vexing scientific question was ever truly addressed. Fearing in that instance the destruction of trees, it is a truism that modification of woodland is nothing new. This chapter aims to explore issues of ecology and human values further in preparation to a systematic account of New Forest history and economic development.

In temperate regions, clearance of interfluve regions between river valleys typically (but not always) dates from at least the Neolithic period, in southern England from about 4000 BC. Then, land was cleared for agriculture and this would have triggered among other problems, soil erosion that accreted on the floodplains as alluvium and would have affected the rivers loading them with sediment.[3] Worldwide, so dramatic has been human-induced environmental change, that scientists have proposed the 'Anthropocene', a geological epoch following from or incorporating the Holocene (or 'Recent'). This is a time from when it is recognised that human activity impacted on planetary systems, including land use change, deleterious impact of biodiversity or climatic influence. Some may prefer to define the new epoch from the start of the Industrial Revolution (in the eighteenth century) on account of human activity changing the composition of the atmosphere and causing climate change.[4] However, the point is that humans have affected significant environmental change on planet Earth.

One way of conceptualising attitudes to woodlands and forests in the west is the apparent dichotomy between 'deep ecology' and what might be dubbed a 'countryside conservation' ethos, manifest in the National Park ethos of the USA and UK respectively. The US has been slow to implement conservation as 'countryside management', as opposed to a deep green or 'wilderness conservation' ethos.[5] The objective has been to conserve the American forests of all kinds, free from human intervention. Philosophically this implies the well-being of ecosystems is paramount, irrespective of the needs of humans.

UK conservation approaches are more pragmatic, recognising the role in humans affecting land cover and in ecological management, and hence their needs in formulating conservation policy. Such conceptualisation is wholly consistent with the notion of the 'Anthropocene' epoch. More specifically, national parks in the UK, following the *National Parks and Access to the Countryside Act* 1949, were established for ecological conservation purposes including the management of historic landscapes in the face of access to the countryside and visitor management. Furthermore, the designation of ecologically defined Sites of Special Scientific Interest (SSSI), more often than not involve 'semi-natural' habitats that requires active management. Such are product of human intervention, albeit often relating to historic management practices including coppicing, grazing or involving land drainage.[6]

'Deep green' thinking over forests is challenged because there is evidence that Native Americans burned forest understories in the management of game animals across the continent,[7] inviting an interesting comparison with the controversy in Europe regarding the nature of the wildwood, and implicitly the impact of humans. With human intervention significant in North American forests, the debate around the nature of European woodlands gives a useful context for the management from the Mesolithic period to modern times, including the first moves towards deforestation leading to the mature (albeit largely medieval and early modern period) surviving landscape of the New Forest. However, whether fire *per se* is plausible as an effective management tool in burning wildwood is open to serious question for temperate environments.

There are other means and these result in 'semi-natural' habitats. For example, ecologists may sanction tree removal where they are maintaining an historic heath community or preventing the 'scrubbing-up' of chalk downland by maintaining grazing pressure. We actually place enormous value on semi-natural habitats set within the landscape, this term is conveniently chosen to imply heavy and continued intervention by humans. It furthermore needs to be made clear the concept is also used in contradistinction with agricultural or forest monocultures where one species, planted and managed by man, is cultivated.

Oliver Rackham, one of the best communicators of landscape ecology in our time, was a woodland specialist whose work continually stresses the interaction of humans and semi-natural woodlands. He reminds us of the importance of the practice of coppicing that commenced in the Neolithic, of the pollarding of woodbanks throughout history and he has discussed the importance of plantation within woods that started in the medieval period.[8] In the New Forest, the importance of coppicing over historic time is questionable, but such practices certainly occurred, even if not in the directly systemised way proposed for elsewhere in England.[9]

Today woodlands are valued for 'ecosystem services', that is anything from amenity, to habitat, to invigorating the hydrological cycle, even sequestering (locking in) carbon from the atmosphere within soil and biomass while providing oxygen for humans and animals through photosynthesis. Deforestation today is

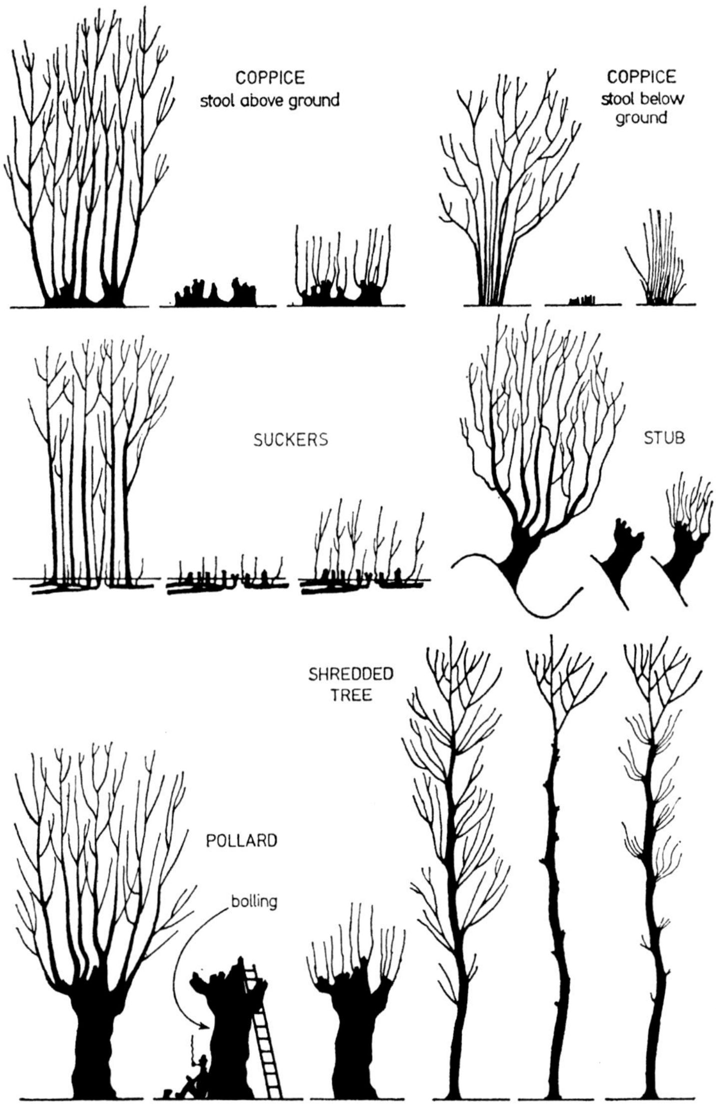

FIGURE 2.1. The impact of management on individual trees.

AFTER RACKHAM 1986, 66

considered an 'environmental crime' in the tropics, yet it occurred progressively from about 6000 years ago in Britain. A comparable negative view is commonly expressed about plantation of conifers during the past 200 years,[10] at least outside their native 'biomes'. A compromise view has it that trees may have market value (commercial forestry and tree crops), non-market values (such as parks) or provide ecosystem services (such as providing habitats) or have nebulous attributes imparted through spiritual, health or recreational value.[11]

In the medieval period, woods were seldom managed as high forest.[12] To do this would reduce the wide options for forest products to largely timber trees produced from 'clear felling' of even-aged plantations. Figure 2.1 shows the impact of management practices on individual trees, as pollards and coppices.

FIGURE 2.2. Landscape of typical wood pasture.

PHOTO: AUTHOR

Pollards are cut at head height or a little above to avoid the destruction of growing shoots by grazing animals. These may be set along the external and internal wood-bank edges and within 'wood-pasture' where there is access to animals, the coppices being cut close to the ground but requiring exclusion of grazing animals. Pollards may also be found along streams and other watercourses. Trees left relatively uncut are termed 'standards', although these might be 'shredded' for larger timber products than are produced from either coppice or pollard. Shredding is effectively coppicing of a standard tree for a time until felling, although it was not especially widespread due to it being a hazardous procedure![13] Beneath the coppice canopy, the low growing plants of the 'ground flora' are often ecologically valuable. The time between coppicing (or of pollarding) is termed the cycle, and the longer this is the thicker and longer is the 'pole' of timber thus grown. Complexity of coppice woodland management, ecology and structures together with a tendency to locate them on marginal soils means they are prone to extremes of waterlogging and drought depending on the soil type.[14]

On the other hand, monoculture stands of conifers provide softwood timber for construction and these became especially economic in the twentieth century. Trees have long been of economic importance, but are also used to show prestige. Many a stately home has limes, beeches or oaks either side of its drive, used to display a landowner's status. Shelter belts cross-cross English private estates providing cover for game birds, signifying a leisured class that was often remote from the day-to-day toil of the ordinary person. Trees form a part of deeper intention of the aristocracy to develop notions of 'Arcadia' in its gardens, as Adam Nicolson reminds us in his accounts of Wilton House, home of the Earls of Pembroke.[15]

Understanding the role of woodland in landscape evolution is not always clear-cut, and there inevitably remains uncertainty about the influence of early man, large herbivores and ecological preference dictated by soil, topography and ambient climate. In historic time it is relatively straightforward to discern a range of roles for woodland including hunting/cover, prestige, ornament and commercial. Yet unlike the general view of coniferous plantation, broadleaved trees plantations, pollards and coppices remain highly valued for landscape amenity alongside their ecological value, even if the original purpose may have been economic. Actually, in the New Forest, neither coppicing nor pollarding proved successful economically or indeed popular over time.

Other forms of woodland were popular in the long-term. Wood pasture, being grazed by animals who could find shelter beneath its trees, presents an open canopy precisely because regeneration is restricted by grazing animals (Fig. 2.2). Such landscapes are familiar from historical sources, including not only the true wood-pasture of medieval commons (these generally became degraded to open areas due to poor management in historic times), but also to 'parkland', generally a landscape created by the nobility and lesser gentry, from the medieval period onwards. Parks were generally not manicured areas, but private game reserves prior to the eighteenth century.[16] At a European scale, lowland forests might have been more like wood-pasture on account of large grazing herbivores, and hence provide an incentive for humans to enter these areas to hunt or later to graze domesticated animals. The other alternative is they presented a far more closed canopy structure that is a fully 'wooded' landscape. The dichotomy is interesting because of implications for contemporary forest management.

Historic woodland forms derive from earlier, more mature, varieties of natural vegetation. A 'high-forest' implies a mature climax vegetation that became established, by stages, as the climate warmed from 11,000 BC, with tree species now familiar migrating northwards and reaching a maximum development around 5000 BC. This implies little human interference but the distribution of dominant tree species (proposed from pollen diagrams from peat bogs) shows the domineering pioneer species of pine and oak to be present in northern Scotland (the northernmost coastal areas probably supported only scrub), while species like lime, oak, hazel and elm,[17] dominated southern Britain.

Hazel would be an important food source for Mesolithic people. Natural regeneration of any given species would occur following the death of individual trees, for example from lightning strikes, and re-colonisation by trees and shrubs after Mesolithic people may have produced a woodland clearing.[18] Hazel, being shade-intolerant, would not thrive or fruit under dense oak canopies in any case, yet it would be capable of shading out re-generating small oak trees. The result could be oak becoming marginalised to less productive sites so that, in this model, oak woods would have dominated less fertile soils.

Britain at the period of 'climax' wildwood provided for Mesolithic peoples with a suitably adapted technology to live, hunt and migrate through the forest, including making temporary clearings. This is supported by some palaeo-ecologists, who think evidence points to a fairly closed canopy, on account of evidence from pollen, beetles and snails but with open areas generated from catastrophic events such as wind-throw. Large herbivores were still present.[19]

Early models for 'wildwood' development for Britain, could suggest that 'a proverbial squirrel could have leapt from Land's End to Ullapool [NW Scotland], without putting a paw on the ground'.[20] Although proposed by Rackham, this view derives from earlier researchers on the historic vegetation of Britain and has been termed the 'Tansley model', after Sir Arthur Tansley.[21]

Geographically, such cover was far from a homogeneous land cover of trees; for Rackham identifies five provinces (Fig. 2.3) where a continuous tree cover was possible.[22]

The dynamics of mature woodland cover have been introduced, but we may ask: what was the nature of the wildwood that preceded the New Forest and how might it have changed? The nearby downlands of Wiltshire and Dorset (including Cranborne Chase) are overlain by very different soils it must be stressed, but they provide clues. Here there is evidence of a light canopy including oak with hazel beneath which deer and humans (the nuts being a staple for Mesolithic peoples) would have prospered together. Around 6000 BC this may have become denser before showing evidence of clearance and soil erosion from 4000 BC.[23] An archaeological section at Down Farm on Cranborne Chase displays one of the earliest known records of substantial landscape change in southern Britain. Here an original (Mesolithic) 'vegetation mosaic' of deciduous, parkland-like land cover (at least containing open spaces)[24] is interpreted as having given way to a more open environment as a result of land clearance perhaps for monument construction and agriculture. The evidence, from a blend of palaeo-environmental sources including plant remains and land snails with archaeological evidence points to a strong relationship with remaining woodland that continues from the late Mesolithic to the Neolithic.[25] This is hardly surprising!

Unfortunately, pollen diagrams can tell us nothing about the age and size structure of the woodland, making the general form of the wildwood a matter of some debate. However, George Peterken[26] helpfully identifies a continuum between 'relatively natural' and 'relatively artificial' woodland, commenting that there is a grey area where (for example) an oak stand is to be found in an area that would naturally have oak woodland as climax vegetation. Wildwood would, pre-human influence, have the property of 'original-naturalness'; his other

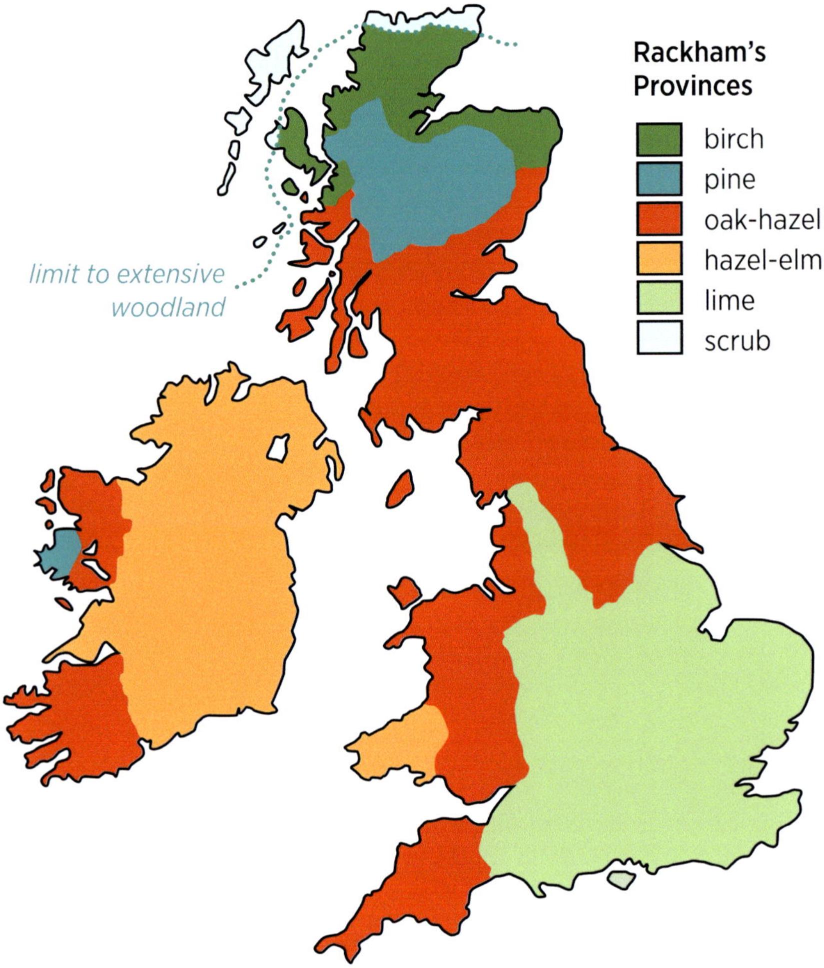

FIGURE 2.3. The mature climax vegetation of Britain during the Atlantic period.

AFTER RACKHAM 2006, 84

considerations relate to what might happen if human interference were to be removed; there is more than one kind of 'naturalness'. Actually, a 'normal forest' would have a wide range of age structures: in the New Forest it seems that this has been maintained by broadleaved planting, too low during 1860–1920, but above requirements 1920–1970.[27] Human intervention would seem inevitable, but what about large grazing mammals?

The Dutch ecologist, Frans Vera[28] questions the wide-spread notion of dense woodland, preferring a much more open 'wood pasture' landscape of sparse tree cover permitting large herbivore grazing beneath. This view has considerable currency among ecologists and conservationists, although as a model upon which to base current conservation objectives it remains uncertain.[29] In essence, Vera points out that large grazing animals, such as deer and wild oxen (aurochs), were present in European forests (as in other forests elsewhere) and that therefore they must have had a significant impact on forest dynamics by browsing trees and eating their seedlings, preventing regeneration.

Large herbivores thus had a strong influence on ancient woodland habitat when it re-colonised the Northern hemisphere after the last Ice Age. Deer, especially, would move in quickly and play a role in grazing and seed dispersal. The pre-Neolithic forests of Britain contained large mammals (wild ox, deer and wild boar) and there is some archaeological evidence for this. Competing influences of grazing herbivores and growing vegetation produced a cycle of succession from trees, then scrub, then grassland and back again in a dynamic equilibrium.

Mature forest trees would decline due to individual tree death, catastrophic storms, bark-stripping, or fire (in pinewoods). Grazing of re-generated shoots and saplings would hinder re-generation of the woodland canopy. Thus created is an open park-like landscape including individual veteran trees. Hence, this alternative hypothesis is that ancient woodlands may have been much closer in appearance to woodland pastures than the imagined primeval forest with continuous cover.

Thorny shrubs such as blackthorn *Prunus spinosa* and hawthorn *Crataegus monogyna* excluded grazing herbivores, into which young trees (both shade tolerant and shade in-tolerant species) in turn regenerate. In this 'regeneration window' events, such as hard winters or drought can cause the grazing animal populations to drop, aiding regeneration. The latter could also be facilitated by the animals where present through soil disturbance and dung deposition. Young trees such as oak or hazel would also invade in scrub areas through introductions of seed by birds, wind and animal dispersal. Hazel, specifically, if shaded out, and therefore not producing pollen, would not survive. By implication, woodlands would have had to be open for that tree to survive.

Next, in the woodland (or grove) phase young trees mature and develop closed canopies, shading out the scrub species. The length of this phase would be considerable and largely dependent on tree longevity. In the break-up (or degenerate) phase, trees die enabling once more the opening up the canopy, allowing grassland vegetation to be re-established. The whole cycle might take some 500 years. In a simulation model for an area measuring 5 × 5 km, Keith Kirby[30] reports that over large spatial scales and a long time period, varied habitat mosaics may be generated by naturalistic grazing regimes. Essentially, his findings are consistent with the Vera model with open elements of forest vegetation co-existing with 'closed-forest' species. There could be continuity of both grassland and woodland-type vegetation, providing niches for a range of different species, including poor plant colonizers, and open conditions for scrub-nesting and foraging birds, conditions that are relevant to modern conservation practices.

One strength of the Vera hypothesis is that plants of open ground and woodland edge remained commonplace, in part by providing cover for the next generation of trees. Such a dynamic is observed in medieval parks and wood-pastures; even coppice woodland cycles strongly echo Vera's ideas, although trees are brought to ground level not by grazing and decay, but by regular and deliberate cutting.

Similarly, natural management of the landscape could be observed in Africa, where mammals graze, control and maintain the open bush and savannah and where humanity evolved. Later, humans in Europe moved into this more 'parkland' landscape'. The question of evidence often relies upon what applied at a specific location, and that would be determined by what was occurring around the mire that supplied a stratigraphic peat column.[31]

Vera draws to our attention the role of large herbivores that may have been underplayed in the high forest hypothesis. The answer may lie between: ecological intuition would seem to support Vera, yet palaeo-environmental evidence can operate to the contrary. It is probably fair to comment that the debate may be one of just how dense was the cover of mature trees, how continuous it was and what was the size and occurrence of clearings.

Rackham is clearly closer to Tansley in his thinking, but acknowledges the points made by Vera whereby first large grazing mammals and later humans influenced woodland development to the point where cycles become defendable. After all, in other predator-prey relationships in ecology, cycles in population numbers of both (the predator numbers lags behind that of its prey) are commonplace. Nature presents many such dynamics. In order to present a clear picture, we are invited to consider the pros and cons of the Vera hypothesis.[32]

Supporting arguments that favour the Vera 'savannah-like' ecological dynamic model include a place for hunter-gathering humans living from large herbivores. In this situation, Neolithic farmers access clearings where they can commence planting. Habitats thereby created are able to support a range of species such as historic trees, butterflies associated with grasslands, a range of habitats for birds of open and closed habitats and, importantly, there are open habitats for plants in the ground flora that do not flower in the shade.

Arguments against the Vera hypothesis include high ratios of tree to non-tree pollen in pre-Neolithic times, although certain non-tree species themselves produce little pollen. Britain and Ireland were similar to continental Europe, and although species composition could be very different after the ice, there is a lack of clear pollen evidence for cycles of vegetation, poor evidence for oak re-generation and not much evidence of common hawthorn, blackthorn or grass pollen before the Neolithic. Long time periods are also identified between the decline of wild herbivores and early records of existing woods. Yet, like Hatfield Forest, the New Forest comprises 'areas of trees, some of many acres in extent, in a matrix of grassland or heath'.[33] It is as if the evolving New Forest land cover may be a rare British example of where Vera's hypothesis may be supported, for he undertook significant research there. However, there are objections to this observation. Linking presumed Mesolithic vegetation to what may have been the (documented) land cover of the Middle Ages is very problematic.[34] Supposed ancient woods may not be the direct lineal descendants of pre-Neolithic vegetation, presumably because humans had been periodically clearing it or otherwise altering it over not centuries but millennia, and this goes for royal hunting forests as for other areas. The next section considers the physical basis of the area.

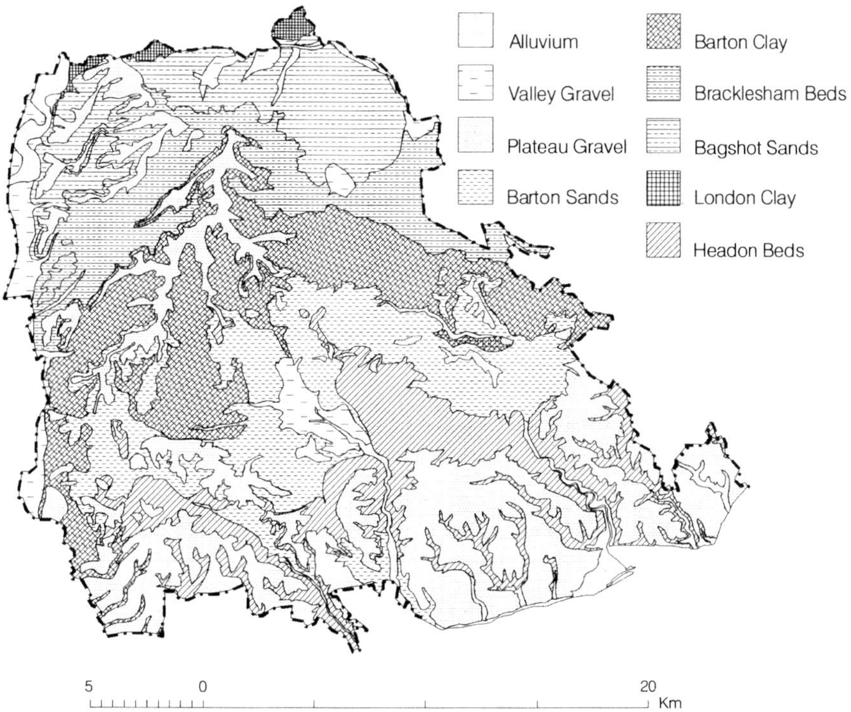

FIGURE 2.4. Geological map of the New Forest.

AFTER SMITH 1999, 4, BY PERMISSION OF HAMPSHIRE FIELD CLUB AND ARCHAEOLOGICAL SOCIETY

Geology, climate and soils

The best geological locus at which to start an account of the New Forest Landscape is with the chalk, that, perversely, nowhere occurs in or immediately adjacent. This pure, soft and mostly whitish, limestone was deposited between *c.*100 and 65 million years ago comprising largely the bodies of microscopic green algae for a warm, subtropical sea in the upper Cretaceous period.

The significance of this deposit is that it immediately underlies the Tertiary rocks that form the 'Hampshire Basin' and includes much of the sands, clays and gravels of the New Forest. The term 'basin' alludes not to any rivers, but to a geological syncline (a downfold) trending west to east, thereby preserving the younger tertiary deposits above the chalk. To the north and west, the chalk forms the ridges of land of the Dorset Downs and also the Salisbury Plain; to the south it re-appears on the Isle of Wight.

Deposition in the chalk sea was brought to an end some 65 million years ago, followed by surface erosion and then a range of clastic Tertiary deposits of sand, pebbles and clay. At some times, such during the deposition of the Eocene London Clay, the entire area was submerged, otherwise there was further periodic uplift and erosion. As a result, the New Forest, is underlain by Eocene and Oligocene sands and clays, the product of marine, deltaic, estuarine and fluvial deposits as the land surface varied with respect to the sea. Most significant was the gentle folding, in the Oligocene, co-incidental with formation of the Alps in central Europe around 23 million years ago.[35]

The geology (Fig. 2.4) has some characteristic surface manifestations that affect the hydrology and soils in the New Forest. Ferruginous (chalybeate) springs emerge from oxidising pyritic and glauconitic sediments in places. The bands of impermeable clays cause an accumulation of acid peat to accumulate as valley mires. The lithology which determines the characteristics of the poor soils is as follows: Bagshot sands are fine sands that succeed the London clay, Bracklesham beds (lithologically very variable, but sandy clays and sands with occasional pebbles and ironstones) and Barton beds (sands and clays) occur on the north side of the forest, while to the south is the Headon Hill Formation. Overall, the strata dip southwards at an angle of 1–2°.

Resting on the eroded Tertiary surface is the range of 'superficial deposits' from the Pleistocene and 'Recent' periods. Major deposits include aeolian sands, 'head' (a range of geological materials moved down slope under periglacial conditons), modern peat and river alluvium. Sub-angular flint gravel terraces of Pleistocene age on the heaths form the poor, acidic soils, or otherwise have been extracted for aggregates.The plateau gravels are variously of fluvial, brick earth and glaciofluvial origins (including river and marine terraces) and there is loess from both local and remote deflation in the late Pleistocene.[36]

The last two to three million years have seen climatic fluctuations that were unprecedented in scale and in frequency during the previous 260 million years or more of Earth's history. To give an idea of the severity of this variation, it is estimated there was variation of average temperature for Britain in the order of 20°C during the past 15,000 years alone.[37] Before then, during the Tertiary geological period (*c.*65–2.0 million years ago) there was an overall fall in mean global temperatures, most pronounced from around 15 million years ago, with massive swings in temperature commencing by the end of the period. The 'Ice Age' or Pleistocene geological period (*c.*2.6 million to 12,000 years ago) inevitably impacted on the natural environment and hence the activities of humans. Constant review of palaeo-environmental information as new evidence comes to light and uncertainty in dating often makes simple statements about soil, water and vegetation difficult, yet it is essential to build a generalised picture of historic and prehistoric landscapes.

Figure 2.5 shows the relative swings in climate affecting Britain over the last 700,000 years. This information is derived from the ratio of Oxygen^{18} to Oxygen^{16} recovered from shells of marine creatures in cores from the ocean floor, considered the most efficacious indicator of global temperatures for the northern hemisphere. In essence, the coldest stages (named Anglian (*c.*500,000–400,000 BC) and Devensian (*c.*115,000–10,000 BC) saw an advance of glaciers into what is today mainland Britain; there were others that affected continental Europe in this way, but are today regarded merely as cold phases in Britain. These were set at approximately 350,000 years ago and just before 100,000 years ago.

Images of ice sheet advance and valley glaciers are totally inappropriate for southernmost England, for even during the Anglian stage solid ice only reached approximately the line of the modern Thames. In the most recent cold phase,

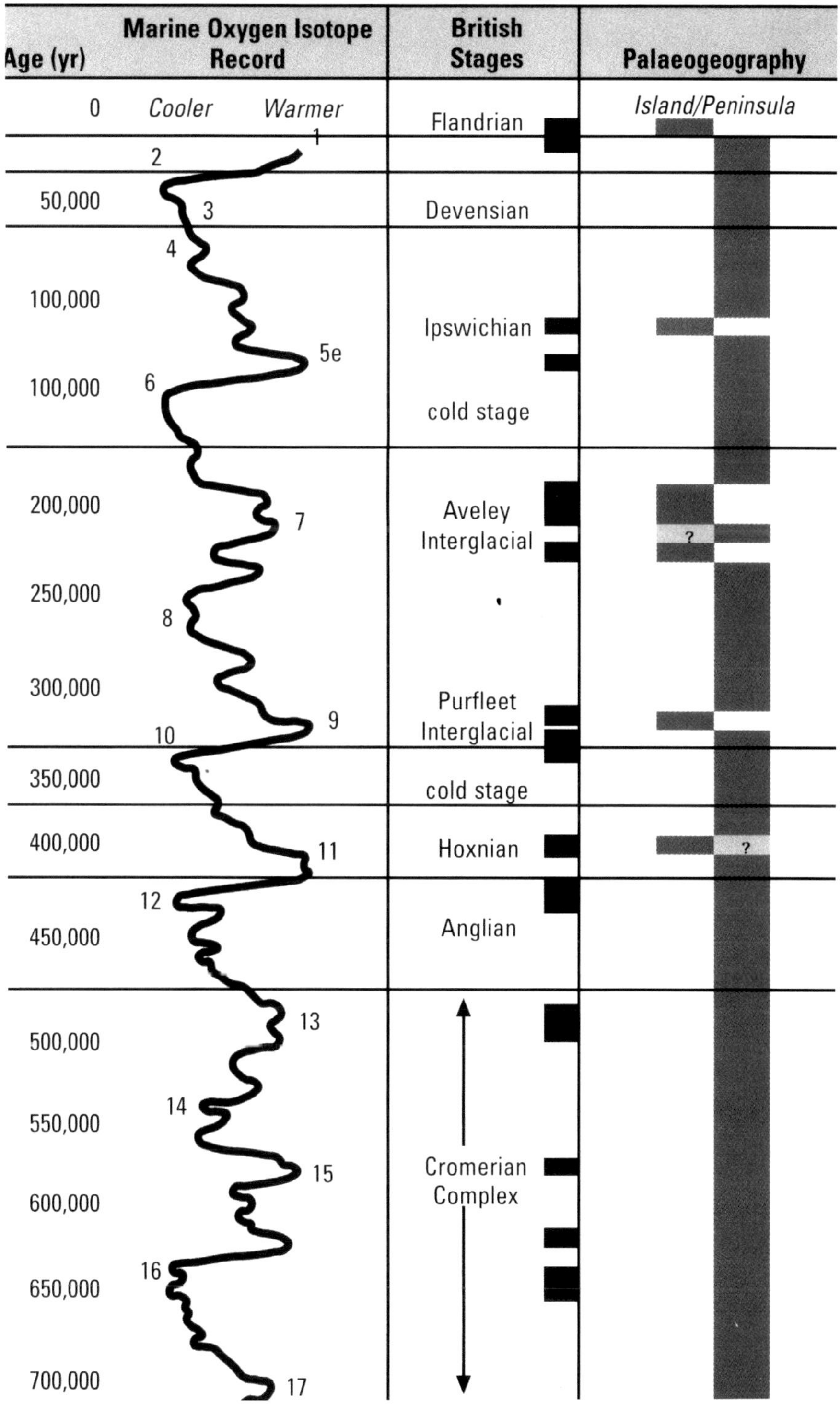

FIGURE 2.5. Relative swings in climate affecting Britain during the past 700,000 years. Numbers 1–17 in the left hand column refer to main isotope stages; the odd numbers indicating warm stages ('interglacials') the even numbers are cold stges ('glacials').

BARTON 2005, 18

the Devensian advance, the ice sheet largely affected only upland Britain, although it did affect the north-east coast as far south as Norfolk. Therefore, extreme physical erosion, including the scraping and removal of soils, cannot have occurred in the New Forest area. There were, however, other cold-phase soil forming processes including 'solifluction'. This is the result of freezing and thawing of topsoil on an annual cycle that breaks up solid geological materials causing downslope fracturing and movement of rock material under permafrost conditions. Solifluction affected, or formed, 'dells' of the New Forest that may be tributary to modern dry river valleys[38] much as it does the coombes of the adjacent chalk downland.

During the Pleistocene meltwaters from further north eroded valleys and deposited 'valley-fill gravels' and flinty river terrace deposits. These are valley-side benches or steps that represent a former level of the valley floor that was cut by lateral movements of an ancient river. These are especially prominent in the lower Avon valley, including the New Forest area, rising between 0.5 m and approximately 100 m AOD.[39] Superficial geological deposition (especially former river terrace and 'plateau gravel' deposits) thus continued throughout the Pleistocene. Wind-blown loess, generally silt grade material, was also transported and deposited on landscapes under these 'periglacial' conditions.

On a scale that affects human prehistory during the past 10,000 years, the climate has certainly not been stable. For instance, there was a 'climatic optimum' in temperature called the Holocene Climate Optimum a warm period approximately 7000–3500 BC, during which time Britain became separated from continental Europe, something that had occurred by 6000 BC. There was an increase in rainfall around 500 BC and a medieval climatic optimum *c.*AD 950–1250. Subsequently, the Little Ice Age occurred between approximately the sixteenth and nineteenth centuries, after which the current global warming period started. The contemporary mean annual rainfall within the New Forest is not particularly high by British standards. A record for Lymington (1976–1988) gives a mean annual rainfall of 782.3 mm; that at Beaulieu (1966–1989) was 860.1 mm.[40] Rainfall is fairly evenly distributed throughout the year, but the months of October to January are overall the wettest.

Soils are the result of geological, topographic, biotic and climatic influences.[41] Subjectively one might comment that the New Forest contains some of the poorest land, agriculturally speaking, in lowland England. Except for a few peripheral alluvial areas, virtually soils all are acidic and nutrient deficient, with large areas affected by seasonal surface waterlogging. In essence, these are sandy or flinty and sandy or coarse loams soils formed from Tertiary sands, head and river terraces. They also include podsols and waterlogged gley soils. Some have clayey subsoils, prone to seasonal waterlogging. Peats occur on seepage slopes and in valley bottoms. Finer textures soils are fine or coarse loamy soils over clay, these are also seasonally waterlogged. The modern hydrology is dominated by relatively impermeable strata, so that the catchments of the New Forest display a quick response to rainfall, manifest in a large fluctuation in river flows.[42]

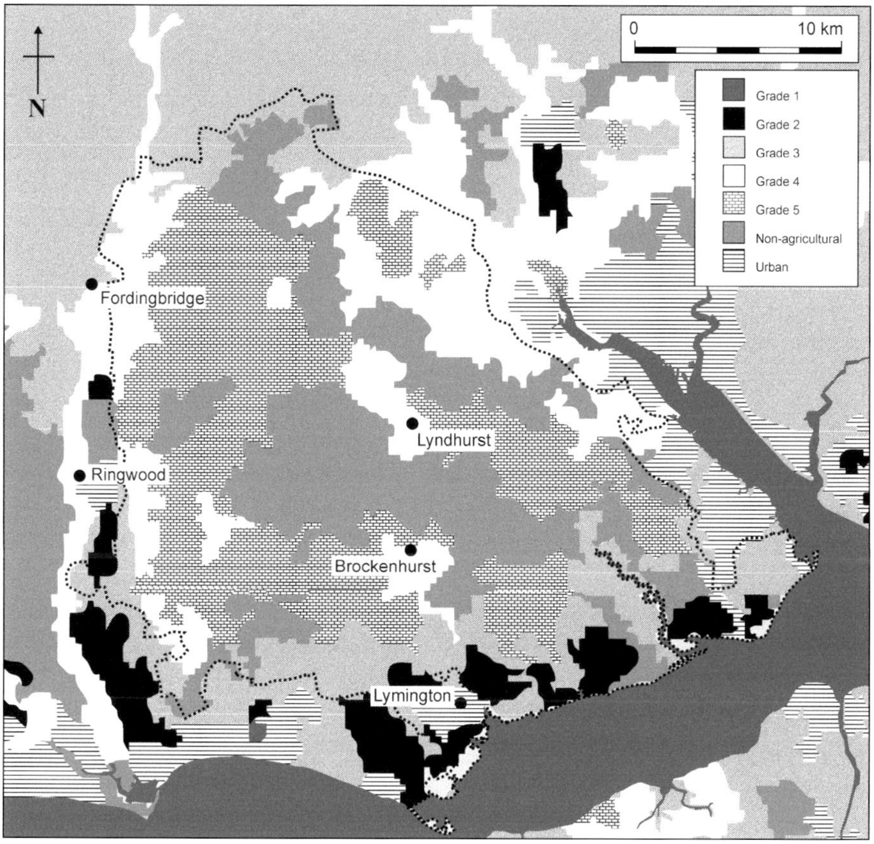

FIGURE 2.6. Agricultural Land Classification for the New Forest area after Defra http://magic.defra.gov.uk. Accessed Sept 2017.

In Figure 2.6, the poorest agricultural land comprises Grade 5 (land with severe restrictions due to factors such as topography, droughtiness, flood risk, stoniness, poor nutrient status *etc.*), and that land considered 'non-agricultural' category (the heathlands for example). These categories dominate the northern forest. Grade 4 is widely distributed, but concentrated on the north east side of the areas and has fewer restrictions. Grade 3 land has moderate limitations which affect the choice of crops, timing and type of cultivation, harvesting or the level of yield, but is suited to hardwood forestry. Finally, and occurring along the southern margin of the forest, where crops are able to be grown, Grade 2 land has only moderate limitations for agriculture between the higher ridges and the sea and along the edge of the lower Avon Valley. Grade 1 land is largely absent. These areas have soils that are river terrace deposits, but with fine and coarse loamy topsoil.

Gravel terraces dominate the geomorphology of the Forest proper. The northern end is on the highest gravel-topped elevations, otherwise the overall topography descends southwards, either towards the Solent or the lower Avon valley[43] in a series of terraces. The main forest watershed runs approximately north–south; six westerly flowing streams descent to the Avon and five more south and east. Along the western margins, terrace gravel underlies large areas of the commons.

Gravelly and sandy soils are poor in nutrient and water retention, with the finer sands on slopes prone to erosion. The Holiday's Hill and Boulderwood associations are developed on Tertiary and Cretaceous sand, loam and clay and Plateaus gravel and river terrace gravel respectively. These include not only soils with peaty tops, but also those displaying gleying (reduction of iron in lower horizons) and podzolisation (see below). The clays form the Wickham 3 and 4 associations[44] characteristically acidic in nature and of low nutrient status, as well as presenting common problems of cultivation of heavy soils.

It is likely the soils of primary woodland were generally 'brown forest soils'. These are impacted on by water draining through the soil profile removing organic matter, clay particles and soluble substances such as nutrients in a process known as 'leaching'.[45] Podzols thus formed are degraded soils where organic matter and certain compounds of iron and aluminium are leached, that is mobilised from the upper to be deposited in the lower part of the soil profile, removing most nutrients that may be present in the topsoil. Podzols are characterised by a leached (very light coloured) horizon near to the surface, something that does not occur in a brown soil, of a kind commonly found beneath a deciduous forest canopy. Podzolisation is probably a consequence of removal of the tree cover however some unenclosed woods overlie undisturbed 'acid' forest brown earths, that is soils that have not been podzolised. This may indicate that that they have never been cleared and farmed.[46]

Similar occurrences have been proposed elsewhere. The archaeology of Ashdown Forest (a former royal hunting forest), is in many ways similar to the New Forest. There was Mesolithic occupation, an elaboration of hunting techniques and prolonged hunting periods during the Neolithic with some occupation (from around 4000 BC). Local clearance around settlements would have taken place on the infertile sandy soils, the heavy clay soils supported thick woodland, an exploited resource. Bronze Age evidence is scarce, but points to some evidence for settlement.[47] The Brecklands of East Anglia were similarly denuded of trees following the Neolithic[48] and land 'broken' for cultivation. That 'brecks' as intakes for un-intensive arable, including fallow periods, were present in the post medieval period[49] gives a possible clue to notions of shifting cultivation on marginal land and gives insight to what may have occurred on heathland in prehistory.

Stability and change

> 'The unenclosed Forest is the largest area of wild, or "unsown" vegetation in lowland Britain and includes large tracts of the formerly common habitats that are now fragmented and rare in lowland western Europe- heathland, valley mire and ancient pasture woodland'[50]

Elsewhere Colin Tubbs can talk of its survival, including a continuity from prehistoric times as 'miraculous' so it comes as no surprise that the area is special. While in this respect, it does not imply the New Forest is unique in an absolute sense, but the narrative is one largely of grazing, of trees and interesting

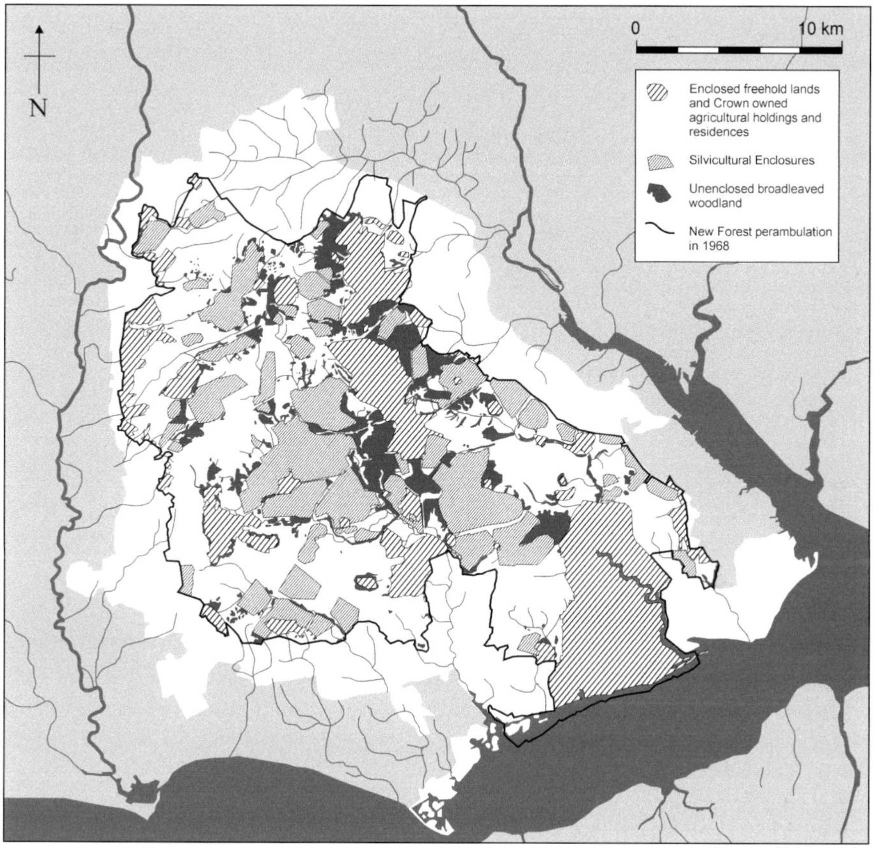

FIGURE 2.7. The modern New Forest boundary and major land covers.
AFTER TUBBS 2001, 21

wetlands, of a separate legal system, of modern recreational pressure and above all, a place within the national consciousness.

Today the perambulation (that is the legal boundary of the New Forest) encloses 145 square miles (37,555 hectares). Figure 2.7 shows the modern boundary and also the major land covers.[51] Of this area: 28% is privately owned (private estates, residential and farming land); 49% is Open Forest; 23% is within Inclosures. The latter two comprise 27,000 hectares owned by the crown and managed by the Forestry Enterprise (part of the Forestry Commission). Of the Open Forest: Bogs and wet heath = 10.5%; Heath = 22%; Grassland with bracken and gorse = 20%; Lawn = 1.5%. Of the Enclosed land: Conifers (plantation) = 17%; Broadleaved trees = 12.5%; Other = 1.5%. Ancient and Ornamental woodland is comprised of: Broadleaved trees = 12.5%; Natural conifer = 2.5%. About 5000 commoners' animals are depastured in the forest, regulated by the verderers; of these about 3000 are ponies, the remainder predominantly cattle with a few donkeys.[52]

The New Forest is therefore an exemplar of what might be done with economically marginal land. It remains to be discussed how hunting gave way to agriculture and why this evidently failed, paving the way to alternative land uses, meaning that it has much in common with marginal land elsewhere. Prehistoric

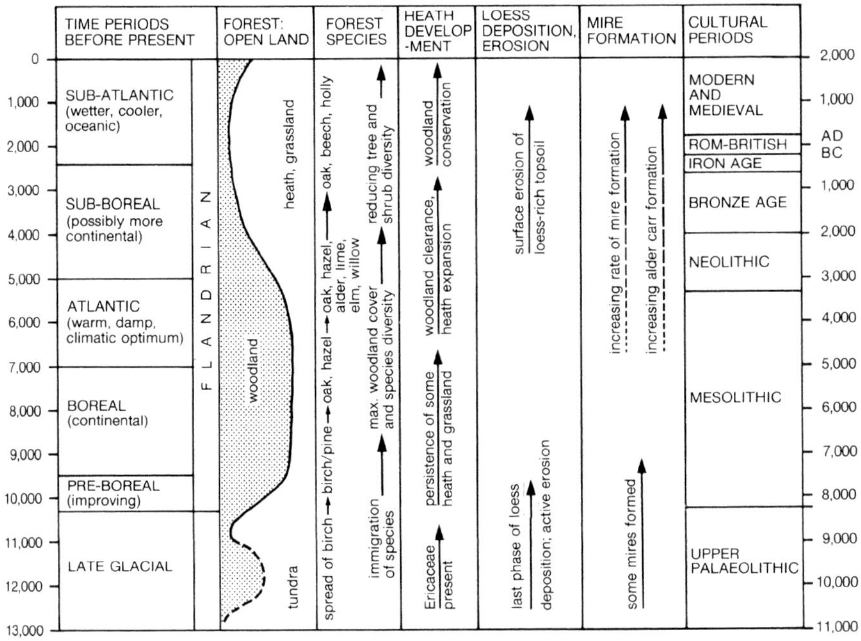

FIGURE 2.8. Timeline for the New Forest.

AFTER TUBBS 2001, 65

dating is never as tight as that expected for historic times. Due to spreading technologies, the technologically-based time periods (Palaeolithic, Mesolithic, Neolithic, Bronze Age and Iron Age) will vary from region to region. Figure 2.8 shows the timeline appropriate to the New Forest.

Within the New Forest there is no evidence of woodland disturbance throughout much of the post-glacial period, at least for the 'core' of the forest. Post-glacial pine (with some birch) was gradually replaced by oak-hazel, elm and then lime by the last centuries BC, only to die out (as did ash) during the Iron Age; these species generally preferring more base-rich soils but they can also tolerate relatively low pH soils. Beech and holly became important in subsequent historic times. Heathland species, notably *Calluna* and *Erica*, only became important during the Bronze Age, and are associated with widespread woodland clearance. It is presumed that, before the pioneering pine and coniferous forests, arctic tundra (and not temperate heath) would have been the dominant vegetation community.[53]

The evidence for the prehistory of the New Forest in terms of detail from the palaeo-environmental record (as opposed to archaeological monuments) is scant. In this area of both continuity and change there is surprising overall continuity of landscape, habitat and land use dating from human prehistory. In the next chapter the emergence of this unusual area is discussed in terms of the prehistoric societies that commenced landscape development, around the details of which there is considerable confidence. A pattern of woodland with glades thus seems to have persisted into medieval times.[54]

Values placed in trees

To develop the theme of human values concerned with forests into historic times, they might be conceptualised around both direct economic and non-market values:

- Natural forests as habitats for plants and animals
- Natural forests as a resource base for hunter-gather societies
- Semi-natural forests as a resource base for agricultural societies
- Semi-natural forests, chases, 'parklands' or forests for hunting by elites
- Plantations and planted trees for amenity and indicating prestige
- Semi-natural forests enjoyed for amenity, spiritual, health or recreational value
- Plantations and forestry for production purposes

The first two apply to the post-glacial wildwood, the third applies to the agricultural phase (largely) from the Bronze Age but pockets of conventional agricultural land use has persisted. The next two are about appropriation of woodland and forest by elites, especially hunting by kings and nobility from Anglo-Saxon times onwards. Next are the more intangible yet very important benefits enjoyed throughout human history. The last theme applies to industrialising societies concerned with construction, ship building, mining and other industrial purposes. It provides a particular emphasis for the post-medieval New Forest with the arrival of the Office of Woods and later the Forestry Commission, representing state enterprise within the royal forest.

The transition to agriculture would have been gradual, and in many societies, hunting has been shown to continue even when the vast majority of the population would be engaged in agriculture. In the New Forest, this transition may have occurred possibly 1500 years later than elsewhere in its immediate environs, notably on the downs. If we can presume there was minimal agricultural activity, the area was merely penetrated by hunting bands much as it had been since the Mesolithic. However this is a presumption based on the negative evidence of hitherto no clear evidence for Neolithic agriculture, monuments or settlement. Forests remained important sources of fuel, charcoal and construction as well as providing habitats in which to hunt animals.

The practice of coppicing is ancient, although the exact systems of underwood exploitation remain a matter of some debate. However, the Sweet Track across the Somerset Levels and Moors includes coppice poles dating from the Neolithic.[55]

Mesolithic peoples in Europe probably used coppice products in construction and in the creation of fish baskets; in Ireland coppicing on an eight-year cycle about 6100–5700 BC has been detected[56] and at Star Carr in Yorkshire (*c.*9000–8500 BC) there is evidence for coppice poles being used.[57] Surviving parts of the wildwood are likely to be coppiced, on account of their species of lichens and mosses. In general, woodlands in the medieval landscape were managed with purpose, of supplying timber from standard trees, and coppice stool products for hurdles, firewood and charcoal. However the continuation of modern 'ancient woodland' directly from pre-Neolithic vegetation has been contested.[58]

A main use of coppice during the Roman occupation was to supply the hypocaust for a Roman villa[59] and the Rockbourne villa is proof of a strong Roman presence in the area, although it does not prove that wood products were taken from the area that would become the New Forest. The Forest also hosted a ceramics industry at this time, although this went into serious decline. Saxon settlement, as evident from place names, shows it possible there were fields cleared from tree cover.

The woodland would appear to have been dominated by oak and hazel (as underwood), with alder along watercourses and birch, holly, beech, ash, lime and probably elm and hornbeam locally. The preponderance of Saxon place names (although there are a few possible Celtic survivals)[60] suggests settlement at this time. Domesday Book records seven hundreds: Bovre, Rodbridge, Rodedic, Sirlei, Egheiete, Rincvede (Ringwood) and Fordingbridge implying strong Anglo-Saxon administration – notwithstanding the economic marginality of the land.[61] The implication of strong Roman and Saxon presence is that there was the political and administrative ability to manage woods from early times.

Rackham reports documentary evidence for coppicing in ninth century England. Having scrutinised the Domesday record, he finds roughly half of settlements mentioned possessed woodland so that 'England was not well-wooded even by the standards of the twelfth century'.[62] The New Forest would seem to buck this trend, although Domesday Book (1086) presents a picture of near economic decline. The Normans maintained a semi-natural condition supporting the needs of the king and nobility, yet the rights to gather wood as well as graze pigs for acorns (mast) and cut turf by ordinary people was codified later in the *Charter of the Forest* (1217). It was regarded as a serious a felony to damage the forest resource, as to take the king's beasts, yet assarting continued into the fourteenth century under some regulation. To the Normans, the establishment of royal forests was one aspect of demonstrating domination and prestige whereby largely illiterate nobility hunted and, one imagines, much business was achieved on hunting trips.

Such evidence suggests a switch in emphasis from prestige hunting forests to recognition as a real economic resource for groups both within and without the perambulation, was going to become significant at some point. Internal colonisation of land from the coming of the Normans through to 'assarts' and 'purprestures' until the calamitous period of the Black Death is well attested.[63]

It is broadly true that the least productive land was placed under forest law. In the eleventh century, it was much more likely that factors, including poorer potential revenue from agriculture, played a role in the selection of land that effectively inoculated it from agricultural development, yet still tightly controlled. In the period until the Black Death, population pressure caused even the poorest areas to be viewed as possible for agriculture. Perhaps inevitably, from the late twelfth century, during and after the times of drastic afforestation by Henry II (Chapter 4), forests became a burning political issue[64] leading to the drafting of *Magna Carta* in 1215 and the *Charter of the Forest* in 1217.

Settlement in the New Forest witnessed this, at least until the fourteenth century when visitations of the Black Death caused a substantial decline in the English population. The proceedings of the justices of the forests record breaches of the forest laws. It may be, in effect, the colonisation of such areas was delayed by around one century, compared with marginal lands outside the forest law jurisdiction. In reality, assarted land could be managed communally, suggesting not only organisation at the manorial level, but also the possibility for institutional conflict between forest dwellers and the Crown.[65]

Evidence suggests a constant tension, then reversion, between the interests of the royal hunting forest because it represented a land reserve and because, in times of high population growth, an economic resource that was to make demands upon the interests of the crown as a hunting forest. Population pressure in agrarian dominated societies leads inevitably to pressure on land. In England this meant the cultivation of wastes, including communal rough grazing and woods[66] and clearance of woodland, and by inference pressure on areas of poor and marginal land. As a generality, progressively more 'marginal' (*i.e.* agriculturally lower grade) land becomes a prospect for cultivation. Outside the forests there would be an expansion of ploughland, within pressure to cultivate the poor soils and that change need not be 'legal' although assarts (and the smaller areas termed purprestures) could be retrospectively licensed.[67]

Another economic function is the simple point that, as a resource, a royal forest could generate revenue for the Crown, perhaps by more conventional means such as commercial forestry. Stagg can talk of the transition of medieval hunting forest into managed silviculture during the period to 1780.[68] Serving the needs of the navy became important, as was supplying domestic needs for construction and repair.

The New Forest went through a subsequent change in the nineteenth century, when it was to be seen as somewhere valued for aesthetic purposes. From this time the conflict between commercial forestry and conservation may be identified, underpinned by significant Acts of Parliament and the Office of Woods. The twentieth century at once saw the forest as being a place of frequent visits by urban dwellers, yet it was not to join the family of national parks until 2005. Measures apparently designed to balance the objectives of the Forestry Commission, of forest dwellers especially in terms of the grazing economy and pure conservation remained in conflict. Notwithstanding the complex history, it is instructive to review the current ecologically defined landscapes, the outcome of millennia of human–nature interactions.

This book will demonstrate that the area that would become the New Forest was late to experience settled agriculture and, with the origins of the extensive heathlands believed to lie in the Bronze Age (a period when the British countryside was under pressure from climatic change and from population pressures) there is evidence showing that extensive, sustainable, agricultural settlement was not only delayed, but that it also failed. This failure would be attributable to the poor soil conditions; something realised perhaps 3000 years before the development of modern soil science! However, land pressures did not go away, and the area was under pressure from population growth through the medieval period to the fourteenth century. Subsequently, in the post-medieval period, pressure is demonstrated by squatters who would be more likely to encroach on marginally economic land than in more fertile areas.

New Forest landscapes

The New Forest is defined – and valued – by its association, or 'mosaic' of land-covers that incorporate semi-natural ecosystems. Developed since prehistory, these have been subsequently managed with objectives of hunting, forestry, agriculture and industry in mind and come to define what the New Forest is, and what it does.[69] It is perhaps interesting to reflect that 'hard boundaries' relate to constructed boundaries including those around 'inclosures'. In the open forest there can often be a gradation, or 'ecotone' from open habitats, such as heath, through scrub, to more-or-less mature woodland. Indeed, this observation is thought to relate to the evolution of more formal wooded areas where trees become protected from grazing pressures.[70]

Forestry

The silvicultural enclosures comprise three elements:[71]

- Relicts of plantations from specific Acts
- The products of (mainly) twentieth century replanting with natural regeneration succeeding the felling of earlier stands
- Pre-enclosure woodland, not felled

Relicts of plantations established after the Acts of 1698, 1808 and 1851 remain, although much broadleaved plantation was replaced by conifers during the twentieth century, including 'verderer's enclosures' that coniferised heathland in the 1950s and '60s. Ironically, by the 1920s, eighteenth and nineteenth century inclosures (once viewed as an intrusion on grazing rights) were valued as oak woods, and there was a public outcry around the partial felling of the Burley Old Inclosure.[72]

The New Forest Act (1877) had provided for leaving woodland for amenity purposes, including leaving self-sown trees and 'gapping-up' in spaces between; by 1928 the Forestry Commission had undertaken to preserve 60% of the inclosures as broadleaved, reducing to 42% at the time of a Working Plan of 1963.

Surviving (in-part) inclosures from the eighteenth century included existing pasture woodland in North and South Bentley, Pitt's, Sloden, Raven's Nest and Long Beech and pasture woodland enclosed in the same century included at least Burley Old, Ocknell, Puckpitts, Coppice of Linwood, Sloden, Raven's Nest and Woodfidley. In a management plan of 1982–1991 the commission made

FIGURE 2.9. Examples of enclosures near to Fritham. OS 1:25000 sheet.

the commitment that no silvicultural work would be undertaken within these enclosures, without agreement of the (then) Nature Conservancy Council. This has since been dropped (Fig. 2.9).[73]

The rise of coniferisation

The 1851 Act allowed for the planting of the poorer soils, regarded as not capable of yielding sufficient quality of beech or oak, paving the way for coniferisation.[74] Between 1940 and 1970, coniferisation mostly involved planting of Douglas fir and larch, Scots pine, Corsican pine and Norway spruce. Coniferisation has been a steady progression from the mid-nineteenth century.

Figure 2.10, from Forestry Commission information, shows the balance between conifers and broadleaved forests since 1770 located within the statutory inclosures. Pasture wood, unplanted areas and some woodland of uncertain date are excluded.[75] Coniferisation ended in 1971 and the recovery of broadleaved areas commenced from 1980. The exact mechanisms of change are complicated, and include factors such as the selective felling of conifers from mixed stands, leaving beech. The outcome of this has been an end to the 'profit motive' expressed through the Forestry Commission for Crown Land, and the rise of a conservation ethic incorporating not only biodiversity, but also landscape and re-affirming traditional land uses.

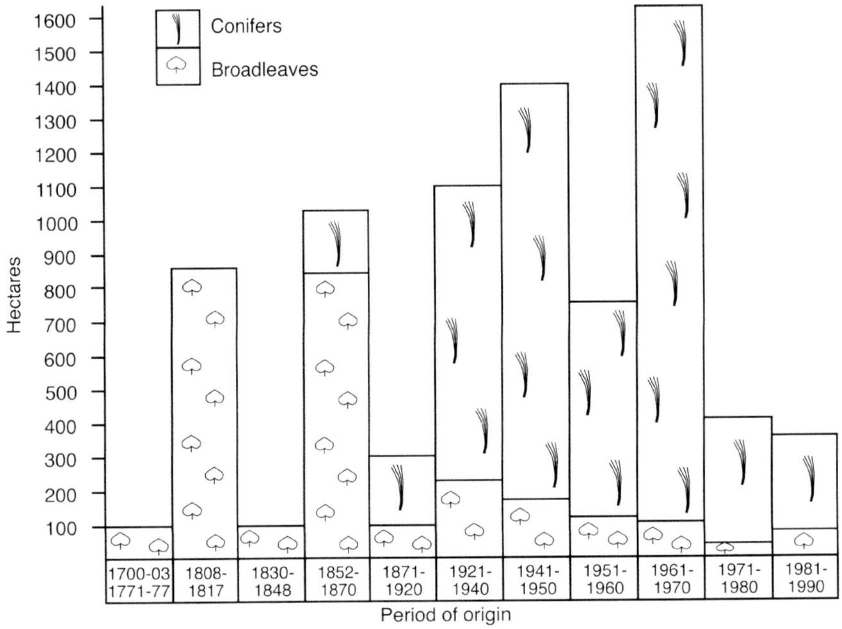

FIGURE 2.10. Age classes and areas of broadleaves in the Statutory inclosures. N.B. Pasture wood, unplanted areas and some woodland of uncertain date are excluded. Constructed from Forestry Commission information.

AFTER TUBBS 2001, 222

Heathlands

New Forest heathlands, both 'humid' and dry, are of international significance. Largely created during the Bronze Age by forest clearance and attempts at agriculture, untouched heaths continue today on account of their unsuitability for agriculture, turf cutting for fuel, grazing and (generally controlled) burning. These are located both on leached, acid and nutrient deficient podsolised soils including those of the gravel terraces, and also on areas of slow permiability caused by the clay content of the subsoil. Typical groundcover is heather (bell heather (*Erica cinerea*) and ling (*Calluna vulgaris*)) with gorse and bracken. Within this variable but low vegetation cover are habitats for small mammals, animals, birds and reptiles. Among the better known are sand lizards, smooth snakes and the Dartford Warbler. There are also ground nesting birds, such as the nightjar and skylarks, are also to be found on some of the New Forest heathlands. They are maintained by herbivore grazing, cutting and by fire.[76] The latter is often deliberate and is effective in controlling encroachment by mature gorse, birch and Scots pine. Ponies and cattle are capable of grazing younger age classes of heather and gorse.

Grasslands

New Forest grasslands are of an acidic composition, and associated with the heather and gorse and are also nutrient poor[77] while these have a complicated management history, including efforts to eradicate bracken, they represent a habitat for the rare plant *Gladiolus illyricus*. This is apparently confined to the more enriched and better drained acid soils. Acid grassland habitats are commonest on southern terraces, and tend to be associated with brown earth (rather than podsolised) soils. Hence, they may represent areas that have lost their woodland cover by burning during the last 300 years and may be associated are scattered holly, hawthorn, oak and yew and scattered woodland ground flora, including bluebells.[78]

Mires and wetlands

New Forest mires and wetlands are also of international significance, having the European designation Special Area of Conservation. They are associated with the low-lying areas of heath, and vary greatly in size. They also support open areas as ponds and attracts a good variety of insect, invertebrate and amphibian life, and provide drinking for ponies, cattle and deer. Wet areas are indicated by rushes, sedges, bog myrtle and sundew and in areas such as valley locations, they benefit from nutrient influx from drainage waters. Where there are permanent ponds and streams, the animal life includes frogs, toads, newts and grass snakes, and other small water invertebrates and insects. Wetland areas are vulnerable to damage from human and animal feet and from drainage and fragmentation.[79]

Lawns

New Forest Lawns are so-named because they comprise short grassland areas maintained through grazing by rabbits and larger animals. Located within woodlands and along stream sides, and the 'ecotone' (transitional communities) between woodland and heaths often comprises grassland, bracken, scrub and trees.[80] These provide early bite grass for animals. Nutrient status of lawns is maintained variously by influxes of exchangeable bases from streams and from recycling of nutrients from animal dung. Yet without human interference, and then human management of the New Forest, such semi-natural ecological systems would not be present, for the New Forest is a complicated mosaic of land use. The next chapter describes the main changes that occurred from the prehistoric period, and how these are central to our understanding of the area we enjoy today.

Tubbs[81] identifies 11 plant communities covering heathland and wetland. These are especially useful, being not only based on observation and experience, but are also able to take some account of transitional communities, and peculiarities of local hydrological conditions, such as seepage mires at the side of valleys. Neither do they conflict with other methods of vegetation survey and classification. These are respectively: dry heath, humid heath (together 8121 ha) tussock heath, wet heath seepage step mire, valley mire (all four 2894 ha), grass heath, acid grassland, improved acid grassland (all three 3993 ha), neutral grassland (353 ha) and re-seeded areas (526 ha). Figure 2.11 shows a model for the valley mires and vegetation classification. Nutrient enrichment is greatest along the 'axis' of the mire and a succession of plant communities occurs outwards from the open water centre.[82] Figure 2.12 shows, by way of complement, valley slope communities.[83]

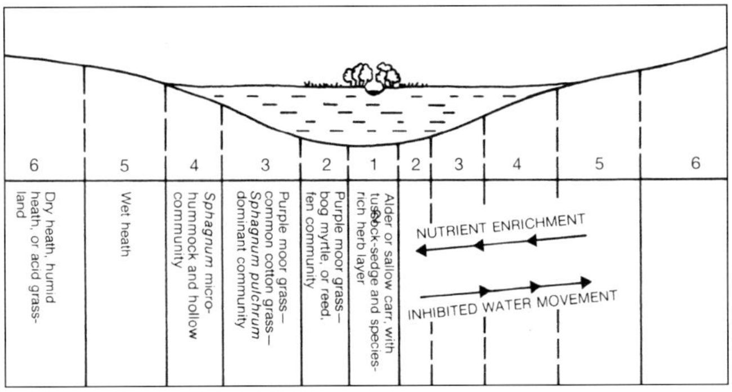

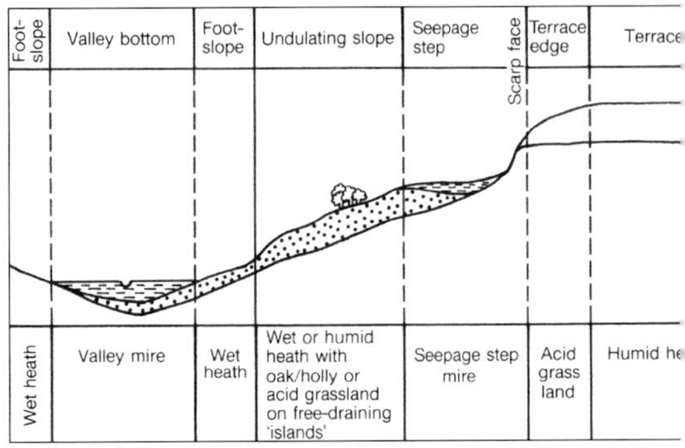

FIGURE 2.11 *(above left).* Valley mire model and vegetation classification.

AFTER TUBBS 2001, 244

FIGURE 2.12. *(above right).* Terrace slope plant communities.

AFTER TUBBS 2001, 246

Ancient and Ornamental Woods

New Forest Ancient and Ornamental Woods as described thus by the *New Forest Act* of 1877 are unenclosed, ancient pasture woodlands of 3671 ha in area.[84] Their origin has been disputed, and may in part result from periods of reduced grazing pressure since the seventeenth century, rather than from medieval coppice.[85] Pollarding was likely practised until the end of the seventeenth century.

The term refers technically to unenclosed woods originating in, or before, the eighteenth century and the cover is mainly oak and beech with an underwood of holly. These areas are semi-natural, the product of original natural vegetation in part (derived from the 'wildwood') and human management such as re-planting, restricting grazing, pollarding, coppicing and the collection of fuelwood, something restricted in recent times to encourage biodiversity. Ancient and Ornamental Woods included trees originally intended for the navy. The total area is 3692 ha of open woodland on the open forest. The *Deer Removal Act* of 1851 reduced the grazing pressure allowing regeneration of oaks and beeches, often creating a dense woodland canopy. These areas are one of the richest locations in Britain for beetles, fungi and other groups which rely on deadwood, both standing and fallen.[86] There was also enclosed 'roughs' or parkland where deer were fed adjacent to hunting lodges. The total area of ancient pasture woodland, a survival of the medieval period, exceeds 4000 ha.[87] Woodland Inclosures (really exclosures) are also a long-established part of the New Forest management and amount to some 344 ha of woodland.[88] These may be ancient pasture woods trapped behind exclosure fences, or else were re-planted (largely in the eighteenth century) on the sites of ancient woodlands.

The challenge for the New Forest Special Area of Conservation is to maintain management of this rare mosaic of habitats, including avoiding scrubbing over, bracken and purple moor-grass infestation restoring wetland and rivers. Grazing regimes are complimented by cutting and burning, maintaining the structure of habitats for the flora and fauna, on both crown lands and the adjacent commons. It remains likely that, given appropriate management prescriptions that present management means will prove sufficient to conserve the landscape.[89]

Summary

The New Forest is the outcome of a complex interplay of natural and human interactions dating back far before the royal hunting forest. The basic form, ecology and economy are determined by poor soils of the higher elevation, ridged areas, be they excessively drained or waterlogged; virtually all are acidic and nutrient poor. However the history of the forest also summarises the development and exploitation of woodlands and forested areas since the establishment of 'wildwood' in the post-glacial period. It is a brilliant example of continual human–nature interaction since pre-history, and furthermore the form it takes would not be possible without management to the present day, meaning that virtually all the values humans place in forests are manifest there. Its history and management deserves a conservation management (rather than deep ecological) approach on account of the persistence of humans in the area.

There have been at least three periods of changing pressure on the land resource. The Bronze Age saw widespread development of agriculture and this occurred again in the later medieval period to the Black Death. The time approximately between the seventeenth and nineteenth centuries saw both plantation of hardwood, then the start of coniferous plantation. Finally, recent centuries saw the rise of introduced 'ancient and ornamental' trees.

The modern landscape reflects all of the needs of hunting, grazing, fuel gathering, construction, industry, silviculture and modern commercial (coniferous) afforestation. Values placed in the forest have varied from hunting and gathering activities throughout the ages on a more-or-less subsistence basis, to leisure pursuits by elites, to industrial development including the development of silviculture and modern forestry on an industrial scale. Viewed in its entirety, the forest is not only valued as a national gem, but is also of European significance in terms of the landscapes developed. The creation of the New Forest National Park is a policy response that recognises the significance of the forest. These themes are developed in subsequent chapters.

Notes

1. T. Hardy (1872) *Under the Greenwood Tree*. Tinsley Bros, London.
2. S. Milligan (1950s) http://www.bbc.co.uk/comedy/thegoonshow/. Accessed Sept 2017.
3. H. F. Cook (2008) Evolution of a floodplain landscape: a case study of the Harnham Water Meadows at Salisbury England. *Landscapes* 9(1), 50–73.
4. J. Zalasiewicz, M. Williams, W. Steffen and P. Crutzen (2010) The new world of the Anthropocene. *Environmental Science and Technology* 2010; 100225131929071 DOI: 10.1021/cs903118j.
5. R. F. Nash (2001) *Wilderness and the American Mind*. Yale University Press, New Haven.
6. J. H. Lawton, P. N. M. Brotherton, V. K. Brown, C. Elphick, A. H. Fitter, J. Forshaw, R. W. Haddow, S. Hilborne, R. N. Leafe, G. M. Mace, M. P. Southgate, W. J. Sutherland, T. E. Tew, J. Varley and G. R. Wynne (2010) *Making Space for Nature: a review of England's wildlife sites and ecological network*. Report to Defra. Available at http://

webarchive.nationalarchives.gov.uk/20130402170324/http://archive.defra.gov.uk/environment/biodiversity/documents/201009space-for-nature.pdf. Accessed Sept 2017.

7. A. Lieberman (1984) Some ecological aspects of Northeastern American Indian agroforestry practices. *Indian Agroforestry.* http://www.daviesand.com/Papers/Tree_Crops/Indian_Agroforestry/. Accessed Sept 2017.
8. O. Rackham (1986) *The History of the Countryside*, 73, 382. Dent, London; (2006) *Woodlands.* Collins, London.
9. R. Reeves pers. comm. (2013).
10. Plantation Woodlands (2005) Hantsweb http://www3.hants.gov.uk/biodiversity/environment-biodiversity-landmanagement/woodland/woodland-hampshires-woodlands/woodland-plantation.htm. Accessed Sept 2017.
11. P. Tabbush (2010) Cultural values of trees, woods and forests. https://www.forestry.gov.uk/pdf/Cultural_value_woods_full_report_March2010.pdf/page19$FILE/Cultural_value_woods_full_report_March2010.pdf. Accessed Sept 2017.
12. G. F. Peterken (1981) *Woodland Conservation and Management*, 66. Chapman and Hall, London.
13. G .F. Peterken (1992) Coppices in the lowland landscape. In G. P. Buckley (ed), *The Ecology and Conservation of Coppice Woodlands*, Chapman and Hall, London, 7; G. P. Buckley (2013) pers. comm.
14. I. P. F Cummings and H. F. Cook (1992). In Buckley 1992 (ed.), *op. cit.* note 13, 52–75
15. A. Nicholson (2008) *The Earls of Paradise.* HarperCollins, London.
16. J. Bond (1994) Forests, chases, warrens and parks in medieval Wessex. In M. Ashton and C. Lewis (eds), *The Medieval Landscape of Wessex*, 116. Oxbow Monograph 6, Oxbow Books, Oxford.
17. V. Gaffrey, S. Fitch and D. Smith (2009) *Europe's Lost World, the Re-Discovery of Doggerland.* Council for British Archaeology Research Report 160, 53–56.
18. Elm was to decline dramatically across Europe from 4000 BC, probably from disease.
19. H. J. B. Birks (2005) Mind the gap: how open were European primeval forests? *Trends in Ecology and Evolution* 20(4), 154–56. Birkshttp://www.knepp.co.uk/Other_docs/Frans%20Vera/Birks%20over%20Vera%20in%20TREE1.pdf.
20. Based on a quotation '…from Blakeney Point to Hilberee: a [red] squirrel could jump from tree to tree…' (*Sir Gawain and the Green Knight*: Blakeney is on the Wash and Hilbere Island is at the mouth of the Welsh Dee). Supplied by G. P. Buckley.
21. O. Rackham (2006) *Woodlands*, 61. Collins, London.
22. *Ibid.*, 84.
23. M. J. Allen (2000) Soils, pollen and a lot of snails, In M. Green, *A Landscape Revealed. 10,000 Years on a Chalkland Farm*, 36–49. Tempus, Stroud.
24. M. J. Allen and J. Gardiner (2009) If you go down to the woods today; a re-evaluation of the chalkland postglacial woodland; implications for pre-historic societies. In M. J. Allen, N. Sharples and T. O'Connor (eds), *Land and People,* 49–66. Prehistoric Society Research Paper 2. Oxbow Books, Oxford .
25. M. J. Allen and J Gardiner (2012) Not out of the woods yet; some reflections on Neolithic ecological relationships with woodland. In A. M. Jones, J. Pollard, M. J. Allen, and J. Gardiner (eds), *Image, Memory and Monumentality: Archaeological Engagements with the Modern World*, 93–107. Prehistoric Society Research Paper 4. Oxbow: Oxford.
26. G. F. Peterken (1981) *op. cit.* in note 12, 42–43.
27. *Ibid.*, 274.
28. F. W. M. Vera (2000) *Grazing Ecology and Forest History*. CABI, Wallingford; D. Lovelace (n.d.) Prehistoric vegetation from the end of the last ice age. The woods of Herefordshire. http://www.bosci.net/prehistory.html. Accessed Sept 2017.

29. K. H. Hodder, M. Bullock, P. C. Buckland and K. J. Kirby (2005) *Large Herbivores in the Wildwood and in Modern Naturalistic Grazing Systems*. Report 648. http://eprints.bournemouth.ac.uk/10330/1/ENRR648.pdf.
30. K. J. Kirby (2004) A model of a natural wooded landscape in Britain as influenced by large herbivore activity. *Forestry* 77, 405–20.
31. F. W. M. Vera (2000) *op. cit.*
32. Rackham (2006) 95.
33. *Ibid.*, 92.
34. P. Szabó (2009) Open woodland in Europe in the Mesolithic and in the Middle Ages: can there be a connection? *Forest Ecology and Management* 257, 2327–30.
35. D. K. C. Jones (1981) *The Geomorphology of the British Isles, Southeast and Southern England*, 55. Methuen, London.
36. D. H. Keen (1980) The environment of deposition of the south Hampshire Plateau Gravels. *Proceedings of the Hampshire Field Club and Archaeological Society* 36, 15–24.
37. R. C. L. Wilson, S. A. Drury and J. L. Chapman (2000) *The Great Ice Age*, 174. Routledge, London.
38. C. G. Tuckfield (1986) A study of dells in the New Forest, Hampshire, *England Earth Surface Processes and Landforms* 11, 23–40.
39. C. M. Barton, P. M. Hopson, A. J. Newell and K. R. Royse (2003) *Geology of the Ringwood District and Geological Sheet* 314, 21–22. British Geological Survey, Keyworth.
40. Supplied by the Environment Agency.
41. D. C. Findlay, G. J. N. Colborne, D. W. Cope, T. R. Harrod, D. V. Hogan and S. J. Staines (1984) *Soils and their Use in South West England.* Soil Survey of England and Wales, Harpenden with key and associated 1:250,000 soil map; R. Allen (2005) chapter 2. http://www.soilandwater.co.uk/index.php?id=33. Accessed Sept 2017
42. Environment Agency (2009) New Forest Catchment Flood Management Plan. http://cdn.environment-agency.gov.uk/geso1008bowa-e-e.pdf. Accessed Sept 2017
43. C. R. Tubbs (2001) *New Forest, the History, Ecology and Conservation*, 39. New Forest Ninth Centenary Trust, Fordingbridge.
44. M. G. Jarvis, R. H. Allen, S. J. Fordham, J. Hazleden, A. J. Moffat and R. G. Sturdy. (1984) *Soils and Their Use in Eastern England.* Soil Survey, Harpenden. Soil Survey of England and Wales Bulletin 15, 299–304 and associated legend and 1:250,000 sheet.
45. Peterken (1981) *op. cit.* in note 12, 44.
46. P. Colebourne (1983) *Ancient Woodlands*, 24. Hampshire's Countryside Heritage 2, Hampshire County Council, Winchester.
47. *Ashdown Forest: History and Archaeology*. http://www.ashdownforest.org/enjoy/history.php. Accessed Sept 2017.
48. O. Rackham (1986) *op. cit.* in note 8, 72, 286.
49. P. M. Dolman, C. J. Panter, and H. L. Mossman (2010) *Securing Biodiversity in Breckland: Guidance for Conservation and Research.* First Report of the Breckland Biodiversity Audit. University of East Anglia, Norwich. http://www.norfolkbiodiversity.org/pdf/reportsandpublications/BBA%20Report%20-%20Main%20Report.pdf. Accessed Sept 2017.
50. Tubbs (2001) *op. cit.* in note 43, 18.
51. R. Daponte (2004) *Introduction to the New Forest.* http://www.forestry.gov.uk/pdf/NewForestFacts.pdf/$FILE/NewForestFacts.pdf. Accessed Sept 2017.
52. G. Cooper (2007) *The New Forest.* http://www.newforest.hampshire.org.uk/today3.html. Accessed March 2013.
53. K. E. Barber (1981) Pollen-analytical palaeoecology in Hampshire: problems and potential. In S. Shennan and T. Shadla-Hall (eds), *The Archaeology of Hampshire*, 91–94. Hampshire Field Club Archaeological Society Monograph 1, Winchester.

54. Tubbs (2001) *op. cit.* in note 43, 21.
55. R. J. Fuller and M. S. Warren (1993) Coppiced woodlands: their management for wildlife. http://jncc.defra.gov.uk/pdf/pubs93_Coppicedwoodlands.pdf. Accessed Sept 2017.
56. M. McQuade and L. O'Donnell (2007) Late Mesolithic fish-traps from the Liffey Estuary, Dublin, Ireland. *Antiquity* 81, 569. http://connection.ebscohost.com/c/articles/27172733/late-mesolithic-fish-traps-from-liffey-estuary-dublin-ireland.
57. Taylor B. Conneller C. and Milner N. (2010) Little house by the shore. *British Archaeology* 115. Accessed March 2013.
58. Szabó (2009) *op. cit.* in note 34.
59. T. Rook (2002) *Roman Baths in Britain.* Shire Archaeology, Princes Risboro'.
60. S. Davies, K. Walke and L. Coleman (1998) *The New Forest Historical Landscape*, Wessex Archaeology. http://www.newforestnpa.gov.uk/__data/assets/pdf_file/0005/27455/new_forest_archaeological__historical_landscape_character_assessment2.pdf. Accessed March 2013.
61. N. Smith (1999) The earthwork remains of enclosure in the New Forest. *Proceedings of the Hampshire Field Club and Archaeological Society* 54, 1–56; Tubbs (2001) *op. cit.* in note 43, 56–57, 170.
62. Rackham (1986) *op. cit.* in note 8, 73–81.
63. M. M. Postan (1972) *The Medieval Economy and Society*, 20. Penguin, Harmondsworth.
64. *Ibid.*, 23.
65. *Ibid.*, 132.
66. M. M. Postan (1966) *The Cambridge Economic History of Europe* I, 183. Cambridge University Press, Cambridge.
67. Tubbs (2001) *op. cit.* in note 43, 83.
68. D. J. Stagg (1989) Silviculture inclosure in the New Forest to 1780. *Proceedings of the Hampshire Field Club and Archaeological Society* 45, 135–45.
69. New Forest National Park. http://www.new-forest-national-park.com/. Accessed Sept 2017.
70. R. Reeves pers. comm. (2013).
71. Tubbs (2001) *op. cit.* in note 43, 215.
72. *Ibid.*, 101.
73. *Ibid.*, 215–16.
74. *Ibid.*, 220.
75. *Ibid.*, 222.
76. *Ibid.*, 26–27, 242–48.
77. *Ibid.*, 249.
78. *Ibid.*, 251–53.
79. *Ibid.*, 26–27, 242–48.
80. *Ibid*, 238.
81. *Ibid*, 238–39.
82. F. Rose (1953) A survey of the ecology of the British lowland bogs. *Proceedings of the Linnean. Society of London* 164, 186–211, modified by Tubbs (2001) *op. cit.* in note 39, 244.
83. Tubbs (2001) *op. cit.* in note 43, 246.
84. *Ibid.*, 162.
85. Smith (1999) *op. cit.* in note 61, 21.
86. R. Daponte (2004) *Open Forest Ancient and Ornamental Woodland.* http://www.forestry.gov.uk/pdf/AncientOrnamentalwoodland.pdf/$FILE/AncientOrnamentalwoodland.pdf. Accessed Sept 2017.
87. Tubbs (2001) *op. cit.* in note 43, 163.
88. *Ibid.*, 163.
89. *New Forest SAC Management Plan, part 1 description* 2001. http://www.newforestlife.org.uk/life2/part1.PDF. Accessed Sept 2017.

CHAPTER 3

A Hungry Land (10,000 BC–AD 1066)

'Everybody must be managed. Queens must be managed. Kings must be managed, for men want managing almost as much as women, and that's saying a good deal.'
Thomas Hardy[1]

Early human activity and the landscape

There are around 2000 archaeological sites recorded as Sites and Historic Monuments of the New Forest and its immediate surroundings within the counties of Hampshire and Wiltshire and it is heartening to read of the protection now afforded to archaeological monuments from the New Forest National Park Authority.[2] Evidence of human activity in the region dates back perhaps 500,000 years, but is sparse from the Lower and Middle Palaeolithic (that ended about 30,000 BC), it would seem to be restricted to the valleys and coastal areas in the region and is based upon finds of implements from the higher gravels; however some evidence may have been obliterated over time.[3] No evidence for Upper Palaeolithic people has come to light in the New Forest, although immediate post-glacial hunting cannot be ruled out, by reference to the broader picture across southern Britain including some sites in Hampshire adjacent to the Forest.[4]

The New Forest presents challenges for the preservation of archaeological material and this is due to erosion of soil and sediment, soil leaching and acidic conditions non-conducive to the preservation of a range of artefacts of archaeological interest. Much palaeo-environmental information is lacking, notably land snails, and there is poor bone preservation due to conditions in soil developed on the sands and gravels.[5] There are further opportunities for preservation associated with the mires and localised alluvial deposition. Nonetheless, the literature provides a reasonably clear picture of an area that, due to its specific geological nature and history, is atypical of the wider 'Wessex' archaeological region such as the chalk downland, the major valleys or the coastal regions.

Given the proven presence of humans throughout most of the post-glacial period, the landscape should, from the first, be seen as the outcome of complicated nature–human interaction. For example, there is apparently no evidence for heathland in the immediate post-glacial in the core of the New Forest, hence heath would appear not to be a part of the natural vegetation succession towards mature, post-glacial forest, starting between 10,000 and 8000 BC. There was infilling from eroded material in the post-glacial landscape that also provided the basis for the mires.[6] This showed a classic post-glacial succession of birch, then pine, then oak-hazel, elm, alder, lime (in that sequence). Beech migration may have been from *refugia* during the colder phases of the Pleistocene.[7] During presumed woodland clearance through human activity, certain areas of remaining ancient woods may still have been affected by human disturbance from an early period[8] perhaps giving them some characteristics of 'secondary (regenerated) woodland'.

In the Palaeolithic and subsequent Mesolithic period (Mesolithic dates are approximately 8500–4000 BC), people hunted in the region under a range of climatic conditions during the Pleistocene and Holocene.[9] Several finds of Palaeolithic hand-axes occurred at high level gravels, at Wood Green, along the southern gravels of the forest, and from the 'Solent Gravels' and in the lower Avon valley[10] that would play a role in north–south communications from prehistory onwards. Although the coastline changed greatly over time in respect of its modern position as sea level fluctuated, hunting and gathering activities were concentrated along the coastal zone before the start of settlement and agriculture. An approximation of the modern coastline of the English Channel (with its 'ria' type inlets) would have been evident from about 6500 BC following post-glacial sea level rise.

Once a forest cover became established, technologies would then then be adapted to hunting in the forests and to fishing in rivers. The earliest forest ('wildwood') thus heralded the arrival of Mesolithic cultures and, following the general pattern across Britain, this contained much birch and pine. Mesolithic peoples possessed tools, especially axes (for felling), burins for bone working, antlers, microliths, arrowheads, and harpoons. They hunted larger herbivores (wild ox, red deer, roe deer, elk, aurochs and horse) as well as beaver, wolf and wild boar. They fished using baskets and weirs, and hunted wildfowl (crane, teal and mallard). For gathering purposes, the woods provided berries, roots, fruit, nuts, fungi, wild seeds, grains, whilst shellfish were taken inland from the coast demonstrating a range of hunting activities into the forest area, although this later changed. Clearings would have attracted grazing animals, notably pigs for pannage and this would continue to the present. It may be there was a tendency, before the introduction of agriculture, for hunter-gatherer societies to migrate away from the sandy areas towards the chalk downland and it may have been there was a pattern of lowland settlement established by the Mesolithic that enabled upland exploitation. Much of the geological materials for tool-making were sourced locally from river gravel flints and pebbles from the Tertiary beds.[11] These become important for flint knapping, evident from 'Open Forest' areas.[12]

In the New Forest, as elsewhere, peat bogs are a key source for palaeo-environmental evidence, especially for vegetation, as they preserve plant tissues, seeds and pollen. Many bog sequences were damaged by peat digging in historic times,[13] making complete sequences rare. However, at Church Moor (SU 247 069) between Boulderwood Grounds and Burley Lodge, a location distant from the main settlements (Lyndhurst, Brockenhurst and Burley) a more complete sequence dates from 8000 BC to the present. Here, in the central forest, there was a mixed cover of pine, birch, hazel, some elm and willow but with oak dominant, reflecting a relatively dry climate. Later dominance of alder, lime *Sphagnum* and *Molina-Sphagnum* communities, when Britain became separated from the continent and a damper climate ensued, due to sea level rise. This situation continued until comparatively recently, although beech became predominant and there were holly invasions; this can be locally invasive on heathlands forming 'holmes' or 'hats' of holly on the tops of hills.[14] Here and elsewhere, there is apparently no suggestion that heathland origin in this area is free from human intervention. Otherwise, species present (beech, oaks, hazel and grasses) reflect the known ecological history.

The pollen record linked with radiocarbon dating of valley mires provides evidence for the post-Pleistocene vegetation and of subsequent clearance of the post-glacial forest, comprising largely oak, hazel and alder with some lime, elm and willow. Mesolithic people probably cleared woodland locally and particulate charcoal is present in cores from bogs, although the latter can arise as much from accidental fire as deliberate human efforts to clear vegetation. Regarding areas now known as the 'ancient and ornamental woodlands' (Chapter 2), the dominant species established after the extreme climatic changes of the Pleistocene were oak and beech, yet enigmatically the dominance of beech in later times probably owes its predominance to human disturbance.[15]

Mesolithic activity, like preceding Palaeolithic activity, is demonstrated by finds on the river terrace gravels in the general area. At Downton, there is evidence of domestic settlement and hunting including tool manufacture. Irregular hollows in gravels had been dug, probably to collect flint.[16] This site continued in occupation into the Neolithic. In the New Forest, isolated finds of flint axes, flakes, knives and scrapers have been recovered on open heath between Godshill, Fritham plain and Denny Lodge, from south of Brockenhurst and dredged from the Solent, where an earlier land surface became submerged.[17] Lighter soils, natural ridges and river terraces were easily cleared by Stone Age people. Distribution of finds in the region would point to some regional economic integration with the trading of artefacts in the Mesolithic,[18] as well as proven settlement at Downton, in the Avon valley – at a site that continued into the Neolithic.

Agriculture and the Neolithic (*c.*4000–2400 BC)

In general, the Neolithic technological revolution produced settled agriculture linked with a burst of associated technologies (pottery, spinning and weaving, advances in building structures and so on). These would supplement existing skills in stone-working, in canoe manufacture, hunting and fishing technologies, weaving and sewing. The usual model for systematic landscape transitions is from a largely broadleaved cover to early agriculture involved a phase of shifting cultivation (often graced with the Scandinavian term 'landnam', meaning clearance of land, generally forested, for agriculture). This was often followed by accelerated arable cultivation as individual cleared land units joined-up.[19]

The expansion of agriculture generally leads to accelerated soil erosion and this is recorded from borings between Hythe and Fawley on the south-west side of Southampton Water,[20] on the periphery of the forest. There was apparently a fall in oak, lime and elm pollen and a peak in herb pollens, supported by radiocarbon dates.[21] These have been ascribed to late Mesolithic or early Neolithic woodland clearance for agriculture.[22] The elm decline that occurred at times around 3750–3580 BC[23] (although authorities vary considerably on the precise dating) may be either preferential felling or the spread of 'Dutch elm disease'; it is generally also strongly associated with widespread land clearance for agriculture.

It may be there was only a gradual replacement of hunter-gatherer societies with more settled agricultural communities; hence hunting and gathering may have remained a form of subsistence far longer than on the chalk downlands. Where farming became established (as the palaeo-environmental evidence suggests that it did) it was relatively small-scale.[24] Outside the forest boundary, at Clarendon Park, is to be found the Fussell's Lodge long barrow suggesting settled communities nearby. In 2009, 6000 year old burials and flint deposits were discovered near to Damerham outside the perambulation and again pointing to Neolithic activity in the area.[25] A long barrow at Braemore Down (the 'Giants Grave') to the north-west has produced axes (included imported examples from Cornwall and Caernarfonshire), suggesting a more settled way of life, as well as the long-distance trading, although this is also known from the Mesolithic.[26] Yet, within the forest itself, there is a striking lack of these or other early Neolithic monuments, while outside there appears a continuity of occupation through to the Bronze Age.

Some late Neolithic pottery has been found in a ditch associated with barrows near Ibsley.[27] Elsewhere in Dorset, Wiltshire and Sussex in the Neolithic period there is an impressive array of monumental structures from throughout the Neolithic! Incorporating both negative and positive evidence, it is considered that the New Forest area was peripheral at a time of initial utilisation of the more fertile soils of downland. It may furthermore be that such a pattern, commenced by late Mesolithic people, actually anticipated problems of poor soil management that would affect agriculture in the New Forest area.[28]

Detailed dating is insufficient to say exactly when agriculture made its impact or how long this lasted. Neolithic people did hunt in the area and there is a limited scattering of artifacts that support this view. Major ecological and landscape changes probably occurred with heathland most likely appearing for the first time and it is probable that soil degradation also first became a problem. The Ibsley barrows might merely point to activity in the late Neolithic, but whether this reflects settlement is unknown. A likely explanation is a subsistence economy where hunter-gathering only gradually gave way to a more settled (*i.e.* less migratory) way of life and an associated increase in economic activity. In the woodland areas too, there is very limited evidence from within the forest itself.[29]

A chronological problem relating the New Forest and to its region is manifest. Simply stated, the overall regional model as understood from the chalk downland to the north, west and east (that experienced dramatic agricultural development that defines the Neolithic economy), does not fit the local picture. This view is supported by the broader pollen record. Most clearance of woodland with its replacement by dominant heathland belongs to the period after 3000 BC.

Bronze Age (*c.*2400–700 BC)

Evidence from the core New Forest area points to there being a time lag in the introduction of agriculture, so that the impact of an agricultural society associated with settlement and monuments, actually only seriously impacts in the Bronze Age. Clearance accelerates from around 1200 BC, suggesting the action of middle Bronze Age to Iron Age farmers that would lead to the creation of heathland.[30]

Throughout Britain, it is the Bronze Age that may be seen as the foundation of the economically forged landscape we see today. While it is true that some of the finest prehistoric monuments belong to the preceding Neolithic, and to that period are ascribed major changes in forest cover (to a more open, farmed landscape), the origins of widespread field systems and sometimes associated dwellings in general belong to the (later) Bronze Age,[31] perhaps something associated with a switch from a pastorally dominated economy towards a more specialised landscape of familiar features: fields, trackways, boundary features with associated dwellings. Prehistoric field systems of uncertain age which may prove early Bronze Age, are to be found nearby on soils away from the chalk yet outside the New Forest.[32] The regular field systems of the Bronze Age suggest a high level of social organisation and associated land allocation.[33]

Figure 3.1 shows Neolithic and Bronze Age monuments and artefact finds in the New Forest area, and the production of bronze artefacts shows there was industrial activity found in 'hoards' in southern England. Some finds may have been meant as votive offerings. In the New Forest, Bronze Age settlers made a significant landscape impact, the evidence pointing towards woodland clearances (*c.*2400–900 BC) probably accelerating after the after the middle Bronze Age (*c.*1500–1100 BC). Stock grazing and arable farming would have both been important, although the fragmentary nature of evidence for enclosures protecting crops makes interpretation difficult.

Settlement is generally implied by the presence of about 250 extant burial mounds (tumuli) – and 300 'boiling sites' (see below).[34] Most round barrows were located on river terraces. While palaeo-environmental evidence is not easy to interpret and there no clear evidence for 'wood pasture' in the Bronze Age, there is evidence beneath Bronze Age barrows for soil deterioration, suggesting earlier disturbance of the woodlands.[35] The three Bronze Age barrows at Mockbeggar Lane (Ibsley, Hampshire)[36] were revealed by aerial photography and excavated in advance of gravel extraction. Two were double ring-ditches, the third had a single ditch, with a causeway. There were a few surviving

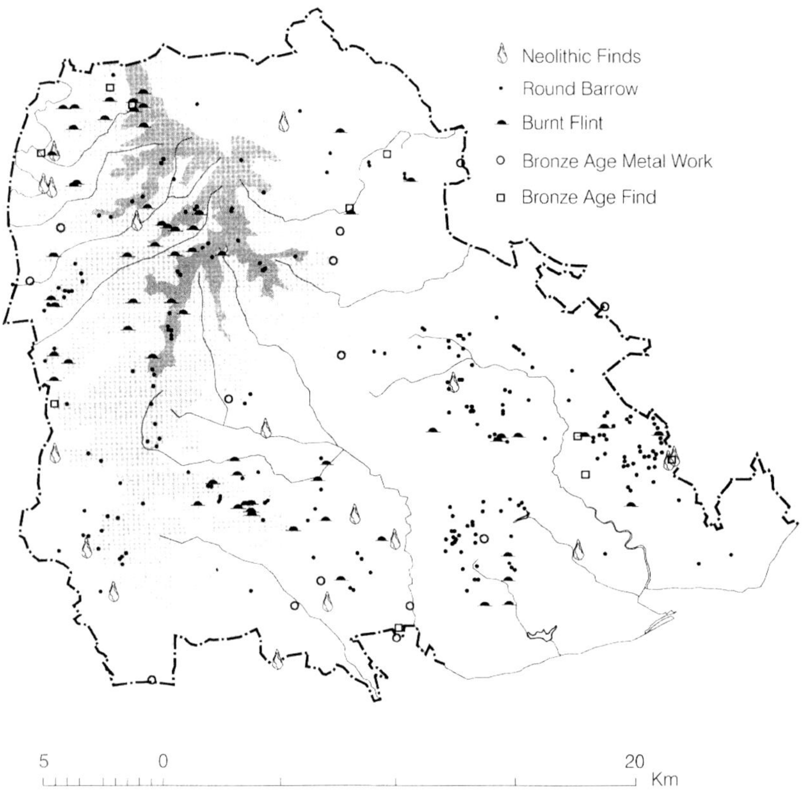

FIGURE 3.1. Neolithic and Bronze Age monuments and artefact finds in the New Forest area.

SMITH 1999, 44, BY PERMISSION OF HAMPSHIRE FIELD CLUB AND ARCHAEOLOGICAL SOCIETY

burial deposits including remains of a cremation and a food vessel, as well as flint-knapping debris. Later linear features at the site were attributed to the Roman and medieval periods. It was suggested that this area, perhaps originally comprising some 30 barrows (and two cremation cemeteries) within about 6 km of the site, on both sides of the Avon valley, was peripheral to an intensively settled area. The barrows, forming a 'necropolis' would have presented as significant landscape features in the Bronze Age, but occupation ceased after the middle Bronze Age when cremation burials were inserted at one of the barrows.

Today, the New Forest is internationally noted for both its wood pasture[37] and its extensive heathland. Heathland probably came to dominate the New Forest landscape from the middle Bronze Age, and at this time impacted on the open forest and river valleys so that it is likely settled valley communities were supported by a mixed pastoral/arable community using the open forest uplands and heaths as convenient grazing.[38] Woodland was cleared for agriculture, although barrows situated in woodland areas may have been another cause of clearance. Those situated on higher ground may have had a role in territorial delineation and subsequently forming a basis for perambulations? There was a likely interplay of forestry and grazing linking pre-historic land uses through to the medieval period, while the paucity of grave goods compared with those of the chalk downland may reflect a poorer society.[39]

These changes would be especially prominent on plateau gravel soils. Any areas put down to crops may well have been on a 'landnam' basis (see above) like the Neolithic, and apparently there was no enclosure construction, although there may have been some boundaries associated with barrows of the late Bronze Age. Funerary activity was present in the Bronze Age, as was hunting and maybe summer grazing. The apparently absent settlements may be buried beneath peat deposits and eroded hillwash material known as 'colluvium'. Additionally to the barrows, there have been cremation burials (probably inserted in the pre-existing barrows) at Beaulieu Heath and Cranbury common.[40] Often termed 'Deverel-Rimbury', the term is now generally restricted to pottery types of the middle Bronze Age that are found within the region, yet these finds may be associated with pre-historic lynchets and round barrows.[41] It is inferred that here landscape of the time largely supported a livestock economy.

Ascribing the age of boundaries to the Bronze Age is not easy. Linear earthworks (a bank and ditch) that could be 'ranch boundaries' are identified running north-east from Whitsbury Castle Hillfort on to the Downs above the Avon valley and outside the New Forest,[42] showing a likely high degree of agricultural development nearby. However, based on pollen evidence within the forest, a small enclosure on Beaulieu Heath at Crockford (SZ 3576 9948) sampled from beneath a bank on Beaulieu Heath, suggests a Bronze Age date and likewise banks near to Dark Hat enclosure banks on field evidence (SU 232 160 and SU 233 161), could also be Bronze Age.[43]

Evidence from the Bronze Age does point to widespread clearance, possibly due to pressure from rising population, heathland development (for which there is no previous evidence) and probable erosion and podsolisation of the soils. There is strong evidence of human settlement not only from barrows, but also from the enigmatic 'boiling mounds'.

Over 300 such sites have been found to date, and comprise low (1 m high), kidney-shaped mounds of calcined flint, with an opening facing a water supply are thought to be where stones were heated up and then dropped into a wooden trough of water to boil.[44] The discarded small stones caused the mound. There were probably fuelled from turf and may approximate the extent of heathland in the Bronze Age; it has been suggested they are associated with migratory camps associated with pastoral activities.[45] Their purpose is unclear; they may have been associated with some form of early sauna![46]

Other economic activity in the area is demonstrated by a (probably) Bronze Age wooden jetty, bridge or causeway and part of a sea-going boat, with a rapier driven into the silts beneath, that has been excavated at Testwood lakes, Totton, in the lower Blackwater valley.[47] There was every possibility for trading outside the forest area, within region and probably further afield, including on the European continent, for subsequent work by Wessex Archaeology at Testwood Lakes revealed the waterlogged remains of timber structures dating from 1600–1450 BC. One significant find was a cleat from a plank boat capable of cross-Channel journeys.[48] Other potential causeways have been noted in Langstone

Harbour.[49] Sea crossings in the early part of the period can be inferred from finds such as the numerous bronze hoards of northern French type.[50]

In the forest, heathland was used for grazing, although earlier there had likely been some cultivation. The economy by the middle Bronze Age was likely based upon settled valley communities supported by a mixed arable/pastoral agricultural economy; the switch towards a more pastoral economy being a likely consequence of soil degradation that created the heathlands, and climate change that was to invigorate valley mire development. Communications were well-established, evidenced by trade, and although evidence for settlement is poor, so it remains likely there were elements of seasonal exploitation of the area as part of a pastoral economy, alongside a (presumed) settled agrarian population.

From 1000 BC (late Bronze Age) there is clearer evidence for a reduction in the woodland area and replacement of woodland by heathland, soil degradation and the development of podsolic soils, suggesting leaching of poor acid brown earth soils due to human agency. Furthermore, towards the end of the Bronze Age there would have been climatic deterioration linked with enhanced peat bog development across southern Britain.[51]

Iron Age (*c.*700 BC–AD 43)

The Iron Age archaeological record suggests further pressure on natural resources evidenced through land clearance and cultivation. Possibly at a time around the Bronze Age/Iron age transition, agricultural systems became fixed as archaeological evidence includes storage pits, field boundaries, small settlements and farmsteads. Probable defensive monuments, material remains of pottery, flint and metals suggest that external interaction and trade were important. The chronology remains unclear, although Iron Age dates are likely, for example the Crockford complex (Fig. 3.2).[52] At Lucy Hill (SU 226 045) denuded banks of prehistoric or Roman age underlie possible medieval field boundaries.

An increase in rates of peat accumulation from around AD 500 has been detected. Furthermore, there was probably accelerated land clearance for agriculture, and this generated more runoff that may have been contemporary with increased precipitation caused by climate change.[53] There may have been further pressure on land resources from people moving from highland areas to lowland as upland farmsteads became uninhabitable due to deteriorating climatic conditions. Economic exploitation probably continued, perhaps with summer grazing. Prehistoric lynchets bear witness to soil erosion and are a way of stabilising slopes for agriculture.[54] Stock may have been allowed to graze, unenclosed, on the open heaths with their owners living in open forest settlements, or in the valleys, yet the possibility of small arable or horticultural fields has not been ruled out. Inferred population pressure during the Iron Age was to continue certain problems manifest by the mid-Bronze Age.[55]

Iron Age and Romano-British finds at Dark Hat (Homy Ridge) relate to a sub-circular enclosure, some 50 m across with denuded banks and yielded pottery from the first century AD.[56] Certain field systems resemble in form that of proven Iron Age system of the chalk downlands.[57] There is thought to have been pottery manufacture from brickearth in the Avon valley, to the north-west.[58] Palaeo-environmental evidence for the Iron Age from the Barrow Moor core is also hard to interpret. There is an increase in particulate charcoal yet also an increase in the occurrence of *Ilex* and *Quercus* pollen.[59]

In general, the nature of the landscape evidence changes from funerary monuments to embanked enclosures and defended settlements or 'hillforts' around the peripheries of the area. These include: Castle Hill, Burley, single rampart and ditch; Roe Wood (Castle Piece), single bank and ditch; Gorley Wood (Godshill Wood); Frankenbury (Godmanscap), single rampart and ditch; Malwood Castle; Tatchbury and Buckland Rings. Many overlooked or secured the main arteries into the open forest and along the coast (Buckland, for example, oversees the Lymington River access to the north; Godshill and Gorley the entry from the middle Avon and Cranborne).[60]

Archaeological evidence from the Iron Age is strongest in respect of 'hillforts' and enclosures, of which there are a number of examples on the crown lands including Castle Hill, Frankenbury, Burley and Castle Piece in Roe Inclosure. There have been seven hillfort-like structures reported of which five were less than 2 ha in area, enclosed by curvilinear enclosures.[61]

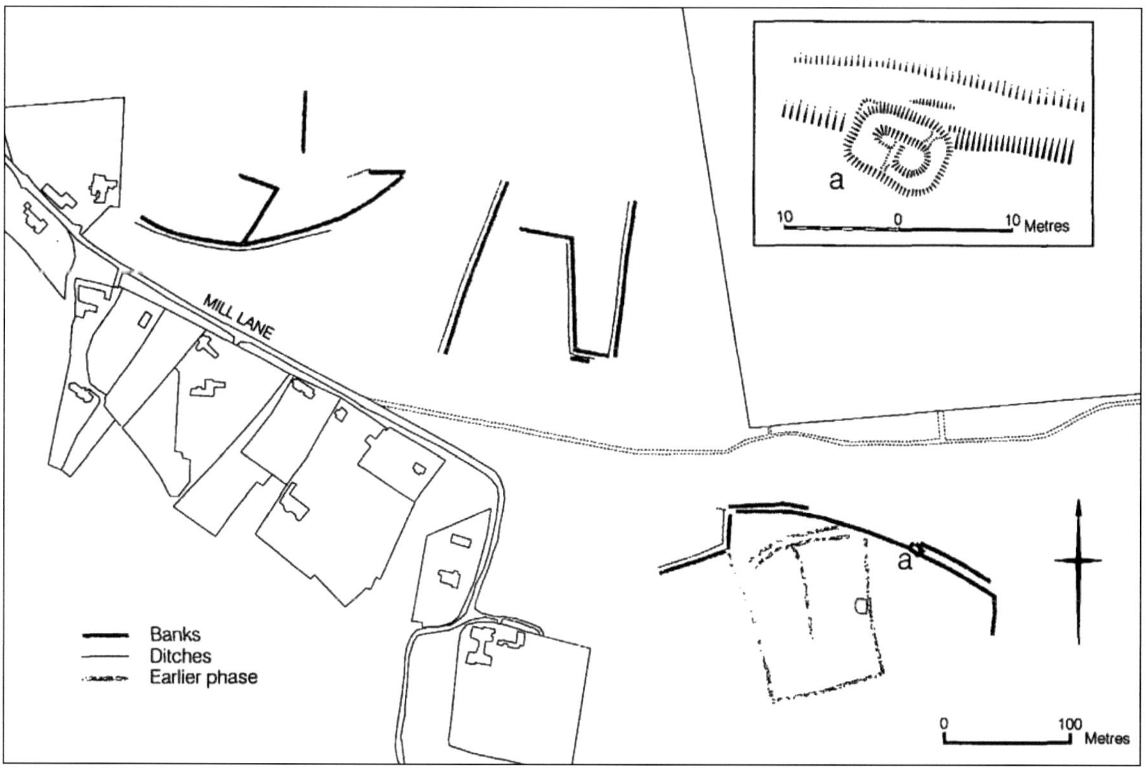

FIGURE 3.2. The Earthworks Complex at Lucy Hill.

Smith 1999, 36, by permission of Hampshire Field Club and Archaeological Society

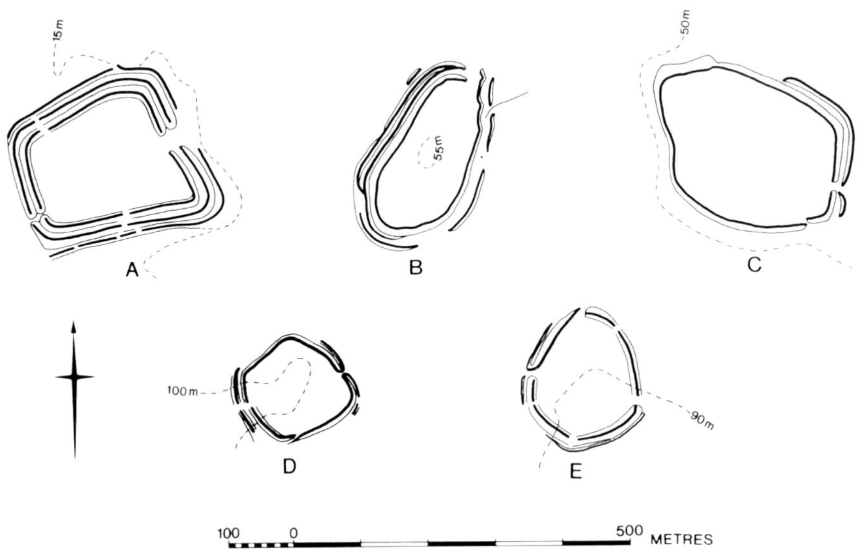

FIGURE 3.3. Iron Age 'hillforts' in the New Forest. A. Buckland Rings, B. Tatchbury, C. Frankenbury, D. Castle Malwood and E. Castle Hill, Burley.

SMITH 1999, 9, BY PERMISSION OF HAMPSHIRE FIELD CLUB AND ARCHAEOLOGICAL SOCIETY

Figure 3.3 shows the forms of Iron Age hillfort enclosures in the New Forest. The term is often misleading as it is now believed many such earthworks did not have a primarily defensive function. Other functions may have been distribution centres for goods and trade, or constraining stock associated with seasonal exploitation of the forest area.[62] The earliest *clear* field systems would appear to be of Iron Age date.[63]

Monuments such as Frankenbury (SU 1667 1520), of unproven age and Castle Hill (SU 166 1617) that was probably (re)-fortified later in the twelfth century AD,[64] would suggest they are part of a defensive system along the western margin overlooking the valley, although settlement within the small hillforts if ever located, would yield more information. This late Iron Age situation points to elites controlling movement and trade and hence opens all kinds of possibilities for the succeeding Roman and medieval periods. However, the largely unexcavated New Forest hillforts have some the characteristics of hilltop enclosures of the Bronze Age–Iron age transition (ramparts with external ditch) that may elsewhere have partly functioned as enclosures of seasonal animal management and maybe corralling over winter.[65] Other factors suggested involve an element of ritual purpose with many New Forest hillforts displaying entrances facing east or south-east, towards the rising sun, to a response to increased notions of land as private property.[66]

The names of tribes or tribal confederations from the later Iron Age are known from classical sources and to a lesser extent from archaeology, particularly Iron Age coinage.[67] On that basis alone it may be that this valley and the area of the New Forest, rather than constituting a boundary in the sense understood in later history, represented more a 'buffer zone' between the Atrebatic culture to the east and the Durotrigic to the west.[68] This can never

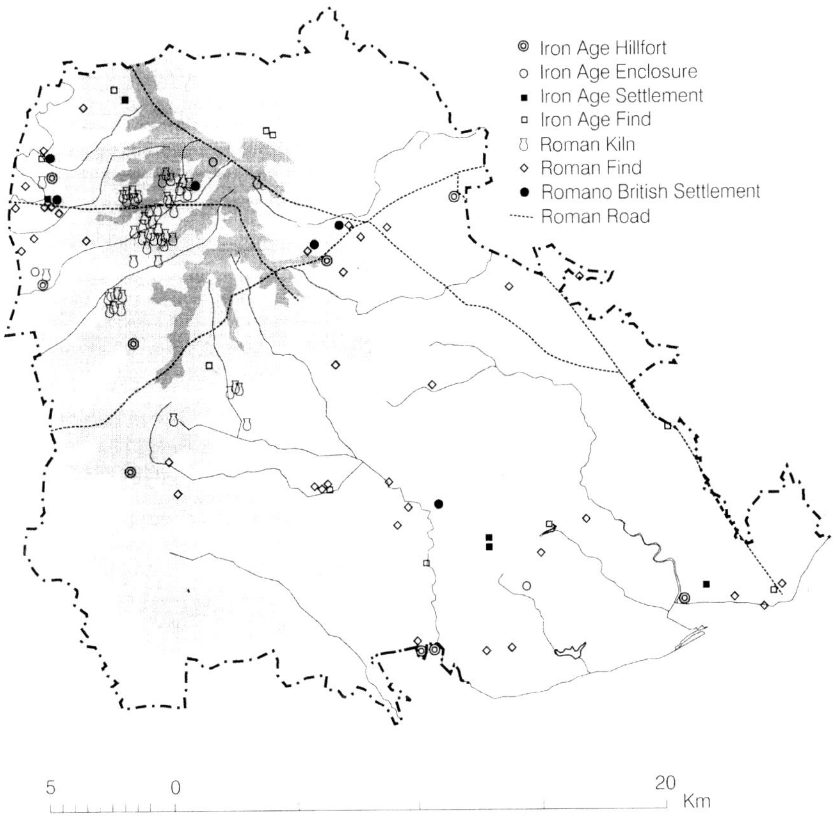

FIGURE 3.4. Iron Age and Romano-British roads, monuments and artefacts.

SMITH 1999, 48 BY PERMISSION OF HAMPSHIRE FIELD CLUB AND ARCHAEOLOGICAL SOCIETY

absolutely clear because Durotrigian coins are found on both sides of the lower Avon, while Atrebatian coins are found east of that river.

Hillforts and enclosures do, however, overlook river valleys (Fig. 3.4). Hence, it is interesting to speculate that they may have been constructed to show the power of a local ruler, and hence they may also have demarked the westerly territory of the Durotriges' tribal confederation (who gave their name to Dorchester) from the Belgae/Atrebatian confederation in modern Hampshire to the east, for Durotrigic coins are known from within the forest.[69]

It may be the distribution of the larger circular enclosures (possibly hillforts in the normally accepted strategic defensive sense) numbering seven in total, are sited to control movement of goods, even people, along the cost and into the Avon valley.[70] The five smaller earthworks, however, are less clear in their function on account of their being located at flatter and hence less defensible, locations. They may have had a function more to do with stock control, or define personal holdings used for arable or market-garden type activities.

The relationship with coastal areas should not be understated. Salt-making occurred on the Pennington marshes, close to Lymington, maybe as a seasonal activity, including grazing along the coast within the economic orbit of the multivalliate Buckland rings (fourth–first centuries BC), probably a late

Iron Age enclosure. However, clear evidence for salt-making is only from the seventeenth century.[71] By the Iron Age trade with the Continent would have been well-established, and in this cross-channel communication and Christchurch Harbour and Hengistbury Head played a significant role.[72]

The presence of long-distance drovers' roads on the chalk downs to the north and west in later history points to the possibility of movement of beasts on a regular basis. The main roads of the forest are almost all on or close to the tops of the gravel and sand ridges, maximising opportunities for transit throughout the year. The vibrancy and degree of integration of the Iron Age economy of the forest into surrounding areas remains uncertain.

However, it is very likely the area continued to be exploited for agricultural purposes, even if a combination of adverse climatic change and soil degradation had made this difficult. Stock is likely to have been let loose to graze on the open heath, either from open forest settlements or from the surrounding valleys. There are some enclosures from the period of uncertain purpose (but stock control is likely) and there is evidence for further settlement, although this is as yet insufficient evidence for accurate dating. The next major economic development was to be industrial.

The coming of the Romans

The motives of the Romans was conquest, development and taxation, yet in natural resource terms there would have been better economic prizes than were to be found in the New Forest. The capture of large hillforts including Maiden Castle and Hod Hill in Dorset by the Second Legion under Vespasian during the Claudian invasion of AD 43, leading to the formation of Dorchester (Roman *Durnovaria*), would have left little doubt that Roman ways were to prevail sooner rather than later, although unexcavated minor 'hillforts' in the forest give no clues whether they were indeed abandoned at this time.

Palaeo-environmental evidence is consistent with clearing woodland, perhaps for fuel and increased grazing activities into the period of Roman occupation.[73] As far as woodland is concerned, it is possible that, during the Roman period, woodlands were exploited, perhaps as coppice, a move that would have sustained resources. It is likely that the Romans probably introduced the planting of sweet chestnut for coppicing. It probably took around 23 ha of coppice woodland products to supply the hypocaust for a Roman Villa.[74] There is no evidence for timber exploitation (as opposed to coppice) in the Roman period, but this does not prove that it did not occur.

However there is overall scant evidence for any large-scale enclosure of land, settlement, villas or cultivation[75] with possibly limited evidence for enclosure in field systems on Ridley Plain (SU 203 063) partly on heath and partly in modern woodland. The conquest did eventually lead to new industrial development, then in the wake of the withdrawal of Roman forces after AD 410, emerging

'Anglo-Saxon' kingdoms would integrate into an England where royal hunting forests would play a political and social role.

The period AD 43–1066 gives perhaps the first tantalising glimpse of the political and economic organisation underlying landscape formation. Located close to the south coast, the Romans would have advanced rapidly into the area following the Claudian invasion, moving swiftly and decisively through southern Britain. They were concerned with forming alliances with local potentates, or where this was not possible, they could otherwise secure military victories. The Romans would have considered the larger hillforts in the region such as Maiden Castle (Celtic *'Mai Dun'* or Great Hill) by Dorchester, and perhaps another at Winchester[76] (Roman *Venta Belgarum*, the market town of the Belgae) comparable to the *oppida* of the nearby continent. Apart from military resistance, such large hillforts actually represent a major shift towards urbanisation, because of the level of settlement within, and the likelihood of them controlling and redistributing goods[77] – as well as demonstrating the power of local rulers.

Romano-British settlement

While larger hillforts may represent proto-urbanisation, the Roman occupation saw the establishment of towns in a modern sense; locally and outside the modern New Forest there was *Venta* and *Durnovaria*. Hitherto, hillfort-like constructions may have permitted the possibility of traders meeting for the exchange of goods. Subsequently, the presence of the Rockbourne villa and industry within the forest evidences significant economic activity and it is undoubted there would have been an increase in economic activity caused by the Roman occupation. Although negative evidence is unsatisfactory, it is likely that significant tracts remained un-farmed.

What has been observed is a transition from Iron Age roundhouses to Roman style rectangular buildings constructed of timber, and a layout of streets in a planned street pattern at a small settlement in Crystal Hollow, Godshill. The immediate local economy was pastorally based during the second century AD and contrasted with the arable or mixed farms of the Avon valley, or indeed the nearby downs. This timber-built settlement was two or three generations later than the wealthier villa complex at Rockbourne on the opposite side of the valley to the New Forest.[78] A regionally significant Roman villa, by the fourth century boasted a courtyard and associated farm buildings from where the owners would have exacted rents from farms and villages from its large estate, until its decline in fifth century.

Evidence of small Roman settlement sites apart from that at Godshill include others on the western margin of the modern forest known from artefact scattering areas in the Fordingbridge area, three enclosures north-west edge of the open forest/Avon valley, enclosures of probable Roman date within the Amberwood Inclosure and at Nursling, these may have been associated with stock-keeping,[79] and also at Church Green, Bignell Wood and near to the Rufus Stone. It may be these were industrially-linked settlements.[80]

Roman roads

Figure 3.4 shows the pattern of Roman roads that came to traverse the forest and so far there is no evidence for it serving major settlements *within the later perambulation.*[81] There was a significant crossing of the road system near to modern Stoney Cross. These roads linked Chichester (*Noviomagnus*) with Winchester (*Venta Belgarum*), Chichester to Bitterne (?*Clausentum,* to the east the River Itchen near modern Southampton), Otterbourne (south of Winchester) to Stony Cross, later extended south-westwards across the area as far as Wattons Ford, south of Ringwood it crossed the lower Avon near to Kingston, from Stoney Cross to Fritham, through the forest potteries, to Fordingbridge. Another linked Cadnam to Buckland rings, a large Iron Age hillfort north of Lymington. Clarke paid particular attention to the road running NW–SE, close to the eastern boundry, Applemore Hill, via Cadnam, to Bramshaw Telegraph and from there to Downton, Harnham near Salisbury and Old Sarum (*Sorviodunum*). In doing so, it passed close to the entrance of the Tatchbury Hillfort west of Totton (a large multivalliate construction) and may have been constructed by the *Legio II* Augusta lead by Vespasian during the early part of the Claudian Invasion. Later, it may also have represented the route of the Anglo-Saxon invasion by Cerdic that established the kingdom of Wessex including a battle possibly fought at Netley Marsh.

Roman industry

An important iron-working site has been excavated at Armsley[82] and it is not impossible that salt-making on the coast continued into the Roman period.[83] Otherwise Romano-British industry in the area was a flourishing ceramic industry concentrated in the north-west of the modern New Forest (Fig. 3.4). All would have required wood products for heat energy. Kilns dated to around AD 250 produced imitations of imported ware although production of more sophisticated wares probably ceased by AD 370 and the industry collapsed by the end of that century. Evidence for workshops or living accommodation for pottery workers has not so far been forthcoming but it has been suggested that ceramic manufacturing was a seasonal (summer) activity[84] meaning that many areas of heath may have remained largely undisturbed until the expansion of silviculture in the eighteenth century.

Industry, in the form of the New Forest ceramic production clustered mostly in the north of the forest,[85] included sites at Pitts Wood, Ashley Rails, Islands Thorns, Crock Hill, Old Sloden Wood, Sloden Inclosure, Lower Sloden Inclosure, Amberwood Inclosure and four areas at Linwood. Transportation to markets may have been via roads northwards towards modern Salisbury and along the Avon valley and like Alice Holt Forest, the indigenous New Forest ceramics industry was of some regional, even national, importance.[86] However, by the advent of the Anglo-Saxons, the domestic ceramic industry had likely collapsed.[87]

Excavation in Jewry Street, Winchester (*Venta Belgarum*) has revealed locally produced New Forest pottery dating from the late third–late fourth centuries. These included imitation of continental 'samian ware' (red-brown fine tableware of the Roman period). The most common items were indented beakers, cups, small bowls and flagons, some decorated. The low population and plentiful local supplies of clay and sand were important factors in the creation of the pottery industry. The design of the pottery kilns in the New Forest is characteristic, yet the closest parallels for the earliest New Forest pots come from north-eastern France and western Germany.[88] The area was therefore open to extensive outside influences. An Anglo-Saxon burial of the sixth century furthermore shows a glass bowl of Frankish manufacture.[89]

Angles, Saxons, Jutes, Danes and the hunt

The 'Anglo-Saxon' conquest of the region involved at least a third Germanic group, 'the Jutes', who probably took their name from Jutland (part of modern Denmark) and are best known for their settlement of Kent, as reported in Bede. They also conquered the Isle of Wight and the adjacent part of what is modern south Hampshire on the opposite side of the Solent by the late sixth century, probably in conjunction with (west) Saxons who conquered from the north.[90] Into the post-Roman period the picture would seem to be one of an area traversed because of its location between important coastal settlements and *Venta* to the east and *Sorviodunum* to the north. The ceramic industry again seems to have been important, but proved transient and agriculture locally important, was muted. There is limited evidence that that certain hillforts in Wessex, including Whitsbury near Fordingbridge, were re-occupied in the immediate post-Roman period, neither can continuity of settlement be ruled out.[91]

Yates[92] notes that, during the development of Kentish Weald, grazing was at first communal in woodlands in the Jutish kingdom of Kent, but subsequently grazing, woodmanship and agriculture were manorialised, that is brought under the direction of the lord of the manor. It is therefore possible by comparison in the New Forest, manorialisation was well advanced by 1066 with some small estates that originated as daughter settlements of swineheards, within the forest gaining independence of their 'mother' settlement.

Interestingly, in the *Chronicon ex chronicus* by a monk of Worcester, the New Forest (or an area approximating to it) is referred to as the *Great Ytene Forest*, apparently, 'Forest of the Jutes'. Even aside from the post-Roman tribal association, this may suggest an identity that pre-dates the Norman Conquest.[93] Yet, in England, it is probable that neither Anglo-Saxon, nor Danish kings made *new forests* for their pleasure although there is good evidence of royal hunting before the Conquest, and it is probable that miscreants were dealt with under the common law, even though these seem extreme by modern comparison. It is furthermore likely that the Saxon kings' rights to hunt were no different from any other 'landowner'. By the reign of Edward the Confessor (1042–1066), there may have existed a nucleus of forest administration, and that his huntsmen held land of him and these may have included the (later) royal forests of Chippenham, Savenake and Clarendon, while his foresters held areas that would become the royal forests of Mendip and Windsor.[94]

We can see the development of not only a political framework from (or similar to) continental Europe, but also the evolution of legal codes and systems concerned with infringements against the forest. Although the formation of the kingdom of Wessex was politically important, both locally and in terms of creating – in a coherent sense – the kingdom of 'England', the Anglo-Saxon period has left little physical evidence within the crown lands of the forest other than local place names, evidence for early settlements associated with this time. There does seem to have been economic continuity with the Roman period[95] including a bias towards valley settlement and burials from the early Anglo-Saxon period, including a cremation urn from Gorley. Fritham, with its quintessentially Anglo-Saxon place name may have its origins at this time as an assart, although the characteristics of this encroachment on the forest in a curvi-linear boundary (including pollards and coppice trees) has characteristics of a medieval vaccary and neither can it be identified in Domesday. The internal sub-divisions of the enclosure at Fritham include a funnel-like feature on its eastern side that may have been for the herding of cattle.[96] In any case, Fritham, being situated in the heads of two valleys, is sheltered and hence more suitable for settlement and agriculture. Most of the human activity at this time was concentrated in valley settlements centred on arable production. The open forest was probably used for grazing.[97] In Figure 3.5, Rockbourne (outside the mapped area) was a royal manor to the west of Braemore. Winkton (not marked and west of Holdenhurst) was partly within the forest.

The pattern of nucleated settlement, by late Saxon times (Fig. 3.5) is recognisable today and probably includes churches, even parish boundaries, that commenced in the seventh century and the majority of place names are of Germanic origin, reinforcing this view. While we have a general idea regarding the form and distribution of settlements there is little guidance on the extent of tree cover and heath area, on transportation networks, industrial activity and conventional agriculture for the first millennium AD. What is more frustrating is that we do not know if the king or nobles hunted in the New Forest.

Carolingian kings on the continent probably felt it expedient to define a boundary within which royal authority was exercised, commencing the process by which a forest could become a royal institution. Within this area, the trees and other vegetation would be managed with a view to providing 'covert' for game. This process would inevitably come into conflict with agricultural interests of fencing fields to constrain livestock, or cutting wood for domestic and industrial purposes. It would furthermore provide for conflict where the

FIGURE 3.5. Presumed Anglo-Saxon Manors at Domesday within the New Forest.

AFTER YATES 1985, 14

ordinary manorial (or similar) governance of the common people and lesser gentry, clashed with that of the crown.

One compelling view of the development of feudalism in north-west Europe during the period between 900 and 1200 is summarised by Baxter.[98] He proposes there was a 'Feudal Revolution' commencing in the mid- to late tenth century that was rapidly realised during the eleventh century. The origins of forest laws may lie within the apparatus of Carolingian government that collapsed due to external military pressures,[99] so that 'an aggressive form of seigneurial lordship filled the resulting political and judicial vacuum'.[100] In effect, local magnates were able to appropriate payments such as taxation, tolls and judicial fines. These were originally paid to the crown (and hence the state) centrally, now they found their way to more arbitrary and exploitative lords who could hone their exploitation of surplus from the peasantry. New techniques of warfare were made available via the *milites* (knights). Castles could be built, and outside forests, the landscape re-ordered. The Open Field Agriculture (OFA) system operating across much of central England (including the required nucleated settlements) enabled strong central control and would fit this pattern well. It is probable that the dukes of Normandy would have adopted Carolingian habits during the tenth and eleventh centuries.[101]

A question relates to the kinds of governance arrangements that may have evolved within the Anglo-Saxon kingdoms. In turn, elements of a political structure may have been inherited from the Roman period, together with a possible underlying 'Celtic' footprint dating from the Iron Age. This would all have to persist beyond the decisive gains of Cerdic over the Britons when establishing the kingdom of Wessex during the first half of the sixth century and may have appeared in customs, but so far it is impossible to tell.

Another possibility, regarding aristocratic tastes and also governance, relates to what developed in response directly to continental influence. The cultural, political and linguistic affinities of the English meant they looked towards the nearby continent. Even if the Normans arrived as new and ready-made continental conquerors, the extent to which their institutions and habits were merely a reflection of the times, or to what extent were they adapting or exaggerating what was already happening, remains a legitimate question.

In economic terms, as 'wastes' fell under the plough, lords may have been keen to preserve their hunting grounds. But what of areas that were destined to become royal hunting forests in by the twelfth century? The evidence, pre-1066, is patchy and conjectural. This relies, in turn, upon considering royal and aristocratic recreational and status-related activities in the kinds of landscapes that are identifiable as falling under forest law by Norman times.

For example active management in 'forest areas' may be indicated by an intensity of change during the Anglo-Saxon period for Epping (formally Waltham) Forest. Then the beech-birch and oak-hornbeam associations of the forest of today replaced earlier lime-dominated woodland; this change is presumed a result of selective tree felling.[102] Anglo-Saxon and Danish kings certainly hunted and it is suggested that parts of the forest woodlands may have been used for that purpose as early as the fifth century; by the eleventh century prior to the Norman invasion, Edward the Confessor owned royal estates at Eling, Ringwood, Lyndhurst and Christchurch.[103]

In the *Life of St Dunstun* (AD 909–988) a miraculous event prevents the king's horse following the stag and hounds blindly over the cliffs at Cheddar Gorge, the outcome of which being that Dunstan becomes Abbot of Glastonbury.[104] It is likely that demesne woods were attached to royal estates, such as that of Cheddar that was to become a poart of the Mendip (or Cheddar) Forest, post-Conquest.[105] The Anglo-Saxon kings evidently hunted in their Wiltshire demesnes, and there were officers appointed for the royal sport. According to Domesday Book, Edward the Confessor gave the huntsman Wulfgeat a hide in the royal manor of Chippenham, and that another, Alvric, held land in the Savernake area and in Cowesfield in what became Clarendon Forest. However, Anglo-Saxon kings do not seem to have exercised hunting rights beyond those enjoyed by any other landowner in his own demesne.[106] At Clarendon Park near Salisbury, Norman kings enjoyed a landscape likely to have been established as a hunting landscape since the late Anglo-Saxon period.[107]

The 'Laws of King Canute', were claimed to have been delivered at Winchester in 1016.[108] Canute was a Dane and king of England some time before the Norman Conquest. The laws support notions of royal forests, presumably where the king could hunt at his pleasure and encompassing penalties for commoners who poached the deer. While these deal with fines, imprisonment, even the death penalty for chasing beasts into a forest, few scholars now regard them as authentic.[109] This position has pertained for over a century, making these 'laws' at worst totally unreliable and a best a reflection of some legal or political agenda, probably in the twelfth century. The likely objective was legitimising the interests of the crown through the supposed 'antiquity' of forest laws.

By the late eleventh century presumed Norman forest laws were something seen as imposed on a subject people. It is not just to certain aristocratic habits that we may look, but to the underpinning legal framework, asking where might the notorious Norman forest laws find origin?

Anglo-Saxons and Normans in transition

In general, deciduous stands and plantations are referred to as 'woods' and where 'forest' refers to a stand of trees often imparting economic value, this differs from historic notions.[110] The first clear evidence of post-conquest royal interest in the area of the New Forest comes in the reign of William I.[111] At this time, specific laws were apparently created that protected crown interest in hunting, and we may presume a boundary (or perambulation) is defined at (or by) this time. Forests in the archaic legal sense comprised extensive uncultivated ground maintained for wild beasts and fowls of forest, chase and warren set within meers (or boundaries). A forest had to have fixed boundaries within which inhabitants were subject to particular laws and these were enforced by appointed officers. In these areas, the landowner claimed exclusively the rights to hunt, however the king only could make a forest (from L. *foresta*), but a noble could, with permission or grant, hold a forest and enact forest laws in his own interest, provided there was support from the crown. For example, the Duke of Gloucester held the Forest of Dean by special grant from Richard II.

It is possible that the Norman 'forest law' was partly their interpretation of an existing continental Frankish legal code[112] introduced afterwards into England. It may not have fully replaced or supplanted existing law but rather reinforced it. Normans merely indulged in an *interpretation* and *reinforcement* of existing legal concepts that derived from continental legal concepts in general, and specifically through contact with the Carolingian empire, as the continental Normans had already done. In any case, under the Anglo-Saxon legal system, *infangetheof* meant that a lord had jurisdiction over a thief caught red-handed within the borders of his estate, and he could hang an offender. Norman rulers were able to create a legal structure that was maybe more efficient than English common law, but was not basically alien; in any case the hunting of wild boar and deer by the aristocracy was commonplace and pre-dated the Conquest.[113]

The prevailing picture, however, is that English (territorial) 'common law' is basically the product of Henry II and his advisers, although detractors from this view would find its origins in among the Anglo-Saxons. Common law is a legal system common to the realm of England, although certain 'obviously privileged areas' perhaps remained outside.[114] This would seem opportunity for such as the forest laws and ecclesiastical courts to make their own arrangements. Common law apparently superseded any customary legal arrangements that might have given clear rights to forest dwellers. Conflict would inevitably occur wherever pressures would be brought through timber gathering, arable expansion or grazing.

If there is a continuity of some legal provision into the post-conquest period, then clues should be sought, although specific pre-Norman forest law survivals are not obvious. Domesday Book (1086) records royal forests and parks in the time of William I, and yet there is no surviving evidence to show how he, or his son William II, administered royal forests although enforcement may have been through the ordinary shire courts.[115] More revealing is an argument that deer parks pre-date the Normans, for they appeared in Domesday (1086) as 'parks' or 'hays' with no evidence for different approaches to deer management before the Norman Conquest;[116] enclosures for deer simply appear as parks post-conquest.

The term *vert*, from the French for 'green', in context referred to not only woodland *sensu stricto*, but also undergrowth and heath[117] and was important in providing cover and food for deer. Management of this relates to serious and direct intervention in woodland management. For example, in south-east England, coppice compartments can be termed 'cants', so that lines of pollards that do not necessarily grow in woodland banks are termed 'cant-markers' and were sought out when coppiced woods were to be auctioned.[118] In Epping Forest, pollarding was the manorial court's responsibility and it is argued this was a hangover from before the imposition of forest law,[119] much as commoners' rights would pre-date the Conquest. However, in the New Forest, pollarding has not always been a common or popular practice. There is no clear evidence for it being the responsibility of adjacent manors at any point; this is perhaps partly because it is often difficult to disentangle the origin of the wood (as being from pollards, coppices or other forms of trees).[120]

In Epping Forest, 'hatches' (gates across roads to constrain livestock) are mentioned in a charter of 1062 for land in the area granted by Edward the Confessor to the monks of Waltham. It is likely that commonable beast grazing predated the establishment of that legal forest around 1130.[121] Similarly, it is likely that commoning rights pre-dated the establishment of the Forest of Bere in Hampshire[122] and there would also have been wood pasture grazed by pigs, oxen and cattle associated with small farmsteads. The more probable explanation of forest rights is that they go back to a time when areas of unenclosed land, including woodland, heath and marsh, were used by nearby settlements for grazing, later to be absorbed into the feudal system as part of privileges and protection enjoyed by tenants in exchange for fealty, services and payments demanded by a manorial lord; in forests these became the 'forest rights'. Claims

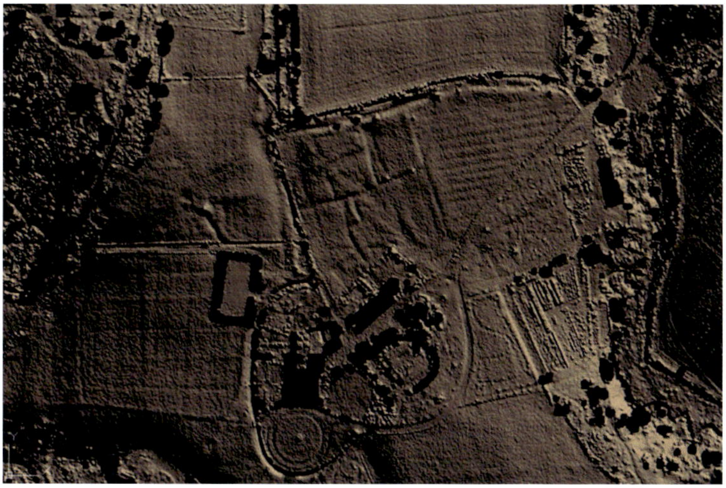

FIGURE 3.6. Lidar Imagery showing the potential site of a deserted medieval village at Landford Lodge, Landford.

© CORNWALL COUNCIL 2013 BASED ON CAMBRIDGE UNIVERSITY TECHNICAL SERVICES AND NEW FOREST NATIONAL PARK AUTHORITY DATA 2011

of forest rights are recorded in the twelfth century.[123] And some surrounding principal manors including Lyndhurst, Christchurch, Eling and Ringwood were crown desmesne at the time of the Conquest, and that royal, seigniorial justice was prevailed distinct from the ordinary justice of the realm, 'even when it is done in the King's name'. Here are similarities with the ensuing forest law.[124]

Another pre-Conquest feature are the 'serjenties' (a property held by provision of military service), and Richard Reeves argues that two of these pre-date the Conquest in the New Forest itself;[125] it is likely they provided accommodation for the king as royal hunting grounds.[126] Yet these serjeanties (Brokenhurst and Minstead)[127] coincided with Anglo-Saxon royal estates at Domesday. The serjeanty of Exbury, on the other hand, may post-date the Norman Conquest. To the Normans, 'grand serjeanties' referred to military service as the condition of tenure; 'petty serjeanties' could be for produce, or for holding cow farms (called vaccaries in the New Forest). These means of holding land may have been stimulated but the proximity of Southampton Castle[128] and grants of serjeanties were essentially a political goodwill gesture.

Lidar imagery furthermore points to ridge and furrow, of likely Anglo-Saxon age, being widespread (Fig. 3.6). These features are especially prominent near present-day Bolderwood and also around Sandhurst.

Although in many instances, the 'woodland' of certain manors lay within the legal New Forest there was evidently an 'ordinary' agrarian economy and this included meadowland that was presumed to have been of some value in order to produce fodder for horses.[129] For example, the Domesday entry for Ringwood (*Rincvede*) located within the forest can list ploughs, a mill, meadows, woodland pigs and pasturage in 1086.[130] The area did provide economic resources before legal afforestation. It comes as no surprise, for Domesday Book (1086) can still allude to ordinary agricultural land uses within the New Forest and despite strong evidence hinting of some depopulation in some areas.

The creation of this large legally forested area provided for the royal hunting forest and its value would otherwise decrease. In the Ringwood Hundred the land was assessed as 28 hides for taxation purposes in 1066, yet in 1086 only six hides are recorded as giving a financial return as the remainder now lay in the forest.[131] The implication is of a decline in agricultural revenue. Then, two manors called *Boldre* were held by a certain Pagen, as they had been held by two allodial owners (free from feudal obligations) in the time of the Confessor. This land, with the exception of 6 acres (2.4 ha) of meadow held by Hugh de Quintin, was taken by the Conqueror into the New Forest, and no further mention of a manor is found.[132] Brockenhurst, apparently outside the forest jurisdiction, on the other hand, apparently doubles in value between 1066 and 1086.[133] Tubbs reports that out of 137 manors in the seven hundreds that were wholly afforested, 47 manors were unassessed for taxation terms, 49 reduced in value and 41 unaffected by afforestation. Compensation to forest dwellers thereby may have taken the form of both tax relief and rights to depasture stock.[134] It is noteworthy that the Normans maintained an administrative system based on hundreds and shires.

In the thirteenth century New Forest, the Swainmote Courts met three times a year to deal with agistment (domestic stock), pannage (grazing by swine) and regulation of the Fence Month (when domestic stock were removed when deer gave birth around midsummer). On account of their concern with communal management, and indeed the clearly Anglo-Saxon name, it is suggested that these arrangements antedated the Norman forest laws[135] and hence it is possible that the New Forest area was used as a royal hunting ground before the Norman Conquest. Furthermore, the presence of two Saxon names (Cola the huntsman and his father Ulviel) among Domesday landowners[136] strongly suggests some continuity of practice; maybe they had served Saxon kings. Among the array of officials known from the medieval forests, Anglo-Saxon royal servants were described as 'woodwards' – that is a forest-keeper or officer.[137] The case can be made for elements of continuity in legal provision from before the Conquest.

It has been noted that nothing specific is known about hunting by Anglo-Saxon nobility in the New Forest, neither do we know much about then likely emerging manorial system for Wessex by the ninth and tenth centuries was leading in the imposition of manors.[138] In any case, Domesday Book shows feudalism to be well developed in 1086. Such local power relations existed within the presumed evolving feudal system including early 'rights' that might be allocated to, and remain with, the commoners.

The feudal system in England existed before the Normans, including outside their regions of direct rule and influence. From medieval times, the real impact of feudalisation (along the lines of continental Merovingian and Carolingian rule), likely saw progressive influence within the economy, society and landscape of Anglo-Saxon England. This continental model, one of fiefdoms carved out to ensure military support for the royal houses from barons, suited the need for military protection of the day and was to prove effective against invasion from such as (ironically) the Normans and the Magyars in central Europe.[139] Feudal relations on the continent seem to have been universalised by Charlemagne.[140]

Circumstantial evidence for the importation of feudal relations before 1066 is compelling. During the reign of Offa, King of Mercia (reigned 757–796), the influence of Carolingian political thought was felt in England[141] so much so that Arnold Baker can state that 'Forest law was probably of Carolingian origin'.[142] Alfred the Great of Wessex (reigned 871–899) achieved a strong centralised authority through his struggle against the Danes. He reformed the currency, legal and military structures in Wessex and created the fortified 'burghs' and is credited with starting the English navy, making the imposition of feudalism easier. If Open Field Agriculture (OFA) is seen, at least originally, as a product of feudal relations, it outlived the feudal system by centuries. Actual direct evidence for OFA in Domesday Book (20 years after the Conquest), is not forthcoming although some earlier tenth century charters may contain clues.[143]

The proportion of allodial landholdings (those of relatively prosperous peasants owing no feudal obligations) fell and there was an increase in the proportion of dependent peasants. In England, the power of central authority would seem to increase as the demand for peasants' resources in terms of labour, cash or kind, became greater as lordly power grew. Yet somewhat contrary to this opinion is the observation that royal authority did not diminish in the tenth and eleventh centuries, it actually seems to have grown,[144] the main exception being the catastrophic period of Stephen's reign when lordly power could be asserted. Subsequently, the restoration of centralised authority during the Angevin period (1154–1216) may have been welcomed, but there were also economic problems for peasants manifest in inflation and in increased taxation. The royal forests, their laws, governance and geographical areas would experience expansion during the reign of Henry II (1154–1189, see Chapter 4). Once economic gains were consolidated, the Anglo-Norman elite relaxed its grip, permitting a tendency for lords to lease estates and commute demesne labour services during the twelfth century. The consequence of King John's intense 'fiscal exaction' and inflation was a major cause of civil war and the making of *Magna Carta* in 1215 and while the barons' power was evident; many lords would favour desmene farming and labour rent over direct management. This arguably was the beginning of the end for true feudalism. In England nonetheless, crown authority remained strong and was to become virtually absolute under the Normans and needless to say a proportion of crown income was to come from royal forests.

Conclusions

It is as if, before the exploitation of the New Forest as a royal hunting ground by William I, various economic experiments had been tried and failed. These related to agriculture (already proving problematic by the Bronze Age), improved communications and industrial development of stone tool manufacture and ceramics. Limited evidence suggests seasonal hunting forays with locally cleared 'landnam' clearances in prehistoric times. Archaeological evidence suggests settlement was peripheral, seasonal or just limited, but no more. Substantial megalithic monuments are all located outside the area, notably, but not exclusively on the chalk downlands. The presumed continuation of hunting as the main activity in the area into the Neolithic, and possibly early Bronze Age, would seem a portent of things to come in the eleventh century AD.

However, aside from the geological bequest of poor soil, the New Forest is well situated for economic exploitation in terms of its location between the coast and the downlands of Wiltshire and Dorset. It was, not geographically isolated and there is evidence for trading since the Mesolithic when settlement would likely be limited to seasonal sites. Then, trade and human migration routes established economic relationships between river valley settlement and interior of the modern New Forest.

During the Bronze Age significant attempts were made to settle and to farm. The podsolization, leaching and erosion of soils would soon present problems for farmers. That there was settlement and a mixed arable/pastoral economy is of little doubt, even if direct archaeological evidence for settlement is lacking. There were abundant tumuli, and the famous 'boiling sites' dating from this time. Exploitation of the forest for agriculture and the wooden jetty in the Blackwater valley at this time can only point to human population pressures that caused the area to experience settlement, communication and agriculture.

Environmental degradation and adverse climate change did not provide a barrier to occupation and exploitation into the Iron Age. Rather, having been brought into the mainstream of landscape development during the preceding Bronze Age, the Iron Age forest leaves a typical, if muted, version of that period also found outside the forest, with pastoral agriculture important and maybe an economy linked to the coastal belt, notably through salt-making. A more mixed agriculture existed in the more fertile soils of the Avon valley.

Enclosures including those for better or worse just about worthy of being graced 'hillforts,' are known most typically on the western edge above the lower Avon, at Frankenbury and Castle Hill, and there is evidence of a tribally organised society from scattered findings of Iron Age coins. Agricultural intensification, if evident from this time, would suggest population pressure once more on more. However, just who controlled the hillforts and smaller Iron Age enclosures remains unknown.

The notion of the New Forest being a 'buffer zone' between tribes is at once reasonable, given its problems in terms of productive agriculture, and also frustrating when speculating on the politics of the period. It also explains why scholars are coy about describing a clear 'political' boundary. If the buffer idea is correct, there is no clear delineation between the Atrebates and Durotriges and the valley was probably not a boundary in any modern sense. Rather, whoever controlled the hillforts along either side of the lower Avon valley controlled traffic and trade in a north–south axis. Given the dominance of their coinage, it is most likely to be the latter tribal group. They would have been powerful, and it is therefore not surprising that Vespasian went out of his way to destroy their centre of power at Maiden Castle, Dorchester.[145]

The Roman period develops aspects of Iron Age geography and material culture. Outside the forest, with an important centre at the hillfort at Whitsbury to the east, a Roman villa estate was developed at Rockbourne. Locally, the general pattern of Roman colonisation and settlement is adhered to, with a postulated Roman road passing Godshill from the east, across the valley to modern Fordingbridge and thence north-west to Whitsbury proving continuity into the Roman period.[146] Yet the timescale of change with a late transition of round to rectangular dwellings and the time taken to establish a 'mature' villa complex by the second century AD requires clear explanation.

The upshot of Roman invasion and occupation was the establishment of the Roman road system within and without the forest. It is possible the second Legion *Augusta* marched up the Avon valley around AD 44 and it can be seen how the coast links with hinterland, and in the process linking the embryonic first century fully urban settlements at Winchester and Dorchester. These centres would open the hinterland for development. The only real new technological innovation for the forest (since the Bronze Age) would seem to be the manufacture of pottery, including the manufacture of Samian ware. It remains a nice point of speculation as to whether the Romans took timber from the forest for construction, including shipbuilding, but they probably also managed coppice in general. The economy here was pastorally based by the second century AD, contrasting with arable and mixed farms in the Avon valley.[147] However, whether it is trade, transhumance of animals or anything else, the area known as the New Forest since the eleventh century did not exist in an economic vacuum, it was always to some degree integrated in an economic sense.

The succeeding Anglo-Saxon period is as disappointing in archaeology as it is in terms of documentary evidence, and hence gleaning information on governance arrangements is very difficult. Any discussion relating to aristocratic and royal hunting is at best circumstantial and at least speculative, but we can be sure the area had a fairly developed, if not very productive, agrarian economy before 1066. We can, however, believe in a long-term developing economy in the locality, relating first to Roman Winchester that becomes the capital of England and hence a locale for the royal Court. Presuming that both the feudal system and the forest laws have continental origins dating from the eighth and ninth centuries, including a 'Feudal Revolution' that would strengthen the power of the king and nobles, the conquest of 1066 would pave the way for strong and potentially arbitrary government. However, it is not as straightforward as that. The next chapter will discuss the Normans.

Notes

1. T. Hardy (1872) *Under the Greenwood Tree.* Tinsley Bros, London.
2. Wessex Archaeology (2010) *New Forest Rapid Coastal Zone Assessment Phase 1.* Main

Report ref.: 72200.02. http://www.newforestnpa.gov.uk/nf_rcza_main_report_final_version_figs.pdf. Accessed Sept 2017.
3. S. Davies, L. Walker and L. Coleman (1998) *The New Forest Historical Landscape*. Wessex Archaeology. http://www.newforestnpa.gov.uk/__data/assets/pdf_file/0005/27455/new_forest_archaeological__historical_landscape_character_assessment2.pdf; http://www.salisburyjournal.co.uk/news/8191595. Accessed Dec 2014.
4. *Ibid.*; N. Barton, S. Ford, S. Collcutt, J. Crowther, R. Macphail, E. Rhodes and A. van Gijn (2009) A Final Upper Palaeolithic site at Nea Farm, Somerley, Hampshire (England) and some reflections on the occupation of Britain in the Late Glacial Interstadial. *Quartär* 56, 7–35. http://www.quartaer.eu/pdfs/2009/2009_barton.pdf. Accessed Sept 2017.
5. M. J. Allen (1996) Landscape and Land-use: priorities in Hampshire, 500,000 BC to AD 1500. In D. A. Hinton and M. Hughes (eds), *Archaeology in Hampshire: a framework for the future*, 55–70. Hampshire County Council, Winchester.
6. K. E. Barber (1981) Pollen analytical palaeoecology in Hampshire: problems and potential. In S. Shennan and T. Schadla-Hall (eds), *The Archaeology of Hampshire*, 91–94. Hampshire Field Club and Archaeological Society Monograph 1, Winchester.
7. O. Rackham (2006) *Woodlands*, 328. Collins, London.
8. *Ibid.*, 331.
9. B. W. Cunliffe (1993) *Wessex to AD 1000*, 5–35. Longmans, London.
10. Davies *et al.* (1998) *op. cit.* in note 3; F. F. Wenban-Smith (2001) *Paleolithic Archaeology of the Solent River. Introduction.* http://eprints.soton.ac.uk/12554/1/W-Smith_%28Solent_C1%29.pdf. Accessed March 2014.
11. J. Gardiner (2006) *Resource Assessment: The Mesolithic in Hampshire*. Wessex Archaeology, http://thehumanjourney.net/pdf_store/sthames/phase3/County/Upper%20Palaeolithic%20&%20Mesolithic/Upper%20Palaeolithic%20&%20Mesolithic%20Hampshire.pdf; Davies *et al.* (1998) *op. cit.* in note 3.
12. Forestry Commission (2008) *B6 Archaeology and Cultural Heritage Plan*. http://www.forestry.gov.uk/pdf/eng-new-forest-b6-archaeology.pdf/$FILE/eng-new-forest-b6-archaeology.pdf. Accessed Sept 2017.
13. K. E. Barber (1975) A vegetation history of the New Forest: a preliminary note. *Proceedings of the Hampshire Field Club and Archaeological Society* 30, 5–8.
14. C. Tubbs (2001) *New Forest, the History, Ecology and Conservation* 67, 168. New Forest Ninth Centenary Trust, Fordingbridge.
15. M. J. Grant and M. E. Edwards (2008) Conserving idealized landscapes: past history, public perception and future management in the New Forest (UK). *Vegetation History and Archaeobot*any 17, 551–62.
16. M. Green (2000) *A Landscape Revealed. 10,000 Years on a Chalkland Farm*, 26. Tempus, Stroud.
17. Davies *et al.* (1998) *op. cit.* in note 3.
18. R. Jacobi (1978) The Mesolithic of Sussex. In P. Drewett (ed.), *The Archaeology of Sussex to AD 1500*, 15–22. Council for British Archaeology Research Report 29, London; Cunliffe (1993) *op. cit.* in note 9, 34.
19. H. F. Cook (2008). Evolution of a floodplain landscape: a case study of the Harnham Water Meadows at Salisbury, England. *Landscapes* 9(1), 50–73.
20. F. Hodson and I. M. West (1972) The Holocene deposits of Fawley, Hampshire and the development of Southampton Water. *Proceedings of the Geologists' Association* 83, 421–44.
21. M. J. Clark and K. E. Barber (1987) *Mire Development from the Devensian Late-glacial to Present at Church Moor Hampshire*, 22–32. Wessex and the Isle of Wight Field Guide, Quaternary Research Association, Cambridge.

22. N. Smith (1999) The earthwork remains of enclosure in the New Forest. *Proceedings of the Hampshire Field Club and Archaeological Society* 54, 45.
23. M. J. Grant (2005) The palaeoecology of human impact in the New Forest. Unpublished PhD Thesis, University of Southampton.
24. Davies *et al.* (1998) *op. cit.* in note 3, 14.
25. http://www.dailyecho.co.uk/news/4418901.Two_6_000_year_old_tombs_uncovered/. Accessed Sept 2017.
26. *Ibid.*
27. S. Coles (2004) Three Bronze Age barrows at Mockbeggar Lane, Ibsley, Hampshire. *Proceedings of the Hampshire Field Club and Archaeological Society* 59, 31–64.
28. Davies *et al.* (1998) *op. cit.* in note 3, 14.
29. *Ibid.,* table 1.
30. Tubbs (2001) *op. cit.* in note 14, 51.
31. D. Miles (2005) *The Tribes of Britain*, 94. Phoenix, London.
32. T. B. James and C. Gerrard (2007) *Clarendon, Landscape of Kings*, 17, 22. Windgather Press, Macclesfield.
33. Rackham (1986) *op. cit.* in note 7, 156.
34. Davies *et al.* (1998) *op. cit.* in note 3, 29; Smith (1999) *op. cit.* in note 22, 52.
35. Grant (2005) *op. cit.* in note 23, 318.
36. Coles (2004) *op. cit.* in note 27.
37. Rackham (2006) *op. cit.* in note 7, 162.
38. Davies *et al.* (1998) *op. cit.* in note 2, 16.
39. Smith (1999), *op. cit.* in note 22, 45–46.
40. Davies *et al.* (1999) *op. cit.* in note 3.
41. Deverel–Rimbury Culture, Oxford Reference 2017. http://www.oxfordreference.com/view/10.1093/oi/authority.20110803095714153.
42. Davies *et al.* (1998) *op. cit.* in note 2, 16.
43. Smith (1999) *op. cit.* in note 22, 20.
44. Tubbs (2001) *op. cit* in note 14, 53.
45. Davies *et al.* (1998) *op. cit.* in note 3, 16.
46. http://www.new-forest-national-park.com/new-forest-history.html.
47. Smith (1999) *op. cit.* in note 22, 45.
48. http://thehumanjourney.net/pdf_store/sthames/Late%20Bronze%20AGE_Iron%20Age%20Hampshire.pdf. Accessed July 2013.
49. D. J. L. Fontana (2000) Survey of wooden structures around the harbour shoreline. In M. J. Allen and J. Gardiner (eds), *Our Changing Coast: a survey of the intertidal archaeology of Langstone Harbour, Hampshire*, 74–80. Council for British Archaeology Research Report 124, York.
50. B. Cunliffe (1978) *Hengistbury Head.* Paul Elek, London.
51. *Ibid.*
52. Smith (1999) *op. cit.* in note 22, 20–21; Tubbs (2001) *op. cit.* in note 14, 54.
53. Barber (1981) *op. cit.* in note 6.
54. H. F. Cook (1994) Field-scale water management in Southern England to AD 1900. *Landscape History* 16, 53–66.
55. Davies *et al.* (1998) *op. cit.* in note 2, 16.
56. A. H. Passmore and K. Fortescue (1989) Excavations at Dark Hat – August 1988. *Proceedings of the Hampshire Field Club and Archaeolological Society,* New Forest Section 24, 14–19.
57. Tubbs (2001) *op. cit.* in note 14, 54.
58. Davies *et al.* (1998) *op. cit.* in note 2, 16.

59. Grant (2005) *op. cit.* in note 23, 318.
60. Davies *et al.* (1998) *op. cit.* in note 2, 16.
61. Smith (1999) *op. cit.* in note 22, 11.
62. *Ibid.*, 10.
63. *Ibid.*, 20–21.
64. *Ibid.*, 14.
65. Davies *et al.* (1998) *op. cit.* in note 2, 16.
66. Smith (1999) *op. cit.* in note 22, 16.
67. M. Papworth (2011) *In Search of the Durotriges,* 55–59. History Press, Stroud.
68. *Ibid.*, 22–26.
69. A. Light and G. Ponting (2001) *The History of Fordingbridge*, 8. Charlewood Press, Fordingbridge; Davies *et al.* (1998) *op. cit.* in note 2, 16.
70. Smith (1999) *op. cit.* in note 22, 10.
71. A. B. Powell (2009) 2000 years of salt-making at Lymington, Hampshire. *Proceedings of the Hampshire Field Club and Archaeological Society* 64, 9–40.
72. B. Cunliffe (1978) *op. cit.* in note 8.
73. Grant (2005) *op. cit.* in note 23, 330–31.
74. T. Rook (2002) *Roman Baths in Britain*. Shire Archaeology, Princes Risboro'; Rackham (2006) *op. cit.* in note 7, 447.
75. Smith (1999) *op. cit.* in note 22, 16, 47.
76. http://www.pastscape.org.uk/hob.aspx?hob_id=230943.
77. Cunliffe (1993) *op. cit.* in note 9, 142, 222–23.
78. Light and Ponting (2001) *op. cit.* in note 69, 10.
79. Davies *et al.* (1998) *op. cit.* in note 2, 17, Smith (1999) *op. cit.* in note 22, 47; Light and Ponting (2001) *op. cit.* in note 69.
80. Smith (1999) *op. cit.* in note 22, 47.
81. A. Clarke A (2003) The Roman road on the eastern fringe of the New Forest, from Shorn Hill to Lepe. *Proceedings of the Hampshire Field Club and Archaeological Society* 58, 33–58.
82. Smith (1999) *op. cit.* in note 22, 47.
83. http://www.lymington.org/history/thesaltindustry.html.
84. Davies *et al.* (1998) *op. cit.* in note 2, 17.
85. Forestry commission (n.d.) http://www.forestry.gov.uk/pdf/eng-new-forest-b6-archaeology.pdf/$FILE/eng-new-forest-b6-archaeology.pdf. Accessed Sept 2017.
86. Davies *et al.* (1998) *op. cit.* in note 2, 17; Light and Ponting (2001) *op. cit.* in note 69, 10; K. A Mew (1997) Through a Glass Darkly: the biography of a Domesday landscape, 97. Unpublished PhD thesis, University of Reading.
87. B. Yorke (1995) *Wessex in the Early Middle Ages*, 11. Leicester University Press, Leicester.
88. Wessex Archaeology (2008) http://www.wessexarch.co.uk/projects/hampshire/winchester/jewry_street/new_forest.html.
89. Independent 2002. http://www.independent.co.uk/news/uk/home-news/rare-glimpse-of-sixthcentury-anglosaxon-life-found-in-new-forest-657643.html. Accessed March 2014.
90. Venerable Bede (*c.*731) *Ecclesiastical History of the English People*, eds D. H. Farmer and R. Latham, trans L. Sherley-Price. Penguin Classics.
91. Yorke (1995) *op. cit.* in note 87, 26, 32.
92. E. M Yates (1985) *The Landscape of the New Forest in Medieval times*, 58. Department of Geography, King's College, London.
93. *Chronicon ex chronicus.* http://www.bsswebsite.me.uk/History/JohnofWorcester/

Chronicle_John2.ht; http://www.envf.port.ac.uk/hantsgaz/hantsgaz/S0004711.HTM. Accessed March 2014.

94. G. Bathe (2013) Of Commoners and Kings. In: Rotherham, I. (ed.) *Cultural Severance and the Environment. Environmental History* vol 2. Springer, Dordrecht, 177–190, DOI https://doi.org/10.1007/978-94-007-6159-9_12; R. Grant (1991) *The Royal Forests of England*, 8. Alan Sutton, Stroud.
95. Davies *et al.* (1998) *op. cit.* in note 2, 17.
96. *Ibid.*, Smith (1999) *op. cit.* in note 22, 21.
97. Forestry Commission (n.d.) *op. cit.* in note 85.
98. S. Baxter (2011) Lordship and labour. In J. Crick and E van Houts (eds), *A Social History of England 900–1200*, 98–114. Cambridge University Press, Cambridge.
99. http://the-orb.net/textbooks/nelson/carolingian_empire_fall.html.
100. Baxter (2011) *op. cit.* in note 98, 98.
101. Grant (1991) *op. cit.* in note 94, 8–9
102. C. A. Baker, P. A. Moxey and P. M. Oxford (1978) Woodland continuity and change in Epping Forest. *Field Studies* 4, 645–69.
103. P. Colebourne P (1983) *Ancient Woodlands*, 22. Hampshire's Countryside Heritage 2 Hampshire County Council, Winchester.
104. http://www.newadvent.org/cathen/05199a.htm.
105. J. Bond (1994) Forests, chases, warrens and parks in medieval Wessex. In M. Ashton and C. Lewis (eds), *The Medieval Landscape of Wessex*, 121–23. Oxbow Monograph 6, Oxbow Books, Oxford.
106. E. Crittal (ed.) (1959) *British History Online 'Royal forests', A History of the County of Wiltshire: Volume 4*, 391–433.URL: http://www.british-history.ac.uk/report.aspx?compid=102825& strquery=severity. Accessed: 21 Dec. 2010.
107. James and Gerrard (2007) *op. cit.* in note 2, 45.
108. B. S. Vesey-Fitzgerald (1977) *Staffordshire Forest Pleas: Introduction, Staffordshire Historical Collections* 5(1) (1884), 123–35. URL: http://www.british-history.ac.uk/report.aspx?compid=52372 Date accessed: 30 November 2010.
109. D. J. Stagg (1979) *A Calendar of New Forest Documents AD 1244–1334*, 5. Hampshire Record Series III, Hampshire County Council, Winchester.
110. Forests and Chases in England and Wales *c.*1000 to *c.*1850 (n.d.) http://info.sjc.ox.ac.uk/forests/glossary.htm#C.
111. Forestry Commission (2012) http://www.forestry.gov.uk/forestry/INFD-6A4KPD. Accessed Sept 2017.
112. Staffordshire Forest pleas (1884) *op. cit.* in note 108.
113. N. Sykes (2010) 1066 and all that. Did the Norman conquest change the nature of hunting in Britain? *Deer* 15, 20–23. http://www.fallow-deer-project.net/img/upload/370/documents/1066%20and%20all%20that.PDF. Accessed March 2014
114. J. Hudson (1996) *The Formation of the English Common Law*, 16–20. Longmans, London.
115. C. R. Young (1979) *The Royal Forests of Medieval England*, 10–11. University of Pennsylvania Press, Pennsylvania.
116. R. Liddiard (2003) The deer parks of Domesday Book. *Landscapes* 4(1), 4–23.
117. D. J. Stagg (1984) *Verderers of the New Forest*, 2. New Forest Association, Fordingbridge.
118. Rackham (2006) *op. cit.* in note 7, 197–98.
119. R. W. Hanson (ed.) (1992) *Epping Forest – Through the Eye of the Naturalist*. Essex Naturalist 11. Essex Field Club, London.
120. R. Reeves and P. Roberts pers. comm. (2014). The term *robora* is a medieval Latin

terms also used for pollard trees http://info.sjc.ox.ac.uk/forests/glossary.htm. Accessed March 2017.

121. Hanson (1992) *op. cit.* in note 119, 18, 26.
122. E. Preston and S. Wallis (2006) *The Forest of Bere,* 14. Devon Books, Halsgrove, Wellington.
123. D. J. Stagg (1986) *Commoners of the New Forest,* 5–6. New Forest Association, Fordingbridge.
124. Stagg (1979) *op. cit.* in note 109, 4.
125. R. P. Reeves (2010) The administration of large holdings in the New Forest 1130–*c.*1430, 59. Unpublished MA thesis, University of Winchester.
126. R. P. Reeves (2013) The Normans, Domesday and the New Forest. Paper delivered to the Hampshire Field Club and Archaeological Society (landscape section) at Peter Symonds College, Winchester 09.11.13.
127. *Ibid.*, Reeves (2010) *op. cit.* 54.
128. *Ibid.,* Reeves (2010) *op. cit.* 64.
129. Yates (1985) *op. cit.* in note 92, 13.
130. The Domesday Book online. http://www.domesdaybook.co.uk/hampshire2.html#ringwood. Accessed Sept 2017.
131. National Archives (n.d.) http://www.nationalarchives.gov.uk/domesday/world-of-domesday/landscape.htm.
132. W. Page (1911) Parishes: Boldre. *A History of the County of Hampshire* 4, 616–23. London British History Online. http://www.british-history.ac.uk/vch/hants/vol4/pp616-623 accessed Sept 2017.
133. W. Page (ed.) (1911) Parishes: Brockenhurst. *A History of the County of Hampshire* 4, 626–29. British History Online. http://www.british-history.ac.uk/vch/hants/vol4/pp626-629. Accessed Sept 2017.
134. Tubbs (2001) *op. cit.* in note 14, 57–59.
135. Yates (1985) *op. cit.* in note 92, 8.
136. *Ibid.*, 58.
137. Grant (1991) *op. cit.* in note 94, 8.
138. The Development of the Manor in Anglo-Saxon and Danish England http://www.ptomng.com/z2001manor.htm.
139. M. M. Postan (1972) T*he Medieval Economy and Society*, 85, 90. Penguin Books, London.
140. *Ibid.*, 90.
141. J. Story (2003) *Carolingian Connections: Anglo-Saxon England and Caroligian Francia 750–850*, 1–18. Ashgate, Farnham.
142. C. Arnold Baker (2001) *The Companion to British History* (2nd edn) 529. Routledge.
143. Rackham (1986) *op. cit.* in note 7, 172–76.
144. *Ibid.*, 110, 113.
145. Papworth (2011) *op. cit.* in note 67, 28.
146. Light and Ponting (2001) *op. cit.* in note 22, 9–10.
147. *Ibid.*, 10.

CHAPTER 4

The Medieval Forest (1066–1500)

According to the *Anglo-Saxon Chronicle*, William the Conqueror

> '...set many deer free, and laid a law upon it, that whoever slew hart or hind should be blinded. As he forbade the killing of harts he forbade the killing of boars, and he loved the stags as if he were their father. He decreed also that hares must go free. The rich complained, the poor lamented; but he was so hard he set their hate at naught...' translation A. Savage[1]

The Normans at work and at play

To the modern mind, hunting a species seems a strange way to demonstrate one's love for it. However, William I was clear about his objectives, almost certainly having learned his leisure pursuits from continental monarchs. Legal afforestation belonged to the reign of William I (1066–1087) although the designation of royal hunting forest does not imply the area concerned was unoccupied. Furthermore, the presence of serjenties, and probable royal hunting grounds, likely demonstrate that royal interest continued post-invasion with a vengeance, in the New Forest as elsewhere. In any case, Lyndhurst belonged to the royal manor of Amesbury in Wiltshire in 1086 but it does not appear in the New Forest section of Domesday Book (1086):

> 'The King himself holds *LINHEST*. It lay in [the lands of] Amesbury, of the King's revenue. Then it answered for 2 hides; now Herbert the Forester has 1 virgate of these 2 hides and pays tax for as much; the others are in the Forest. Now ether is nothing except 2 smallholders there. Value 10s; before 1066 the value was £6'[2]

If the establishment of the New Forest at some point between 1066 and 1086 by William I makes the forest internationally famous, the account of the death of his sons William II ('the Rufus') and Richard makes it notorious in popular imagination. The memorial near to Cadnam (SU 2716 1255) commemorating the death of William II is unlikely to mark the spot of the accidental killing or assignation in AD 1100, one modern theory being the location was actually in the Beaulieu area.[3]

That afforestation, and hence hunting, was a major objective of Norman governance is demonstrated by the contemporary *Anglo-Saxon Chronicle*.[4] By 1215 there were at least 143 royal hunting forests in England[5] including (not only) the well-known royal forests of Dean, Epping and the New Forest, but also extensive areas of Devon, Essex and Huntingdonshire, so that somewhere between 20% and 25% of England was probably involved.[6] These areas would be generally on poor soils, in a kingdom otherwise wealthy on account of its soils and developed agrarian economy. Domesday names such as *-hurst* (a wooded slope of hill) or *-ley* (a forest clearing) strongly suggest a forest-type economy. It is argued that, upon afforestation, land held by individuals became grazing land, because it could no longer become enclosed.[7]

It is interesting to speculate as to just why the Normans felt the need to place so much land under forest law. The Normans are rightly regarded as arrogant and repressive, but also practical. One description has the Conqueror as: 'that Al Capone of English History' who was 'the leading representative of a collection of generally illiterate opportunistic thugs' (meaning the Norman aristocracy) – who 'enjoyed exclusive privilege of the chase'.[8] Perhaps a more sympathetic description may be to liken them to yesteryear examples of proverbial 'Essex Men' with added aristocracy, keen to impress and flaunt power and *nouveau riche* wealth, yet also feeling insecure in a new – and resentful – kingdom. In the long term, elites of Norman origin in conquered territories had to blend in so as to become the rulers of subject areas. England was to prove no exception and perhaps there was little other option to this integration.

Scholarship has postulated that the Norman (and later) kings may or may not have themselves enjoyed hunting, or even been any good at it as individuals, generally employing huntsman to kill animals for the royal household.[9] However, once in effective command of large tracts of land and being at the top of the feudal system, the king could then allocate hunting rights as a status symbols, even wealth on favoured subjects.[10] By way of illustration, the royal hunting forest of Malvern, whereabouts in pre-Conquest times bishops had hunted became a royal hunting forest under William I. Subsequently, Robert Fitzroy, the illegitimate son of Henry I, was declared lord of the Chase of Malvern, although later forest rights reverted to the crown so that Charles I was able to dis-afforest the area in the seventeenth century in order to raise revenue.[11]

The last chapter ended with the hypothesis that royal hunting forests were not a native English concept, although Anglo-Saxon kings and nobles certainly hunted over large geographic areas. This chapter covers the main features of the period 1066 to the late fifteenth century, when a greater certainty regarding the roles, rules and production of the forest can be appreciated alongside changes in fortunes of the common people. Neither is it likely there was large-scale depopulation, as was once thought, yet the evidence is clear for some. Sometimes termed 'physical afforestation', population loss did occur and it likely affected an agricultural economy that would have been weak on account of the poor quality of the land.

Certainly, by 1086 the forest was a legally defined entity constrained within a perambulation that had existed for around seven years. The New Forest community would have been aware of its situation through the imposition of the Norman administration and this may have fostered a more self-aware and maybe inward looking attitude than before, especially as there is evidence for limited depopulation including the removal of settlements at around that time. It may be that afforestation was in fact more piecemeal, at least by 1086.[12]

The crown did not to miss any opportunity to exact revenue, be that from monasteries or via such taxes as 'chiminage' for those merely traversing the area. The sacrosanct attitude towards venison enacted by the crown suggests good reason for protection of the 'vert' (that supported the deer population) and constituted woodland, undergrowth and heath,[13] yet this did not prevent its exploitation to raise revenue for other purposes, albeit under tighter control than applied to areas outside the New Forest.

In the succeeding centuries, English laws and institutions would evolve, and within the forest, a balance between the needs of those within the forest (generally those whose livelihood depended upon it) and that of the crown and nobles, or the state, had to be sought until the fourteenth century catastrophic population decline. There is a discernible long-term trend away from Norman hegemony imposed at afforestation, towards at least guarantees of customary rights for commoners and others. There has also been debate as to the relationship between common rights and forest law (Chapter 3), it is likely these rights pre-existed due to use of the area for grazing that survived the Norman Conquest.[14] However, forest rights would likely have evolved from Anglo-Saxon customary rights, though there is clear evidence that these rights were restricted and standardised, and were likely not granted by the crown in compensation for the imposition of the forest.[15] The ordinary manorial court process continued within the New Forest, co-existing with forest laws and supplementing the common law rather than replacing it,[16] and common law pleas and forest law pleas were heard in forest courts,[17] begging questions regarding the relations between manorial and other courts.

Domesday Book specifically names the New Forest (L. *Nova Foresta*) but otherwise does not give the names of individual forests. A forest included not only the 'king's demesne woods' but it also contained manors held by private lords. The relationship is therefore imposition of a layer of governance above that of the ordinary manor. Affected lords could not convert their land from pasture into arable, neither could they cut down nor make assarts (clearings) or make enclosures to exclude game. Assarting refers specifically to the bringing of uncultivated, land (such as woodland) into agricultural production. Unenclosed waste thus affected in an illegal action is referred to as 'purpresture'.

Commoners' cattle had the right of pasture within the forest, although existing rights were further restricted by the imposition of forest law. The common people had certain rights to gather from the forest and rights to graze beasts within the perambulation of the forest, although this was often a matter of contention. Forest laws applied therefore not only to crown land, but to 'private' land within the perambulation[18] and, within these areas, the common people were liable to financial demands (for such as grazing or arable agriculture) and were subject to constant annoyance from forest officials. Crimes under forest law were essentially two kinds: those of 'vert', infringements against the vegetation, and those of 'venison', poaching or otherwise adversely affecting the beasts.

There are other considerations regarding social control. For example, whatever the wider mythic or political meanings underpinning the Robin Hood legends, it is easy to see how outlaws could hide in forest areas and harass the better off members of society. Normans valued their security; they had to in their new land. Not having means of control of 'masterless men' would be most undesirable. Yet, although royal hunting forests would, for reasons of revenue, best be located in areas where agriculture was not profitable, removing the population – and hence social structures – *en masse* would give shelter to outlaws.

There was, inevitably, a bad start. The *Anglo-Saxon Chronicle* for 1088 refers to a plea for assistance from the Conqueror's son, William II:

> 'Then he sent for Englishmen and explained his need of them and asked their help, and promised them the best law that there had even been in this country, and forbade every unjust tax and granted people in the woods and hunting rights – but it did not last any time'.[19]

Clearly resentment arose from taxation by the Crown. With the imposition of forest laws to protect the 'venison and the vert' and with a capacity for the dispossession of some individuals, a colourful, if dubious, account is provided by Ordericus Vitalis (1075–*c.*1142):

> 'Now, reader let me explain why the forest ... is called "new". That part of the country had been populous in earlier days, and was scattered with hamlets providing support for settlers. Indeed a dense population thoroughly tilled the county of Hampshire, so that the southern district provided the city of Winchester with all kinds of country produce. But after William I conquered the realm of England, so great was his love of woods that he laid waste more than 60 parishes, forced the peasants to move to other places, and replaced the men with beasts of the forest so that he might hunt to his heart's content. There he lost two sons, Richard and William Rufus, and his grandson Richard ... by which the Lord plainly showed his anger.[20]

Unpopular the Conqueror was, and so much so that writers could invoke his unpopularity with the Almighty! However, this passage is the origin of the once widely held belief that forest laws gave the occasion for considerable depopulation of the New Forest. Yet, clearly there are sites that were probably removed and that were recorded in Domesday. For example, Cildeest (modern Childenhurst, the name is no longer in use), last recorded in the medieval period) with earthworks suggesting a field system, including probable Anglo-Saxon ridge and furrow.[21] Some sites may furthermore have been within lands later granted to the Cistercians at Beaulieu in 1204, and lost since.[22]

Norman arrival in 1066 was to be as conspicuous across the land as their political and military presence was soon felt. Many cathedrals and abbey churches were re-built in the wake of conquest, while the Harrying of the North (1069–1070) is an extreme example of their propensity for merciless suppression of dissent. Hastily erected 'motte and bailey' castle constructions followed the Conquest, demonstrating their intent and near to the New Forest, the re-fortification at Old Sarum was to create a Norman fortress town within an Iron Age hillfort. Actually, enactment of savagery within the New Forest remains a matter of conjecture. The chroniclers relate the forest laws as harsh and corporal, even capital, though by the mid-twelfth century, fiscal fines had become the norm. Perhaps because minor infringements did not present a threat to either state or to the *status quo*, miscreants may have been treated relatively leniently. Yet, widespread imposition of hunting forests on a vast scale and the associated legal system can only be matched by legal ostentatiousness. The Normans required a legal framework for their deeds and has been noted, there remained much administrative continuation in both the secular and ecclesiastical realms.

Feudalism, economy and the law

Royal hunting forests cannot nationally be seen in isolation from considerations of the feudal system that dominated western Europe between about AD 900 and 1200 (Chapter 3), although this existed in fluid form, adaptable in local conditions and over time.[23] In England, the feudal system has uncertain and contested origins, yet the ability to extract the surplus of peasant labour through tithes, obligations to work on the lord's demesne land and to provide military service remained long after 1066 and there were probably elements present before that date.

The feudal system not only had the crown as the administrative and governing head of state but it was also the ultimate owner of the country, and remains so today; freehold tenure refers to the *right to hold land without payment to another,* for a freeholder is free to dispose of his land without reference to a higher authority. In the middle ages, freeholders still paid rents in cash or in kind. Similarly, the term 'British subject' today remains constitutional currency, implying that the 'citizen' is actually a subject of the crown, another feudal hangover. In practice, under the feudal system, the monarch distributed land to his 'tenants-in-chief' who in turn permitted lesser gentry, and ultimately villeins or other un-free men to hold land, although the latter generally paid cash in rent and for other purposes.[24] Therefore, while notions that ownership, in the modern sense of proprietarily commanding one's freehold land, dates largely from the mid-seventeenth century,[25] in the agrarian society of the middle ages, land was more accurately said to be 'held' in exchange for military obligation, at least as observed for the eleventh and twelfth centuries.

Feudal relations are complicated by another factor: alongside the obligation-led feudal system, a market economy element operated, largely in the towns and cities. The latter would emerge strongly in the later medieval period as a factor in economic historical development in both England and Europe. Market economic elements were not *laissez faire* as might be understood today, for example sizeable town markets required charters to operate. There were also monopolistic and 'restrictive practices' included regulated in guilds that controlled labour markets.[26] Economic developments in the forests would seem a long way from either a largely feudal countryside or emergent markets around urban areas, for royal forests remained a private fiefdom of the crown.

For example, John, son of Ralph de Bokland, in 1347 obtained a grant of a weekly market on Tuesday in his manor of Brookley and a yearly fair to last four days.[27] This may have become redundant after the Black Death.

The frequently poor prospects for agriculture in areas subsequently recorded as royal hunting forests meant that the Domesday survey (1086) observed relatively low populations and few plough teams.[28] While it is also probable there was limited depopulation following legal afforestation, inhabitants were still permitted to exercise commoners' rights, including turning stock out into the waste as legal rights. While it may be assumed these rights had pre-Conquest origins,[29] forested areas have been described as 'foreign territory outside of the ordinary law and administration'.[30] As noted in the previous chapter, areas already under royal control were likely to become royal hunting forests; for example north of the New Forest, near Britford, Wiltshire, woodland that may have become incorporated in Clarendon Forest was in royal hands.[31]

From Norman times, there would appear to be unclear roles within the prevalent legal systems with no clear demarcation between 'administration' and 'justice'.[32] Communal courts were inherited from pre-Conquest arrangements, there would be one in each shire that in time would become the county courts; shires were subdivided into hundreds (sometime in the north of England, 'wapentake' was the name used), each with their own court and each seemed to have both civil and criminal jurisdiction. Even after the Conquest, freeholders were obliged to attend and to sit as judges, although hundred courts would gradually loose influence as the king increased his in the Shire courts.[33] The sheriff controlled the shire court, the bailiff the hundred court, the vills could have their own version of the hundred court. This all meant the king had some influence over the judicial system.[34]

There were also feudal courts where a lord had a right to hold courts for all those who held land from him. The king held a court of honour for the 'mesne' lords who were, in feudal terms, beneath him. Manorial courts belonged lower down in the system concerned with a lord's demesne and a court baron was for the free tenants and court customary for un-free villeins who had customary land rights; later it came to administer 'copyhold tenancies'.[35] The manorial courts were thus concerned with the administration of seigniorial justice, those of direct concern to the lord of the manor and largely concerned with agriculture and land tenural matters.[36]

The ecclesiastical courts administered canon law and the Normans had set out to strengthen these. They were concerned with such 'abuses' as the benefit of clergy (whereby clerics retained a right to be tried for offences by the said courts and no other, and disputes over which caused the martyrdom of St Thomas Becket). The general population's moral or religious offences were also tried in these courts but these were also concerned with economic interests for the church, generally involving the payment of tithes.[37]

As Norman kings began to assert their authority, perhaps in their own terms 'modernising' English administration and jurisdiction, and eventually also pulling away powers from feudal lords, something realised in the early thirteenth century. The Norman kings started to develop the concept of the 'exchequer'. By the time of Henry I, officials visited the counties as justiciars, the king's officials,[38] to review events and in particular to collect taxes due to the king and hold pleas.

This was, by nature, a General Circuit Court, or an 'eyre'. An eyre called by Henry II (likely date 1178) was called the General Eyre and it met every 7 years. These would visit a hundred, or vill, and ask a local jury about a particular dispute.[39] Various commissions to hear various legal disputes, for example the Assizes of Clarendon under Henry II (1166) had confirmed itself the watchdog of crown interests. Initially the terms 'assize' probably referred to a court 'sitting', but later it referred to the ordinances (laws that were thus produced) from that sitting.[40] Henry was concerned with more than clerical wrong-doing, he placed his ideas in the hands of itinerant officials who were responsible with the instigation of trial by jury and oath-taking in court.[41]

The central state developed the *Curia Regis* or royal court, becoming eventually fixed at Westminster. Then there could be specialist courts including the Court of Common Pleas (1178)[42] and also the Courts of Exchequer, Courts of Chancery and King's Bench concerned with crime and keeping the king's peace, and later civil matters. The Court of Chancery (the court of the Lord Chancellor) administered justice and required a writ to commence any case in the royal justice system.[43] In theory displaying a mechanism for mitigation of either crown or common law, this would seem in contrast to the notorious later Star Chamber (from about 1474 and abolished by Oliver Cromwell) which was concerned with the rights of powerful people, and came to represent arbitrary power for the monarch.

The Court of Exchequer was concerned with the Royal Exchequer and revenue matters[44] and chancery courts mitigated inequity of the common law and was concerned with trusts and land law. With the centralisation in London came a gradual fading away of feudal courts and until the later twelfth century trial could be heard in the country (in circuit) or in London for the more wealthy and appeals became increasingly heard in London. The justices involved were likely the same individuals.

'Common law' was thus the system that developed from the operation of these royal courts, the term implies a system that is common to the whole country, *as opposed to localised law deriving from communal courts of earlier times.* Initially therefore, the common law was enforced throughout the land by the itinerant justices and professional administrators trained for that purpose. It is likely that those in land disputes would prefer the common law courts to those of the feudal or manorial courts due to entrenched local interests and powers; it is probable the forest law was additional to common law.[45]

As part of their 'acculturation' into the practices of the western European nobility, continental Norman rulers (originally of Scandinavian descent) would have restricted the cutting of trees in order to provide covert for game and took profit for 'forest pleas', that is those presented at forest courts for alleged transgressions of aristocratic hunting interests. Desmesne land would have reserved ducal rights over the 'vert' and the 'venison' (actually all livestock). Similar administrative arrangements were to emerge in England by the thirteenth century, including a system of officials whose job it was to administer the 'forest law', including collection of taxes, rents and fines.

What becomes clear is that, even from before the charters of 1215 and 1217 (see Chapter 2), the Royal Exchequer benefitted from forest income. Forest eyres were profitable and from the reign of Henry II income was regularly brought to the exchequer by the sheriff and by forest officials. Revenue-raising was in part due jurisdiction lying outside the normal rule of law and subject to the personal authority of the king.[46] Therefore the final legal system remained of economic as well as other importance. This being the forest, courts were to enforce the forest law, including preserving game for the crown and this was unique, in that it had geographical extent and is described below.

In essence, in forest areas the English common law became superseded by Norman forest laws, and likewise manorial courts became subject to another, higher, layer of administration and jurisdiction, but it continued to administer people and land on a day-by-day basis. While the severity of the resulting punishments may be exaggerated by the chroniclers, apparently punishments for hunting the lesser animals were not excessive, *nor were they especially repressive when viewed in respect of the common law of the eleventh century*. Hunting with horses and dogs, in the king's forest, required considerable resources and might be considered a rebellious act against the crown rather than simply the theft of more basic resources. Punishment would be by fine, imprisonment or, for a bondman, some form of corporeal punishment. Killing a royal beast apparently resulted in the death penalty for a bondman, merely causing it to become out of breath could result in the man becoming an outlaw.[47]

The legal entity of a forest was to determine the development of the area – almost to the exclusion of other factors, yet with the caveat that there were communities within who not only had to make a living themselves. This matter will be returned to in Chapter 5.

Within the perambulation

The boundary of a legal forest was defined in order to differentiate areas where crown forest interests applied above those outside that were merely subject to the Chancery, and of course the manorial courts. As a legal entity, a royal hunting forest can only be removed by statute and unlike most others, the New Forest was never 'dis-afforested', this is a legal process would enable private land sales within a perambulation. Today the only other remaining English royal hunting forest, in the full legal sense, is the Forest of Dean.[48]

Norman forests were the preserve of the king although nobles had the right to hunt in 'chases'. In other, comparable, areas were parks and free warrens,

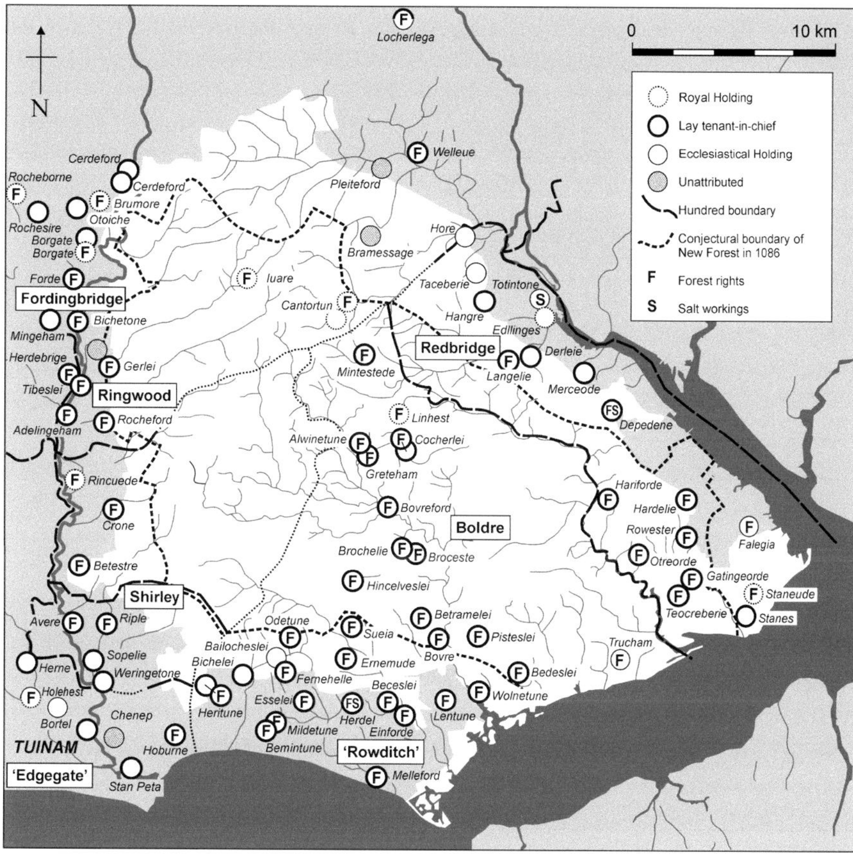

FIGURE 4.1. Domesday (1086) holdings in the New Forest and surroundings, showing those with forest rights.

AFTER DAVIES *ET AL.* 1998, 20

generally held by many lords of the manor outside the bounds, or with permission of the crown. As has been described, 'forest' in reality exhibited a range of land covers including woods, scrub, heath, grassland and wetland. There are visible remains of deer park pales, coppice banks, lodges, settlement pattern and buildings. However, Domesday Book actually supplied the first consistent documentary evidence that points to ownership and management.[49] Subsistence activities have left visible remains including settlement pattern suggested by artefact scatters in enclosed lands. Unusual governance is a factor that has largely preserved the present form of the landscape, certainly more than any other.

There must have been a recorded perambulation in Norman times that approximated to that presented in Figure 4.1. Actually, the earliest known formal perambulation of the New Forest was undertaken in 1217–1218 in the reign of Henry III, although we may presume that boundaries were defined earlier. It is believed this perambulation remained more or less unchanged until 1964.[50] To quote D. J. Stagg:

> 'An expansion of the original New Forest boundary took place during the 11th and 12th centuries, predominantly during the reign of Henry I. One of the earliest known perambulations of the New Forest was made *c.*1215–1216 subsequent to Magna Carta,

> another dated 1217 was made following the Charter of the Forest. These reduced the boundary with the reintroduction of the original 1086 bounds (Small Bounds). This was revoked in 1227, and was replaced by the pre-Magna Carter boundary (the Large Bounds) which remained in force until 1299 when it was replaced by the original bounds, represented by the perambulation of 1300–1301. The bounds represented by the perambulation 1300–1301 were again revoked in 1306 and replaced by the large bounds. The Large Bounds was replaced with the small bounds when the Charter of the Forest was finally implemented in 1327.'

Fluctuations between the large and small bounds would still have been of practical interest, while the large bounds brought in more revenue, because more people would be under the jurisdiction of forest law.[51] These boundaries would likely have included some 25 hides granted by King John to the Cistercian order at Beaulieu in 1204.[52] Afforestation undertaken by an enthusiastic Henry II was furthermore reviewed and certain areas returned to cultivation, although dis-afforestation does not imply a return to cultivation as afforestation does not, of itself, imply an end to cultivation in the first place. It would be the poor soils of the New Forest that evidently led to extensive retention of the forest law.[53] It is thus certain that the perambulation varied over time; areas that became known as 'purlieu' were dis-afforested at the time of the *Charter of the Forest* (1217). As the interest (or power) of the crown diminished, so did the area; another mechanism being the sale of the privileges abrogated (that is abolished) by the imposition of forest law.[54] The accession of Edward III in 1327 is regarded as the end of the long struggle for dis-afforestation of purlieu, in that respect it was a turning point.[55] It should be noted there is an enclosure of around 200 ha comprising a double ditch separated by a bank between Denny Lodge and Culvery Farm, just south of Beaulieu station, marked as 'The Bishop's Dyke' by the Ordnance survey (sometimes called 'The Bishop's Purlieu').[56] While it may relate to thirteenth century land grants to the Bishop of Winchester, its exact dates and purpose remain uncertain, although it may have been a medieval deer park.

Where sufficiently detailed maps are absent, the ability of boundary reconstruction from a record of minor landscape features is difficult because these may have vanished or changed names. Only a general impression can be gained from other sources.[57] An attempted identification of the boundary features was undertaken by Arthur Clarke but the manuscript and maps were never published.[58] It does however correlate closely the medieval bounds with the pre-1964 bounds. Yates (following Stagg) identifies alternative evidence, including vills that were required to provide representation at the assizes (when listed) and even the location of homes of forest officers, notably the regarders and freemen within and without the forest who constituted the boundary (Fig. 4.2).[59]

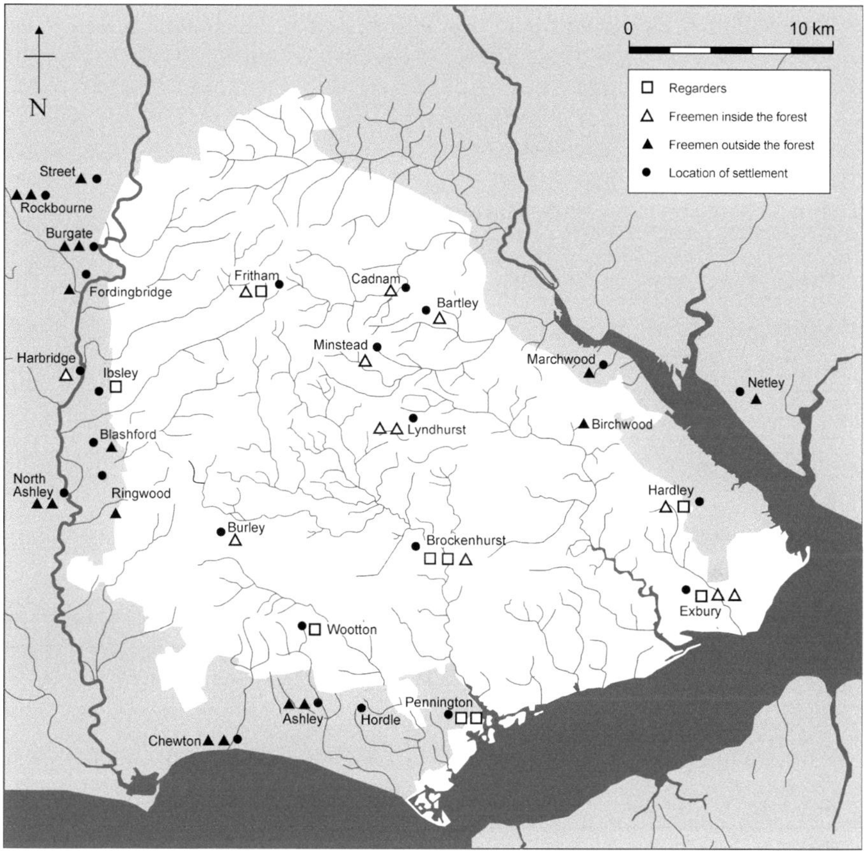

FIGURE 4.2. Approximate perambulation of the New Forest in 1344.

AFTER YATES 1985, 16

Economic development

Even if the afforestation caused a long-term 'economic recession' in that part of the conventional agrarian economy that was set within a perambulation, there was also a subsequent long-term move away from the provision of leisure pursuits for the king and nobles. Initially, diversification of activity seems to relate to support of the itinerant Royal household; but the rise of economic importance of the vert for other than hunting becomes clear well before the end of the middle ages. There were certain areas that were no longer under cultivation, perhaps because of the near impossibility under forest law of protecting them from deer, yet only limited evidence for depopulation.[60] Small areas of meadow were permitted to be fenced to exclude deer, so there could be hay crops. It is likely there was compensation in the form of exemption from taxation, with commoners' rights allowing for an element of self-sufficiency, as cottage husbandry. Livelihoods continued but manorial life was evidently under stringency within the perambulation.

The New Forest therefore was never 'enclosed' in the normally accepted agricultural sense that would produce a continuous system of modern fields or 'closes'. However, there are limited but conspicuous areas of enclosure associated

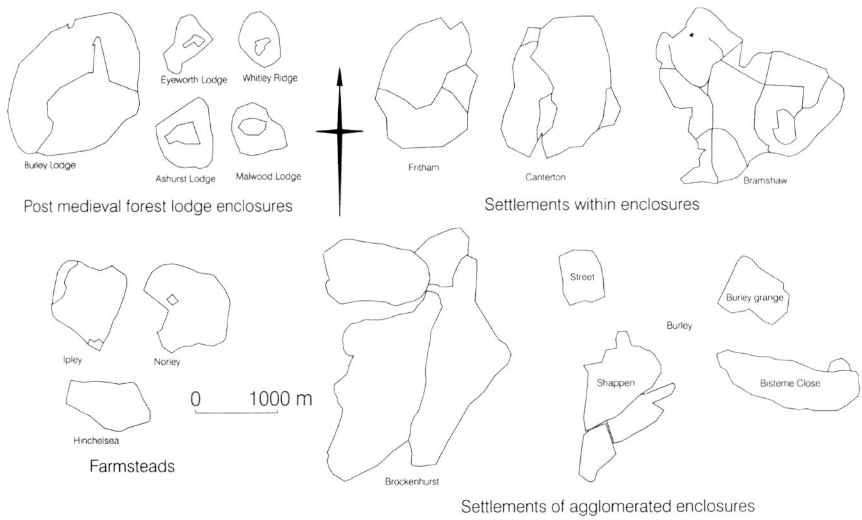

FIGURE 4.3. Areas of private enclosures within the New Forest perambulation.

AFTER SMITH 1999, BY PERMISSION OF HAMPSHIRE FIELD CLUB AND ARCHAEOLOGICAL SOCIETY, 23

with towns, villages and farmsteads that have likely developed from woodland clearances ('assarts') and hence display curvilinear boundaries. They have may had both agricultural purposes or be later inclosures that came to be established for silvicultural purposes (Fig. 4.3).[61] Although there is generally only limited evidence for plantation within woods in the middle ages, notably by monastic houses,[62] no such evidence relates to the New Forest, although there were coppices within the woods such as the Bentley Inclosures (see below) and also managed by the monks of Beaulieu Abbey.[63] This Cistercian house produced an informative record concerning coppice products from an estate that was concentrated in the historic New Forest. In accounts of 1269–1270, 1 acre (0.4 ha) of coppice was recorded as being cut every 20 years, and provides quantification of products in the form of firewood bundles, bushels of vine-sticks or fencing rods, oven faggots with waste wood going for charcoal burning.[64]

Crown interests were clearly tied up with interventions in management, governance and economy of the New Forest, from the turn of the twelfth century until the start of the fifteenth century. For the period 1105–1254 there was great need to supply the royal court.[65] Although documentary information is limited, venison was regularly sent to London and elsewhere for Christmas feasts, although locally, Clarendon was less relevant as it could supply its own needs from its own forest.[66] The New Forest provided four specific 'economic' services in the middle ages, specifically hunting for the king, free from interference, provide for a supply of meat, provide revenues for the exchequer and, from the fourteenth century at least, provide income from the sale of timber and underwood products from 'coppices' within the perambulation.[67]

The significance of serjeanties has been noted in Chapter 3; the granting of these to favoured individuals who were held in fee (*i.e.* hereditarily) implies economic interest (as it does continuity into the Norman period). For example, the creation of vaccaries (cow farms, or rather not cow farms *per se* but petit serjeanties held by managing a head of cattle) was overseen by the Warden of Fee, who would be keen to collect fixed rents. However, it is possible that, because there is no evidence that the forest vaccaries were created by the Warden, they may have predated the forest system, for fixed rents were accounted for by the Sheriff and therefore did not reach the Warden.[68]

Interestingly there is early evidence of a crisis in timber supply, at least for tall trees by the end of the twelfth century when England was importing tall timber from Scandinavia.[69] Regional evidence points to a timber shortage for construction; a dendrochronological study of Salisbury Cathedral spire demonstrated the timber used was imported from Ireland during the fourteenth century.[70] While there had been a dispute between the chief carpenter Godardus and the warden of nearby Clarendon Forest, it is surprising the oaks around Dublin, then relatively recently under English control were sourced, rather than from local forests. Later still, in the fifteenth century, domestic timber prices fell when timber began to be imported from the Baltic region.[71]

Crown interest continued, and if anything strengthens into the post-Norman period, although the interests of the royal family remain to the fore in intervention in forest affairs. In 1254 the New Forest was granted by Henry III to his son, later Edward I (1239–1307, 'Longshanks') then, in 1270 the forest was granted in 'dower' to Eleanor of Castile, to provide income in the event of her husband's death. In the process of her administrations, the hereditary officers were ejected, the Lyndhurst Bailiwick was sub-divided and there was the creation of lodges for accommodation.[72] Eleanor acquired holdings at Lyndhurst (that became a high status settlement), Godshill, Linwood and Fritham; her death in 1290 lead to a loss of interest in the forest by the royal family.

The reign of Henry III (1216–1272) saw a shift of emphasis from the deer to the greenwood, and interference with the vert such as felling of saplings. At this time, lopping of boughs was dealt with vigorously by the justices of the forest, although this may have occurred at an earlier time because there is a lack in survival of earlier legal documents. Some of the land around the New Forest was re-afforested and the old bounds were reinforced and there were complaints against the rigours of forest law, and its administration. In the following century there were problems relating to diminishing crown interest.

An investigation into manorial payments from *Lyndhurst*, *Godshill*, *Fritham*, *Lindwood*, *Burleigh* and *Batramesley*[73] shows that for the period between 1291 and 1300, certainly pannage and pasture are significant land uses. Large sums were also collected for turf cutting and it is likely that such activity impacted on the landscape through ecological damage and in maintaining/expanding healthland. Such would have supplemented the use of the vert for fuel. Actually, peat was not part of the right, legally only heather turves were included within turbary and although no longer practised was apparently carefully regulated.[74] Consequently, the right of turbary cannot easily be established as an origin of the pools within the New Forest mires, although evidently peat was recorded as being cut in the eighteenth century (Chapter 7).

An Ordinance of the Forest in 1306 could state: 'the People of our Realm are by the Officers of our Forests, miserably oppressed, impoverished and troubled with many wrongs, being everywhere molested.' This being attributable to the excesses of forest officers, powers were to be controlled. In the interests of better justice, sworn juries were introduced for cases of trespass of the vert or venison. At this time, there were two courts operating under the ordinance, namely the Attachment Court and Swainmote Court.[75]

The forest was 'farmed out' from approximately 1313 to the wardens in exchange for a fixed rent in a fashion analogous to the farming of demesne land on other feudal estates outside the perambulation.[76] Implicit is a reduction of interest by the Crown,[77] something continuing into the period 1358–1400 that saw a general decline in the forest system. This decline is a consequence of the introduction of more general taxation including lay subsidies, a tax imposed on persons according to the reputed value of their estates. Renewed interest returned during the reign of Edward III (1327–1377) who reinvigorated hunting and upgraded accommodation including the manors of Lyndhurst and Brockenhurst and appointed high status wardens, but there remained little interest in management.[78]

Some inclosures within the forest are irregular,[79] perhaps following older assart or purprestre where the new boundaries avoided large trees, and where the boundaries are irregular because they likely only enclose the land wherein the underwood was exploited for the first time, possibly enclosing the whole wood as in the case of Ridley. Later enclosure tended to display straight boundaries, wood banks are common. Sizes ranged from 5.7 ha to 73 ha. Some existing unenclosed woods in the New Forest were enclosed and coppiced during the Middle Ages, including Ridley Wood, while Bentley Old Inclosure may have been enclosed wood pasture.[80] It may be that there is confusion between the coppicing as generally understood in a modern sense and the coppicing in the forest in medieval times, which was little more than sporadic underwood exploitation.[81] Therefore, it is likely that all coppices were derived from pasture woodlands and 'The Bentleys' were medieval coppices, later converted into inclosures (Chapter 6).

Erratic exploitation of the underwood therefore led to a somewhat *ad hoc* system that resembled coppice management. A record of 1389 relates to the exploitation of underwood such may have occurred at *Sandhurst*, *Rowe* and *Guisely* and the creation of boundaries was no more than the enclosing of the area of underwood which had been felled. However, the systemised, often compartmentalised management of coppice management of the classic type practised in East Anglia and elsewhere in England, where the woodland resource was in great demand, is unlikely in the New Forest. Exploitation of the underwood related to domestic use and in supplying small-scale wood crafts. Following enclosure of wooded areas upon leasing to an individual and after 7–9 years being thrown open again for grazing and while wood was cut and removed, the compartmentalisation and cyclical cutting and re-growth from ancient coppice stools is not known.[82]

'Coppicing' however, is first mentioned in 1389 but the records of wood sales are unclear about earlier times. Under Richard III (reigned 1483–1485), the *Encoppicement Act* of 1483[83] responded to a renewed threat. This act is not relevant to the forest coppices, but it would relate to private woodlands within forests, for example a woodland within the manor of Brockenhurst would be covered, coppices in the forest proper would not. We may, however, infer that similar measures were in place within the legal forest.[84] Trees such as hazel, ash and underwood, once cut, suffered from animals grazing saplings and hence inhibited re-growth. Clearly only modest coppice production had occurred in the late medieval period and prior to Tudor times the need to legislate for wood production as coppice, small though it was, might have been a portent of what was to follow, albeit largely in areas without the perambulation.

The *Encoppicement Act* 1483 encouraged the enclosure of private forest 'coppices' within the bounds of forests for 3 years (after cutting as standard) and extended the period to 7 years to keep excluding grazing animals.[85] Enclosures thus created had a ditch and bank topped with (un-sharp) palings.[86] Thorns could then be planted on the inside of the enclosure to deter grazing. Concern was not so much for the tall trees, but the underwood – that is in effect the coppice. Coppices were leased to individuals by the crown, although the interest for these would have been largely underwood; standards being harvested to the benefit of the treasury, with the Surveyor of Woods presenting annual accounts to the treasury. These changes are not to be seen as systematic wood production rather the aim was to preserve the underwood for domestic fuel and charcoal, both significant aspects of the forest economy for its inhabitants.[87] Athough private coppices were protected; parallel activities were likely applied in crown coppices such as Broadstone, Castle Hill and South Bentley that, in 1595, were leased to individuals.[88] Coppices remaining in the crown land were actually not affected by the legislation of 1483.There must have been a developing interest in large timber production, specifically for the navy, and something that would be a portent of state interest in the forest, for earlier, in 1416/17, the New Forest supplied timber for Henry V's flagship, *Grace Dieu*.[89]

Settlements and enclosures

The term 'settlement' in historic geography implies merely a place where a group of people have established a group of dwellings for a protracted period of time, or permanently. A 'settlement' is distinct from a single house and imparts a sense of community, although this does not have to be large. It can also contain a descriptor that tells of the appearance or function of a settlement, or can impart a relationship with local topography. Economic descriptions are commonplace, for example a 'mining-' 'farming-' or 'industrial-' settlement, as does 'market town'. A monastic settlement may be part economic and part cultural in purpose, while a 'gap town' or 'spring-line village' implies a relation to the physical environment as 'nucleated-', 'dispersed-' or 'linear-' imply form taken by the settlement. They may not always haven been occupied, but hunting settlements, be they from the Mesolithic or the medieval period (seen as hunting lodges), would still satisfy the criteria of a settlement.

To the above can be added notions of legitimacy. For example, in the medieval period, certain tenant farmers of the manor of Forde (modern Fordingbridge) had rights to grazing within the New Forest[90] and that, with part of the manor of Fordingbridge within the New Forest, once included the right of Turbary. Such rights would have reduced pressure in areas otherwise operating an open field system on the better soils, such as those on river terraces adjacent to the forest in the Avon valley. These grazing rights demonstrate strong economic relations with and without the perambulation, and the likelihood is these had continued from prehistory (Chapter 3).

Agriculture could be practised around the periphery of the forest and in designated areas within. The Crockford complex (near the Norley enclosure) is a system of embanked fields covering over 80 ha of Beaulieu Heath on gently sloping land at around 30 m AOD and probably medieval in origin, but with prehistoric antecedents. The scale of the system, where small rectangular fields abut larger ones, is suggestive of a managed estate, rather than individual encroachment.[91] However, the date remains uncertain, and planned field systems are commonplace at proven Bronze Age sites.

While the term 'assart' relates to winning land (such as 'waste') for cultivation or pasture and it may be enclosed by fence or bank, this may be sanctioned by the manor. The term 'purpresture' relates to the appropriation of land for private use (agricultural or domestic) that may have been intended for communal use, including tracks and common land and lacks legal sanction. Such may not only be the origin of land use change, generally to agriculture, but also provide the basis for the genesis of a settlement. On the other hand, a squatter encroachment on land belonging to the crown, or with commoners' rights, may have been established with the complicity of the local community, or the manor where revenue followed encroachment[92] and to them may be added settlements with industrial purpose that were established in the post-medieval period.

Many settlements are presumed to date from the Anglo-Saxon period or later, and Domesday gives us a picture of a relatively mature settlement pattern (Fig. 4.1). The settlement types were diverse: villages, farmsteads, moated sites, agglomerated enclosures, common edge settlements and hunting lodges. Often these have curvilinear outlines suggesting an origin as assarts, or otherwise as agglomerates of clearings. For example, Fritham may be of Anglo-Saxon origin, but it may have operated as a vaccary (cow farm) during the high medieval period.[93] Supporting evidence seems to come from its funnel shape that facilitated the diversion of cattle into enclosures.

Modern Fritham shows signs of having been a nucleated settlement, but with satellite farms to the east and south and a secondary settlement to the west, against the forest boundary. It furthermore displays external ditches with pollards in places. Hinchelsea was also a vaccary.[94] The 'curvilinear' boundaries are taken as an indication of settlements annexing and reclaiming for agriculture more and more land. Brockenhurst was not legally afforested. The enclosed and often curvilinear fields are on the south-west side ('The Weirs') and include boggy land, with clear attempts at drainage today. This may have had a directly agricultural function, being outside the forest jurisdiction.

Fourteenth century subsidies show the area to have a low population, even prior to the Black Death, although major settlements were established at Lyndhurst, Burley, Minstead, Boldre and Brockenhurst. Ipley, for example, was a small settlement first recorded in 1210, then later in Lay Subsidy rolls (taxation on lay estates) of the fourteenth centuries and it appears as a vaccary held by Beaulieu Abbey. The enclosures may have resulted from population pressures, prior to the Black Death.[95]

Moated sites, probably rare examples of moated homesteads in Hampshire, are to be found at Royden Wood, Holbury Manor and and Old Charford and date from the twelfth–fourteenth centuries.[96] Otherwise, small square or sub-rectangular enclosures represent the sites of former hunting lodges;[97] these are approximately 50 m in area and although little is known of them from the early period before 1300 although King John gave a lodge to Beaulieu Abbey.

Early sites are often erroneously known as 'Church Place'. Today they are situated in areas of permanent afforestation although this was not always the case. Figure 4.4 shows six examples identified. They were partly fortified, in order to protect crown property within, by palisades and earthworks. Overall, lodges were maintained into the fifteenth century, becoming more elaborate over time.

Work is recorded on lodges in 1200, and these would have been maintained by keepers within the forest, although there was considerable royal interest.[98] This is reflected by expenditure during the reign of Edward III,[99] and also by Richard II at dates between 1387 and 1390. Richard evidently invested in lodges at Helmsley, Hatherburgh and Studley and also in the head of the pond at Lyndhurst Park.[100]

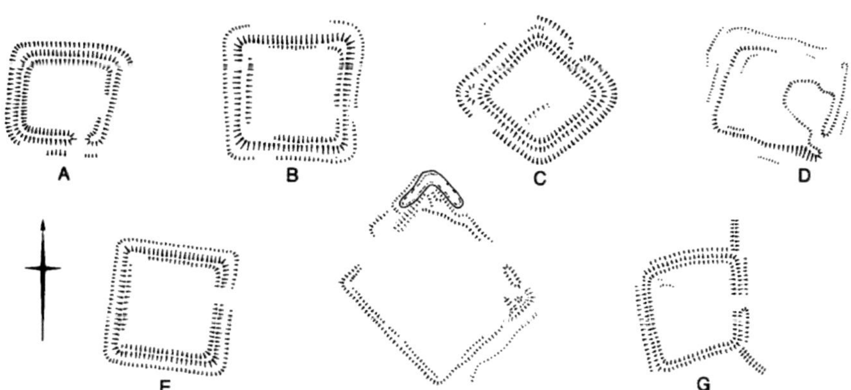

FIGURE 4.4. Earthwork remains of New Forest Hunting Lodges. A. Church Place, Denny; B. Church Place, Ashurst; C. Church Place, Sloden; D. Boulderwood; E. Studley Castle, F. Queen Bower; G. enclosure at King's Passage, Matley.

AFTER SMITH 1999, 5, BY PERMISSION OF HAMPSHIRE FIELD CLUB AND ARCHAEOLOGICAL SOCIETY

Deer parks were enclosures with paling fences or 'park pale', banks and ditches (often water-filled) that was surmounted with wooden pales that were commonplace in medieval England.[101] Red and roe deer were generally hunted on horseback, as these became increasingly rare, fallow deer were increasingly reared in deer parks from the thirteenth century. Deer were thus raised for release into the open forest. Inside the paling they could be either wood pasture, or else were un-compartmentalised so that deer could freely graze with trees pollarded for protection against grazing. Compartmentalised trees enabled separation between trees and grazing.[102] In the New Forest, there seems to have been a simple distinction between areas open to grazing and those 'inclosed' to protect the trees. According to Liddiard,[103] parks like certain of the settlements may have pre-dated the establishment of royal hunting forests, although they are generally regarded as quintessentially Norman. The best example in the forest is at Lyndhurst Old Park, also termed 'the King's Park'.

Edward I had visited Lyndhurst and enclosed the park.[104] A park was attached early on to the manor of Lyndhurst and by 1299 it covered an area of 500 acres (202.4 ha), with profits accrued from honey. The 'close of Queen Margaret at Lyndhurst' is mentioned in 1313 and later in that century, the sheriff of Southampton was ordered to provide transport for the work of inclosing the King's park at Lyndhurst. Also in the fourteenth century, John de Beauchamp (1358) was charged to sell timber from there to cover the expense of making four lodges and ridings in the forest. Subsequent payments were made for the fencing and repairing of the palings.[105]

There were other enclosures for other purposes that give insight into a wider agrarian economy of the New Forest. For example, pig pounds were found in the forest,[106] a possible example being at Sloden Wood (SU 2165 1255). Specific stag parks were often found associated with keepers' cottages. The latter persisted in the post-medieval period as is evidenced by Charles II's creation of a deer park for imported deer from France. Sheep enclosures were most likely associated with the Cistercians of Beaulieu.[107]

Conclusions

This chapter describes the origins of legal and institutional New Forest that has come down to us. The extent to which of Anglo-Saxon kings or nobles hunted there remains a matter for speculation, but it is clear that the hard-nosed Normans were keen to set aside a large area of agriculturally marginal land, and whatever the presumed economic loss arising from their actions, it cannot have been a major consideration. Neither does there appear to have been widespread de-population, although there were evidently moves in that direction. To turn the entire forest over to being essentially a game reserve would have raised questions for law and order, management and have raised questions for staffing the maintenance of the royal household, and all that implies.

Economic imperatives shifted away from the concerns of elites for recreation and the trappings of power enabling moves towards timber production. Even on such poor quality land, there grew a realisation of the need for wood products where other, ordinary agricultural products, would not yield well. There was a loss to the legal forest of substantial areas in the south to the Cistercian order at the turn of the thirteenth century; predictably this constituted the better agricultural land within the early perambulation.

The maintenance of the New Forest landscape would, after all, require the labour of lesser men and women whose interests would have to be protected against arbitrary power of the crown and its officers. Settlement patterns included not only moated sites and hunting lodges for elites, but also clearly identifiable settlements today that reflected the parallel economy of forest dwellers such as at Fritham, while Lyndhurst operated as foci for the administration of forest.

The landscape as a whole contains features that are to be found outside the perambulation, including encroachments by squatters. However, the paucity of archaeological evidence can make it hard to ascertain the age of particular enclosures and field systems. We may surmise that the appearance of much open forest was much as it is today, although inclosures for 'silviculture' were likely to have more the appearance of coppice. The next chapter looks more closely at forest governance.

Notes

1. http://www.newforest.hampshire.org.uk/history1.html.
2. T. Hinde (ed.) (1985) *The Domesday Book*, 118. Guild Publishing, London.
3. http://www.new-forest-national-park.com/rufus-stone.html.
4. D. J. Stagg (1974) The New Forest in Domesday Book. *Proceedings of the Hampshire Field Club and Archaeological Society*, New Forest Section 13, 20–24.
5. O. Rackham (1986) *The History of the Countryside*, 131. Dent, London.
6. R. Rutherford-Moore (n.d.) Recreating a Royal Hunt in Sherwood Forest. http://www.sthubertsrangers.org/royal_hunt.htm.
7. S. Davies, L. Walker and L. Coleman (1998) *The New Forest Historical Landscape*, 1920. Wessex Archaeology, Salisbury.
8. P. J. Neville Havins (1976) *The Forests of England*. Robert Hale, London.
9. J. Bond (1994) Forests, chases, warrens and parks in medieval Wessex. In M. Ashton and C. Lewis (eds), *The Medieval Landscape of Wessex*, 126. Oxbow Monograph 6, Oxbow Books, Oxford.
10. P. Hurle (2007) *The Forest and Chase of Malvern*, 13. Philimore, London.
11. *Ibid.*, 9, 73.
12. K. A. Mew (1997) 'Through a glass darkly': the biography of a Domesday landscape – the *Nova Foresta*. Unpublished PhD thesis. University of Reading.
13. D. J. Stagg (1984) *Verders of the New Forest*, 2. New Forest Association, Fordingbridge.
14. D. J. Stagg (ed.) (1979) *A Calendar of New Forest Documents AD 1244–AD 1334*, 31. Hampshire Record Series III, Hampshire County Council, Winchester; Peter Roberts pers. comm. (2014).
15. R. Reeves pers. comm. (2013).
16. P. D. A. Harvey (1979) Forest laws. In D. J. Stagg (ed.), *A Calendar of New Forest*

Documents AD 1244–AD 1334, ix. Hampshire Record Series III, Hampshire County Council, Winchester.

17. D. J. Stagg (1979) Common law in the New Forest. In D. J. Stagg (ed), *A Calendar of New Forest Documents AD 1244–AD 1334*, 3–4. Hampshire Record Series III, Hampshire County Council, Winchester.
18. Stagg (1979) *op. cit.* in note 14, 36.
19. E. M. Yates (1985) *The Landscape of the New Forest in Medieval Times*, 1. Dept of Geography, King's College London.
20. M. Chibnall (ed.) (1975) *Ecclesiastical History*, Vol 5, 285. Clarendon Press, Oxford.
21. R. Reeves (2012) The Great British Story – The New Forest. Broadcast on BBC1 South Today, 12 June 2012.
22. P. Roberts pers comm. (2014).
23. P. Vinogradoff (1924). Feudalism. In J. B. Barry, J. R. Tanner, C. W. Previte-Orton and Z. N. Brooke (eds), *Cambridge Medieval History* Vol 3, 458–84. Cambridge University Press, Cambridge.
24. M. M. Postan (1972) *The Medieval Economy and Society*, 66. Penguin Books, London.
25. C. Hill (1972) *The World Turned Upside Downside*, 15. Penguin Books, London.
26. M. M. Postan (1972) *The Medieval Economy and Society*, chapter 12. Penguin Books, London.
27. *Victoria County History* http://www.british-history.ac.uk/report.aspx?compid=56898.
28. Bond (1994) *op. cit.* in note 9, 123.
29. The New Forest History. http://www.newforest.hampshire.org.uk/history1.html.
30. C. Arnold Baker (2001) *The Companion to British History*, 529 (2nd edn). Routledge, London.
31. Bond (1994) *op. cit.* in note 9, 123.
32. R. Clements pers. comm. (2013).
33. F. W. Maitland (1908/1909) *The Constitutional History of England*, 44. Cambridge University Press, Cambridge. https://books.google.co.uk/books?id=MQaHL9s_xRwC&printsec=frontcover&source=gbs_ge_summary_r&cad=0#v=onepage&q&f=false.
34. *Ibid.*, 24.
35. *Ibid.*, 49.
36. Yates (1985) *op. cit.* in note 19, 5–8.
37. *Ibid.*
38. Maitland (1908/1909) *op. cit.* in note 33, 63–64.
39. *Ibid.*, 69.
40. *Ibid.*, 12.
41. J. Hudson (1996) *The Formation of the English Common Law*, 130. Longmans, London.
42. Maitland (1908/1909) *op. cit.* in note 33, 68–69.
43. *Ibid.*, 114.
44. *Ibid.*, 63.
45. *Ibid.*, 13–14; P. Roberts pers. comm. (2014).
46. http://www.le.ac.uk/elh/whittlewood/forest.htm
47. Staffordshire Forest Pleas: Introduction, *Staffordshire Historical Collections* 5(1) (1884), 123–35. http://www.british-history.ac.uk/report.aspx?compid=52372. Accessed 6 July 2010.
48. K. Jones (n.d.) Forest of Dean. http://www.katherinejones.co.uk/work/forest_of_dean_framework.pdf. Accessed August 2012.
49. Davies *et al.* (1998) *op. cit.* in note 87, 20.
50. C. J. Tubbs (2001) *New Forest, the History, Ecology and Conservation*, 57. New Forest Ninth Centenary Trust, Fordingbridge.

51. D. J. Stagg (1974) A perambulation of the New Forest 1217–1218. *Proceedings of the Hampshire Field Club and Archaeological Society*, New Forest Section 13, 26–27.
52. *Ibid.*
53. A New Forest History. http://www.newforest.hampshire.org.uk/history2.html.
54. Yates (1985) *op. cit.* in note 19, 17.
55. D. J. Stagg (1983) *A Calendar of New Forest Documents: the Fifteenth to Seventeenth Centuries*, xvi. Hampshire Record Series V, Hampshire County Council, Winchester.
56. Pastscape 'Bishop's Dyke'. http://www.pastscape.org.uk/hob.aspx?hob_id=226270#aRt <accessed Nov 2015> http://www.newforestexplorersguide.co.uk/heritage/history-in-the-landscape/bishops-dyke.html. New forest explorer's Guide http://www.newforestexplorersguide.co.uk/heritage/history-in-the-landscape/bishops-dyke.html <accessed Nov 2015>.
57. Yates (1985) *op. cit.* in note 19, 15.
58. R. Reeves pers. comm. (2013).
59. Yates (1985) *op. cit.* in note 19, 16–17.
60. Stagg (1974) *op. cit.* in note 4, 20–24.
61. N. Smith (1999) The earthwork remains of enclosure in the New Forest. *Proceedings of the Hampshire Field Club and Archaeological Society* 54, 23.
62. O. Rackham (2006) Woodlands, 447–48. Collins, London.
63. R. Deakin (2008) *Wildwood: a journey through trees*. Penguin ebooks, London.
64. Bond (1994) *op. cit.* in note 9, 129.
65. R. P. Reeves (2010) The administration of large holdings in the New Forest 1130–*c.*1430, 61. Unpublished MA thesis, University of Winchester.
66. R. Reeves pers. comm. 2013.
67. P. Roberts (2002) *Minstead: life in a New Forest community*. Nova Foresta Publishing, Lyndhurst.
68. R. Reeves pers. comm. (2013).
69. Postan (1972) *op. cit.* in note 26, 212.
70. Salisbury Cathedral (2004) http://www.salisburycathedral.org.uk/news.archive.php?id=105.
71. Postan (1972) *op. cit.* in note 26, 256.
72. Yates (1985) *op. cit.* in note 19, 23, Reeves (2010) *op. cit.* in note 65, 62.
73. Yates (1985) *op. cit.* in note 19, 21.
74. http://www.newforest.hampshire.org.uk/today1.html.
75. http://www.newforest.hampshire.org.uk/history2.html; Stagg (1983) *op.cit.* in note 55, xx.
76. Postan (1972) *op. cit.* in note 26, 107.
77. Reeves (2010) *op. cit.* in note 65, 62.
78. *Ibid.*, 63.
79. Smith (1999) *op. cit.* in note 61, 38.
80. G. F. Peterken (1981) *Woodland Conservation and Management*, 16. Chapman and Hall, London.
81. R. Reeves pers. comm. (2013).
82. *Ibid.*
83. http://www.newforest.hampshire.org.uk/history2.html.
84. R. Reeves pers. comm. (2013).
85. C. Tubbs (1964) Early encoppicements in the New Forest. *Forestry* 37, 95–105.
86. http://www.newforest.hampshire.org.uk/history2.html.
87. *Ibid.*
88. R. Reeves (2008) *To Enquire and Conspire, New Forest Documents 1533–1615*, xxxv. New Forest Record Series V, New Forest Ninth Centenary Trust, Fordingbridge.

89. *Ibid.*, xxiv.
90. A. Light and G. Ponting (2001) *The History of Fordingbridge*, 8, 28–29. Charlewood Press, Fordingbridge.
91. Davies *et al.* (1998) *op. cit.* in note 7, 21; Smith (1999) *op. cit.* in note 79, 20.
92. www.sjc.ox.ac.uk/forests/glossary.htm.
93. Smith *op. cit.* in note 61, 21–22.
94. *Ibid.*, 22.
95. *Ibid.*, 23.
96. *Ibid.*
97. *Ibid.*, 23–24.
98. R. A. Brown, H. M. Colvin and A. J. Taylor (1963) *History of the King's Works* Vol. I, 60. HMSO, London.
99. *Ibid.*, Vol. 1, 162.
100. *Ibid.*, Vol. II, 985–86.
101. Rackham (1986) *op. cit.* in note 5, 122.
102. *Ibid.*, 125.
103. R. Liddiard (2003) The deer parks of Domesday Book. *Landscapes* 4(1), 4–23.
104. Brown *et al.* (1963) *op. cit.* in note 98, 984.
105. *Victorian County History Lyndhurst* http://www.british-history.ac.uk/report.aspx?compid=56900.
106. Smith (1999) *op. cit.* in note 61, 30–31.
107. *Ibid.*, 37.

CHAPTER 5

Forest Governance in Medieval Times

Of Geoffrey Chaucer's yeoman forester character:

> 'A thief of venison, that has abandoned
> His greedy appetite and all of his old craft
> Can keep a forest better than any man'[1]

Officers of the forest

Problems were to emerge from the *Divisum Imperium* in the mid-sixteenth century, from the creation of the post of Surveyor General of Woods, Forests, Parks and Chases until the abolition of the post of Lord Warden in the nineteenth century. The inevitable governance clash between anciently defined officers and that of emerging state interest was to handicap the running of the New Forest for centuries; the new officials appointed by the exchequer were much resented. There follows an account of the historic forest administration that came under the control of the Lord Warden, appointed by the crown.[2]

The Lord Warden oversaw a wide range of officials concerned with the protection of game and forest habitats, including a hierarchy of keepers.[3] The first recorded Warden of the New Forest was Waleran Fitz William who, in 1130, accounted for both the New Forest and Clarendon Forest. These areas remained in a single keepership until 1216; the wardenship being hereditary until the thirteenth century.[4] Eventually Clarendon Forest would be divided.[5]

Naturally the role of officials varied from time to time and from place to place. An early account of officers of royal forests at afforestation is recorded from the Staffordshire Forest Pleas (1262) concerning Cannock Chase (actually a royal forest).[6] All the officers of the forest listed below had the power of arresting malefactors and they comprised:

1. The Steward or Chief Forester
2. The Foresters (actually a diverse group)
3. The Verderers
4. The Reguarders
5. The Agisters
6. The Woodwards

The Preservators (see below) were a post-medieval addition. What follows is a list applicable to the New Forest who operated within the perimeter of the forest law, although rangers had powers without the perambulation. Responsibilities were as follows:

1. The Steward, Seneschallus, Chief Warder, Custos, Chief Forester, *Capitalis Forestarius*, for he is described by all these titles on the records, held an office of great honour and authority. It was always held in fee by grant of the crown and could be a hereditary office.

2. The foresters were of various classes: the foresters in fee, *Forestarii de feodo*, held a hereditary office. Besides these there was the *Forestarius equitans*, ryder or ranger. These appear to have been appointed by the king, and held their office for life or during pleasure.

The riding forester[7] is an officer found in many forests who acted as an intermediate officer between the forester and his foot foresters. The only bailiwick that merited such an appointment on account of its size was was the Lyndhurst bailiwick. His mounted status allowed him to cover the whole bailiwick to oversee the foot foresters who prevented the poaching and theft of wood and timber. Under the foresters in fee were thus an inferior class of forester whose duties corresponded to those of the modern gamekeeper – that is patrolling and policing the forest. These offices were ministerial, and had no judicial functions (bailiffs of a bailiwick).

The rangers,[8] on the other hand, were in practice foresters with duties outside the bounds of the forest. Instituted by the early fourteenth century, the rangers protected the interests of the crown in areas that had been dis-afforested under the *Forest Charter* of 1217 yet where certain rights still existed. These included Hale Purlieu and Dibden Purlieu. Of their specific duties the rangers were appointed to drive the deer back into the forest from the purlieus where the landowners were allowed to hunt them. They were also charged with calling the local inhabitants in and around the forest to help harbour the deer when the king chose to hunt in the forest. Other duties included calling the townships to appear at the Swainmote Courts and also to transfer prisoners from the court to the king's jail at Lyndhurst.

3. The verderer, *viridarius*, was a judicial officer of the forest chosen by the crown, later by the freeholders of the county. Verderers enforced forest law which was to protect the vert and venison among other duties. There was a court, comparable with that of a coroner that after 1698 tried petty offences.[9] A verderer was sworn to maintain the laws of the forest and to receive and enrol the attachments (the legal process of seizing property to ensure satisfaction of a judgment) and presentments of all manner of trespass within the forest, whether of vert or of venison. The reconstituted verderer's court meets in Lyndhurst to the present.

4. The 'reguarders' (regarders) were officers of the forest appointed by the king or by the Chief Justice in Eyre of the forest and later elected by the freeholders of the county. Originally 12 in number their duties were to keep a roll on which was written all the ancient assarts, wastes, and purprestures (unauthorised use

of crown lands) and changes thereof. A regard included vert, eyries, mines and forges, ports, harbours and the wood they shipped, dogs, nets and weapons; swarms of bees, wax and honey were also included in the charges of the 'swanimote' and eyre where regards were enrolled.[10] The regarders, originally of knightly class, by the sixteenth century were drawn largely from the yeomanry and younger sons of local landowners and were under the control of the Justice in Eyre. These appointments were made to fill vacancies due to death, ill health and negligence.[11]

Specifically in the New Forest, the roles of the regarders included:

- Perambulate the boundaries and present them at the Swainmote and then at the next eyre (justice seat)
- Survey old assart and purpresture lands
- Record persons using common pasture
- Buildings erected
- Encroachment and enclosures on the kings's land
- Record new assarts
- Record damage to woods, including amount cut down and carried away, and by whom
- Report on failure to repair bridges, obstacles and nuisances, digging 'marlpits' and other damage
- Account of ditches and hedges
- Report insufficiencies of foresters and woodwards, deputies, servants in respect of offences against the vert or venison,
- Account for aeries (nests) of hawks
- Possession of weapons
- Survey ports and creeks where products such as charcoal, wood and timber may be carried away
- List ale houses
- Account of dogs

Regarder surveys were originally at three-year intervals, including the boundaries, prior to a forest eyre.[12]

5. The agisters in effect regulated grazing and received and accounted for the money paid for the herbage and pannage of the king's demesne lands and woods. This was paid for the herbage of the woods and pastures, and the mast (acorns) of trees, the latter was called pannage. The agisters were also concerned with trespass done by cattle and assisted by foresters their responsibilities included making agreements with inhabitants regarding the number of swine that could be fed.

6. The woodward (wodewardus) looked after the woods and vert, although the origins of the post are unclear. In the medieval period he was a private forester looking after the king's rights in *private woodlands*. The activities of the woodward were regularly recorded by the preservators (see below), while the payment of those regarders undertaking the duties formerly executed by the preservators is accounted for by the woodward.[13]

7. The office of the preservators[14] has its origin in the exchequer's drive towards control of wood sales on crown estates and is post-medieval because commission to set up the office was published in 1567. Indeed, their presence in the New Forest was not realised until comparatively recently,[15] although they played a significant role, often overlapping with that of regarders, surviving until about the start of the seventeenth century. Preservators therefore represented a significant manifestation of the *Divisum Imperium* between the older governance under the Lord Warden (including the regarders) and the Deputy Surveyor, dating from Tudor times. Up to 18 preservators were appointed by verderers, it would seem, from among the regarders or the yeomanry. They were apparently not well paid and pay could be intermittent, and with a primary purpose of ensuring that timber destined for defensive or civil engineering projects was not corruptly diverted by other forest officers, upon whom checks were made. One weakness, however, was that they reported to the treasury and not the justice system, and their role came to be seen as superfluous. Needless to say, there is confusion between the role of preservator and that of regarder, and by the eighteenth century the latter was responsible for marking all timber for felling for any purpose and to value any non-naval timber or wood sold in the forest and also attend the sales and deliveries of the same.

They in effect herald the arrival of a new administrative structure in royal forests and are part of a hierarchy that is later, and parallel to that of the Warden, the chief forester who was subservient to the Chief Justice of the Forests (Chapter 4).[16] That year, the exchequer had gained complete control of wood sales in the forests. Before that, control was split between the exchequer and the justices of the forest. The exchequer gained its interest from the creation of the wood sales department in the office of General Surveyors. The central task consisted of undertaking monthly views of the forest to certify all trees or branches which had fallen during the year, as well as answering a number of other articles relating to the woodland management in the forest. Preservators were appointed from amongst the regarders, however due to the size of the New Forest, the role of preservators evolved into a separate office that was extinguished during the reign of James I, when the role was passed over, once again, to the regarders.[17]

The forest laws

Forest laws were restricted to specific areas and were fundamentally about securing preservation of game for the crown.[18]

Although scholars argue about dating and the provenance of material included within them, the earliest known version of the forest laws probably relates to the Assize of the Forest (or Woodstock, a major royal hunting lodge for the midlands) from 1184, thought to be from the reign on Henry II.[19] The assizes of this reign were concerned with producing evidentiary legal system, and hence is significant in the development context for English law. Outside the jurisdiction of the forest laws, the impact of Henry's 'assizes' would have devolved power to the lords, and hence would have strengthened actions by the manorial courts.[20]

The first article states:[21]

> 'First he forbids that that any one shall transgress against him in regard to his hunting rights or his forests in any respect; and he wills that no trust shall be put in the fact that hitherto he has had mercy for the sake of their chattels upon those who have offended against him in regard to his hunting rights and his forests. For if anyone shall offend against him hereafter and be convicted thereof, he wills that full justice be exacted from the offender as was done in the time of King Henry, his grandfather'

Article 8:

> 'And the king has commanded that if his forester has desmesne woods of the king in his custody and those woods shall be destroyed, and he cannot show any just cause why the woods were destroyed, the person of the forester himself and not something else, shall be seized.'

And Article 10:

> Item: 'The king has commanded that his "assarts", both new and old, are to be inspected, and likewise both purprestures and wastes of the forests; and that each shall be set down in writing by itself.'

This gives a sense of retrenchment of ancient laws and it meant that officially only royal officials can change land use. Henry II enforced the forest laws fiercely and furthermore expanded the area under forest laws, partly because he enjoyed the chase, but also because there was a parallel need to raise revenue. For, while farm rents were fixed, revenue from feudal obligations (including revenue raised from from desmene lands and from forest eyres) could be changed.

Henry's financial policy included increasing the money supply to pay bills from the civil war prior to his reign and benefit trade within the Angevin empire, although fixed rents were a problem during a time of inflation.[22] The Assize of the Forest would seem to summarise previous laws. Punishments included blinding and mutilation, but it is debatable whether these were ever followed through, the main objective being to raise revenue for the crown.

These laws are probably more or less those established by the Normans.[23] It is stated that the purpose of the assize is the protection of the forests and forest game, and had the approval of the nobility, bishops and archbishops. 'No-one shall place confidence in the fact that he [the king] has hitherto been moderate in his punishment of offenders against his forests and his forest game, and has taken from them only their chattels in satisfaction for their offences.' There was to be no bows, arrows, hounds or harriers in his forests, except by licence from the king or other duly authorised person (by the crown). No owner of a wood within the forest shall sell or give away anything out of the wood to its wasting or destruction, beyond his own needs. Demesne woods were protected on penalty of its 'answering with his own body' and not payment of a fine. Indeed, all males over the age of 12 who were resident in a protected area were to take an oath for the protection of game. Clerics were not exempt. Night-time hunting is specifically mentioned, including in areas that were formally protected or dis-afforested. There are clearly elements of protection of the resource, as well as protection of wild animals, and it is probable that the connections and social standing of a felon helped to determine his fate.

It has been argued that offences of poaching did not merit the death penalty under the forest law that preferred fines, yet under common law, theft could be a hanging offence. Because common law also pertained within the forests, this may have led to the confusion. Furthermore, in 1280, the terms of appointment of the justices of the forest eyre were

> 'to inquire of all robberies and homicides, arson, and other offences whatsoever both within the boundaries of our New Forest and also outside, hearing and determining these offences according to law and custom at these appointed days, let inquests be held at Winchester and Southampton'.[24]

The forest may have been different from other royal forests in maintaining the common law. It may furthermore have remained so because it was an ancient royal demesne from before 1066 – Lyndhurst, Christchurch, Eling and Ringwood were all crown manors at that time and may therefore have remained outside the normal, national system of justice, policing and finance. Royal justice remained inside. The actual mechanism for common law survival is unclear, but it may have been linked to royal bailiffs presiding over courts of common law within royal demesnes, thereby preserving elements of common law jurisdiction where they might least be expected.[25] It may furthermore have been advantageous for tenants of the crown not to be answerable to the county court or pay taxes at that level. Instead they may have preferred *tallage* (a form of arbitrary taxation levied by kings on the towns and lands of the Crown) that would have been paid directly to the king, thereby increasing his revenue.

The forest courts

The judicial system in forests was complicated and uncertainties remain. The court of Swainmote has an Anglo-Saxon name although the entire system would seem to reflect the legal *modus operandi* of Norman kings in administering justice; the names of courts ('eyre' and 'regard') clearly have Norman-French origins.

The court of 'justice-seat' or eyre was the highest of the forest courts and was held every three years, presided over by a Justice in Eyre, who held the magistrate position under forest law and presided over the only court of record capable of entering and executing judgments against offenders, in theory. It had an investigative function as well. Stagg[26] draws the distinction between the general eyre concerned with criminal and civil proceedings and the forest eyre concerned with forest offences. Actually some very serious offences against the person were tried at the forest eyre as crown pleas, including rape and murder[27] and this court was able to impose the death penalty by hanging on guilty parties.[28] In 1257 it was also possible to be hanged for theft resulting from offences against the venison.[29] For example:

> 'It is presented and proved that on the Monday before the feast of St Nicholas in the 32nd year [2 Dec. 1247] John the son of Edonis de Lyndhurst and Simon le Theyn were taken by the foresters with bows and arrows for harming the deer. Afterwards they were hanged for theft ...'

Evidently caught red-handed, this was not always the case for offences against the venison, although the fear would cause many to become outlaws.[30] On a more lenient note, the pleas of the vert tried in that same court in 1257 were both numerous and settled by fines of 1s or 2s.[31] The justices in eyre, or their deputies, continued down to 1635.

Apparently in the thirteenth century there is only direct evidence for two courts, those of Swainmote and the higher forest eyre. However the Court of Attachment[32] must have existed as it enrolled cases before the Swainmote, and the Court of Regards must also have existed because otherwise there would have been no need for regarders.[33]

The system was to separate forest officials from the judiciary.[34] The lower courts were the Swainmote and Wodemote (known locally as Attachment) that met in the Verderers' Hall at Lyndhurst. A generalised account of the roles of the four courts at the end of the medieval period follows.[35]

Court of Attachment or 'Woodmote' was presided over by verderers and the warden (or his deputy) and concerned those who had committed crimes against the forest law. They were enrolled, but the court did not possess the power to try or convict individuals who were passed upwards to the Swainmote, or the court of justice seat.

The Court of Regard was held every third year to enforce the law requiring the regulation and planting of food crops within assarts (that could be taken into the hands of the king) and more mundane actions such as the declawing of dogs within the New Forest.[36]

The Court of Swainmote was the court of freeholders living within the forest and similar in its constitution to the Hundred Court outside. In the same fashion as the chief bailiff of the hundred presided over the Hundred Court, so the Chief Warden of the Forest (or his deputy verderers) presided in the Swainmote Court. Foresters and agisters were in attendance and its role was to regulate agistment, pannage and to try offenders before a jury of 'swains' (freemen of the forest). This was re-established in the New Forest in 1877.[37] Its meeting was limited by the *Charter of the Forest* to three times per year with dates fixed by the same. The first Swainmote was held 15 days before Midsummer Day, when the agisters met to fawn the deer; the second court was held 15 days before Michaelmas, when the agistment of the woods began; and the third court on the Feast of St Martin in November, when the agisters met to receive the pannage. All the officers of the forest had to be present, including the verderers, reguarders, agisters and woodwards.

A court of Swainmote was held on 9 February 1487; it recalls many infringements of forest law, but most concern offences against the venison and often involve dogs. For example:

'Henry Erlesman, the forester of the bailiwick of Battramsley attends and he presents that on 24th June 1485 [or 1484] William Holcombe, a gentleman recently of Lymington, had entered the New Forest at Lady Hill within the said bailiwick of, and with greyhounds had taken and killed a buck, one of the King's beasts, and he carried away the flesh without permission or warrant'.[38]

Other miscreants were not only described as gentlemen, there were also clergy and yeomen. Of the lower orders:

'Also on the 10th June 1485 Thomas Gaylpryn, a labourer recently of Canterton, with a bow and arrow has shot and killed a buck at the end of the king's road called Canterton Lane in the North Bailiwick, and had carried away the flesh without warrant'.[39]

Actually the system was bound to evolve and reform; the seeds of this lay in the thirteenth century.

Governance and reform

State administration between the thirteenth and later sixteenth centuries divided the New Forest into nine bailiwicks, these were called North, Inner, South and East carved from the older Lyndhurst bailiwick, the other five were Godshill, Fritham, Linwood, Burley and Battramsley (Fig. 5.1).[40] Godshill, being based largely in the Bagshot sands and plateau gravels, was the poorest, Burley on the Barton Clay the overall best endowed (see Fig. 2.4). The remaining are of mixed land quality. Nonetheless, regardless of land quality, they were also under forest law, yet to understand the 'governance' it is important to go further than the confusing matter of two major jurisdictions operating in one geographical area.

The term 'governance' relates to how things get done and naturally includes what in modern terms is understood as the 'regulatory environment'. Notions of governance relating to corporate, public or community engagement may be described as the interaction of four factors: of hierarchies, of networks, of communities and of markets.[41] While a modern conception, all of these facets were present in medieval England. The role of markets in the towns has been outlined, and forest products were sold under market conditions.

From 1066, the rule of the Normans was through strong hierarchical government, and that was set to change, albeit slowly. Forest governance overall was complex, multi-level and incorporated non-feudal elements, notably both manor and parish that operated at a community level. There were also strong vested interests, those of local magnates, both lay and ecclesiastical that constituted networks capable of exercising power, as well as commoners who would often find themselves at variance with more powerful interests.

The manor was, in theory, a kind of legal, administrative and economic expression of the medieval 'vill'. The existence of the manor did not exclude other, more informal channels of expression and communication among the people, including guilds,[42] a kind of network. Although a 'one size fits all' model for the English manor existed nowhere, it was for present purposes both

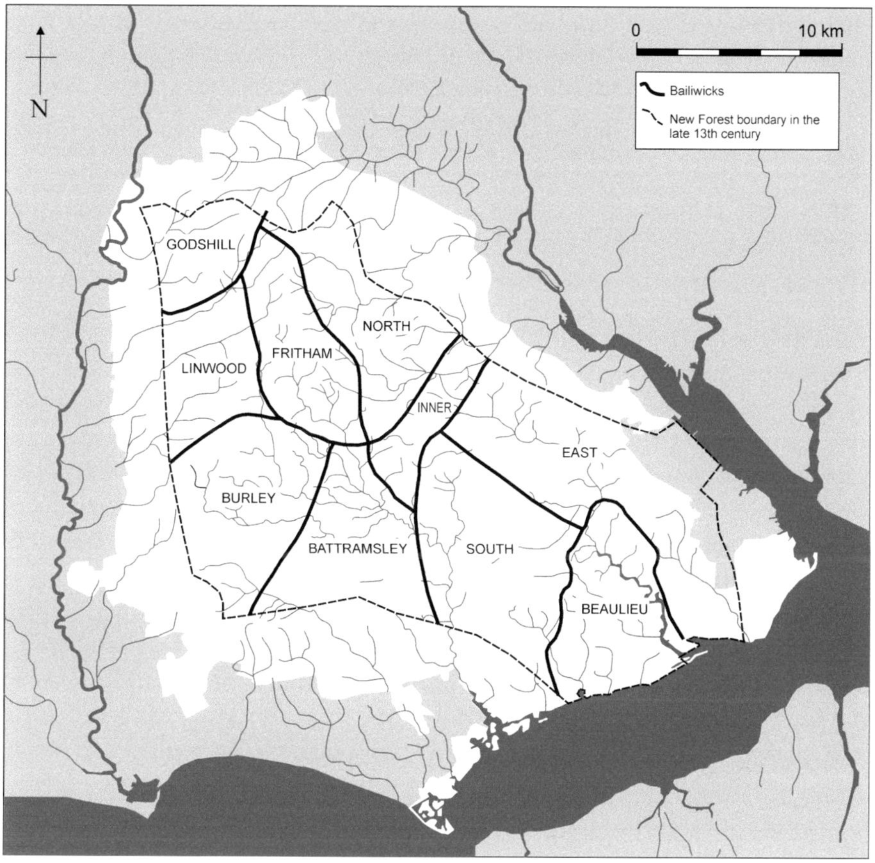

FIGURE 5.1. Bailiwicks in the New Forest.

AFTER YATES 1985, 22

powerful in the lives of ordinary people and the lesser gentry alike. It may also be viewed as a kind of early 'environmental agency' because for it regulated tenural conditions, marshalled natural resources and organised communal agriculture (especially in nucleated, open field agriculture-based manors). Land in a typical manor was of three kinds: the lord's demesne land, that of dependent villeins or surfs and that of free men who nonetheless were still subject to the customs of the manor and fell under its court's jurisdiction.

Questions may be asked relating to the functions of different courts, and most particularly to the relationship between the ordinary manorial courts and to the forest law. Ordinary agriculture continued in royal hunting forests, albeit in muted form due to poor soils with royal interest explicit, for Lyndhurst was itself a royal manor.[43] The margins of cultivation probably shifted with population pressures, notably before the mid-fourteenth century,[44] and in times of population pressure assarts and purprestures created arable land within royal forests. Clashes of interest over land use between crown and manor in this situation would be inevitable, to say nothing about the interests of common people caught between them. The forest law can be seen as a source of conflict with the interests of the manor, its gentry, villains and freemen alike. The reign of Henry II (1154–1189) may have started to restore local power but forest courts effectively functioned well into the seventeenth century. For much of this time, it was the forest courts that prevailed, at least in respect of infringements of vert and of venison.

Forest laws became the greatest manifestation of 'top-down' government; but as we have seen, its courts did not represent the only legal system. Neither were they destined long to remain unaffected by legal and constitutional reform. The Assizes of Clarendon under Henry II (1166) had confirmed itself the watchdog of crown interests, and mentions both duties and officers viz: justices, wardens, chief foresters, leepers (couriers?) and stewards; the wardens might also have been justices.[45] The four verderers acted much as magistrates, being able to hold inquiries and preliminary hearings of offences, even acting as coroners in crown pleas. There were 12 regarders to survey the forest every third year and who had a particular interest in purprestures. Otherwise, the wardens (or keepers) were appointed by the king for day-to-day running of the forest and were able to appoint lesser officers, these were the foresters-in-fee (hereditary officers) in each of the six bailiwicks of Lyndhurst, Godshill, Burley, Linwood, Battransley and Fritham.

The narrative of the New Forest is not entirely one of arbitrary power. Rather, from Henry II onwards, it is one of steady decline within the presumed crown authority in favour of other groups gaining increasing influence. These were the commoners, forest officials and those who were concerned with the direct management of the forest and its trees. In the *Charter of the Forest* (1217) can be seen a more significant development in terms of rights for the ordinary person in England. Magna Carta sought to provide a solution to grievances concerning law and justice, including access to that justice,[46] as well as redressing issues between the crown and the barons. However, the more famous Magna Carta during the reign of King John (1215) is also concerned with forests and their governance. Sections 44, 47, 48, 52 and 53 are concerned with the forests:[47]

> 44. Men who dwell without the forest need not henceforth come before our justiciaries of the forest upon a general summons, unless they are in plea, or sureties of one or more, who are attached for the forest.
>
> 47. All forests that have been made such in our time shall forthwith be disafforested; and a similar course shall be followed with regard to river banks that have been placed 'in defense' by us in our time.
>
> 48. All evil customs connected with forests and warrens, foresters and warreners, sheriffs and their officers, river banks and their wardens, shall immediately by inquired into in each county by twelve sworn knights of the same county chosen by the honest men of the same county, and shall, within forty days of the said inquest, be utterly abolished, so as never to be restored, provided always that we previously have intimation thereof, or our justiciar, if we should not be in England.
>
> 52. If anyone has been dispossessed or removed by us, without the legal judgment of his peers, from his lands, castles, franchises, or from his right, we will immediately restore them to him; and if a dispute arise over this, then let it be decided by the five and twenty barons of whom mention is made below in the clause for securing

> the peace. Moreover, for all those possessions, from which anyone has, without the lawful judgment of his peers, been disseised or removed, by our father, King Henry, or by our brother, King Richard, and which we retain in our hand (or which as possessed by others, to whom we are bound to warrant them) we shall have respite until the usual term of crusaders; excepting those things about which a plea has been raised, or an inquest made by our order, before our taking of the cross; but as soon as we return from the expedition, we will immediately grant full justice therein.
>
> 53. We shall have, moreover, the same respite and in the same manner in rendering justice concerning the disafforestation or retention of those forests which Henry our father and Richard our brother afforested, and concerning the wardship of lands which are of the fief of another (namely, such wardships as we have hitherto had by reason of a fief which anyone held of us by knight's service), and concerning abbeys founded on other fiefs than our own, in which the lord of the fee claims to have right; and when we have returned, or if we desist from our expedition, we will immediately grant full justice to all who complain of such things.

Here is regulation within the forests, freeing those without the perambulation of the forests from being tried under forest law, restricting recent afforestation, outlining the possibility for sworn men to abolish 'evil practices' associated with forest officials, even with the crown and finally restoration of justice where feudal appropriation has prevented it.

Major aspects of the feudal system, despite early thirteenth century reform guaranteeing the 'rights' of certain classes, survived largely to the later fourteenth century, when relations of villagers to the manor started to change. Feudalism was by then disintegrating, yet various courts (especially of the manor) survived, as did officials of the forest as representatives. Networks of interests existed through the appointed officers in the forest, and through institutions of the vill, the church, guilds and informally among those with common interest in, for example, forestry and agriculture. The whole vill would constitute a local community, although details of community among ordinary people are largely lost to us. Finally, and perhaps most interesting in terms of economic change are markets. There was a strong market element in English medieval society as we have seen and this was regulated within the towns and cities. From manors, surplus produce sold in local markets was sold to markets in the towns, that represented places of exchange of goods and services.[48]

Almost a century later than the charters, there remained great cause for concern. In 1306 the *Ordinance of the Forest* stated: 'the People of our Realm are by the Officers of our Forests, miserably oppressed, impoverished and troubled with many wrongs, being everywhere molested.' The excesses of the forest officers (foresters, verderers, agisters *etc.*) were controlled through sworn juries who were introduced for cases of trespass of the vert or venison.[49]

Unlike the other components of governance, markets are a sensitive reflection of the ups and down of the medieval economy, reflecting aggregate demand from changing populations, the capacity of agriculture and the amount of money in circulation.[50] In the half-century or so until about 1350 demand was strong, reflected in expanding trade at home and overseas. However, such considerations are also tempered by knowledge that certain aspects of labour were controlled by the guilds, or by feudal bonds, and there were limited constraints on importation and exports. Markets for commodities have to be seen in the context, not only of local versus national (or international) markets, but also of timescale. The year-by-year economic management of the manor would be short-term when compared with the concerns of the forest, be it in terms of beasts, of forest products, of pressure on land-use in relation to human population or finally, of wood products.

For ordinary goods, it is likely that population levels determined demand for both agricultural products and hence land is required for cultivation, providing for encroachment on to marginal land of the forests. For trees, it is probable that by the twelfth century there was a shortage of tall trees for timber, as seen by the importation from Norway.[51] Indeed between the later twelfth century and early seventeenth century, oak for quality carving was often imported from the Baltic region (English oak being often used for frame timbers).[52] This suggests that trade in timber was not merely about size of tree or sufficiency of supply.

There were other feudal interests, other than the crown, lords and peasantry. It is interesting to note that the marginality of many royal forest lands made it suitable for donations to monasteries in the twelfth century. The grant of land to Beaulieu Abbey (1203–1204) for the Cistercians in the southern New Forest by King John is one such example. Actually, much of this area did not contain the poorest in the New Forest and today the Beaulieu estate includes much land of reasonable grade, occupied originally over 5000 ha[53] and today it supports productive farmland.

As well as official grants of land, another cause of encroachment, and once more difficult to quantify, is that of assarts (clearance of waste for cultivation) and purpresture (unlawful acquisition of land). The creation of enclosures for cultivation would have been especially commonplace in the thirteenth and early fourteenth centuries, prior to the population reduction wrought by the Black Death, including those made by the monks of Beaulieu Abbey.[54] Population pressure in agrarian dominated societies leads inevitably to pressure on more marginal land. In England this meant the cultivation of wastes and clearance of woodland. As a generality progressively more 'marginal' (*i.e.* agriculturally lower grade) land becomes a prospect for cultivation. Outside the forests there would be an expansion of ploughland within pressure to cultivate the poor soils and that change need not be 'legal' although assarts (and the smaller areas termed purprestures) could be retrospectively licensed upon payment of a fine.[55] Such required a complicated system of regulation. In 1257 there are examples of assarts and the 'waste of woods' being taken by individuals 'without warrant', although the crown merely took back the land.[56]

Under Henry III, the crown established ten vaccaries (directly managed stock farms) in the New Forest, and by around 1300 a survey revealed there were 12.[57] These tended to become small holdings in the present; as such they represent a move towards a more conventional agricultural economy in the forest, although their purpose was most likely to support the royal entourage times of residence.[58]

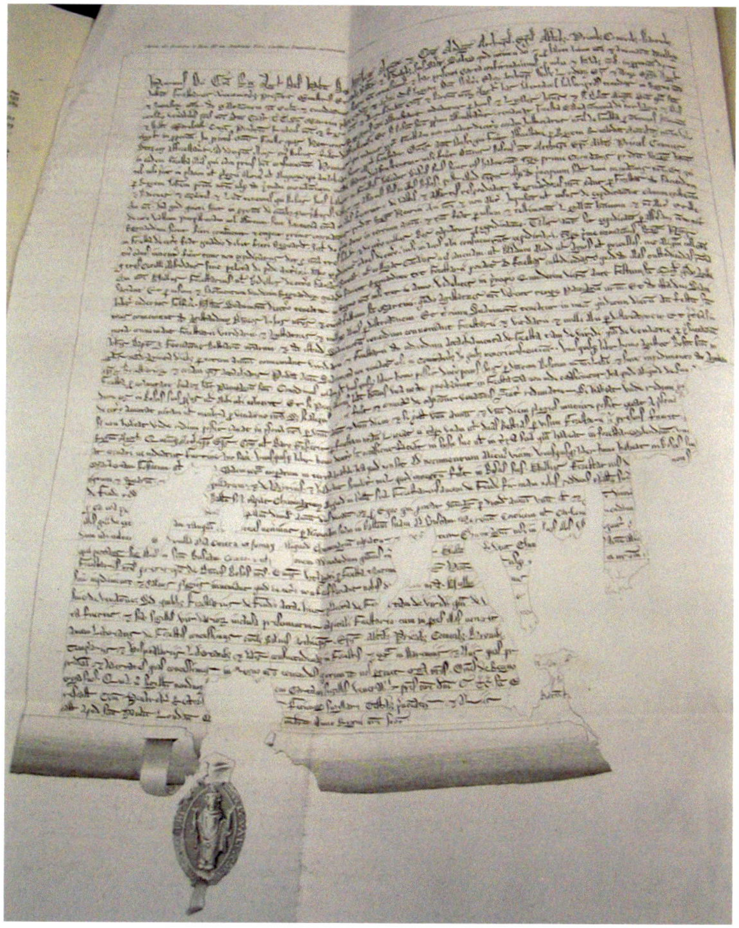

FIGURE 5.2. The *Charter of the Forest* 1217.

HTTP://INFO.SJC.OX.AC.UK/FORESTS/CARTA.HTM, FROM ROTHWELL (ED.) 1975, NO. 24, 337–340

One legal change saw the replacement of customary law to be enshrined in a legal framework, starting with the *Charter of the Forest* of 1217. In some instances, this change enshrined the rights of those resident on the forest, in terms of commoners grazing and rights to gather fuel. In other instances, it merely replaced the forest law by *de facto* comparable constraints that represented the interests of the state. Such are enclosing and restricting grazing.

Charter of the Forest

The *Charter of the Forest* 1217 (Fig. 5.2) dates from the rein of Henry III and deals with matters closer to the interests of ordinary people than Magna Carta. Seen as an extension of its immediate predecessor,[59] the *Charter of the Forest* provided a right of common access to (royal) private lands. It also repealed the death penalty for taking royal game and abolished mutilation as a lesser punishment (although the extent to which these punishments were actually enacted is open to question). It remained in force in England until superseded by the *Wild Creatures and Forest Laws Act* 1971. Men who lived outside the forest need not come within the justices of the forest. The Swainmote was restricted to meeting three times in a year and free men could keep eyries of birds of prey within their woods and this may signify an institution that pre-dated royal forest[60] and there were concessions to those made outlaws.

Inappropriate afforestation under Henry II and John was to be reversed, Article 1 states:

> 'In the first place, all the forests which king Henry our grandfather made forest shall be viewed by good and law-worthy men, and if he made forest any wood that was not his demesne to the injury of him whose wood it was, it shall be disafforested. And if he made his own wood forest, it shall remain forest, saving common of pasture and other things in that forest to those who were accustomed to have them previously'.

And, Article 3:

> 'All woods made forest by king Richard our uncle, or by king John our father, up to the time of our first coronation shall be immediately disafforested unless it be our demesne wood'.

Such activity was to be policed by the regarders, while free men had the right to agist his own wood in the forest and exercise pannage. And, Article 12:

> 'No one shall henceforth lose life or limb because of our venison, but if anyone has been arrested and convicted of taking venison he shall be fined heavily if he has the means; and if he has not the means, he shall lie in our prison for a year and a day; and if after a year and a day he can find pledges he may leave prison; but if not, he shall abjure the realm of England.'

Rights of the aristocracy are clear, but restricted to those enjoyed during the reign of Henry II:

> 'Archbishops, bishops, abbots, priors, earls, barons, knights and freeholders who have woods within forests shall have them as they had them at the time of the first coronation of the aforesaid king Henry our grandfather, so that they shall be quit forever in respect of all purprestures, wastes and assarts made in those woods between that time and the beginning of the second year of our coronation. And those who in future make waste, purpresture or assart in them without license from us shall answer for wastes, purprestures and assarts'.

There are still privileges for the ruling classes:

> 'Any archbishop, bishop, earl or baron whatever who passes through our forest shall be allowed to take one or two beasts under the supervision of the forester, if he is to hand; but if not, let him have the horn blown, lest he seem to be doing it furtively'.

There is also a hint of animal welfare, as greyhounds, mastiffs and great currs were later recorded as being used as hunting dogs:

> 'And he whose dog is then found not expeditated shall give as amercement three shillings, and in future no ox shall be seized for failure to expeditate. The manner, moreover, of expeditating by the assize shall generally be that three claws of the forefoot are to be cut off, but not the ball. Nor shall dogs henceforth be expeditated

> except in places where it was customary to expeditate them at the time of the first coronation of king Henry our grandfather.'

Article 12 states that

> 'Every free man may henceforth without being prosecuted make in his wood or in land he has in the forest a mill, a preserve, a pond, a marl-pit, a ditch, or arable outside the covert [high closed canopy] in arable land, on condition that it does not harm any neighbour.'

This suggests that assarting was permitted under certain circumstances, and may have provided a spur to industrial activity. Much later, in 1280 at the Pleas of the Forest held at Winchester it was reported that the Prior of Brummore (Braemore) has newly assarted 4 acres (1.6 ha) of the king's wood at Godeshull (Godshill) and included it with a ditch.[61] Otherwise the planting of arable crops in old assarts was generally dealt with by the imposition of a fine; for example 'At Depedene Cecily who was the wife of Robert Brut holds ½ acre planted twice with winter corn and twice with summer corn, 1s 6d'.[62]

Also in the late twelfth century, tanners were not permitted to live within the forest.[63] Evidently by 1276 (in a report of inquisitions held at the forest eyre held in Romsey) there was concern about demesne woods being destroyed by charcoal burners and one Thomas de Foxcote had a customary right to burn beech and other trees within his bailiwick, to make potash for the drying of cloth. Otherwise, foresters of fee retained for themselves all the honey found in the bailiwicks.[64]

The *Charter of the Forest* was re-issued in 1225 with only minor changes to the wording. This charter, therefore, represents a progressive 're-definition' of the feudal system under the legal and political changes of Conqueror, and Henry I and Henry II.[65] As far as afforestation is concerned, the process is put into reverse, so that areas thereby dis-afforested became referred to as purlieu land, for example 1305 in the New Forest, dis-afforestation purlieus were returned to the common of pasture rights. Where the crown had granted purlieu, common of pasture rights were re-established.[66]

The charters of the early thirteenth century may to some degree reflect tensions between crown and barons that arise from interests residing in the feudal court (representing the barons) and the royal courts described above. It is clear from the *Charter of the Forest* that, with the rights of the aristocracy stated, but circumscribed; the commoners' rights are also guaranteed. A process of dis-afforestation had begun under Richard I (reigned 1189–1199), apparently to raise money for the crusades. The crown claimed money for assarts, and for ploughing and cultivating the soil. He also sanctioned encroachments after payment of fines for unofficial assarts.[67] The Assizes of Richard I, however, do prohibit the grazing of cattle or pigs during the fence month; offences against venison could be met by mutilation, not the case for offences against the vert. Offences of vert included stripping peat, cutting trees or branches, digging turf, cutting underwood, making assarts, making new purprestures, even renewing mills and making new watercourses, pasturing livestock, even cutting hay outside a hedge or ditch. A regard was made every three years to determine which assarts had been planted with corn or legumes. The revenue interest is clear, new assarts were appropriated by the king, old assarts were taxed at 1s per acre, 6d for an acre of oats, barley, beans, peas or other legumes.[68]

Under the *Charter of the Forest*, anything made forest during the reign of Richard I, or that of John's (1199–1216) was to be dis-afforested, apparently with the exception that it had become royal demesne (Article 3). And that:

> 'shall remain forest, saving common of pasture and other things in that forest to those who were accustomed to have them previously' (Article 1).

Article 9 states that:

> 'every free man shall agist [graze cattle in exchange for rent] his wood in the forest as he wishes and have his pannage' [grazing pigs], be it in Royal demesne land or elsewhere'.

Article 17, as if to summarise, states:

> 'All these aforesaid customs and liberties which we have granted to be observed in our kingdom as far as it pertains to us towards our men, all of our kingdom, clerks as well as laymen, shall observe as far as it pertains to them towards their men.'

The commoners had specific rights and these relate to the management of resources in the forest. While the heaths date from the Bronze Age, their maintenance and expansion would have been a result of turf cutting and wood product removal, while grazing animal would help by eating shoots. Commoners' rights in the late medieval period were subject to small payments, these were local administration charges, rather than a tax for the exchequer. The origin of these is unknown, although they had mostly lapsed by 1789.[69]

To summarise, the historic six rights of common were:

- **Common of pasture of commonable animals** (horned cattle, ponies, horses and donkeys). Maintaining grazing and browsing at a suitable level has been a matter of some debate.
- **Common of pasture for sheep** is attached for certain lands and not commonly exercised.
- **Common of mast (or pannage)** allowing pigs to feed on acorns, and beech mast and other nuts in the late autumn. The 'pannage season' extends from 25 September to 22 November.
- **Common of turbary** was the right to take turves for fuel (although not usually peat). This was regulated to prevent lasting damage to grazing and to vegetation.
- **Common of fuel wood or estovers** The right to take sufficient wood for the commoner's house or holding; usually limited to smaller trees, bushes and fallen branches. Largely uneconomic in the present.
- **Common of marl** the historic right to take clay for marling land is no longer practised and the marl pits are long redundant.

Others, such as the cutting of bracken for litter and fodder, were not mentioned, and may not been considered of significance. Turbary rights most likely made a contribution to heathland development both during and after the medieval period, although this was regulated by the foresters, but the availability of coal brought an end to the practice.[70] Copythorne Common was such a 'turbary common'. The common of marl, another obsolete practice, was collected in the south part of the forest, presumably from better quality land with more loamy soil, although to find soil within easy reach that was in the modern sense calcareous would have been difficult.[71] Rights were attached to a property rather than individual, but differed between properties. Estovers as the right to receive a free supply of a fixed quantity of firewood annually is today granted by the Forestry Commission. The right is highly prized, but fewer than 100 houses now benefit from it.[72]

Grazing has been the most extensively exercised common right throughout history. Common of pasture for commonable animals were for ponies, cattle, donkeys and mules. Common rights are attached to land from Millbrook, into the Bournemouth area and to Cranborne in the west. Northwards they extend almost to Salisbury. The common of pasture for sheep is confined to the south-east and is associated with certain former monastic properties,[73] recalling the Cistercians at Beaulieu but also Christchurch, Breamore and the Bishop of Winchester. Indeed, in a record of the pleas of the forest at Winchester 14 January 1280, pasture in the New Forest was overgrazed, for:

> 'It is presented *etc.* that the Abbot of Beaulieu pastured in the Forest so many horses, mares, cattle, sheep and other animals that they are ignorant of the numbers, to the surcharging of the pasture of the King's beasts and to the injury of the whole district during 4 years to the damage of £2 for which the abbot is answerable. Also that the forest and district is much surcharged by the animals of the prior of Christchurch and the prior of Bromhore. Therefore in mercy'.[74]

It paid to be a monk. Such grazing would have been strictly controlled using shepherds and dogs.[75] By the thirteenth century, there appears to have been a relaxation in the strict uses designated for land and payments were being made instead of removing stock from the forest during the fence months; By 1537, manors within the forest paid no dues except the month money[76] and by 1670, money was paid for both turbary and grazing.

Dwellers within the forest

Changes were evidently wrought by creation of the forest during the reign of William I; these inevitably impacted on the ordinary folk. Domesday recorded 137 holdings (manors) within the seven hundreds of south-west Hampshire (Bovre, Rodbridge, Rodedic, Sirlei, Egheiete Rincvede and Fordingbridge). The New Forest was carved mainly from Bovre and Rodbridge. Of the manors, 47 within the forest itself were unassessed for taxation, although their pre-Conquest values were given, 49 were reduced in value (probably because their outlying woods and wastes were afforested) with 41 unaffected by afforestation. Of the larger enclaves of enclosed land, only Fritham and Linwood cannot be identified in Domesday, while 'Juare' (possible Eyeworth Lodge) and 'Slackham' (possibly Sloden Enclosure) may represent precursors to Fritham.[77]

Within the New Forest, Domesday Book shows that some 30–40 vills (this was the geographic and topographic settlement) were without ploughs, peasants or value in 1086, and a further 40 or so partially included within the forest and therefore presumably with reduced resources and populations. Manors were established at Lyndhurst, Burley, Minstead, Boldre and Brockenhurst with scatters of holdings at Sowley, Beaulieu, Exbury and Cadland. Yet there was, in 1086, a low population density in the region (presumably reflecting inherently poor natural resources) and this remained evident throughout, into the fourteenth century.[78] That William I actually 'laid waste' to large areas of Hampshire is, in reality, open to question – and probably seldom occurred. Rather, an area of poor soil that supported largely woods and would present problems sustaining highly productive agriculture would be unable in the long term to support a high density of population.[79] Unfortunately, the Domesday survey does not give sufficient detail relating to holdings and their assets, to be absolutely clear about this point.[80]

Forest dwellers were therefore subject to both manor and forest law.[81] The *Charter of the Forest* had provided for the Attachment Court and Swainmote to be held every three years, and the 'rights' listed above were provided for. Evidently the role of the forest officers, especially the regarders, enabled a degree of auditing and hence enforcement. Payments for such as grazing rights and month money could be enforced. In theory, infringements of forest law by commoners and others were under due judicial process, and the petty annoyance of forest officials controlled. Actually, the penalties for forest offences were not that severe and it seems that hanging was not used. Small fines were generally imposed for infringements of the venison and vert; assarts and purprestures were similarly controlled. This had been assures in the *Charter of the Forest* in any case.

One interesting midwinter transgression reported in the forest eyre of 1280[82] involved, on 21 December 1256, Simon Fletcher and Thomas Passavoinet, a servant of the Vicar of Boldre, who killed a doe and carried it to the vicar's house. The vicar illegally sheltered the poachers, then took the venison to Salisbury the following night. Thomas was caught by forest officials and imprisoned at Lyndhurst. Offal and entrails were found in the vicar's house. The miscreants were put on trial and fined £2, a sum paid by the vicar who apparently was not charged. This event, post-dating the charter by a long time, suggests no savage punishment, yet the vicar was apparently not tried by any court and strongly suggests benefit of the clergy.

But what of the overall agrarian economy? As one might expect from the quality of the land, the picture in the thirteenth and fourteenth centuries appears 'one of marginal subsistence'. Winter fodder (in times before the widespread cultivation of root crops) would have been limited, depending on the availability of hay, and limiting the number of non-breeding animals that could be kept alive after the traditional slaughter at Michaelmas. Fertilisation of the soil would thus be restricted to the amount of dung produced. This provides a context for the production of venison, salted for the royal household and also for victuals of many military expeditions. In the south, however, better soils and climate would have permitted some over-wintering livestock within the forest and this is evidenced by payments for winter pasturage associated with the 'fence month' and collected, together with produce such as eggs, and for rights such as turbary and pannage, honey and geese.[83]

Stagg suggests that, around the close of the thirteenth century, there was a rise in lawlessness, including the creation of illegal assarts and the waste of the woods. A stature of 1293 was passed that dealt with trespassers in forests, chases, parks and warrens. A forester would not have to answer if he killed a trespasser who would not surrender, but fled or sought to defend himself. An ordinance of 1305 was passed after some dis-afforestation had occurred, and eventually commoners were allowed to graze these purlieus.[84] These were difficult times in the New Forest for ordinary folk.

Conclusions

The period to about 1500 saw not only the full establishment of the royal hunting forest, but the beginnings of significant reform representing a move away from conventional feudal 'top-down' governance. The Normans created the legal entity of the New Forest from land that was of limited value for conventional agriculture. They blatantly managed it for their own ends through a hierarchy of officials, although subsequently feudal power in England was challenged and would change. Henry II, despite his zeal for legal reform, was keen on the forest law and extended the area subject to them. From the early thirteenth century, there was progress in the rights of commoners and other 'ordinary folk' and, importantly, changes in emphasis of forest management from concentrating on the venison towards that of the vert.

Reform as affected the people of the New Forest (as elsewhere) away from top-down occurred during the reigns of John and subsequently Henry III. These came to signify the rights of commoners, seeing that those within the perambulation of the forest had access to resources such as turbary, pannage and other animal grazing. It is as if legal and institutional reforms associated with the New Forest were to play a role in both the establishment of the modern English legal system, that is, demanding evidence and trial by jury.

There was a new legal and governance structure before the thirteenth century, creating ultimately courts of Swainmote and the senior Justices in Eyre and also courts of Attachment and Regard. These operated while the manorial system continued, albeit concerned with seigniorial matters around agriculture and land tenure. By implication this was of limited influence within the forest as a whole, for it did not only relate to common law courts. With the forest legal system, came the plethora of officials, whose roles may not always be clear. Governance must have been more complex than outside the perambulation. However, the link between the Justices in Eyre and the Exchequer, for whom funds were raised, is one that continued beyond the medieval period into the seventeenth century.

Within the perambulation there were – or remained – deer parks, plots of arable land, and there is evidence that lend moved into, and out of, agriculture. The description of purprestures and purlieus in part bear witness to land use change, and in part to the waxing and waning of the strength of the king and of the enforcement of forest laws. In 1217 the power of the monarchy is called to account and certain rights of forest dwellers are thereby established by statute. However, during the medieval period, there is clear evidence that England's forests were not up to supplying timber for large construction projects, something that was a portent of change in the forest economy. This would start to be seriously realised in the sixteenth century, or to put it another way, things had to change.

Notes

1. L. C. Lambdin and R. Lambdin (eds) (1999) *Chaucer's Pilgrims: an historical guide to the Pilgrims in the Canterbury Tales*, 33. Praeger Publishers, Santa Barbara.
2. R. Reeves (2008) *To Enquire and Conspire, New Forest Documents 1533–1615*, xxxviii. New Forest Record Series V, New Forest Ninth Centenary Trust, Fordingbridge.
3. History of the Crown Lands (n.d.) http://www.forestry.gov.uk/pdf/eng-new-forest-b2-history.pdf/$FILE/eng-new-forest-b2-history.pdf. Accessed Sept 2017.
4. D. J. Stagg (ed.) (1979) *A Calendar of New Forest Documents AD 1244–AD 1344*. Hampshire Record Series III, Hampshire County Council, Winchester.
5. J. Bond (1994) Forests, chases, warrens and parks in medieval Wessex. In M. Ashton and C. Lewis (eds), *The Medieval Landscape of Wessex*, 116. Oxbow Monograph 6, Oxbow Books, Oxford.
6. Staffordshire Forest Pleas (1262) Introduction, *Staffordshire Historical Collections* 5(1) (1884), 123–35. http://www.british-history.ac.uk/report.aspx?compid=52372. Accessed 13 July 2010.
7. R. Reeves (2007) *Preservation and Decay*, xliv. New Forest Record Series 3, New Forest Ninth Centenary Trust, Fordingbridge. http://www.newforestcentre.org.uk/uploads/publications/6.pdf.
8. *Ibid.*, xlv.
9. P. A. J. Pettit (1968) *The Royal Forests of Northamptonshire: a study of their Economy 1558–1714*, 23. Northampton Record Society, Northumberland Press, Gateshead; D. J. Stagg (1984) *Verders of the New Forest*, 2. New Forest Association, Fordingbridge.
10. Forests and Chases in England and Wales, *c.*1000 to *c.*1850. http://info.sjc.ox.ac.uk/forests/glossary.htm; D. J. Stagg (1983) *A Calendar of New Forest Documents: the Fifteenth to Seventeenth Centuries*, xvi. Hampshire Record Series V, Hampshire County Council, Winchester.
11. Reeves (2007) *op. cit.* in note 7, xxxvi.
12. D. J Stagg (ed.) (1983) *A Calendar of New Forest Documents: fifteenth to seventeenth century*, 230–32. Hampshire Record Office, Hampshire County Council, Winchester; P. Roberts (2001) Elizabethan conservators of the New Forest, *Hampshire Studies* 56, 246–53.
13. Stag (1983) *op. cit.* xxx.

14. Stag (1983) *op. cit.* xxxiv
15. Roberts (2001) *op. cit.* in note 12.
16. Pettit (1968) *op. cit.* in note 9, 19, 28.
17. R. Reeves (2007) The Use and Abuse of a Forest Resource, xxxiv. New Forest Record Series 1, New Forest Ninth Centenary Trust, Fordingbridge. http://www.newforestcentre.org.uk/uploads/publications/3.pdf.
18. E. M. Yates (1985) *The Landscape of the New Forest in Medieval times*, 6. Department of Geography, King's College London.
19. Stagg (1979) *op. cit.* in note 7, 7.
20. M. M. Postan (1972) T*he Medieval Economy and Society*, 110. Penguin Books, London.
21. D. C. Douglas and G. W. Greenaway (eds) (1981) English Historical Documents (2nd edn), 451–53. David & Charles, Exeter.
22. R. Abels (n.d.) *Medieval Kingship in Late Twelfth- and Early Thirteenth-Century England: the Reigns of King Henry II and King John*. http://usna.edu/Users/history/abels/hh315/feudalkingship.htm. Accessed Sept 2017.
23. P. J. Neville Havins (1976) *The Forests of England*, 24–26, Robert Hale, London.
24. Stagg (1979) *op. cit.*. in note 7, record 336.
25. *Ibid.*, 4.
26. *Ibid.*, 16.
27. *Ibid.*, *e.g.* record 287 p. 121, record 34 p. 58, record 44 p. 60.
28. *Ibid.*, record 287 p. 121, record 43 p. 60.
29. *Ibid.*, record 69 p. 70.
30. *Ibid.*, record 72 p. 71.
31. *Ibid.*, records 64–65 pp. 65–69.
32. 'Attachment' normally refers to a court being able to seize a person's private property, but under forest law it refers to the capability to hold an individual for 'enrollment', but not conviction of a case against the venison or vert, this was the role of the Eyre or Swainmote http://www.deanverderers.org.uk/glossary.html.
33. R. Reeves pers. comm. (2013).
34. C. Tubbs (2001) *New Forest, the History, Ecology and Conservation*, 67, 80. New Forest Ninth Centenary Trust, Fordingbridge.
35. 'Staffordshire Forest Pleas: Introduction', *Staffordshire Historical Collections*, vol. 5 part 1 (1884) 123–135. URL: http://www.british-history.ac.uk/report.aspx?compid=52372. Accessed Sept 2017.
36. Stagg (1979) *op. cit.* in note 7, 8.
37. *Ibid.*, 8, 31.
38. Stagg (1983) *op. cit.* in note 12, 1. Record Series V, Hampshire County Council, Winchester.
39. *Ibid.*, record 27 p. 5.
40. Yates (1985) *op. cit.* in note 18, 23.
41. J. Pierre and B. G. Peters (2000) *Governance, Politics and the State*, chapter 1. Macmillan, Basingstoke.
42. Postan (1972) *op. cit.* in note 20, 124.
43. Yates (1985) *op. cit.* p. 6.
44. J. Thirsk (1997) *Alternative Agriculture,* 10. Oxford Univeristy Press, Oxford.
45. Stagg (1979) *op. cit.* in note 7, 20–21.
46. J. Hudson (1996) *The Formation of the English Common Law*, 224. Longmans, London.
47. The Magna Carta (2012) http://www.constitution.org/eng/magnacar.htm.
48. Postan (1972) *op. cit.* in note 20, 233.
49. http://www.newforest.hampshire.org.uk/history2.html. Accessed March 2014.

50. Thirsk (1997) *op. cit.* in note 44, 10.
51. Postan (1972) *op. cit.* in note 20, 212.
52. O. Rackham (2006) *Woodlands*, 232. Collins, London.
53. Tubbs (2001) *op. cit.* in note 34, 82.
54. *Ibid.*, 83.
55. *Ibid.*
56. Stagg (1979) *op. cit.* in note 7, 75.
57. *Ibid.*, record 388 p. 141; N. Smith (1999) The Earthwork remains of enclosure in the New Forest. *Proceedings of the Hampshire Field Club and Archaeological Society* 54, 21.
58. Tubbs (2001) *op. cit.* in note 34, 72.
59. Stagg (1979) *op. cit.* in note 7, 5.
60. Yates (1985) *op. cit.* in note 18.
61. Stagg (1979) *op. cit.* in note 7, record 265 p. 117.
62. *Ibid.*, record 261 p. 115.
63. *Ibid.*, 9.
64. *Ibid.*, record 148 pp. 84–85.
65. Postan (1972) *op. cit.* in note 20, 166.
66. Stagg (1979) *op. cit.* in note 7, 13.
67. http://www.newforest.hampshire.org.uk/history2.html.
68. Stagg (1979) *op. cit.* in note 7, 8.
69. Tubbs (1981) *op. cit.* in note 34, 79, 87, Forestry Commission (1947) *The Baker Report*, 46–50. HMSO, London cmd 7245.
70. New Forest Association (n.d.) http://www.newforest.hampshire.org.uk/today1.html; D. J. Stagg (1986) *Commoners of the New Forest*, 7–9. New Forest Association, Stockbridge.
71. M. G. Jarvis, R. H. Allen, S. J. Fordham, J. Hazleden, A. J. Moffat and R. G. Sturdy. (1984) *Soils and Their Use in Eastern England*. Soil Survey of England and Wales Bulletin 15. Soil Survey, Harpenden.
72. New Forest Association (n.d.) *op. cit.* in note 70.
73. *Ibid.*
74. Stagg (1979) *op. cit.* in note 7, record 191 p. 93.
75. *Ibid.*, 32.
76. Tubbs (2001) *op. cit.* in note 34, 80; Smith (1999) *op. cit.* in note 57, 20.
77. Tubbs (2001) *op. cit.*, in note 34, 56–57.
78. Smith (1999) *op. cit.* in note 57, 21.
79. D. J. Stagg (1974) The New Forest in Domesday Book, *Proceedings of the Hampshire Field Club and Archaeological Society* New Forest Section report 13, 20–24.
80. R. Reeves (2013) The Normans, Domesday and the New Forest. Paper delivered to the Hampshire Field Club and Archaeological Society (Landscape Section) at Peter Symonds College, Winchester 09.11.13.
81. Stagg (1979) *op. cit.* in note 7, 27–37.
82. *Ibid.*, record 232 p. 108.
83. *Ibid.*, 38.
84. *Ibid.*, 13.

CHAPTER 6

The Increase and Preservation of Timber (1500–1700)

'He's chased the deer now him before
And the doe down by the den
Till the fattest buck in all the flock
King Henry he has slain.
His huntsmen followed him to the hall
To make them burly cheer,
When loud the wind was heard to sound,
And an earthquake rocked the floor…'

Traditional and released by Steeleye Span in 1972

Henry VIII heralds a new regime?

The above verse is taken from the folk song collected by Francis J. Child and re-interpreted by the well-known folk-rock band. It concerns an unidentified royal personage who probably never existed in any historic sense, being linked to beliefs about the annual cycle of fertility. It is, in context, a great pity the king in question is most unlikely to be Henry VIII (reigned 1509–1547). Neither are the (wooden) stag's heads in the Great Hall at Hampton Court his handiwork; they date mostly from the 17th century, although the antlers are real. Yet, like the song, these might as well be in homage to King Henry VIII.

The last chapter described the governance of a New Forest emerging from the middle ages. This chapter covers the time from the end of the Wars of the Roses to the turn of the eighteenth century, when inevitably great changes would take place. Richard III, he of Leicester car park fame and the last Plantagenet (reigned 1483–1485), lived at the end of the Middle Ages, while the seventeenth century saw the birth of the modern world in the English Civil War and the age of Enlightenment.

The early part of this period is dominated by two famous Tudor monarchs, Henry VIII himself and also one of his daughters, Elizabeth I (reigned 1588–1603). Significantly, there was a rise in England as a naval power and conveniently the royal hunting forests remained institutionally and economically under crown control. Then the chapter covers New Forest in the English Civil War period (1642–1651), the restoration of Charles II (1660), the problematic reign of James II (1685–1688), his flight and effective abdication and the following reign of William III (1689–1702).

Henry VIII's treatment of women, tyrannical impulses and opportunistic religious views are well known, as is the destruction and massive state land grab at the Dissolution of the Monasteries. While his attitude towards hunting may have been consistent with his predecessors, we may ask of his real motivations regarding the forests? Henry stands between medieval monarchical arrangements and the newly emerging English state of the sixteenth century while the rise of naval power caused a decisive switch in *raison d'etre* for the New Forest from royal hunting forest to providing some timber for the navy.

It is macro-economic and international politics that shed most light on Henry VIII's motives. He inherited a buoyant treasury from his father Henry VII, experienced friction with both France and Spain, and the English economy progressively suffered during his rule. It is the excavation of his impressive (largely oak constructed) flagship, the *Mary Rose*, from the Solent that sank during action against a French fleet that reminds us of these problems. Henry VIII invested heavily in the English navy, and hence would be concerned with reforming governance of this royal hunting forest.[1] The royal forests become both a strategic source of timber, and also a source of revenue for the exchequer.

For Henry, hunting probably provided a chance to escape, with his friends, from the cares of politics. He even had a specially made breach loader, for hunting birds, although guns of the day would not have been as accurate as a crossbow. In early Tudor times, hunting was deemed a symbol of knighthood and marked out the true gentleman. Interestingly, a few humanists such as Sir Thomas More objected to the hunt.[2] However, Henry hunted in the New Forest, and even tried to increase the size of ponies by ordering all horses less than 14½ hands high to be killed. This effort in selective breeding did not work, as local people apparently favoured smaller ponies.[3]

Henry's reign did produce a real local political and managerial achievement in the *Orders and Rules of the New Forest in the County of Southampton.*[4] The document outlines its management describing common practices (formalised later as Common Rights) and it identifies a hierarchy of officers. It specified procedures within the forest, including procedures for hunting. It is dated 1537:

> 'And if it shall please the Kings Majesty to hunt within the Forest, the Lord Warden may command his Rangers to Summon all the Country, as well within the Forest as upon the Borders of the Forest, to come unto a Place assigned to wait upon the Lieutenant and other Fosters to wendlas [windlass – intercept] the Deer, and to bring them to such places as the Kings Majesty may take his Pleasure, and the same People shall compass and stand in a Stable until such time as the hunting be done.'

The document displays concern over forest management, for a crisis of function was emerging in the New Forest. However, the evolution in governance observed by commentators is one of regulation of traditional forest practice and privileges and exclusion of strangers, thereby protecting commoners' interests.[5] From being almost completely concerned with the pleasure of the ruling elites prior to the sixteenth century, the exchequer's interest arose from generating revenues from elsewhere – hence forest governance came under scrutiny. Actually, there was much interest from the Exchequer manifest from the thirteenth century, although the assumption would seem that the forest's function remained for hunting.[6]

The role of the New Forest subsequently diversified with the rise of 'sylviculture' (modern spelling 'silviculture') – that is, the forerunner of modern commercial forestry. Yet, hunting by monarchs continued into the reign of the flamboyant Charles II, said to have been the last monarch to hunt in the New Forest. The succeeding reigns of James and William actually saw rolling programmes of broadleaved afforestation to provide timber for the navy. The forest would meet direct 'state interests', as understood in the modern sense.

The switch of function was slowly realised. For example, an offence against the venison is recorded from 1488[7] and timber for the navy had been gathered long before – in 1416/17[8] for Henry V's flagship *Grace Dieu*. Tudor monarchs were concerned to manage the forests in order to increase revenue for the Exchequer, and in this context we see the rise of notions of environmental auditing. Early in the reign of Henry VIII we find the establishment of the Office of General Surveyor in 1512,[9] subsequently there were concerns over the sale of wood with the establishment of the Court of General Surveyors in 1547. These developments, almost exactly spanning Henry's reign, were to pave the way for a *Divisum Imperium* where the exchequer would nuzzle in on the ancient system of governance inherited from Norman times.

In an Act of 1542, management of crown woods for timber was formalised and thus created was the Court of Surveyors and the post of Surveyor General of the King's Woods who were assigned to manage 'forest districts'. These precursors of the 'Office of Woods'[10] (ultimately the modern Forestry Commission), were instigated to increase the commercial function of crown woodlands under the direction of the exchequer. These new arrangements had responsibilities for creating through timber, 'profit of the king'.[11] The Surveyor General was answerable to the exchequer and hence often in conflict with the responsibilities of the Lord Warden, who continued to administer the forest laws, and whose duty was to preserve the game, something that would cause conservative actions in respect of forest management.[12] The creation of the post of Surveyor General in turn gave rise to a second hierarchy of officers, known as 'Deputy Surveyors'. The ensuing *Statute of Woods* in 1544[13] extended the period of enclosure to seven years in order to exclude grazing animals from woods over a 24-year growth period, and woods of lesser age for shorter periods. This effectively recognised the value of woods in an economic sense – distinct from hunting.

The *Statute of Woods* (1544) was effectively a working plan for coppice management and this was perhaps the first recorded 'regularisation' of silviculture, as opposed to mere protection of the vert for hunting. Yet, by the reign of Elizabeth I (1558–1603), the New Forest was poised to become predominantly a supplier of commercial timber. Coppice management also developed into the reign of Elizabeth I, when coppice clearance was extended to nine years (see below). The regarders reported markets for products were for charcoal, fuel, fence stakes and house repairs. The demand for large timber trees was not apparent, or at least there may not yet have been a supply problem.

This value highlighted by the regarders (although the confusion of function with that of the preservators was noted in Chapter 5) was not only in timber, for in many parts of the country wood was used for charcoal production, including for smelting iron. The statute provided for 12 standels (standard trees) to remain per acre, through several coppice cycles to provide for large timber. A later Act of 1588 extended the length of enclosure after felling to nine years. In 1595 coppice was present at Castle Hill, Broadstone and South Bentley Coppice.[14] Preservators' returns show the coppices were leased to groups of individuals described as 'wood seller tenants' at between £3 and £4 per acre, although one William Hobbes let 5 acres (2 ha) near to Harmansgrove. These could cut the hazel underwood and lop pollarded oak for fuel, charcoal, fence stakes, hurdles, house walls, baskets, barrel hoops, frameworks for bee skeps or hives and general house repairs. Fuel wood and charcoal were remnants not used for any other purpose. However, sapling oaks had to be left to mature for use by the navy, coppicing is not helpful when large ship's timbers are called for. Two coppices are shown in a survey of 1655, and although demand for underwood products was slackening nationally, demand seems to have held in the New Forest. The coppice system on crown lands ended with the Act of 1688.[15]

Monarchs may have become progressively less interested in hunting, but ordinary forest dwellers still sought livelihoods and presented a potential threat. It is clear that, during the sixteenth century, strong penalties for transgressors remained. By way of illustration in nearby Buckholt Forest (one of the forests in the orbit of Clarendon) supplied venison and timber in the middle ages.[16] As the hunting declined, so agriculture (including rabbit warrens) increased, including 'informal enclosure', changing open fields with common grazing to enclosed farmland, made possible by overall better land quality than in the New Forest. Although the term 'forest' may be legal in origin, the term 'forestry' came to describe the cultivation of trees, supplanting the earlier – and more attractive – term 'silviculture' in use during and after Tudor times.

Re-organisation and the rise of auditing

In the last chapter it was noted that the role of 'regarder' was to inspect and record encroachment on the forest. The rise of fuller resource auditing in the New Forest arose with the Deputy Surveyors and may thus be associated with the inevitable rise of the *Divisum Imperium*, a governance issue dated to 1533.[17] The Commission of Inquiry of that year continued into the following century, and is seen as an attempt by the exchequer to gain a better understanding of how the forest was managed and could be improved. It also brought to light 'long established and questionable practices' that, indeed, were to be remarked upon to the end of the eighteenth century. A jury was summoned by the sherriff, and the inquiry included an investigation into felling and sales from the forest resource. In its wake, a large number of cases were brought against forest officials, including the Surveyor General of Woods of the time.[18] It was alleged there was a confederacy to cover for questionable practices among the officials.

The Tudor period saw an elaboration of officers and new roles that were to lead to confusion in the long term.[19] While there is no mention of agisters – who originally collected money on behalf of the crown – they do re-appear in the Eyre of 1608.[20] The Swainmote was convened by the verderers and heard by a jury at which forest presentments for minor forest offences (involving fines or obtain sureties) or referred for sentence to the eyre that had both judicial and investigative powers and was the higher court.[21] The *Charter of the Forest* had provided for the Swainmote to be held every third year (like the eyre) and this operated as a court of allotment, concerned with grazing and pasturing, and also undertaking surveys. However this court did not settle long-standing controversies. There were instructions for dealing with felons and vert and venison. The Orders and Rules established an annual cycle of management. Dues were collected, animals were rounded up and marked, and unauthorised grazing was dealt with by fines.

The *Orders and Rules of the New Forest* from 1537 provides a clear insight into the officers' roles.[22] The New Forest, the Manor of Lyndhurst and the Royalty of the Hundred of Redbridge 'and all Issues and profits of the same, is part of the Livlode belonging to the Crown'. In these *Order and Rules*, the chief officer is the Warden, the Earl of Arundell (authorised by crown and parliament) and he was to enjoy all manner of rents, issues and profits. Under him are a Lieutenant, Steward, Auditor, two Rangers, eight Yeoman foresters (of eight bayliwicks), the Bowbearer, one Verminer, two Riders, one Bailiffe of the Hundred of Redbridge, all paid for by the Warden of the Forest. There is a reference to 'The Verderer chosen by the King's Writt directed to the Sheriff of the Shire' suggesting crown oversight. Although the Office of General Survey dated from 1512, it was 1517 when the Exchequer gained control of the forest's resources as they now controlled sales of wood from the royal forests.

The intriguing position of 'verminer' probably relates to someone engaged in small mammal containment. Although forest development and administrative arrangements differed, at nearby Clarendon Park[23] there is a record in 1650 of small feral animals including mice, rats, squirrels, voles and moles (these were regarded as particularly problematic, and in the sixteenth century, 'wontodoge' or mole-catching had been a designated task), while larger management of fox, badger, marten, otter and squirrel could be hunted as vermin, probably by the warrener. Today, foxes, stoats, weasels, mink, rats and grey squirrels remain vermin to hunting interests.[24] In the eighteenth centuary there are references to verminers, from 1712:

> 'The case of Trafford Smith Verminer of New Forest in Hampshire. At a court held 22 May 1711 it was ordered that the verminer should have all trees out of which vermin were taken. All former verminers took such to their use ...'[25]

The profession evidently had its perks. A further irony is that today, even deer may be regarded as vermin to farmers and gardeners.

Many of such positions would have been sinecures for the gentry.[26] When this governance structure was fully operational it was possible for the crown to seek to optimise revenue. However, there was also a system of oversight where maladministration, corruption and oppression were possible. Here is a role for the Regarders, although these officers are not specifically mentioned by name in the *Order and Rules*. Times for paying rents were also stipulated, including for those living without the forest but grazing cattle due on quarter days, and chimmage (tolls) for carters crossing the forest.[27]

The king appointed the Riding Foresters (and Forester) of Burley, their wages coming from the Sheriff of the shire. The Lieutenant agreed with the warden to appoint his deputy, otherwise he had the authority over appointments of 'groomes' (assistants) for the eight foresters and two rangers. The Steward and his clerk held courts of the forest at Lyndhurst every three weeks, representation was from the lieutenant or his deputy, the rangers and their men, the Riding Forester or his man, the forester of Burley and his man and the other eight foresters or their representatives, the bowbearer and the rangers and their men, two riders who were responsible for stray beasts who could be sold for the Lord Warden. The court dealt with transgressions committed within the previous three weeks. Until 1827, the wardenship of the New Forest had always accompanied the grant of the manor of Lyndhurst, but then the court baron was held by the Steward of George Harrison, Lord of the Manor (but not Lord Warden, this was William Sturges-Bourne in 1827[28]), whose last court was to be held in 1831. At this date the crown appears to have resumed possession of the manor, and henceforth the courts were held by the successive Stewards of the manor.[29]

The activities of the forest officers were thus checked, including Regarders, who recorded fallen trees and inspected coppices. The verderers particularly took their offices seriously, however, apparently the woodward less so. Complaints were soon made against the forest officers particularly in respect of the preservation, viewing and marking of wood.[30]

The foresters specifically included the Riding Foresters (who could cover relatively large areas) and the foot foresters. These officers have their origin in the medieval period and belonged to the Lord Warden's department. Hitherto, the office of forester was the backbone of the forest system,[31] being responsible for protecting the vert and venison in their respective areas of jurisdiction. In the New Forest the foresters operated within bailiwicks, which had become fixed by 1300. The foresters replaced the foresters of fee in the thirteenth century. By the sixteenth century, the foresters were often termed keepers and they had oversight and direction of the under foresters or groom keepers in each bailiwick and whose lodges became established in the early seventeenth century.[32] Bailiwicks had been established as administrative areas in the later thirteenth century.[33] In Tudor times, each bailiwick in the New Forest had a master keeper and a hunting lodge. The master keeper was responsible to the crown with groom keepers beneath him who were responsible for the hunting lodges and who lived there or else in a village nearby.[34] And there were also substantial freeholders within and around the forest. Rangers originally had responsibilities outside the forest, in the purlieu areas, where landowners were permitted to hunt deer.[35]

By 1567 the exchequer was in full control of sales of wood from the New Forest.[36] A commission reporting in that year brought a new office, that of 'preservators' into being. These new officials produced returns between 1570 and 1609, the period of existence of the office.[37] Apart from record keeping, the preservators' duties included powers relating to the unlawful exploitation of the woods, importantly this related not only to by local inhabitants but also forest officers. Their powers included stop and search of wood carts, requesting information relating to the origins of the wood.[38] Prior to that, control was split between the exchequer and the justices of the forest. The exchequer had gained its interest from the creation of the wood sales department within the office of general surveyors, thus protecting its interests.[39]

The switch in emphasis from venison to vert demonstrates the early phase of management for timber products. The New Forest was clearly suffering a crisis of function and confusion in its governance along the lines of whether the crown or the exchequer would hold the most influence. Although it may be demonstrated that, before 1500, there is evidence the crown was looking to timber products as a means of boosting the exchequer, monarchs were evidently no longer all committed to preserving large areas of England solely for their own pleasure.

The end of monastic interests

England's financial problems during the reign of Henry VIII have been mentioned. It is revealing that, in the 1537 *Orders and Rules of the New Forest*[40] published during the dissolution of the monasteries (1536–1540), records extortion exacted on the religious houses to the benefit to the foresters:

> 'The riding Foster, the Lieutenants, and all the Fosters of the Forest shall have at Christmas of the Prior of Christchurch a Supper, and Horse meat, and Lodging all night, and the next day their Dinner, and when they have dined every Gent. Yeoman and Grooms after their Degree shall have Money as of old times hath been used 46s 2d.'

Similar arrangements pertained to Breamore with a payment of 33s 2d and at Bewley 46s 8d. However, by April 1540 no monastic institutions remained in England and Wales, yet the New Forest had been ringed by monasteries. The closest had been Augustinian: at Christchurch, Breamore, Ivychurch (Alderbury) and Mottisfont. Most were twelfth century foundations, although the Benedictine Abbey at Romsey had been founded in AD 967 and there were also assorted secular canons, hospitals and friaries thereabouts. The Beaulieu Abbey estate (1204–1538), a Cistercian house, had its origins in a grant of forest land from King John. It had a daughter house in Netley Abbey, across Southampton Water and the remains of the monastic grange can be seen at St

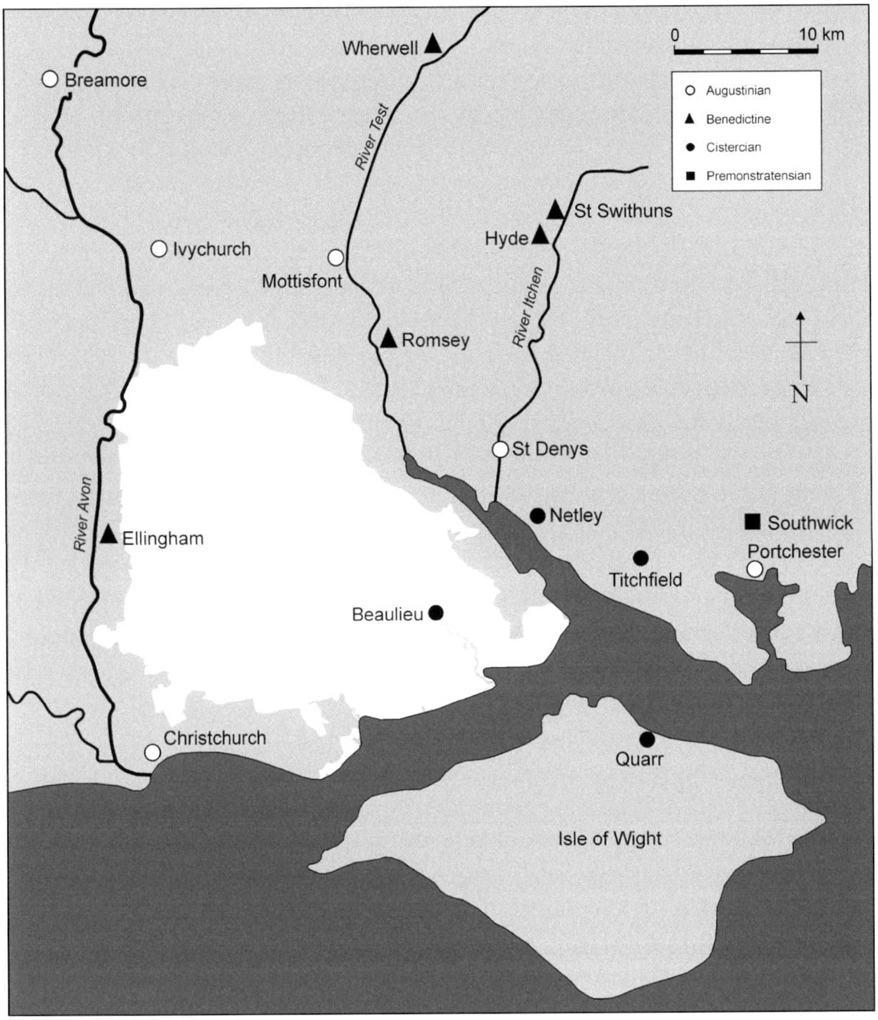

FIGURE 6.1. Monastic foundations in and around the New Forest.

AFTER YATES, 1985, 42–43

Leonards.[41] The Abbot of Beaulieu grazed 80 horses, 200 oxen and cows, 1300 pigs and 50 pigs within the forest. The Abbot of Netley grazed 10 horses, 60 cows and 40 pigs within the forest.[42] Roydon Woods is a complex area with a diverse history (Fig. 6.1). This enclosure may form a part of a thirteenth century grant to Netley Abbey, and this may extend westwards.[43]

It is probable that only Cistercian and Premonstratensian estates were managed directly by the religious houses themselves. The grant of land at Beaulieu may have dated from 1203 when King John made the grant to the house of St Mary of Citeaux, as the head of the Cistercian order, upon the condition that a monastery should be built there. The new monastery was founded in the New Forest St Mary of Beaulieu with provision for 30 monks.[44] The grant endowed the Cistercians with additional manors beyond the forest. Monks of Faringdon in Berkshire were transferred and Faringdon was made a cell to Beaulieu. John gave the monks a hundred marks towards the construction of the abbey, a gold chalice, and 100 cows and ten bulls for their dairy in 1204. Henry III enlarged Beaulieu and, in 1217, he instructed the keeper of his herd of horses in the New Forest to hand over all the profits to the monks. Royal patronage continued and Beaulieu undertook significant trade, especially in wool and corn. Trade links with Gascony, from where wine was imported, were also very important.

The advowson of the church of Ringwood was granted to the abbey in February 1329 by Edward III. Monasteries typically appropriated the rectoral tithes, leaving a small amount to support a vicar. With these went grazing rights in the forest. Examples are: Eling appropriated by Mottisfont Priory, Boldre, Milford and Sopley by Christchurch, while Hale chapelry and Charford chapelry were included in the possessions of Breamore. Further afield, St Swithin's Priory (the Cathedral) and the Bishop possessed the manors of Exbury and Fawley. The relative poverty of the ordinary parishes compared with some monastic houses has also been noted, while the monastic remains give good indication of their considerable landscape impact in the Middle Ages.[45]

Under the Act of 1536 that dissolved the lesser monasteries, more than two-thirds of the Cistercian abbeys were suppressed. The religious were, as a rule, transferred to the larger houses of their order. In March 1536, Abbot Browning died and Thomas Stevens became abbot of Netley. Yet, in the following February, Netley was suppressed, and the community transferred to their mother house at Beaulieu. Then, on 2 April 1538, the Abbot Thomas Stevens surrendered Beaulieu Abbey to the royal commissioners; he and the monks receiving pensions. At the time of the dissolution, the monastery also held several manors in Hampshire, the Isle of Wight and beyond. The site was immediately granted to Thomas Wriothesley (afterwards first Earl of Southampton) who benefitted enormously by obtaining lands from the dissolution of the monasteries.[46] During the 1530s, records show shows new crown lessees taking wood in the forest by virtue of the old rights that belonged to the religious houses which they had since occupied.[47] Rectoral beneficiaries upon dissolution also fell into lay hands.

The Tudor state was increasing in complexity and there was a consequent call for rationalisation. There emerged a need for new systems of management. The Court of Augmentations (established to handle monastic property and revenues appropriated by the State) represented part of a new system. The Court was subsequently amalgamated in the Office Surveyor General and represents a new administrative structure in parallel with the 'traditional' governance structures for the forest. These new arrangements would affect the sale of wood products.[48] Monastic lands confiscated due to the 'treason' of their abbots were administered by the Court of General Surveyors. Other monastic estates came under the Court of Augmentations (1536). This was amalgamated in 1547 with the Court of General Surveyors and Court of First Fruits and Tenths, as the 'Court of Augmentations and Revenues of the King's Crown' and subsequently absorbed into the exchequer in 1553.[49]

Coppicing: a New Forest experiment?

The *Statute of Woods* 1544 has been mentioned. Until the fifteenth century, forestry (in a productive sense) would have been a secondary consideration to management for deer. Furthermore, the reluctance of medieval foresters to plant even age stands and let woods run to 'high forest' has also been noted.

Timber and coppice products would be required for maintenance of lodges within the forest, however 'Without doubt, by the late-sixteenth century the practice of coppicing in the New Forest was in a state of disarray'.[50] This is attributed to actions of forest officers at the local level, who seem to have lost interest in the practice,[51] possibly because the Lord Warden gained the right to take profit from sales of coppice after a period of seven years following enclosure, and also the *Divisum Imperium* – between exchequer and crown – at a higher level. There were actually 1308 acres (528 ha) recorded in 1608/9, probably distributed in 18 individual coppices, and it is debatable as to whether this is an increase in number since the 1560s.

Yet, the antiquity of coppices is suggested by the irregular boundaries of the coppices (particularly in Ridley Wood (SU 2022 0600) and Sloden (SU 2165 1255) where the irregular earthwork is within a larger, later inclosure, although that may have had another function linked with livestock[52]). North and South Bentley Inclosure boundaries follow the line of old coppice enclosure south of Fritham (see Fig. 2.9). These had been recorded as coppiced until the early 1700s, and display characteristic irregular outlines and it is likely they maintained coppicing later than elsewhere in the forest.[53] After that they were wholly or partly cleared and planted with acorns of sessile Oak. Tubbs[54] finds them not to have been recorded under the 1698 *Enclosure Act for the Increase and Preservation of Timber in the New Forest* during the reign of William III, when timber was required for the navy (see below). The Bentley Inclosures may therefore contain some of the oldest surviving planted oaks in western Europe. However, the 1698 *Act* reintroduced the regulation to remove stock from the forest during the midsummer 'Fence Month' and during winter heyning (22 November–4 May) when winter forage was low.[55] At these times, domestic animals should have been removed when deer were calving in June and to winter fodder for the deer. Indeed, by 1700, coppice areas were being planted with acorns alongside the timber following the 1698 *Act*.

The practice of coppice management is prehistoric (Chapter 2) and was undertaken since at least the late medieval period, proven by the legislation passed as the *Encoppicement Act* of 1483, encouraging enclosure of private forest 'coppices' within the bounds of forests (Chapter 4). Such management would seem to have continued until the seventeenth century.[56] This must not be confused otherwise with underwood management up to the seventeenth century, although coppices may have originated as a by-product of opportunistic underwood exploitation.[57] It should not perhaps be considered as ordered as the more coppicing familiar elsewhere, nor should coppice management be confused with the deliberate plantation of trees from the seventeenth century.

It seems the crown sought to increase its revenues at a time of inflation and crown debts[58] when deer were of no longer of any great value, and by the time of Elizabeth I, a survey of 'encoppicements', that is coppiced enclosures, was made. Deriving from the 'first law affecting silviculture', the *Encoppicement Act*, in 1483,[59] 5800 acres (2359 ha) had been encoppiced although there were evidently problems with their management and condition. The Queen, concerned about the supply of timber for the navy, took considerable care of forest management, something that neither the Stuarts nor the period of the Commonwealth was to take seriously. Indeed, it is likely there was neglect even to pay the officers of the forest during the reign of James II.[60] Unfortunately for the crown, coppicing was not to prove as successful as tall timber trees; encoppiced areas suffered neglect by tenants and officers alike, with deer permitted to graze upon the young hazel shoots.[61] Perhaps this reflected the loss of fuel markets to coal.

Alongside the coppicing of woods *per se*, that of aldermoors and withies in the New Forest also deserves mention. Wet woodlands were fast growing (because of better nutrient availability and no drought stress when compared with the forest soils in general) and also they were also cost-effective as they required no fencing, being generally limited to areas of around 3 acres (1.2 ha). The practice, presumably ancient and once used to pay keepers' wages, albeit in conflict with deer management, ceased in the 1950s.[62]

Issues of timber and coppice production in the New Forest, being close to the 'establishment' of the day would have played a part in the development of early scientific and legal enquiry. Next it is the rise of substantial texts on forests that is considered.

Manwood and Norden

Around the turn of the sixteenth century there was evident concern for the maintenance of forests, due to both their physical state and as the bad practice that was attributed to corruption. These are precursors to John Evelyn's post-Restoration interest in silviculture. Like Evelyn, with his motives apparently pro-monarchy and pro-aristocracy, the earlier John Manwood (d. 1610) was not only aptly named, but his book *A Treatise of the Laws of the Forest* published originally in 1598 (Fig. 6.2) ran to several editions. A barrister by profession, Manwood had been Justice in Eyre of the New Forest under Elizabeth I and his book provides valuable information on medieval forest laws, offices, beasts and customs.[63] The function of the Chief Justice in Eyre was basically to fix the fines and punishments of those who had been previously convicted at the Swainmotes. The justices in eyre, or their deputies, continued down to 1635; they were virtually ended by the *Act for the Limitation of Forests* (1640), although Charles II attempted to revive them.[64]

The Appendix of Manwood's book contains the discredited *Charter of Canute* (Chapter 3) as well as the *Charter of the Forest* (1217). Manwood confirms that protected animals are the hart, hind (red deer), boar, hare and wolf. Protection

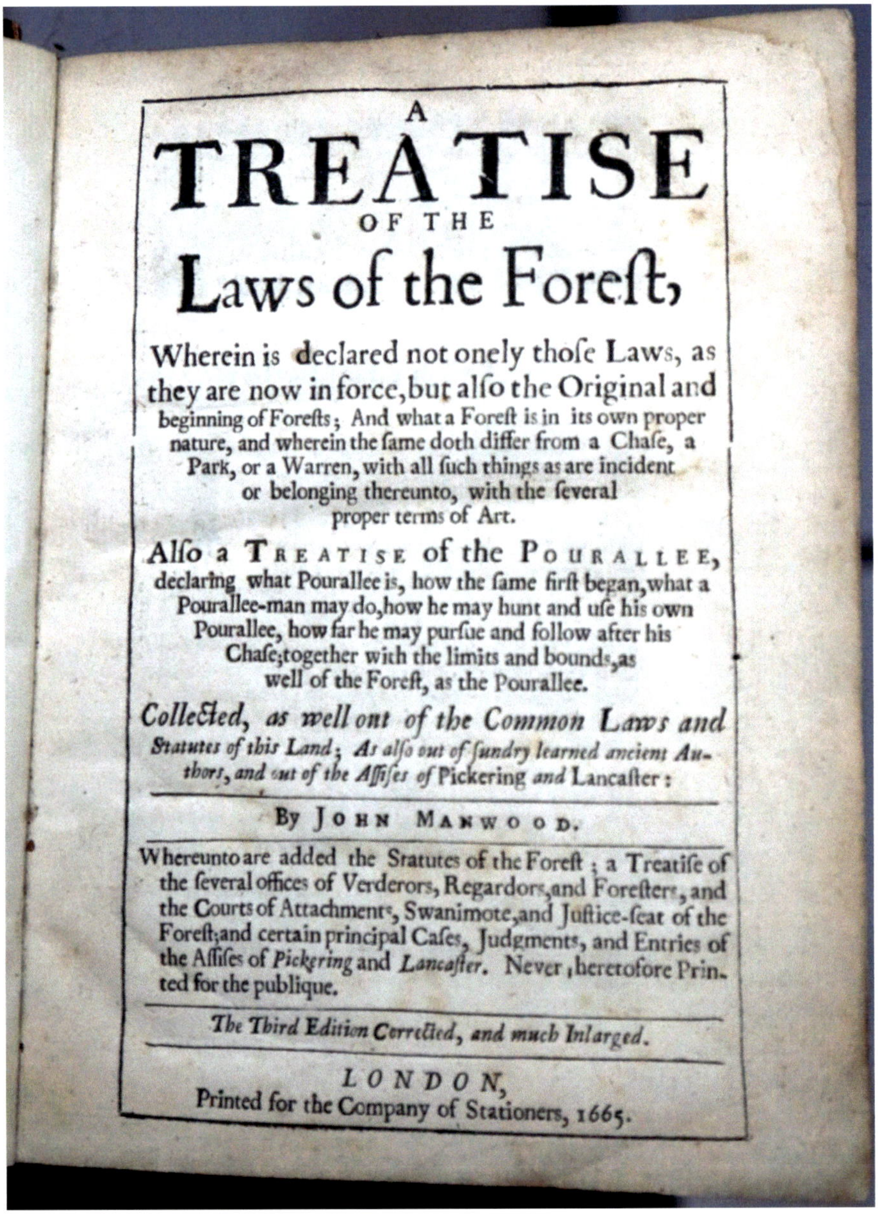

A
TREATISE
OF THE
Laws of the Foreſt,

Wherein is declared not onely thoſe Laws, as they are now in force, but alſo the Original and beginning of Foreſts; And what a Foreſt is in its own proper nature, and wherein the ſame doth differ from a Chaſe, a Park, or a Warren, with all ſuch things as are incident or belonging thereunto, with the ſeveral proper terms of Art.

Alſo a TREATISE of the POURALLEE, declaring what Pourallee is, how the ſame firſt began, what a Pourallee-man may do, how he may hunt and uſe his own Pourallee, how far he may purſue and follow after his Chaſe; together with the limits and bounds, as well of the Foreſt, as the Pourallee.

Collected, as well out of the Common Laws and Statutes of this Land; As alſo out of ſundry learned ancient Authors, and out of the Aſſiſes of Pickering *and* Lancaſter:

By JOHN MANWOOD.

Whereunto are added the Statutes of the Foreſt; a Treatiſe of the ſeveral offices of Verderors, Regardors, and Foreſters, and the Courts of Attachments, Swanimote, and Juſtice-ſeat of the Foreſt; and certain principal Caſes, Judgments, and Entries of the Aſſiſes of *Pickering* and *Lancaſter*. Never heretofore Printed for the publique.

The Third Edition Corrected, and much Inlarged.

LONDON,
Printed for the Company of Stationers, 1665.

FIGURE 6.2. First page of the 1665 edition of Manwood's *A Treatise of the Laws of the Forest*

was also said to be extended to the beasts of chase, the buck, and doe (fallow deer), fox, marten and roe deer and also of the warren, hare, coney, pheasant and partridge. Manwood was furthermore concerned with conservation of flora and fauna, indeed one of his motives has been likened to that of a modern conservationist:

> 'the necessity of the preservation of the Coverts of the Forest, forasmuch as the destruction of the coverts, doth banish the wild beasts from the forest, and the exile of the wild beasts from the forest doth make the same no Forest at all in the end.'[65]

And:

> 'a forest must always have beasts of venery abiding in it, otherwise it is no forest: and if there be no beasts of forest, nor beasts of chase in the same, then may men fell their woods that they have within the forest and destroy their covers.'

His contemporary, John Norden (*c.*1547–1625), was surveyor of crown lands and published *The Surveyor's Dialogue* in 1618. In this he referred to 'desert forests' where:

> 'idleness, beggary and atheism ... wherein infinite poor, yet most idle inhabitants have thrust themselves, living covertly without law or religion ... among whom are nourished and bred infinite idle fry, that coming to ripe grow vagabonds and infect the commonwealth with a most dangerous leprosy'.[66]

Whether dialogue or diatribe, we may reflect on the whole notion of 'masterless men', whose belief system and habits were apparently at odds with those of a surveyor of crown lands. Netzloff[67] further comments that Norden's concern for enclosures of land and destruction of woodland was something apparently causing concern for decades. Specifically in the New Forest, in 1609, Norden undertook a survey of New Forest coppices. This new and innovative level of auditing and presumed intervention would support the claim that the forest law was *de facto* in decline by the sixteenth century.[68] Coppices were let to woodcutters who cut the underwood and pollards but not saplings; for Norden expressed his concern that these be left to grow to tall trees.[69]

The rise of silviculture

The practice of coppicing, albeit rather erratic, subsequently declined during the seventeenth century to be replaced by crown interest in timber production.[70] Nonetheless, overproduction from coppices is believed to have saturated the local markets.[71] The Elizabethan and Stuart treasuries were evidently keen to develop the potential of economic exploitation of the royal forests. This might be approached through revival of medieval rights, sale of wood products as things stood, or development of the potential[72] of the woodlands. One example, resulting from the activities of one Otto Nicholson who from 1600 leased assart land in Northamptonshire, Buckinghamshire and Huntingdonshire, then sought out 'concealed assarts' in the king's interest so that the Commission for Assarts appointed in 1604 (including a Justice in Eyre) could sell assarts in 'fee farm', a form of freehold that still involved an annual rent being paid.[73] The resulting 'improvement of assarts', involved both fee farm and granting of new leases. As far as the Hampshire forests were concerned (the New Forest, Alice Holt and Wolmer) by 1623 they had generated respectable income for the Exchequer from fines and rents over some 8771 acres (3552 ha) of assart.

Between 1570 and 1677, the reported inadequacy of the coppice system for preserving timber has been noted.[74] Coppices were leased by 'wood seller tenants' who could cut the hazel underwood and lop pollarded oak for fuel, charcoal, fence stakes and house repairs, but sapling oaks had to be left to mature. Yet, the value of underwood sales around the end of the sixteenth century was still greater than that of timber.[75] In 1609, the Deputy Surveyor General produced a list of existing coppices and also potential sites with the likely intention of expanding the practice, yet in the following year, with him serving on a Commission of Enquiry, both advocated increase and preservation of woods within the New Forest, while not recommending further coppice creation for, in that respect: 'nothing hath ensued but expense of money and spoil of timber trees and the intended coppices never were finished nor at all preserved'. There had evidently been problems with coppice production, possibly of Setthorns Coppice, and in subsequent decades, Bentley Coppice and King's Coppice were felled in the 1660s, although the Bentley North and South Coppices at Fritham were retained and converted to timber trees.[76] Tenants, minor forest officers and commoners seem to have come to abuse underwood trees while local communities resisted the change so that by the end of the seventeenth century, coppicing was no longer a favoured policy. In the seventeenth century, and despite the efforts of the previous century, coppicing was in terminal decline. Indeed at that time, there was even hostile criticism for the reason that common rights were seen as an obstacle to profit. Larger farmers wanted the commons for their own cattle. Commoners were also accused of moral degeneracy and idleness.[77]

The resources of harvestable timber on crown land were in decline. The earliest attempts to make permanent enclosures (of doubtful legality before the 1698 *Act for the Increase and Preservation of Timber in the New Forest*) at Holmhill, Aldridgehill and Holidays Hill between 1670 and 1673 were 'for the nursery and supply of timber', but met with uncertain success. Demand for timber continued to rise due in part to demands of the navy.[78]

Furthermore, during the second half of the sixteenth century and early seventeenth century, government officers began looking at ways to gain greater control over the management of the woodland resource and better preserve them. However, they were to some extent failed by those very officers to whom they committed the care of the woodlands.[79] The verderers' powers were actually increased during the seventeenth and eighteenth centuries on in order to address offences undermining the planting and preservation of oak for shipbuilding (*e.g.* breaking inclosures, encroachment on crown land), and also powers were granted to deal with trespass and abuses by other forest officers.[80]

Royal forests had supplied hardwood to local markets for centuries; oak for fittings and furnishings and beech for furniture.[81] The deliberate planting of oaks and (to a lesser extent) beech in order to supply the navy was a priority. The policy under William III (reigned 1689–1702) was to plant 2000 acres (810 ha) of oak, increasing by 200 acres (81 ha) per year for 20 years, until an area of 6000 acres (2430 ha) was achieved.[82] Actually only slightly over 1000 acres (414 ha) were planted in 15 years,[83] following the 1698 *Act for the Increase and Preservation of Timber in the New Forest*. With the practice of pollarding was made illegal;[84]

presumably full tree growth was preferred. This Act also gave Verderers powers to fine miscreants £5 for the breaking of Inclosure fences, burning heather and fern, destroying covert (apparently a catch-all offence) and stealing wood.[85] Venison offences could be dealt with by the (apparently harsher) common law.

The 1698 Act of Parliament actually made it illegal to start new pollarding on any more (specifically) oak trees within the New Forest, because this would not have produced timber suitable for shipbuilding. Those that had been pollarded were permitted to continue until the *Deer Removal Act* of 1851, when it was seen as no longer necessary to provide winter fodder for the deer, ponies and cattle. Today, holly pollarding still occurs each winter to provide additional food for ponies. Some young oak and beech trees may have to be revived in certain areas to help maintain the aesthetic value of the woods.[86] Pollarding, however, continued until the end of the seventeenth century, so that any pollard trees in the forest would generally be over 300 years old,[87] although the practice was allowed on existing pollard trees until the 1851 *Deer Removal Act*. Cutting was typically at a height that would have been achieved by a man standing on a wagon.

There would also be a 'revolution' in agriculture that would include more scientific approaches to the cultivation and management of crops, including trees and would form a major part of the 'Scientific Revolution'. The New Forest was finally to lose its *de facto* importance as a royal hunting forest, to be replaced by the interests of silviculture. Otherwise controversial for what today is regarded as a neo-liberal view of economic history, the agricultural historian Eric Kerridge[88] could declare that the 'Agricultural Revolution' occurred prior to the eighteenth century. The seventeenth century was certainly a period of innovation, although the increase in food production was not realised until the following century when agriculture expanded to meet a growing British population.[89] All in all, from the seventeenth to mid-nineteenth century, the chief interest in the New Forest *was* economic rather than leisure for elites, or anybody else, and this observation lay in its capacity to produce timber for the navy.[90] Strategic interest would cement state interest.

Before 1600 there had been a reform of forest administration and several efforts to improve coppice production, including an effort at 'privatisation' on crown lands. Preservators' returns between 1570 and 1610 and again during the 1670s, find inadequate timber conservation using the coppice system.[91] Planting was certainly increasingly regulated, demonstrated by the (already noted) rise of surveying and auditing. Yet any crisis in timber production was slow in being realised. The naval threat at, and after, the time of the Spanish Armada (1588) seems actually to have caused little felling in the later sixteenth century; the only known Elizabethan felling involved 200 trees for John Smith, the Navy Purveyor, in 1601/2. Otherwise timber was used by royal carpenters; it was a known resource. There was, however, concern about felling coppice during the reign of James I (reigned in England 1603–1625) who caused an arbour to be built near Linwood to commemorate the killing of his first New Forest stag. Royal interest in hunting evidently continued.[92]

Sufficient oak and pine were likely available during Tudor times,[93] but during the following two centuries demand grew for timber and wood for domestic building, repairs, ships, coopering, charcoal burning and fuel on a small scale. The literature presents an element of debate about how significant the New Forest was to become, in respect of its ability to supply timber to various sectors of the economy. Stagg[94] can describe the transition from medieval hunting forest to 'managed silviculture and inclosures', describing the birth of modern forestry in a context of wider agrarian improvement including forests and waste land.

Advances in scientific understanding occurred during the turbulent seventeenth century despite yet another period of conflict with the English Civil War. The Civil War captures the imagination today, for it not only temporarily toppled the monarchy as an institution, but it occurred in a world that was rapidly evolving towards a modern political, social and economic outlook. The war can be described in terms of various competing interests, be they economic, constitutional or religious. Aside from conflict, the century would also see an end to interest in the New Forest for hunting. In February 1649 a committee was appointed to bring in a bill for the disposal of forests, parks and chases, but the Committee for the Navy sought the protection of timber for the construction of ships.[95] Cromwell toyed with selling off the royal hunting forests, although apparently the New Forest was not a prime candidate.[96]

In England at large there were momentous changes in agriculture, as in politics and economics. These are given context in the mid-seventeenth century by Walter Blith[97] in *The English Improver Improved*:

> 'All clearely demonstrated from Principles of reason, Integrity, and the late but most Real Experiences; and held forth at an Inconsiderable charge to the Profits accrewing thereby, under Six Peeces of Improvement.
>
> 1. By floating and Watering such Land as lieth capable thereof
> 2. By Drayning Fen, reducing Bog and regaining Sea-lands
> 3. By such enclosures as prevents Depopulation, & advanceth all Interests
> 4. By tillage of some Land lost for want of, and pasturing others destroyed with Plowing.
> 5. By a Discovery of all Soyles and composts with their nature and use
> 6. By doubling the growth of Wood by a new Plantation'

These six 'Peeces' of improvement embrace the entire seventeenth century 'Agricultural Revolution' (excepting new and improved varieties of crops and breeds of animals). The New Forest was itself affected. A number of potential post-medieval water meadows and associated drainage systems have very recently been identified within the valleys of the River Blackwater, the Cadham River and tributaries of the Beaulieu River. In many cases, although main drainage channels were already partially marked on the OS First Edition maps, none had been previously recorded.[98] Land reclamation became a common theme to the present, notably through drainage for forestry (Peece 2 and see Chapter 9), something seen as worth reversing in the present.

Blith, a former Parliamentarian army captain from the Midlands, addressed his book to both Houses of Parliament and was concerned not only with matters technical, but also with social impact of good husbandry (Peece 3). Although it seems unlikely Blith would have had much time for royal hunting forests managed at the pleasure of the monarch, he nonetheless reflects concerns of earlier commentators, in term of cultivation practices. Specifically, plantation was set to replace coppice. Yet it is the last 'Peece' which is often skipped in discussions of seventeenth century agrarian advancement.

John Manwood had sought to clarify what must have been regarded, by the early seventeenth century, a muddle of laws, judgements from a range of courts, customs and vested interests. It was the latter that were changing. His opinion is that 'very little, or nothing, as yet is extant', something with which Stagg takes exception.[99] Forest offences, at the time, with the exception of minor offences against the vert, could only be determined at the forest court of eyre (1166–1670). This might be viewed as basically a financial assembly concerned with revenue, rather than the general eyre that had dealt with criminal and civil proceedings since 1166.[100] In reality the *Preservation of Timber Acts* of 1765–1766 would end offences under forest law. The period would also to see the rise of modern conceptions of forestry as a commercial venture. Pioneers included Arthur Standish, writing in the 1610s, who believed the supply of timber and wood was declining (apparently not an increase in demand). He counselled in the first decade of the seventeenth century that farmers should plant hedges and quarter-acre plantation in the corner of each field. This approach would, in his opinion, produce so much firewood that within 30 years existing coppice could be converted to tillage and pasture.[101]

During the seventeenth century forest officials would have to reconcile two differences: a growing shortage of timber (largely, but not exclusively for ships) and pressure on the forest resources from both insiders and outsiders. There was, and has never been, a Parliamentary *Act of Disafforestation* so the New Forest could not be fully 'privatised'. The New Forest supplied timber for ships, together with other royal forests at Alice Holt, the Forest of Dean and the nearby Forest of Bere in Hampshire.[102] However, the preponderance of beech in some woods is likely due to the selective felling of oaks, with only limited beech planting.[103] The unsettled seventeenth century was also largely a period of decline in the management of the New Forest. Before the Commonwealth, Charles I (reigned 1625–1649) may have hunted in the New Forest, yet he allowed progressive dis-afforestation and leased royal forests to raise revenue to support his foreign policy. Hence in the New Forest, the oldest generation of oak, beech and holly dates mainly from the period 1620 to 1760, although a few giant oaks may be older.[104]

Apparently, the New Forest was 'in a shameful condition' during Charles I's reign.[105] As for the period of the Commonwealth (1649–1660) John Evelyn could talk of neglect of England's woods,[106] yet Stagg can find 'a remarkable degree of continuity' in the operation and landholdings within the New Forest.[107] Although between 1660 and 1670 heavier fines were being imposed than earlier in the century, the re-printing in 1665 of Manwood's *Treatise* may have re-enforced the view that the forest laws were already obsolete.[108]

The mid-seventeenth century actually presents a picture of an active economy within the forest. Although deer were still being taken with bows and arrows and dogs, guns were coming in. The emphasis on cases presented at forest courts were heavily on the side of infringements of 'vert' and there may have been a loss of dominance by venison officers. Other offences concerned the illegal placing of beehives in the forest, with the construction of small enclosures, cutting of turf for fuel, depasturing of sheep, unringed pigs, illegal buildings and, significantly, large numbers of oak and beech trees were stolen, including those for use by shipwrights.[109]

Charles II, probably influenced by Evelyn's *Sylva*, caused a further survey to be made finding the neglected forest containing little that was useful for shipbuilding[110] and caused further enclosures for the planting of oaks. However, from 1669 the level of new forestry was legally questionable.[111] That king may have been interested in hunting deer but he had other, better known interests. Inclined to give woods away to those at court, he infamously made a grant of coppice to one Winifred Wells, a mistress and one of the queen's maids of honour. Such is hardly a decisive management move, and during his reign the perception is one of decline.[112] An exception may have been to authorise one John Norton to enclose 300 acres (121 ha) in 1669 for young oak; the expense was defrayed by the selling of decayed wood. Later, during the 1690s, woodwards are recorded as accounting for the cutting and sale of faggots from King's Coppice and they sold standard trees. There is therefore a lack of consistency in forest policy that points to a switch of function from hunting ground to timber production. But what of other land uses?

Grazing

With the switch of emphasis towards timber production, conflicts with grazing interests were bound to continue due to the need to protect stands of trees or the potential for conversion of grazing to trees. There is consequently clear a sense of division of labour and interests within the forest including responsibilities for the regulation of grazing. While agisters are not specifically mentioned in the sixteenth century, their role is represented by the officers named, and the regular court meeting was there to enforce money paid for 'herbage and pannage'. The 'riders of the forest', foresters and rangers would seem to be likely candidates for enforcement on the king's lands; they appear to be doing the work of agisters in the seventeenth century.[113] It was not until the 1698 *Act* that there was the first statutory recognition of Common Rights.[114]

It was considered important to restrict access during the Fence Month when does were fawning, typically this was fourteen days either side of Midsummer Day. Then, grazing by cattle and access was restricted unless 'month money' was paid. This naturally smacks more of economic opportunity to gather revenue, than protection of the venison. Grazing by the manors was otherwise free, but dues were paid for summer grazing by manors outside the forest and a few outside manors could graze in winter in exchange for payment, this apparently being a concession purchased 'of old time'.[115] Regulation of grazing of common lands did not require payment and remained regulated by manorial courts. Apparently potential for double subordination was managed by supremacy of the forest court system. Transgressions by poaching venison or grazing of the vert led to being presented at the Court of Swainmote to be tried by verderers. Guilty parties were imprisoned in the 'blindhouse' at Lyndhurst (presumed to have been an associated windowless prison) followed until sureties were given, or a fine paid to the Lord Warden.[116] There is a large nineteenth century painting of the Lyndhurst Blindhouse by Sir Charles Burrand hanging upstairs in the New Forest Centre.

Removal of oak and beech trees within the forest required permission of the Lord Warden who was also responsible for protection of the venison. Creation of new coppice or coppice hedge (layered hedge) required the same permission. However, for seven years a fee of 4d was due for every length and after seven years, profits from the hedge were due to the Lord Warden. Presumably by this time, the hedge would be effective as a fence as well as supplying poles. Then, at some point during the reign of James II of England (1685–1688) the Keepers of the Forest apparently went unpaid, resulting in further managerial decline including slippage into corruption.[117]

Governance of the New Forest was facing a crisis, variously associated with managing timber production against illegal removal, pressures from grazing (notwithstanding legitimate rights of commoners) and a general decline into corruption. There was not only friction between the Lord Warden and the Deputy Surveyor, but also local resistance, especially the breaking down of inclosure fences. That there is good evidence the governance system not working is shown by a number of inquisitions in the seventeenth century following the Civil War period.[118]

It was at this time that North and South Bentley Inclosures were cleared and planted with acorns (apparently without statutory recognition), and seven new legal inclosures created between 1700 and 1703.[119] It was likely the growing of timber for the navy that caused the decline of interest in coppice, pressure on grazing would be felt from the rolling inclosures and from population growth.

Seventeenth century pressure on land

For a second time in English recorded history, landscape evidence shows a response to a known increase in population. In the mid-fourteenth century the population had fallen calamitously during visitations of the Black Death, with sustained recovery likely from about 1500, so that by the seventeenth century there was once more pressure on land, the perceived contribution of commoners has already been noted. In the New Forest there were an estimated 4000 dwellers in the late sixteenth century and this must have pressurised land abandoned as a result of the earlier Black Death to be re-cultivated. Subsequent population growth led also to the growth in the number of cottages.

Much can and has been made of the conflicting interests of crown (or its agencies) and the commoners' rights. What should not be forgotten in conflicts between crown, commoners and silviculture, is the plight of the landless poor, and the apparent failure of the historic system of governance to accommodate their interests. We are reminded of the late Christopher Hill's thesis regarding the turbulent years of the 'English Revolution'[120] during the mid-seventeenth century. There was not just the dispute between old aristocratic interests and an emerging mercantile-cum-bourgeois class of pre-industrial England, but a revolution within, involving the interests of the poor. This would-be 'proletarian revolution' evidently failed under Oliver Cromwell, but it provides context.

Grievances among the landless poor included opposition to dis-afforestation and to enclosure;[121] this interesting observation regards factions who sought to maintain their traditional rights within the forest law system. This failed attempt to accommodate the grievances of the poor would be reflected by the (often romanticised) 'diggers', who sought to address the needs of the landless labourer by (famously in 1649–1650) cultivating marginal land (wastes and commons) and provide for a communal living. This development appeared to challenge notions of absolute property rights, and was quickly suppressed.[122] Otherwise the period has been seen as one where absolute property rights came to be, as understood in a modern sense.[123] Hill can talk of a fear of the marginalised by the appellation of 'masterless men' as of those with no knowledge of religion[124] as well as no relationship with land tenure. Masterless men, in various guises, were to be present in the New Forest well into the nineteenth century. In reality, in the New Forest many of the poor had religion, albeit of the non-conformist kind, which is witnessed by the large number of chapels.[125]

The wood pasture for one would have provided opportunity for masterless men to make a living. At the beginning of the seventeenth century there is mention of certain arable land and woodland commonly called 'The Old Park of Lyndhurst'.[126] By the 1640s, the population may well have exceeded the estimate of 4000 people.[127] Yet, there was further demographic complexity. The Great Plague from 1665 would slow population growth, but thereafter overall population would have grown more or less exponentially. In any case, by this time, any notion that the New Forest functioned fully as a royal hunting forest, was over once and for all – even if Charles II led the occasional foray.

Ensuing management change had favoured tall timber production making plantation the preferred way forward. Areas planted were restricted with commoners' rights enforced. Evidently, the Stuart kings who allegedly had neglected forest management were keen, nonetheless, to maximise revenue, and to that end, justice seats were held in the New Forest between 1622 and 1670.[128] Fuelwood gathering would continue; by the eighteenth century this wood was used extensively to fire kilns.[129]

The establishment of illegal small enclosures has been mentioned. At the sessions of the Swainmote Court held at Lyndhurst on 9 June–22 July, 1635 'before the foresters, verderers, regarders, agisters [*etc.*] of the forest',[130]

> 'Thomas Norton, yeoman, recently of Brockenhurst, on the 10th June 1635 at Brookley in Battramsley bailiwick had enclosed with a large ditch and high hedge a close of meadow containing half an acre… <fine 20s.>.'[131]

Lower down the social scale, an entrepreneurial:

> 'Nicholas Thomas, labourer, recently of Searchfield, on the 1st June 1635 upon a mount near Crowsnest [SU 2416] in North bailiwick, cut down and dug three thousand turves worth three shillings for various inhabitants of Downton <fine 20s.>.[132]

And solving her housing problem:

> 'Elizabeth Tymothy, spinster of Brockenhurst, since the last regards of the forest had built a house or cottage where no house was previously, at Brockenhurst on the fee of Robert Knapton… <fine £3>'.[133]

One has a sneaking respect for:

> 'Hugh Wiseman, husbandman, recently of Wootton, on the 10th June 1635, had enclosed with a hedge a parcel of the king's demesne containing twenty perches, and upon this had built a house or cottage where no house was previously <fine £3>.'

In 1670, it was claimed, before the grand justice of the court of eyre (in the last recorded sitting), that 'from time out of mind the commoners have had common of pasture for their cattle throughout the fence month' in return for payment.[134]

As with the fourteenth century, there is evidence for encroachment, this time not so much from assarts, but rather more from small paddocks and associated cottages at the edge of the forest affecting heathland margins. Indeed, in the later medieval and post-medieval periods, encroachment on the edge of the commons often took this form. The presentments of the regarders made at the king's court called the Swainmote held at Lyndhurst on the 27 June [1670], a perambulation was made by the foresters, verderers and regarders.[135]

In a sitting of the eyre that September, Arthur Oxford (a gentleman[136]) found he was a luckier man than Thomas Amyes:

> 'Arthur Oxford a forester for copperage timber. <pardoned>
> Arthur Oxford for cutting browsewood. <pardoned>
> Arthur Oxford, 13th February 1660, one oak *etc.* <pardoned>
> Thomas Amyes, 11th August 1660, for timber oak 10s., the cart and horses £5, and £5 for the fine, process immediate. <£10 10s>
> Arthur Oxford , 13th February 1660, a beech. <pardoned>[137]'

Perhaps more illuminating of the state of the forest is:

> 'we present that there has been both before and since 25th April 1660 great destruction and spoil made in the king's woods and coverts, but who made the same we do not know, saving only the greatest spoils have been made by the Foresters of

> keepers by their unlawful browsing in the winter, more for their own benefit and advantage than for the preservation of his majesty's deer…'[138]

There follows a list of the kings's demesne woods.

Subsequently, Thomas Butler and Giles Tarver of the bailiwick of Battramsley were presented for:

> 'Erecting and continuing sine the Act of Indemnity each of them a cottage on the freehold land of Nicholas Lambert of Battramsley'.

Also presented was

> 'Nicholas Durrant of the said bailiwick for erecting and continuing a cottage and enclosing twelve luggs of ground since the 25th April 1660'.[139]

In the 17th and 18th centuries, encroachment took place to the west in the Newtown area and to the north at Stoney Cross with London Minstead (east of Minstead) also an encroachment.[140] It may have been that encroachment from 'outsiders' were not so welcome, but nonetheless, it seemed commonplace in mid-seventeenth century, where for example, in October 1635 at the Minstead manorial court one Robert Whitehorn, who had apparently squatted on the manor common, was ordered to 'take away and level the Fence' and lay open four lugs (about 100 m^2) suggesting enclosure was by a bank and ditch. Actually, he evidently stayed, for the property is again recorded in 1655.[141] The economy, as indicated by records of the preservator from the regarder's return, was essentially pastoral and based in woodland industries, although there was limited arable production. Manorial control was seen as in retreat, but yet would be important if the forest system, at least as realised in the Middle Ages, was experiencing problems.[142]

At Minstead[143] there was evidently considerable activity during the seventeenth century that reflected a developed 'forest economy'. This was primarily concerned with charcoal production, with some families coming to specialise in in charcoal making, but also included a summertime saltmaking industry located on the coast, as well as iron making at Sowley (near to the Solent that would come to supply the Portsmouth Dockyards) and tin smelting (charcoal was shipped to Cornwall).

Indeed, over-zealous producers were brought before the forest courts for illegally cutting and coppicing crown woods, and there can be talk of a 'black economy' involving cutting, carting and sale of coppice products, although markets for underwood products were to decline throughout the seventeenth century. Illegal sales were commonplace. One John Martin was accused of selling two loads of 'cooper's boards' and so much cleft timber as five horses could draw to Salisbury or Fordingbridge as well as keeping 'buckett timber, for sale at his house (that is wood assigned for his own use, and not for sale).[144]

Encroachment was gathering pace in the eighteenth century.[145] However this was whether 'sanctioned' by authority or not (as in the case of 'squatter' encroachments) such developments show attempts to settle and even undertake

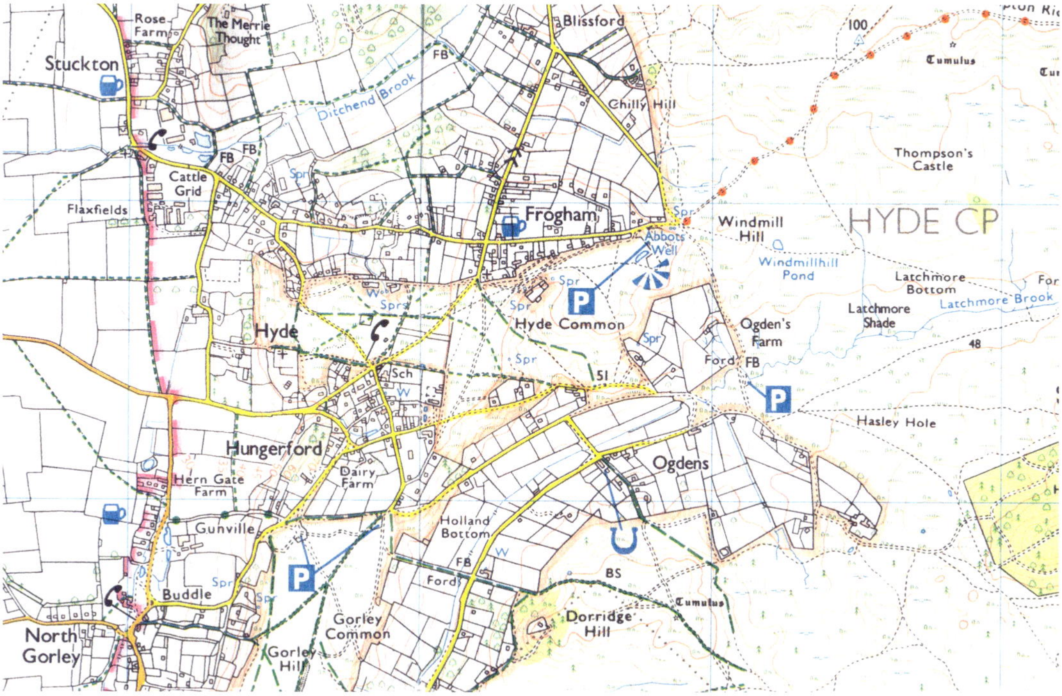

FIGURE 6.3. Examples of encroachment on the forest margins around Frogham from modern (1:25,000) OS mapping. The grid squares are 1 km.

agricultural activity in places from where they were previously excluded. The matter of encroachments will be returned to in the next chapter, for it continued into the eighteenth century.

Figure 6.3 shows encroachment at the forest margins, presumed to date from the seventeenth or eighteenth centuries. Discrete parcels of land, today individual cottages or as rectangular plots within the boundary of Hyde common but close to its boundary, are presumed to be the work of squatters. The three areas on the south side of Frogham and the larger area on the south side of the common are all associated with springs or wells for water supply. Such activity would seem to be a response by the poor to population pressures on land.

Conclusions

At the start of the time period covered by this chapter, monastic interests came to an end and by the latter part of 1540 there were no monastic houses left in England. However, apart from Beaulieu, direct impact on the landscape within the perambulation established by the Normans would be limited. Incomes hitherto appropriated by monasteries fell into lay hands, and with them such rights as grazing. The increasing complexity of the Tudor state is manifest in not only enquires, but the establishment of the post of 'General Surveyor of the King's Woods' and the like, together with their associated institutional arrangements, not only created the notorious *Divisum Imperium* but heralds real state intervention in forest resource management.

With Charles II the last monarch recorded as hunting in the New Forest, there was a general and steady decline in this activity by kings and nobles since at least Tudor times. With elements of commoners' rights preserving the interests of many forest dwellers encapsulated by the *Charter of the Forest* (1217) and recorded under statute in 1698, grazing pressures continued through the period covered in this chapter. The seventeenth century, one of tumultuous change in English society, brings pressure on land from squatter encroachments and possible from an increase locally in the amount of ploughland.

Crown interests would come into potential conflict with those of the more financially astute exchequer with a new governance system represented in the Office of General Surveyor. This was to create the famed *Divisum Imperium* that has its origin with its origins in the early sixteenth century. From then onwards, the traditional system (with the Lord Warden at its head administering the forest laws) would be at variance with more direct state interest.

With dramatic changes in governance, it might be expected that there would be more forward thinking in management and auditing. In some ways this seems true, for rigorous quantitative surveys appear at this time as do learned treatises on the forest law and early silviculture. Yet, with sometime neglect from the monarch to pay traditional officials and with the exchequer becoming responsible for sales of timber during the sixteenth century, options for corruption seemed to have grown significantly.

It is as if an Elizabethan experiment with 'coppices' managed in some form, was doomed to fail, something that would impact on poorer members of society, for state interests that favoured tall trees moved in. The landscape displays only former coppice enclosures and the practice of creating new pollards was banned. Tall forest trees, mainly oak, were cultivated for battleship construction with often ambitious plans for 'rolling inclosure' that was never to be popular with graziers, but at least their interests became enshrined in statute. The New Forest is to witness something almost anathema to the medieval mind: the deliberate cultivation of tall trees on an even-age plantation system. This is the rise of true 'forestry' as is understood today.

Notes

1. D. J. Stagg (1974) The *Orders and Rules of the New Forest* AD 1537. *Proceedings of the Hampshire Field Club and Archaeological Society*, New Forest Section report 13, 33–38.
2. Animal rights history: Sir Thomas Moore. http://www.animalrightshistory.org/animal-rights-c1450-1660/renaissance-m/mor-thomas-more/1516-utopia-hunting-hawking.htm. Accessed March 2014.
3. Henry VIII in Hampshire and the Isle of Wight. http://news.bbc.co.uk/local/hampshire/hi/people_and_places/history/newsid_8157000/8157452.stm. Accessed Sept 2017.
4. New Forest history. http://www.newforest.hampshire.org.uk/history2.html. Accessed Jan 2014.
5. C. R. Tubbs (2001) *New Forest, the History, Ecology and Conservation*, 52. New Forest Ninth Centenary Trust, Fordingbridge.
6. See Chapter 4.

7. R. Reeves (2008) *To Enquire and Conspire. New Forest Documents 1533–1615*, xxxiii. New Forest Record Series 5, New Forest Ninth Centenary Trust, Fordingbridge.
8. *Ibid.*, xxiv.
9. *Ibid.*, xviii; R. Reeves (2007) *Preservation and Decay. New Forest Documents 1565–1624*, xl. New Forest Record Series V. New Forest Ninth Centenary Trust, Fordingbridge.
10. See also Chapter 7.
11. D. J. Stagg (1989) Silvicultural Inclosures in the New Forest to 1780. *Proceedings of the Hampshire Field Club and Archaeological Society* 45, 135–45.
12. New Forest history *op. cit.* in note 4.
13. History of the Crown Lands (n.d.) https://www.forestry.gov.uk/pdf/eng-new-forest-b2-history.pdf/$FILE/eng-new-forest-b2-history.pdf. Accessed Sept 2017.
14. Reeves (2008) *op. cit.* in note 7, xxxv.
15. P. Roberts (2002) *Minstead: life in a New Forest community*. Nova Foresta Publishing, Lyndhurst.
16. M. Baskerville (2009) The use of land at Buckholt, a Hampshire Royal Forest from 1200–1900. *Proceedings of the Hampshire Field Club and Archaeological Society* 64, 200–22.
17. Reeves (2008) *op. cit.* in note 7, xxxviii.
18. *Ibid.,* xvii.
19. Stagg (1974) *op. cit.* in note 1, 33.
20. Reeves (2008) *op. cit.* in note 7, xl.
21. Tubbs (2001) *op. cit.* in note 5, 80.
22. *Ibid.*, 81.
23. Stagg (1974) *op. cit.* in note 1.
24. T. B James and C. Gerrard (2007) *Clarendon, Landscape of Kings*, 115. Windgather Press, Macclesfield.
25. http://www.kwacs.org.uk/vermin.htm. Accessed Jan 2014.
26. Calendar of Treasury Papers 1708–1714, 1712 about 24 Feb? [in margin] CLVIII 54. Supplied by Peter Roberts.
27. Tubbs (2001) *op. cit.* in note 5, 80.
28. Stagg (1974) *op. cit.* in note 1, 34.
29. http://www.historyofparliamentonline.org/volume/1820-1832/member/sturges-bourne-william-1769-1845.
30. Parishes: Lyndhurst. In *Victoria County History, Hampshire* 4 (1911), 630–34. http://www.british-history.ac.uk/report.aspx?compid=56900 Accessed 25 September 2010.
31. Reeves (2007) *op. cit.* in note 9, pxxxvi.
32. *Ibid.*, xl.
33. *Ibid.,* xli.
34. E. M. Yates (1985) *The Landscape of the New Forest in Medieval Times*, 23. Dept of Geography, King's College London.
35. Reeves (2007) *op. cit.* in note 9, xl.
36. *Ibid.*, xlvi.
37. *Ibid.*, xxxiv.
38. *Ibid.*, xix.
39. *Ibid.*, xxxv.
40. *Ibid.*, xxxvi.
41. Stagg (1974) *op. cit.* in note 1.
42. R. Midmer (1979) *English Medieval Monasteries*. Hineman, London.
43. Yates (1985) *op. cit.* in note 34, 26.
44. New Forest Association (n.d.) *A History of the New Forest and its Adjacent Commons*, New Forest Association, Fordingbridge.

45. Victoria County History, Hampshire and the Isle of Wight 2 (1912), 144–45.
46. Yates (1985) *op. cit.* in note 34, 43.
47. England Under the Tudors (2012) http://www.luminarium.org/encyclopedia/wriothesley.htm. Accessed Sept 2017.
48. New Forest Record Series. http://www.newforestcentre.org.uk/uploads/publications/6.pdf. Accessed Sept 2017.
49. *Ibid.*, xviii.
50. National Archives (2012) http://www.nationalarchives.gov.uk/records/research-guides/dissolution-of-the-monasteries.htm. Accessed Sept 2017.
51. Reeves (2008) *op. cit.* in note 7, xxxiii.
52. *Ibid.*, xix.
53. See Chapter 3.
54. Tubbs (2001) *op. cit.* in note 5, 216.
55. Tubbs (2001) *op. cit.*, 79.
56. History of the Crown Lands (n.d.) www.forestry.gov.uk/pdf/eng-new-forest.../eng-new-forest-b2-history.pdf. accessed Sept 2017.
57. Reeves (2008) *op. cit.* in note 7, xxxii..
58. *Ibid.*, xvii–xviii.
59. Preservation and Decay. http://www.newforestcentre.org.uk/uploads/publications/6.pdf. Accessed Sept 2017.
60. B. Vesey-Fitzgerald (1966) *Portrait of the New Forest*, 93. Robert Hale, London.
61. *Ibid.*, 95.
62. Tubbs (2001) *op. cit.* in note 5, 85.
63. Reeves (2008) *op. cit.* in note 7, xxiv.
64. Seeing the Forests for the Trees (n.d.) http://info.sjc.ox.ac.uk/forests/tw.html. Accessed Oct 2012.
65. *Encyclopaedia Britannica* (1911) http://www.1911encyclopedia.org/New_Forest.
66. http://web.mac.com/calhounabode/Manwood/Intro_to_Manwood.html; J. Manwood (1665) *A Treatise and Discourse on the Laws of the Forest.*
67. M. Netzloff (ed.) (2010) *John Norden's A Surveyor's Dialogue 1618: a critical edition.* Ashgate, Farmham.
68. Tubbs (2001) *op. cit.* in note 5, 81.
69. http://www.newforest.hampshire.org.uk/history2.html. Accessed March 2014.
70. Tubbs (2001) *op. cit.* in note 5, 81.
71. C. Tubbs (1964) Early encoppicements in the New Forest. *Forestry* 37, 95–105.
72. P. A. J. Pettit (1968) *The Royal Forests of Northamptonshire: a study of their Economy 1558–1714*, 37. Northampton Record Society, Northumberland Press, Gateshead.
73. *Ibid.*, 74–80.
74. Tubbs (2001) *op. cit.* in note 5, 85.
75. Pettit (1968) *op. cit.* in note 72, 104.
76. Reeves (2007) *op. cit.* in note 7, xxii.
77. D. J. Stagg (1986) *Commoners of the New Forest*, 9–10. New Forest Association, Stockbridge.
78. Tubbs (2001) *op. cit.* in note 5, 85–86.
79. Reeves (2007) *op. cit.* in note 7.
80. Verderers' Court. www./.verderers.org/court.html.
81. J. Bond (1994) Forests, chases, warrens and parks in medieval Wessex, 121–23. In *The Medieval Landscape of Wessex*, M. Ashton and C. Lewis (eds), 130. Oxbow Monograph 6, Oxbow Books, Oxford.
82. D. Cobb (1974) Forest trees and ships. *Proceedings of the Hampshire Field Club and Archaeological Society*, New Forest Section Report 13, 28–29.

83. NFNP (n.d.) www.newforest.hampshire.org.uk/history3.html. Accessed Jan 2014.
84. G. F. Peterkin (1981) *Woodland Conservation and Management*. Chapman Hall, London.
85. Tubbs (2001) *op. cit.* in note 5, 82.
86. *Ibid.*
87. R. Daponte (2004) Open forest http://www.forestry.gov.uk/pdf/AncientOrnamentalwoodland.pdf/$FILE/AncientOrnamentalwoodland.pdf. Accessed Sept 2017.
88. E. Kerridge (1967) *The Agricultural Revolution*, 15. Allen & Unwin, London.
89. M. Overton (2011) Agricultural Revolution in England 1500–1850 http://www.bbc.co.uk/history/british/empire_seapower/agricultural_revolution_01.shtml.
90. New Forest Committee (1947) *The Baker Report*, 8. Forestry Commission cmd 7245, HMSO, London.
91. Tubbs (2001) *op. cit.* in note 5, 85; P. Roberts pers. comm. (2014).
92. Reeves (2007) *op. cit.* in note 7.
93. Cobb (1974) *op. cit.* In 82.
94. Stagg (1989) *op. cit.* in note 11.
95. Pettit (1968) *op. cit.* in note 72, 70.
96. Roberts (2002) *op. cit.* in note 15, 19.
97. W. Blith (1649/1652) *The English Improver Improved, or the Survey of Husbandry Surveyed* (2nd edn). Printed for John Wright, London.
98. The National Mapping Programme 2013. Report No: 2013R47. http://www.newforestww2.org/uploads/publications/52.pdf, 60–61.
99. D. J. Stagg (1979) *A Calendar of New Forest Documents AD 1244–1334*, 5. Hampshire Record Series III, Hampshire County Council, Winchester.
100. *Ibid.*, 6.
101. O. Rackham (2006) *Woodlands*, 448. Collins, London.
102. E. Preston and S. Wallis (2006) *The Forest of Bere*, 20. Halsgrove, Wellington.
103. Peterken (1981) *op. cit.* in note 84, 17.
104. *Ibid.*, 16.
105. http://www.newforest.hampshire.org.uk/history2.html.
106. Chapter 6.
107. D. J. Stagg (ed.) (1983) *A Calendar of New Forest Documents: the fifteenth and sixteenth centuries*, x. Hampshire Record Series, Hampshire County Council, Winchester; P. Roberts pers. comm (2014).
108. Stagg (1983) *op. cit.* xxxi–xxxii.
109. *Ibid.*, x.
110. J. R. Wise (1883) *The New Forest Its History and Scenery*, 44. Sotheran, London.
111. Historic legacy and Management http://www.forestry.gov.uk/pdf/eng-new-forest-b2-history.pdf/$FILE/eng-new-forest-b2-history.pdf.
112. Reeves (2008) *op. cit.* in note 7, xxxv.
113. P. Roberts pers. comm. (2014).
114. *op. cit.* note 93
115. Stagg (1974) *op. cit.* in note 1, 33.
116. *Ibid.*, 35.
117. http://www.newforest.hampshire.org.uk/history3.html.
118. P. Roberts pers. comm. (2014); TNA PRO E 178/6453.
119. http://www.newforest.hampshire.org.uk/history3.html p86. Accessed March 2014.
120. C. Hill (1972) *The World Turned Upside Down*. Penguin History, London.
121. *Ibid.*, 54.
122. E. Vallance (2009) *A Radical History of Britain*, 172–202. Abacus, London.
123. Hill (1972) *op. cit.* in 120, 15.

124. *Ibid.*, 320.
125. P. Roberts pers. comm. (2014).
126. Victoria County History (1911) *op. cit.* in note 11.
127. Yates (1985) *op. cit.* in note 34, 36.
128. Tubbs (2001) *op. cit.* in note 5, 82.
129. Tubbs (1964) *op. cit.* in note 71.
130. Stagg (1983) *op. cit.* in note 107, note 414, p. 67.
131. *Ibid.*, p. 88.
132. *Ibid.*, p. 90.
133. *Ibid.*, p. 95.
134. Tubbs (2001) *op. cit.* in note 5, 80.
135. Stagg (1983) *op. cit.* in note 107, 232–37.
136. *Ibid.*, p. 130.
137. *Ibid.*, p. 204.
138. *Ibid.*, p. 238.
139. *Ibid.*, p. 237.
140. http://www.newforestnpa.gov.uk/fcsforweb.pdf. Accessed March 2014.
141. Roberts (2002) *op. cit.* in note 15, 36.
142. *Ibid.*, 116.
143. *Ibid.*, chapters 5–6.
144. *Ibid.*, 94.
145. N. Smith (1999) The Earthwork remains of enclosure in the New Forest, 34. *Proceedings of the Hampshire Field Club and Archaeological Society* 54, 1–56.

CHAPTER 7

Decline of the Old Ways (1660–1900)

'Bygone Acts of Parliament, and Reports of Select Parliamentary Committees appointed to enquire into this or that burning question, are not generally read once, twice & again' Heywood Sumner *c.*1930.[1]

Planting and counting the hearts of oak

The period covered by this chapter is from the late seventeenth century to approximately 1890. It presents changing values towards 'production forestry' and closer integration in the national economy, and begins a scrutiny of the relationship of the forest with the surrounding economy. While remaining a discrete area with a clear identity, the New Forest moved towards better economic integration with the national economy precisely because it was tasked with timber production. Once the preserve of kings, the forest became a part of the national land resource; the question was now how to optimise its assumed economic function of growing trees.

The impact of John Evelyn's book *Sylva* (1664)[2] was profound. It had been produced and promoted by the Royal Society at a time when timber was being replaced by new fuels such as coal. Evelyn, we infer, was from the other side of the contemporary political spectrum to the parliamentarian supporter and 'improver' Blith (Chapter 6) and very much a 'restoration man'. He expressed concerned about neglect, and hence lost opportunity for profit from more economically marginal lands[3] with the aim of maximising timber production in the national interest, and the widespread establishment of plantations was advocated.[4] Where the barrister Manwood had sought to shed light on the forest laws, and the surveyor Norden had engaged in some systematic environmental auditing, Evelyn was very much in the scientific agricultural improver mould. Certainly the intellectual equipment was now in place for a thorough development of silviculture at a time when the country was concerned about the strength of its navy.

Evelyn's book on forest trees and the propagation of timber (Fig. 7.1) was originally delivered as a paper to the Royal Society. Probably the first treatise on timber production, it reflects the concerns of the day. The author castigated the decline of England's woods during the Commonwealth, and was clearly responding to a need to produce more timber. Evelyn was furthermore a friend of that other diarist, Samuel Pepys, who held the offices of clerk of the office of Privy Seal and clerk of the acts of the navy from 1660.

Probably the most embarrassing event in British naval history (and worse

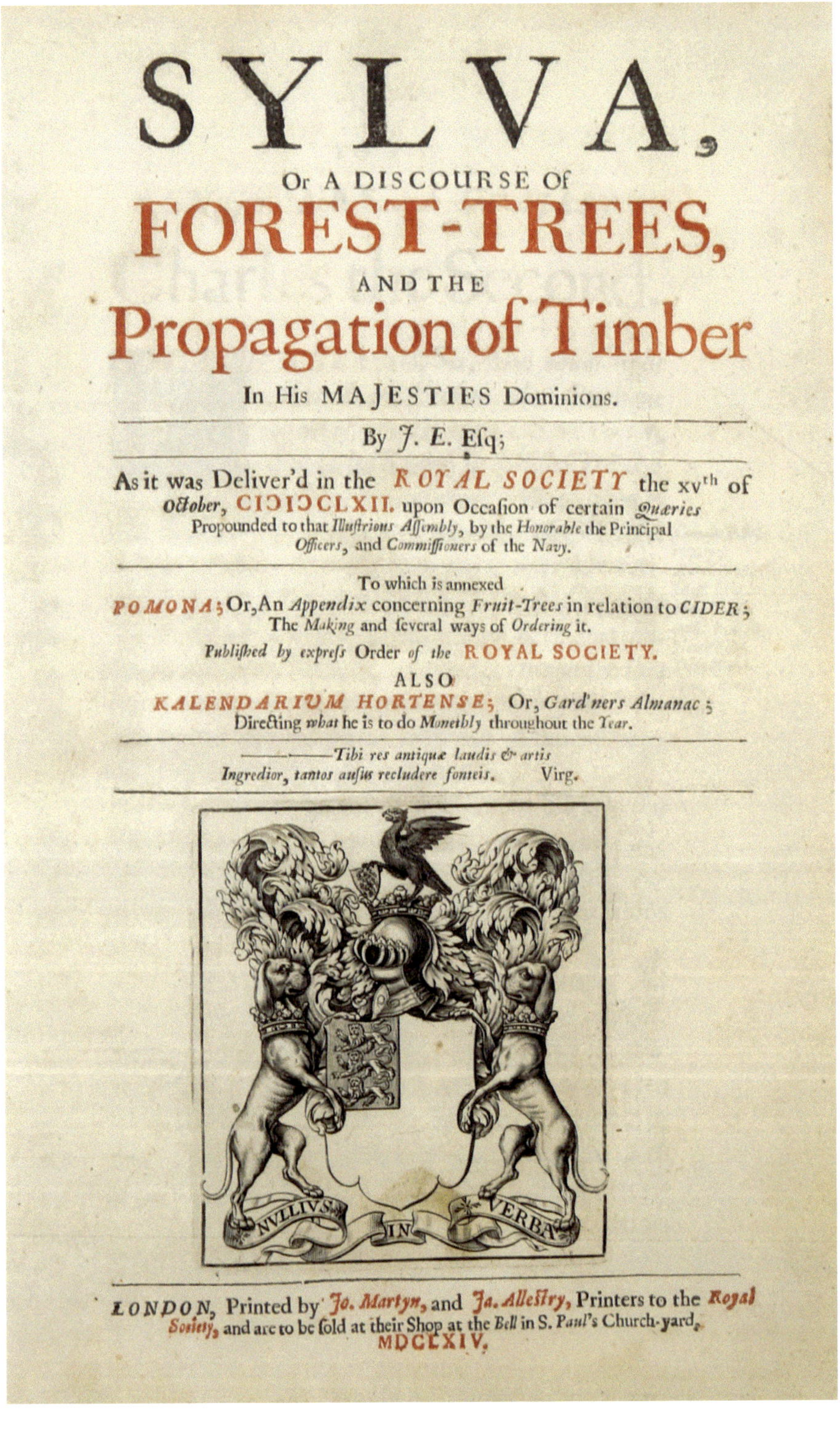

SYLVA,

Or A DISCOURSE Of

FOREST-TREES,

AND THE

Propagation of Timber

In His MAJESTIES Dominions.

By *J. E.* Eſq;

As it was Deliver'd in the *ROYAL SOCIETY* the xvth of *October*, CIƆIƆCLXII. upon Occaſion of certain *Quæries* Propounded to that *Illuſtrious Aſſembly*, by the *Honorable* the Principal *Officers*, and *Commiſſioners* of the *Navy*.

To which is annexed

POMONA; Or, An *Appendix* concerning *Fruit-Trees* in relation to *CIDER*; The *Making* and ſeveral ways of *Ordering* it.

Publiſhed by expreſs Order *of the* ROYAL SOCIETY.

ALSO

KALENDARIUM HORTENSE; Or, *Gard'ners Almanac*; Directing *what* he is to do *Monethly* throughout the *Year*.

——*Tibi res antiquæ laudis & artis*
Ingredior, tantos auſus recludere fonteis. Virg.

NVLLIVS IN VERBA

LONDON, Printed by *Jo. Martyn*, and *Ja. Alleſtry*, Printers to the *Royal Society*, and are to be ſold at their Shop at the *Bell* in S. *Paul's* Church-yard, MDCLXIV.

FIGURE 7.1. The front cover of John Evelyn's (1664) *Sylva, or a Discourse of Forest Trees.*

BY PERMISSION OF PHILIP SERRELL AUCTIONEERS

than the loss of the *Mary Rose*) occurred in June 1667, when the Dutch fleet crippled the Royal Navy in a raid on the Chatham Naval Dockyards on the Medway in Kent.[5] He was consequently determined to reverse the decline in naval fortunes, and in 1673, he was promoted secretary for the affairs of the navy. From 1684, he oversaw a great recovery in the navy, so that the number of ships increased from 24 to 92 three years later.[6] More and taller timber trees would be needed, but there were also many problems that would conflict with that objective.

The requirements of the navy for timber superseded the effective breakdown of the forest law. The commoners had claimed the right to de-pasture stock on the forest throughout the year and were not apparently constrained by the Fence Month. Daniel Defoe passed through the forest around 1720, remarking that there was plenty of timber on the shore of one river that was bound for the Portsmouth shipyards; prior to that there had been much felling during the reign of William III.[7] Defoe could find 'no signs of decay of our woods, or of the danger of our wanting timber in England', something that conflicted with the official (government) view of resource scarcity.

Timber production through plantation had won the land use conflict over hunting, pollarding and coppice, but the locals would continue to experience difficulty in this brave new world. The first statutory inclosure was in 1700 at Vinney Ridge, following the 1698 enclosure legislation (Chapter 6).[8] Further Acts were to follow to ensure timber production. Unfortunately, on 26 November 1703, a great storm hit southern England. Evidently, this was of the same order of magnitude as that of 15/16 October 1987 and uprooted around 4000 oak trees.

In all, four surveys of resources had been undertaken between 1608 and 1783 because estimates of trees considered fit for the navy stood at 123,927 in 1608, falling to 12,476 by 1707 (a survey prompted by the storm). This decline was attributed to devastation during the Civil War period. Subsequently, an increase to 19,836 by 1764, then a fall once more to 12,447 by 1783 failed to impress the commissioners writing the *Fifth Report*.[9] There was a crisis in production, and furthermore inquisitions into New Forest governance and management during this period cried out for reform, the consequences reached far into Governmental and crown interests. If, in the early seventeenth century the New Forest contained almost 124,000 timber trees, 24,000 could be spared. There were 118,000 loads of 'Fyrewood and decayed Trees'. By then, coppice amounted to only some 1304 acres (520 ha) and there were reported 96 acres (39 ha) of Aldermoore. Between about 1670 and 1673 some 100 acres (40 ha) of coppice was enclosed at Holmhill, and a further 300 acres (121 ha) at Aldridgehill and Holiday's Hill, for 'nursery and supply of timber'.[10]

Inclosure areas with trees of sufficient size were opened for grazing and elsewhere further areas were subsequently planted. This was 'rolling afforestation' and inevitably it would lead to friction between commoners and the Crown. There was also evidence of neglect. After 1760 management was in decline and, apparently, the resulting record levels of grazing prevented natural regeneration, tending the forest towards a mature canopy of trees. This situation was to continue until 1851 when it was noted the understory dominated by holly developed.[11] There were two further enabling Acts; one for 'statutory inclosures' in 1808 and the *Deer Removal Act* 1851,[12] so the total area under statutory inclosure (Table 7.1) amounted to 7023 acres (2844 ha) in the mid-nineteenth century, and was rising. Actually, while these figures are indicative of land use change, some enclosures were thrown open for grazing and subsequently wholly or partly re-enclosed.[13]

There were to be dramatic changes that reflected the demands of forestry from within crown lands, to encroachment on the commons, and industrialisation on a scale perhaps not hitherto experienced. As an illustration, between 1775 and 1815, the displacement tonnage of the Royal Navy doubled for ships greater than 500 tons, to peak around in 1810, estimated at above 600,000 tons,[14] exceeding that for other European power at the time. The following period saw a move away from timber ships towards iron hulls and, as if by compensation, there was an observable rise in the perceived aesthetic value in the forest. In addition to shipbuilding, there was construction-based industry and the manufacture of small domestic items. There was also a heavily taxed salt-making industry around Lymington that may have dated from the Iron Age in the seventeenth and eighteenth centuries.[15]

TABLE 7.1 *(below and opposite)*. Statutory Inclosures formed under the *New Forest* Acts of 1698, 1808 and 1851 (1 acre = 0.4047 ha).

HTTP://WWW.FORESTRY.GOV.UK/PDF/ENG-NEW-FOREST-B3-INCLOSURES-PLAN.PDF/$FILE/ENG-NEW-FOREST-B3-INCLOSURES-PLAN.PDF

Inclosures made under the 1698 New Forest Act			**Inclosures made under the 1808 New Forest Act**			**Inclosures made under the 1851 New Forest Act (Deer Removal Act)**		
Date	*Name*	*Acreage*	*Date*	*Name*	*Acreage*	*Date*	*Name*	*Acreage*
*c.*1700	Priors Acre	136	1808	Hurst Hill	181	1852	Frame Heath	420
	Salisbury Trench	100		Wootton	410		Broadley	176
	Puckpits	77		Holly Hatch	150		Island Thorns	492
	Rhinefield Old	177		New Copse	281			
	Burley Old	122				1853	Park Hill	694
	Woodfidley	295		1809 Broomy	225		Oakley	823
	Roe Old	93		Wilverley (reinclosed)	500			
				Rhinefield Sandys (reinclosed)	224	1859	Dames Slough	358
*c.*1751	Etherise	102		Aldridge Hill (reinclosed)	128		Vinney Ridge	359
	Blackbush	34		Stockley	131		Pound Hill	236
	Pignal	94						
			1810	Godshill	384	1860	Shave Green	246
*c.*1768	Aldridge Hill	132		Burley New	330		Brockis Hill	160
	Ocknell	248		Lodge Hill	138		Denny Lodge	280
	Pitts	121		Church Place	177			
	Sloden	250				1861	Milkham	394
	Coppice of Linwood	289	1811	Norley Wood	163			
				Holmsley	345	1862	Slufters	371

Inclosures made under the 1698 New Forest Act			**Inclosures made under the 1808 New Forest Act**			**Inclosures made under the 1851 New Forest Act (Deer Removal Act)**		
Date	*Name*	*Acreage*	*Date*	*Name*	*Acreage*	*Date*	*Name*	*Acreage*
*c.*1775	Furzey Lawn	79		Anderwood	169	1864	Sloden	306
	Long Beach	146		Roe Wood	342		Busketts Lawn	342
	Wilverley	480		Set Thorns	318			
	Raven's Nest	74		Holidays Hill	164	1866	Perry Wood	794
	Rhinefield Sandys	225		Northerwood	16			
						1867	Deer Leap	302
Total		**3274**	1817	Amberwood	214		Knights Wood	563
				Holm Hill	285			
				Ramnor	107	1868	Kings Garn	304
				King's Copse	159			
				Shepherd's Copse	12	1869	Highland Water	786
				Folds Gate Hill	22	1870	Denny	462
				Stubby Copse	112		Hawkhill	394
				Woosen's Hill	84			
				Bramshaw Wood	63	**Total**		**9262**
				Costilcles	45			
				Black Knowle	6			
				Over Corner	6			
				Fletcher's Hill	74			
				Ivy Wood	20			
				Ramnor New	30			
				Appleslade	87			
				Little Holm Hill	38			
				Bratley	46			
				Backley	42			
				Beech End	77			
			1843	Buckford	38			
				Clumber	48			
				Ferny Knapp	21			
				New Stubby Copse	132			
				King's Hat	66			
				Foxhunting	90			
			1848	Linford	203			
				Hasley	90			
				Pignal Hill	30			
			Total		**7023**			

Source: D. Stagg, *Proceedings of the Hampshire Field Club* vols 45, 46, 48.
N.B. Records of inclosure dates vary slightly between different sources.

The 'Drivers', their map and the General Surveyor

The driver (both literally and metaphorically) was now timber production and it was state interests that would conflict with both traditional forest dwellers and also the marginalised poor. *A General View of the Agriculture of the County of Hants*, written by Abraham and William Driver and published in 1794, objectively states that:

> 'The New Forest is situated on the south side of Hampshire; it was formerly bounded on the east by Southampton River, and on the south by the British Channel, being near thirty miles in length, and ninety in circumference; but since the disafforestations of Henry the Third and Edward the First, its boundaries are much reduced, and now only extends from Godshill, on the north-west, to the sea, on the south-east, about twenty miles, and from Hardley, on the east, to Kingwood, on the west, about fifteen miles; containing within those limits about 92,365 acres, the whole of which does not now belong to the Crown: as several manors and freehold estates, to amount of 24,797 acres, are private property; about 625 are copyhold, belonging to his Majesty's manor of Lyndhurst; 1004 acres are leasehold, held under the Crown; 902 acres are encroachments; 1193 acres are held by the master-keepers and groom-keepers, attached to their respective lodges; and the remaining 63,844 acres are the woods and was land of the forest. In all the freeholds subject to the regard of the forest, which are of the nature of purlieus, the Crown reserves certain rights'.[16]

Published through the Board of Agriculture, *A General View* reiterates the forest was a discrete entity within a clear perambulation. It also displays the preoccupations of the late eighteenth century. These were land ownership (a modern economist would prefer to term 'property rights'), a desire for accurate surveying, resource survey and even a preoccupation with Britishness (for the adjective 'English' is replaced by 'British' for the Channel!) The 902 acres (365 ha) of encroachments are 'chiefly [made] by poor people', or otherwise by neighbouring estates (Chapter 6).

There is an impressive list of forest officers: The Lord Warden (The Duke of Gloucester), The Lieutenant, The Riding Forester, a Bowbearer, two Rangers, a 'Woodward', an Under Woodward, four 'Verdurers', a High Steward, an Under Steward, 12 Regarders, 9 Foresters or Master Keepers or Master keepers (of the nine Baliwicks) and 13 (lately 15) Under Foresters or Groom Keepers 'of the 15 walks'. There were also a Surveyor General of the Woods and Forests (but not only to the New Forest), his deputy, a Purveyor of the Navy, paid by the Navy Board and appointed by the Portsmouth dockyard.

The Drivers, who were apparently not prepared to list in detail the expected duties of each officer, comment:

> 'if each officer were to do his duty, without considering his private emolument, it would tend much to the increase and preservation of the timber in this forest; whereas on the contrary, it is important that the interests of all the inferior officers so clash with that of the forest, that it is vain to expect either a preservation of the timber now growing in the forest, or an increase from new plantations, while the present system remains, as it clearly appeared to us from the survey we made of the New Forest in 1787, by order of the Commissioners of Land Revenue ...'[17]

The diatribe was aimed at the under-keepers. These were petty officials who obtained emoluments from deer, sale of browse wood, rabbits and swine considered inimical to the preservation of timber. The authors blamed insufficient salaries for these under-keepers. Then the forest was, in their opinion, badly overstocked with deer, neither were the crown lands clearly demarked from those of the commoners. Timber production was being impaired by the crown officials not working in any interest other than their own. Elsewhere, this would have been regarded as blatant corruption.

Legislation supporting timber production was strengthened. The *Preservation of Timber Acts* (1765–1766) ended offences under the forest laws,[18] although penalties for transgression now included transportation and it has been noted that forest courts were, by now, infrequent. At the highest level, by 1780 the Whig statesman Edmund Burke's economic reforms achieved considerable success.[19] A part of this process was a reform of the Civil List, the list of individuals to whom money is paid by the government. Consequently, upon his accession in 1760, George III surrendered the hereditary revenues from the crown estates to Parliament; it was decided that Parliament would assume responsibility and pay the expenses of the royal household and some of the costs of the civil government. This process has been repeated ever since.[20]

The British establishment was worried. In 1789, a Royal Commission published *The Fifth Report* and accompanying map on the New Forest at a scale of 4 inches to 1 mile (1:15,840).[21] The commissioners of the Land Revenue painted a bleak picture for the governance of the New Forest. It related to the perambulation during the reign of Charles II 'from Godshill on the north-west to the sea, on the southeast about twenty miles, and from Hardley on the east to Ringwood on the West, about fifteen miles [24 km] and contains within about 92,365 acres [37,408 ha], statute measure.'

The Fifth Report recalls earlier perambulations, but it was not found easy to account for the reduction of the forest area of the New Forest in the reign of Edward I, although dis-afforestation had occurred during the reigns of Henry II, Richard I and John. A 1:63,360 scale map of Hampshire had been published in 1791 by Thomas Milne (see Fig. 8.1) but more detail would be required. There was concern at a high level for the management of the forest, with surveys undertaken in 1786/87 by four surveyors and generally known as 'Drivers' map'; for the first time there was an accurate account of the forest boundaries.[22]

Figure 7.2 shows a segment of this map, second edition published in 1814. The formal title of the map is:

> 'A Plan of His Majesty's Forest, called the New Forest, in the County of Southampton. Laid down from surveys undertaken by Thos. Richardson, Wm. King and ABm. and Wm. Driver. By order of the Commissioners of the Land Revenue, appointed by Act of Parliament passed in the 26th year of King George IIId. Engraved and published by order of the said Commissioners, by William Faden, Geographer to the King, MDCCLXXXIX'.

FIGURE 7.2. The segment of the Drivers' map depicting Burley Manor. The Wilverley Inclosure is in the south-east, Burley Lodge is on the eastern magin and the manor abuts those of Bisterne and Ringwood to the west. See also Table 7.1.

HTTP://WWW.NEWFOREST.HAMPSHIRE.ORG.UK/HISTORIC_MAPS/MAPS_INTRO.HTML

The Drivers emerge as typical surveyors and resource auditors reflecting the contemporary concerns over natural resources. Timber production joined food security in time of war. One political manifestation of this concern to audit and manage natural resources was the governmental Board of Agriculture established in 1793 and considered interventionist. This was the time of intervention in corn importation and export, the well-known 'Corn Laws'. The great fear was disruption of food supply through naval blockade, as the British establishment wrestled with fears around the permeation of ideas arising from revolutionary France.[23] The forest was bound to come under great scrutiny for its ability to grow timber, and conveniently close to the south coast of England that was accessible by river.

There remained problems arguably greater than those that beset food production. At best, the forest system was seen as an unreformed medieval legal system, at worst, there was identifiable corruption exacted by forest officers. Yet, ironically, a commission of enquiry advised against dis-afforestation of the New Forest, probably because the crown award (compensation) would have been small, compared with that which might have been received by the commoners. However, the Crown was in favour of powers to increase silviculture. The Commissioners of Woods, Forests, Land Revenues, Works, and Buildings (under that name since 1832), or to be short the 'Office of Woods', was to strengthen its powers over the next 70 years, a recipe for conflict caused through re-enacting lapsed powers and reducing commoners' rights.

Intent to reform was seen in the *New Forest Bill* of 1792. Introduced by William Pitt to further increase the preservation of timber, it proposed limited compensation for loss of common rights; this showed intentions, however it was not taken to an Act of Parliament, although the role of the Surveyor General of Woods was strengthened eventually to the detriment of the Lord Warden's Office.[24] This would appear a late manifestation of the *Divisum Imperium* between the offices of the Lord Warden and the Surveyor General in the Office of Woods.

Not all the area in the *Fifth Report* was, in fact, crown land. The commissioners report several freehold estates (24,797 acres or 10,043 ha) as well as manors. There were leasehold, copyhold and remaining customary tenants, 901 acres (4432 ha) of purprestres (encroachments). Master keepers and groom keepers had enclosed almost 1200 acres (486 ha). In all there was still 63,845 acres (25,857 ha) of woods and waste land. 'Incroachments' comprised mostly cottages and small adjoining plots of land by poor people. 'The Incroachments are held at present without paying any rent or acknowledgement to the Crown; but having generally, if not in every Instance, been presented at the Forest Courts and ordered to be pulled down and laid open…'. Evidently crown ownership was to be presumed to remain owners and the squatters were miscreants. Furthermore, in addition to complaints about the state of the inclosure fences, the stealing of young trees or branches for charcoal hearths and irregular cutting of fern, heath, furze, turf and peat.[25]

The *Fifth Report* also reveals a lapse in hitherto common practice:

> 'to those who have a right of common, swine and cattle of all kinds, commonable or not commonable, are suffered to go into the Forest at all Times, without Regard to the fence Month and Winter Haining and without any restrictions as to Number, or Proof that they belong.'

The plight of the poor taking advantage of slack governance was one thing; corruption by forest officers quite another. Officers of the forest had been found to be 'counteracting judicious plans since 1608'.[26] For example, the regarders chosen (like the verderers) from among the freeholders and whose duty it was to survey the forest resources, were themselves marketing trees to be felled. In the Bailiwicks of Godshill and Linwood[27] forest rents had, for many years, been let out or farmed out to under-keepers for a sum paid to the use of the Lord Warden. The latter apparently also benefited from agistment or profit for herbage and pannage (via his steward) that the commissioners regarded as being due to the Crown. Apparently, no agisters or verminers had been appointed for close to a century,[28] although there is a record of a verminer in 1712 and again in 1756.[29] Percival Lewis, writing in 1811, mentions agisters,[30] but only in an historical context. He too is greatly concerned with the poor condition of the forest and calls for legislation to provide for better management in the interest of the navy.[31]

The survey notes that accompany the *Fifth Report* are clear:

> 'We propose that a nursery should be established in a central part of the forest for the production of different kinds of forest trees and firs that a proper person should be appointed to reside on the spot who undertakes the mode of cultivation the different species of plants required and planting in general: that he should have a proper assistance according to the size of the Nursery, which need not exceed ten acres and should have a proper salary allowed him and not suffered to make any advantage whatever of the produce to himself'.[32]

John Evelyn would have been agreed that scientific investigations into timber production were called for, and moves were clearly afoot to improve both timber production and to improve governance by reducing inefficiency and corruption. The *Fifth Report* is angling to solve a dual problem of poor pay for officials (allegedly leading to corruption) with incentivised nursery cultivation for young trees.

Office of Woods and the arrival of big government?

Politically, the *Divisum Imperium,* that is the division of powers between the Lord Warden to 1850 and the 'Office of Woods', was to be a source of significant political strife such that one would have to give way. Institutional and legal reform would bring the balance firmly to favour governmental interest or to be specific, the interest of timber production before the rights of commoners were re-asserted. Much as Britain evolved a Ministry of Agriculture to support agricultural production (today subsumed within the Department for Environment Food and Rural Affairs) from the Board of Agriculture in the late eighteenth century[33] forestry institutions were to evolve in parallel. The Office of Woods would become the Forestry Commission in 1919.[34]

The Crown, as sovereign landowner, retained the ancient officers including the Lord Warden until 1850 and would use the ancient forest laws to enforce its interests, although by this time game conservation was a thing of the past. The Crown was to become, for reasons of strategic naval warfare, a promoter of tall trees, then a maximiser of profit by providing for a range of timber into various domestic markets. The Office of Woods was to usurp this role. The commoners, who jealously guarded their rights of grazing and fuel-gathering, saw this as a conflict. In this dispute, the governance changed with the verderers coming to largely represent commoners' interests,[35] apparently, accommodation was reached. It is symptomatic of the drive for timber production that the Office of Woods, comprising officials under the Crown, charged with the management of crown lands longed to end the Fence Month and winter heyning, in pursuit of the conservation of timber resources although payment was to continue into the nineteenth century. In any case, payments of the Lease Fee for summer grazing and Hocktide Money (Chapter 5) ceased during this century, although those on the forest borders were turned out all year.[36]

The Office of Warden and the Justice of Eyre were to vanish upon the death of the incumbents, so that by 1850 powers of the ancient officers were effectively destroyed. In 1851 the Crown relinquished any official interest in deer. Fences, hedges and ditches surmounted by fences remained to exclude deer. Pollarding, it should be recalled, was forbidden in leases, but was probably practised. However, the shift towards 'commercial forestry' had been underway since the late Middle Ages. As will be described in Chapter 8, 'Big Government' was at hand such that, since 1924, along with the Forest of Dean, the crown lands of the New Forest have been managed by the Forestry Commission on behalf of the Secretary for State.[37]

As the demand for timber for ships declined, so in the mid–late nineteenth century, there emerged a great appreciation of the New Forest as a proverbial 'national treasure' and there was implicit value placed in its 'mozaic' landscape of woodland, heaths, lawns and bogs. This complexity hides the context of an agro-ecosystem role to which the forest was central. Historically the floodplain supplied fattening pasture and hay to a pony-based economy within the forest. It is, however, likely that historic access for cattle to the Forest from surrounding areas was reduced in the 1960s by the new perambulation and providing cattle grids for the roads in and out of the area. The arable was enclosed in the eighteenth and nineteenth centuries[38] to produce a landscape dominated by small, irregular, rectilinear fields on the river terrace that are associated with parliamentary enclosure.[39]

Mid-century saw an unprecedented event: an effort to remove deer from the royal hunting forest. In the late 1840s, widespread corruption was uncovered within the crown management, leading to an overhaul of local administration and abrogation of the forest law. A select committee re-enforced this view in 1848. The Crown took for itself large areas of inclosures, supposedly in compensation for not stocking the forest with deer.[40] Commoners and landowners alike resisted these changes, because rents were higher from land carrying common rights (and reduced by inclosures). In effect, the 1851 *Deer Removal Act* starts the process of full statutory arrangements for the forest.[41]

By the nineteenth century, the forest wastes were said operate as the cottager's farm, and:

> 'the source of his livelihood, or of his comforts and of his capital. The rights if turbury, pannage and grazing still important to domestic economy that raised animals including skimmed milk from butter production used to fatten pigs whose manure in turn boosted the hay crop'.[42]

At its core, the *Deer Removal Act* 1851 (something that would have been anathema to Norman kings) reflected three opinions.[43] First, the Treasury (acting for the Crown) found maintenance of a herd of 2000–4000 deer expensive. Second, the commoners favoured deer removal as it would reduce grazing competition for their animals, and there would be a reduction in need for boundary fences, thereby reducing cost. Finally, and at the core of some of these problems was the powers of rolling inclosure dating from the 1698 legislation that caused the Crown to gain power to inclose 6000 acres (2430 ha) on a rolling basis, a far from popular move with the commoners.

This legislative counterpart from 1851 provided for a further 10,000 acres (4050 ha), technically making 16,000 acres (6480 ha) in all. These were to be 'freed from all forms of Common and other rights'. Two years later, deer were considered to have been removed, except for remnants in certain woodland areas. Yet the Crown still retained the rights to the Fence Month, and to 'winter heyning' when, at these times, domestic animals were obliged to be removed because the deer were calving in June, and during the 'winter heyning', to winter fodder for the deer.

The 1851 *Deer Removal Act* was an attempt finally to switch the emphasis in land use towards forestry, and so new silvicultural inclosure continued to 1877 (see Table 7.1).[44] The *Act* did not remove restrictions on commoning, and claims of over one-third of commoners against inclosure (and the interests of the Crown) were rejected. Conflicts of interest required resolution, so a House of Lords select committee in 1868 expressed concern over the extension of 'rolling powers of inclosure' and found the interests of crown and commoners were at variance.

During these deliberations, dis-afforestation was (surprisingly) to be rejected as an option, yet this was also the period of growing interest in the amenity of the New Forest. In short, its economic value was shifting from one of local economy at variance with a particular national interest, by now well on the wane (timber production for ship building), towards something reflecting anything from Victorian romanticism to genuine ecological interest. One is furthermore left pondering whether the popularity of the British monarchy at this time of empire and growing world dominance left their lordships with a convenient echo of past monarchical splendour.

A lost reflection on the latter period of the New Forest's governance and management has been recovered, edited and published by Le Pard.[45] This article reports an unpublished article by the lawyer turned archaeologist Heyward Sumner, dating between 1928 and 1934. The main purpose is to review the New Forest *Deer Removal Act* 1851 into the twentieth century. The quotation at the start of this chapter tells us a lot about where this writer was coming from.

Sumner's account[46] recalls a Commons select committee in 1875 that was to further 'inquire into and report upon the present condition of the affairs in the New Forest into the operation of the Deer Removal Act'. The pressure on the commoners was recognised, but also the crown interests be allowed to continue. During the enquiry process, it was acknowledged during evidence presented, that crown officers would prefer to take the best land for growing trees. And for the commoners, it was recognised that the verderer's court should be reconstituted.[47]

The *Deer Removal Act* 1851 had therefore been about more than eliminating grazing pressure on the forestry, there was an unjust objective by which the State tried to remove commoners' rights through rolling enclosure, presenting a threat to the open landscape. Recognising poor market conditions for large oaks, the *Act* also extended planting to trees of any kind. Had this trend continued, the New Forest would likely become like the Forest of Dean today; that is mostly covered by trees. Legal redress of the balance would be required if the interests of forest dwellers, particularly commoners, were to be upheld according to their ancient rights. For once there is a sense of emerging democracy.

If deer management had provided one nineteenth century concern, another was coniferisation, for the state continued to seek new means of profiting from commercial forestry. It was, in any case, believed that the poorest of the soils available produced inferior oak and beech, the *Act* effectively extended plantation to conifers. Monotonous plantations of Scots pine (also once known as 'Scots Fir', botanically *Pinus sylvestris*), and of other confers such as the Corsican pine (*P. laricio*), Weymouth pine (*P. strobus*) and Douglas fir (*Pseudotsuga* sp.) were established commercially. Areas inclosed 1852–1870 included former wood-pasture within inclosures established in the eighteenth century, such as Puckpitts and Burley Old Inclosures (Table 7.1). This all suggests a dramatic landscape and ecological change.[48] The balance of woodland type in statutory inclosures 1700–1990 is shown in Figure 2.10,[49] something that continued, despite the fellings in the two world wars. From 1971, conifers were no longer protected in favour of broadleaved plantation; felled areas did not have to be replaced by conifers (Chapter 8).

Drastic coniferisation may be traced to around 1820 with larch and Scots pine used as nurses for edges of inclosures. By mid-century, conifers register as a significant area and by the 1870s it may be seen that, not only has broadleaved area fallen once more, but conifers dominate. At this time, concern was expressed by among others Deputy Surveyor Gerald Lascelles that the 'old forest' was under threat, yet progress of fir enclosure replacing hardwoods continued. Short rotational thinning of oak plantations had been established in the nineteenth century and there were also chestnut areas on a rotational basis, traditionally this produced the bent timbers, the 'crooks and knees' demanded by shipwrights. Another incentive by mid-century was the high price of tan bark; perhaps this masked the real economic problem that was the near collapse of markets for the shipyards and today, there are several widely spaced, even-aged plantations of oak dating from this time.[50]

The New Forest Association, commoning and inclosure

No doubt, the *Deer Removal Act* 1851 caused resentment among those who enjoyed the former privileges within the forest. To recap, crown interest in deer was relinquished, followed by a partially successful removal programme. Compensation took the form of a generous allocation of land for silviculture as well as land enclosed under Acts of 1698 and 1808. They also presumed to claim unprecedented rolling power to enclose; this was limited to 16,000 acres (6478 ha) being fenced at any time.[51] Common right claims were officially registered, and the old hierarchy concerned with deer management was disbanded, leaving only agisters and verderers. The Office of Woods nonetheless attempted an attack on common rights by enforcing the Fence Months. The blanket application of enclosure continued to impact on the landscape of wood, heath, bog and lawn.

The outcome also produced widespread opposition that led to the formation of the New Forest Association (NFA) in 1867. This new organisation was to petition parliament and resolve conflicts between commoners and crown[52] as well as protecting local interests. The objective of the Office of Woods[53] was allegedly 'the complete destruction of the New Forest', to be achieved by depreciating commoners' rights through inclosing 'every acre which the legislation permitted', for other royal hunting forests had experienced partition between the landowner and the commoners, as enclosure in severalty. A recommendation of the 1868 select committee was for dis-afforestation of the New Forest that promoted dis-afforestation and partition of land rights. NFA can realistically claim to be one of the oldest conservation bodies and pressure groups in the World!

Actually, there is much that is unknown about details of common rights in and around the New Forest. Here, as nowhere else, are there potential problems around customary rights creating a legal imperative for record keeping. Into such uncertainty comes the modern countryside ethos, for the clash between forestry and conservation has since been partially resolved, although Tubbs reports conflicts of interest as late as the 1990s.[54] NFA was capable of galvanising growing public opinion. Here, for the first time, is the coming together of pragmatic politics from within the forest. The protection of traditional rights against state interests is followed by a re-enforced conservation ethic through the first publication of Wise's *The New Forest, its History and Scenery* in 1863, later running to five editions.[55]

The years 1851–1877 also saw a steady increase in inclosured area, and in the size of the inclosures thereby created. New inclosures contained large areas of conifer of variable age as well as broadleaved/conifer mixtures. The great Douglas fir avenues in Oakley and Park Hill, and elsewhere, date from this time. Pressure on the commissioners of woods increased and at least a policy of clearing all the ancient trees from an inclosure site, prior to replanting, was abandoned. Today, much ancient woodland is found in late inclosures, for example at Denny (1870), Highland Water (1869) and Knightwood (1867).[56]

Smaller enclosures continued, much in the fashion of the 1698 *Act*: Slufters Inclosures (1862) was on land of mixed quality; its 371 acres (150 ha) included very poor heathland together with the site of an ancient coppice, at its south-western end.[57]

The increase in the rate of afforestation was questioned on aesthetic grounds, for John Wise's book very much reflects the rise of a view that the forest was of national aesthetic and historical value. Meantime, the resentment around the Crown's behaviour grew with significant landscape impact caused by modern forestry. The renewed creation of inclosures that excluded grazing animals, often have established banks and ditches, essentially proving their description as historic boundaries. Fences constraining commoners' stock only had to exclude ponies, cattle and pigs; while between 1808 and 1851 the proportion of inclosures thrown open rose from 24% to 83% (latterly in anticipation of the *Act*); it fell dramatically to below 40% in the 1840s.[58]

It was not only the commoners who were disgruntled. By the summer of 1870, the local gentry were in open revolt against the Crown and not unsurprisingly this had effect. The following year, a resolution of the House of Commons blocked any more felling of ornamental timber in the New Forest and any further inclosures, pending a full inquiry. The eventual outcome was the report of the select committee in 1875 upon which the *New Forest Act* of 1877 was based;[59] the *Act* that would eventually check inclosure. Once more, national legislation was to intervene, a further step in punctuating the dramatic changes in the history of land use and management in the New Forest.

The consequence of various impasses was *New Forest Act* 1877. For the purposes of the *Act*, 'the forest' is defined as:

> '...lands whereof Her Majesty is seised in her domain as of fee [that would mean as inherited by the Crown], subject to the rights of commoners therein or thereover, situate within the within the boundaries of the New Forest in the county of Southampton, including all such lands as may at the commencement of this Act be inclosed in pursuance on any commission issued in pursuance of the Act of 1698, the Act of 1808 & the Act of 1851, or any such Acts. Register of common rights made in pursuance of the Act of 1854 means the register of decisions of claims of rights of common & other rights in& over the New Forest made by the Commissioners...'[60]

The *New Forest Claims Act* 1854 had provided for the registration of common rights in the forest. Tree husbandry had to recognise the 'picturesque character of the ground' including recognition of the value of ornamental trees. Its special value in its locality was also made clear. The Office of Woods took rolling powers of inclosure from the Crown only to be limited to that of the *New Forest Act* 1877, or areas inclosed prior to that time, such areas were 'free' from common rights and had protected public rights of way. The Verderer's Court was reconstituted, tightening regulation, and the Fence Month and winter heyning were protected by payment from the verderers of the sum of 20 shillings (£1) each 14 January. This secured for the commoners the right to turn out animals during the Fence Month and made statutory provision for preserving the amenity of the forest.[61] Although the medieval governance had all but effectively ended by 1850, the reconstituted verderers regulated 'vert' and, importantly, also championed the commoners' interests. This dramatic switch recognises a famous switch from top-down crown interests to an altogether more level and democratic form of governance.

Commoners' rights were now re-defined, making Heywood Sumner liken it to the *Charter of the Forest* of 1217; he also comments there is a public interest.[62] The interests of the Crown could be balanced with those of public interest, including amenity. It is believed that active silviculture had been effectively stopped by the 1877 *Act* with no further inclosures and clear felling of both the old broadleaved woodland and the 'ancient and ornamental woods'. The passing of this *Act* means this land cover category has statutory protection (Chapter 2). Actually, this became effective only into the early years of the twentieth century.[63] Between 1882 and 1889, around 3000 ornamental trees comprising 13 species were planted in and around the unenclosed forest, including turkey oak, sweet chestnut, sycamore, lime, maple and scarlet oak. Although most were planted on roadsides and around villages some were planted within the forest and there has been since a legacy of secondary regeneration.[64] Evidently, the local gentry favoured ornamental trees.

In effect, realised by the 1877 *New Forest Act*, crown land had effectively become state land. While overt efforts to 'nationalise' large tracts of land elsewhere were recommended but never enacted in the post-second World War period,[65] the New Forest saw a *de facto* public ownership and here can be seen the rise of the conservation ethos, to be expanded on in the next chapter. The forest by the close of the nineteenth century, was well positioned to balance economic, landscape, ecological and social interests for the future. The verderers, in legal terms, became a Body Corporate with powers of litigation, maintaining registers of common rights, employing officers and passing by-laws for the protection of stock. They were (and are today) guardians of the commons, the commoners' rights and indirectly, the forest landscape.[66]

The *New Forest Act* 1877 was in effect the rescuing legislation for the modern New Forest, largely because it restricted inclosure to 17,645 acres (7144 ha), ending 'rolling powers'.[67] Much as the *Charter of the Forest* (1217) had restricted geographically the area under forest law (to that in the reign of Henry II), so inclosure was to be restricted to that defined in the *Acts* of 1698, 1808 and 1851, remaining crown common land (45,000 acres, 18,376 ha) was to remain unenclosed and the verderers were to pay for the right to graze their animals during the Fence Month. The Verderer's Court was to be reconstituted and their number, increased from four to six, swore no oath to the Crown (although the Official Verderer was to be a crown appointment). The remaining were elected by commoners and parliamentary voters within the forest parishes.[68] The verderers continued to be responsible for all such unlawful activities as illegal enclosures, purprestres and trespass.[69]

Despite reform, there would inevitably be friction between the Office of Woods and the verderers after 1877, notably over their rights to control unenclosed forest, including permitting sawmills and military activity.[70] The *Baker Report* (1947) reports a dispute over the erection of sawmills by timber merchants (with Crown permission) that was opposed by the Verderers on account of damage to grazing interests. The the Office of Woods supported the sawmills, resulting in an out-of-court settlement in 1892 involving designation of sawmill sites, at considerable cost to the Verderers.

The verderers maintained that the Office of Woods should recognise commoners' rights absolutely, and that no activity should impede them without recourse to the verderers. Resulting litigation was expensive, with no clear legal resolution of the issues.[71] While the state had reached accommodation with those who had defined rights within the forest, there is a further narrative concerning those on the margins of society.

Encroachment, enclosure and property rights

Prior to the 1850s and in keeping with the mores of the day, it had become a general social duty (if also a lucrative one) for landowners to enclose and improve their waste or common lands and the Crown was no exception. It persisted in a fairly ruthless manner to maximise its revenues, and inclosures from commercial-scale silviculture continued. Inevitably, conflict arose because commoners exercising grazing rights and fuel gathering were in conflict with silviculture. Under the *New Forest Act* of 1808, there was even legislation against the breakdown of inclosures[72] and this was followed by pulses of inclosure, the more important around 1810, 1815 and 1848 serving to aggravate the problem.[73] Subsequently, the cost of maintaining enclosures is reflected in the motivation for the *Deer Removal Act* 1851.

In 1819, an Act for the regulation of common pasture in the New Forest provided for fixed penalties for illegal depasturing of stock. This may be a response to pressure on the grazing grounds,[74] perhaps associated with inclosure, with rising population, or both. A Right of Common enables the occupier of a plot of land to certain rights. These may be specified material or products from another's land. Today, the principal product is grazing and the owner of the land is the Crown. Land with common rights may be outside the perambulation, with many holdings in villages on the periphery of the forest.[75] In the New Forest, rights are generally attached to a particular property. Historically for commoners, estovers (fuel cutting) continued to be exploited in the period covered by this chapter; evidently there was conflict between the needs of local people, and timber plantation.

Yet, the association of 'commoning' with property rights would effectively exclude an underclass of landless poor. From the middle of the eighteenth century, the population of England was set to rise continuously. This would place pressure on land resources, including the role of 'squatting' in peripheral areas. Encroachment on common land before the eighteenth century certainly occurred (Chapter 6), most likely due to population pressures. Later, it became both a matter of concern and record. The 1789 report of the commissioners refers to 902 acres (365 ha) of mostly cottages, gardens and small fields on the edge of crown lands.[76] It should be noted the subsequent period to 1819 experienced high food prices,[77] thus likely incentivising heathland cultivation.[78]

While the situation was aggravated by the seemingly relentless march of enclosure, such matters were patently not addressed and the only recourse for many poor people who remained in rural locations was to 'squat', that is encroach on someone else's property. Rich farmland in singular private ownership was out of the question. Odd pockets of unimproved common land, effectively held in severalty in marginal areas, was the best bet and the forest had an abundance of it. Actually, encroachment was commonplace and the Crown often displayed lax controls over encroachment, making it commonplace in the first half of the eighteenth century. From cases presented at the Swainmote Court (1749–1752), the legal cost of eviction was greater than the value of the land.[79] By 1819, the report of the commissioners could claim that encroachment was halted, something further prevented in the *Deer Removal Act* of 1851.

An earthwork survey[80] included a multi-period field system at Lucy Hill (SU 226 045) cut on their eastern side by Burley New Inclosure, that is known to have been created in 1810 (Table 7.1). These appear part of an extensive system of fields extending southwards to Mill Lawn. It is uncertain, but these fields may relate to an attempt to extend a manorial site to the north of Burley. In 1802, Burley Manor had attempted to claim a large area of open forest by virtue of long usage and custom; this claim was rejected by the Crown. Alternatively, these boundaries may be evidence of piecemeal encroachment for cereal growing in the seventeenth century. This example alone suggests not only pressure within the forest to create ordinary agricultural land, but also created tension between crown and manor over possible 'illegal' assarts. Percival Lewis could record that the majority of encroachments were made by 'the lower order of persons' but a few had been made 'by the proprietors of neighbouring estates' who added them to their own property.[81]

Romany population

The Romany or 'Gypsy' population has been discussed by Len Smith[82] and has been a notable feature of the New Forest for centuries. While 'Egyptians' (Romany people did not originate in Egypt) are known to have been in England in the sixteenth century,[83] there are records of them in the area in the seventeenth century and associated with the Nomansland area during the eighteenth and nineteenth centuries.[84] More mobile by lifestyle and culturally distinct from long-term settled groups, or those such as squatters *who sought to settle*, Romanys nonetheless operated within the forest economy. A record of 1893 states: 'They are makers of tin ware, tinkers, umbrella menders, chair bottomers, clothes peg makers, beehive and basket makers, chimney sweeps, rag and bone collectors *etc.*'.[85]

The New Forest, as other forested areas, was home to the Romany population, in part due to it being abundant in herbs and other medicinal plants, wild game and also springs of fresh water.[86] The forest would also represent a comparatively large area of land relatively free from intensive settlement and agriculture, although there has always been a strong tradition of governance meaning any nomads were frequently moved on. Gypsies famously also told fortunes and entertained and engaged in herbal and similar 'cures' for ailments including warts, although it was horse trading that represented a significant part of the domestic economy alongside seasonal agricultural or horticultural work, and scrap metal dealing. At the end of the nineteenth century Romanys lived in tents and wagons at Shave Green, Godshill, Copythorne, Longdown, Thorney Hill, Bransgore and elsewhere deep in the forest. Outside the forest, Bournemouth, Blackhill near Wellow and also near the railway town of Eastleigh were popular locations. Traditional camping areas were replaced in the twentieth century by compounds[87] that were subsequently removed.

Extent of encroachment

The term 'encroachment' tends to be preferred to the emotively loaded term 'squatters', for that has come to imply infringement of property rights, at least in the popular press. Encroachment is the action of occupying land without official sanction and generally for purposes of agriculture, industry or dwelling. Despite low population densities and economically marginal land quality, it sheds light on both efforts to constrain land use change and on the changing labour markets at the dawn of the Industrial Age. Neither was encroachment a model for one-way land use change. Much seventeenth and eighteenth century encroachment was subsequently abandoned to the forest,[88] no doubt due to changing economic circumstances, including lower post-Napoleonic food prices. However, certain villages today are able to trace their origins to encroachment; including East Boldre, Norleywood, Bull Hill, Nomansland and Woodgreen. Later sales of heathland by the Crown consolidated certain villages in the south. A study of the enclosure pattern on the wastes of Bramshaw (these were privately owned) suggests much less pilfering of land, presumably because of tight control by resident landowners.

To attribute the fortunes of encroachments simply to population pressure and food prices, while clearly a factor, may be over-simplification. Other factors included housing needs for shipyard workers on the Beaulieu River and other industrial concerns generating a need for housing – there was also industrial development in the north of the forest. As opposed to earlier periods therefore, the motives for squatting in the forest were as much to do with industry as with more established agricultural activities. And there are cultural and lifestyle choices that must be considered.

Perhaps the New Forest's most unusual profession was that of snakecatcher.[89] Harry 'Brusher' Mills (1840–1905, the nickname probably came from his employment to clear wickets) had this intriguing day job which involved catching adders, grass snakes and smooth snakes for sale to the London Zoological Gardens (Fig. 7.3). Brusher presumably lived as a squatter into the early twentieth century, occupying a hut that was burned down following an order to leave it. He went elsewhere for a change of clothes and even the occasional bath. It has been presumed this hostile action was to prevent him gaining squatter's rights. A less confrontational explanation may have been that 'the authorities' (probably the local council) were concerned for his health and hence operated in his own interests, probably not wanting to deal with a dead body in the forest. This edifice was likely a former charcoal burner's hut, near to Sporelake Lawn, just north of Holland's Wood campsite.[90]

Harry is described[91] as a short, stocky man with a 'mahogany face', two overcoats, creased trousers and gaiters (no doubt a concession to gentility), heavy boots and a faded neckerchief. His body was 'hung about with sacks and bags and his pockets were stuffed with tins, boxes and bottles'.

FIGURE 7.3. Harry 'Brusher' Mills.

COURTESY OF THE NEW FOREST NINTH CENTENARY TRUST, CHRISTOPHER TOWER NEW FOREST REFERENCE LIBRARY. HAMPSHIRE RECORD OFFICE: 20M92/2/Q49

Nomansland

The place-name 'Nomansland' often invokes curiosity. In medieval England there had been little room for manoeuvre when creating assarts or purprestures (the encroachment on a public area for the benefit of private utility including agriculture and the construction of a dwelling) that was not officially under manorial control or to be found within a royal forest. Land was thus subject to some form of governance, while the loss of woodland to arable being a loss of one resource in favour of another. Yet if all land ultimately belongs to the Crown, even unnoticed encroachment represented transgression of someone's perceived land rights, including those of the Crown itself! Outside the New Forest this evidently was not taken into consideration.

Nomansland is a settlement that provides a surprise. Its origins are far from prehistoric, Anglo-Saxon or even medieval, belonging in the period of the Napoleonic wars. Figure 7.4 shows the form of the present-day settlement on the edge of the New Forest. Here, one John Shergold apparently erected a charcoal burner's cabin on crown land at sometime around 1795, on what

FIGURE 7.4. Modern day Nomansland from modern (1:25,000) OS mapping. Note the high density of settlement to the northwest of the Bramshaw Inclosure.

today may be the site of the present *Boundary Cottage* at the southern side of the junction where North Lane meets The Green at Forest Road. In a court case at Lyndhurst, 23 October 1802, apparently in the absence of forest officials and plaintiffs (a bureaucratic mix-up is blamed), and presided over by three Parliamentary Commissioners, the location of Shergold's claim as within the forest could not be established. Several people testified to hunting birds and animals including deer suggesting there was no control over hunting. The court did not believe he was on land belonging to the Bishop of Winchester, and so on account of this negative evidence, he was discharged.[92]

The date when a legal dispute was settled is thereby taken as the foundation of Nomansland. There was an immediate rush by would-be occupiers because the land apparently belonged to no identifiable landlord – hence the name – and claimants are said to have walked, run or ridden on that very day to claim land without penalty. The new settlers may have built mud houses (clay and chopped heather) with thatched roofs and it is likely that the early houses were built by single men who married once they established themselves.

By 1807 Nomansland was a group of cottages standing on common land in Downton Parish beside the Wiltshire–Hampshire border near Bramshaw Wood (Fig. 7.4). South Land was recorded in 1817, in 1841 Morgan's Vale was recognised as a village in the common between Ridge and Vale roads with the commons enclosed in 1822, further land being provided for small building allotments. Its boundaries, defined by the inclosure award, enclosed a roughly square area of 14 acres (5.7 ha). Nearby, industrial activity at Redlynch included broom-making, up until the Second World War, smithies and an iron foundry, with a further foundry (in 1855), lace and shoemaking at Woodfalls. Two brickworks were located in Morgan's Vale in 1837. The church dates from 1837, the school 1839.[93] The settlement was first mapped by the Ordnance Survey in 1807–1808 (published 1811) and later information may be gleaned from an Enclosure Award map 1822 (Nomansland itself was outside the area enclosed) and the Tithe map of 1838,[94] although being outside either of two parishes of the Parish of Downton no tithe was due. While uncertainty surrounds the extent of the area at this time and even the number of dwellings that were recorded, in 1841 the population was 140, reaching a maximum of 173 in 1851 but falling thereafter, at least into the 1930s.[95] It became a part of Redlynch Civil Parish in 1934. Figure 7.4 shows the modern-day settlement, with common land to the north and a strong demarkation along the road separating it from the New Forest.[96]

The period from the mid-eighteenth century to the close of the nineteenth century therefore saw increasing state intervention via crown interests and its proxy Office of Woods, the precursor to the Forestry Commission. The fortunes of the ordinary forest dwellers continued to demonstrate pressure of land resources, manifested as squatting and also disagreements over the traditional rights. The common of estovers for commoners was gradually bought out by the Office of Woods and later the Forestry Commission from about 1810, so few have the right today.[97] Otherwise the New Forest Association protected commoners' rights and limited inclosure. Alongside such changes, comes the rise of an aesthetic and ecological concern for the landscape into the twentieth century. Battle lines were subsequently redrawn between the conservation and commercial forestry interests.

On Hyde Common (Fig. 6.3), many cob cottages and hovels were located on the edges of the heaths and commons and there are a few dispersed settlements within the common area itself. This allowed cultivation, managed woodlands and small paddocks with associated squatter development. During this period, settlements such as Gorley, Woodgreen and Hatchet Green expanded.[98]

Encroachment at the Common's edge is probably later eighteenth century with small island enclosures containing two or three paddocks and associated squatters' cottages. These are today The Cottage, Badger's Haunt and Edgehill; that containing Ogdens Farm is probably nineteenth century. Hungerford developed at a similar time and displays a series of small enclosures. A late encroachment was that for the construction of the Church of the Holy

Ascension (1854/5), its associated churchyard and the original parsonage. There was also limited gravel extraction from the east side of the Common, close to Abbot's Well.

East Boldre

East Boldre (Fig. 7.5), a squatter settlement, was established between 1700 and 1900, and thoroughly researched by Jude James.[99] The earliest settlement name was Beaulieu Rails because a settlement had grown up along the wooden railings atop the earthen bank defining the western boundary of the manor and parish of Beaulieu. This bank may have its origin in the early thirteenth century when King John granted land to the Cistercian order. East Boldre is a linear settlement, merging with East End in the south making the developed area some 4.5 km from north to south. Its eastern boundary was defined by a an earthen bank and ditch, supporting oak trees. The western boundary is defined by a road, unenclosed over much of its west boundary, abutting Bagshott Moor, and areas of open heath. The settlement, however, was situated entirely on waste lands of the New Forest (rather than manorial commons), geologically on plateau gravels. Clays beneath these ensure a water supply from pools or

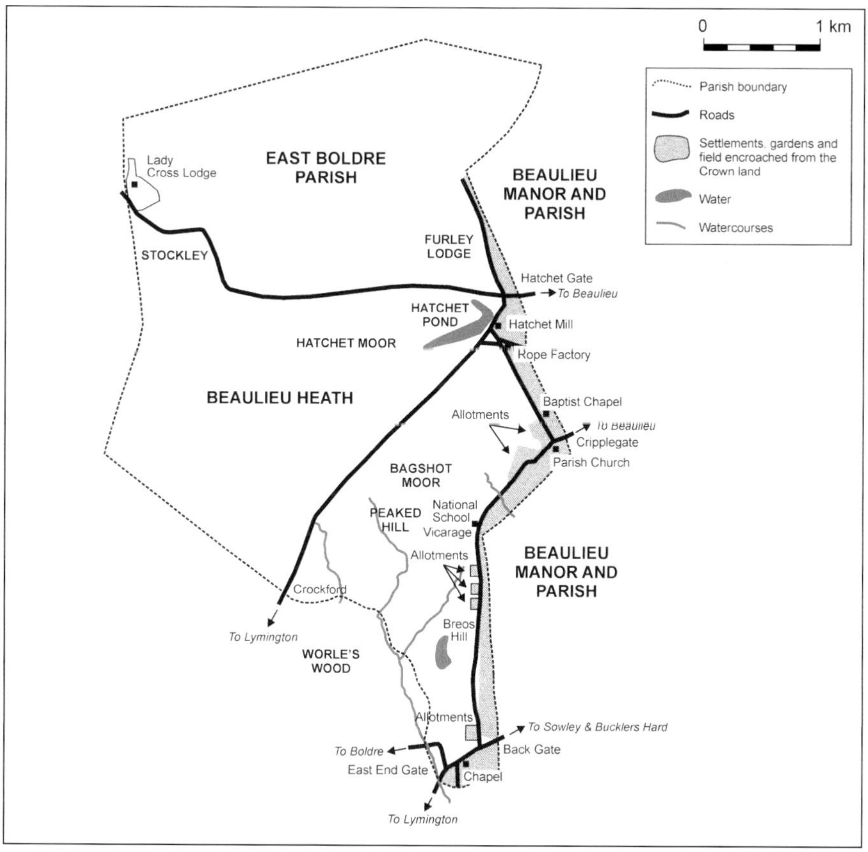

FIGURE 7.5. East Boldre and Beaulieu Manor and Parish Boundary.

AFTER JAMES 1994, BY PERMISSION OF THE NEW FOREST RESEARCH AND PUBLICATIONS TRUST IN ASSOCIATION WITH THE NEW FOREST SECTION OF THE HANTS FIELD CLUB AND ARCHAEOLOGICAL SOCIETY

wells in the gravel. Soils, variable in quality, can be improved by marling. The centre is some 6 km WSW of that of Beaulieu. The settlement became a parish only in 1839, hence the records are bound up with the parent parish. However, East Boldre, abutting Beaulieu parish, is evidently older.

The Tithe Schedule of 1851 shows the village occupied a total area of 290 acres (117 ha), about equivalent to 'two small/medium sized farms in the southern New Forest area'. While most squatter encroachment was agriculture linked, the economic circumstances of East Boldre lie first in its proximity to the Beaulieu estate and village that could provide many employment opportunities, and furthermore in the common land, apparently unused for any tangible purpose, so it would become available for exploitation. Actually the shipbuilding industry became a major employer

The Rev. William Gilpin, vicar of Boldre Parish (1777–1804), reported that the Duke of Bedford (then Lord Warden of the Forest) tried to remove the settlement, but was resisted by some 200 men who were determined that he should not, so he withdrew. The reverend gentleman clearly saw nothing wrong with this 'trespass on the waste' providing 'for large families with ease'. Not everyone agreed with this view; however it is clear there were concerted efforts in the 1790s to establish mud cottages. Furthermore, between 1812 and 1817, Rev. Henry Comyn, curate of Boldre reported that East Boldre had grown in response to the employment needs of the shipbuilding industry at Bucklers Hard; this flourished between the 1740s to about 1818. More casual employment included agricultural labourers, rope making, brickmaking at Pitts Deep and Baileys Hard and in the ironworks at Sowley; in essence it was landless labourers who caused the encroachments, although apparently a system of rental also developed whereby tenants paid rent to those who had previously encroached. There may also have been an element of collusion from farmers who found themselves short of labour during the Napoleonic wars. There was additionally conflict regarding who was responsible for the poor rate. Boldre was the parish within which East Boldre rested, yet it was the Beaulieu estate that benefitted from the labour, especially during the Napoleonic wartime, and hence benefited economically. In an ensuing and costly court case, Beaulieu took responsibility for 13 out of 50 properties in respect of the Poor Law, Boldre had the remainder. Beaulieu, however, remained negligent in respect of its responsibilities to the poor.[100]

In the villages

'Squatting' was therefore well-established in rural areas, where subsistence agricultural activities were linked with whatever local industry or service was appropriate to support a poor family. Indeed, Postan[101] comments upon smallholders in the Middle Ages engaging in a range of non-agricultural activities. The apparent land shortage of the early fourteenth century had led to an expansion of assarts (clearance of 'waste' land or of forest land for agriculture), but it would be eased by the Black Death. By the seventeenth century through to the nineteenth, population pressures would cause the same problem. Poor relief was available and may have led to a labour surplus in certain rural areas between 1600 and 1834.[102] Parish housing was often available,[103] however, housing was an issue in the forest.

The most drastic and unpopular (among the poor at least) solution of the day was to ensure that every parish was incorporated into a Union (workhouse) under the *Poor Law Amendment Act* 1834 that would admit paupers from the participating parishes.[104] This would have been the fate of many in and around the forest during the nineteenth century, with a New Forest Union Workhouse erected in Ashurst for unfortunates from among others Lyndhurst, Minstead, Fawley, Eling, Beaulieu and Bramshaw.

While there has been considerable debate around rural migration, impact of the earlier welfare state based in the Poor Law, and even despite some provision of social housing prior to 1900, poor people had to be opportunistic. The hackneyed cliché 'On yer bike' evidently applied, at least on a local scale, when new industrial opportunities for work presented themselves in the New Forest during the Napoleonic period. This seems to have applied across much of the forest area, but was especially important within striking distance of the Beaulieu River shipyards.

It is also important to outline changes affecting rural settlement in the nineteenth century. Stephen Ings talks of relationships between 'master and man' for those with a direct stake in the economy of the forest, for example the ruling elites, established church and the labouring classes.[105] For, within the impoverished communities of the New Forest, throughout the reign of Victoria (1837–1901) until the outbreak of hostilities in 1914, the majority of labourers lived in mud-walled cottages on scraps of waste land. Their employers, on the other hand, were more likely to be farmers who, as tenants of the gentry, had links to the established church. This would contrast with squatter settlements, such as Nomansland that was beyond the reach of such economic and religious relations. For labour became scarce as men took up arms, often never to return home, driving up wages and challenging relations between master and man.

Even in the late nineteenth century, there was a flood of urban residents into the villages of the New Forest and it surroundings, commencing an erosion of the number of traditional inhabitants. While the First World War and the 'Spanish flu' outbreak immediately after would inevitably create massive change in both attitudes and in the labour market, rural life would change, not least due to a protracted rural economic recession.[106]

Conclusions

Following a protracted period of uncertainly and neglect, the period 1700 to 1890 saw functional success and the operation of the forest as a reasonably successful economic entity. Hitherto it had been the pre-occupations needs of the royal household that had predominated, thanks to William III's interest in silviculture for the navy. Then, experimental silviculture was advocated. State interest predominated, so the result is the first serious local industrial phase since the Roman period, arising out of the Scientific Revolution (Chapter 6), albeit largely in the service of the British navy. The outcome of scientific enlightenment and state engagement was a conscious effort to account for forest resources and governance fully through state agency. Sadly, the eighteenth century was also corrupt and this continued into the following century. However, thanks to Edmund Burke, revenues became truly 'public'. Subsequently, any vestige of the traditional system of governance came to an end with the death of the last Lord Warden.

None of the above really changed the plight of the forest poor. True, gypsies were free to roam and to trade, but the commoners came into conflict with the interests of silviculture/forestry. Landless poor could be forced to squat in order to engage in both agricultural and industrial activities associated with the shipyards, supported in part by the Poor Law system.

Just as the navy no longer required large oak and beech timbers in profusion, the forest enters Victorian consciousness as a special case of the English Rural Idyll. Efforts to remove deer in the interests of timber production were not effective, and with the local gentry in rebellion, the ancient system was reformed to give the modern system of verderers and agisters. Progressive inclosure of trees was to be prevented and the interests of commoners protected. The next chapter will demonstrate on the one hand the emergence of totally modern economic and cultural interests in terms of forestry, recreation and conservation, on the other hand the forest would be long in becoming a National Park.

Demographic change from the later nineteenth century would be associated with a loss of the ancient relationships between classes and institutions. Certainly within the timeframe of this chapter, the economy of the forest changed dramatically and with it both the legal framework and governance systems changed to match. And with it, attitudes at all levels from national government to the village scale underwent dramatic change, something that will be explored further in Chapter 8.

Notes

1. Heywood Sumner (*c.*1930). Article ed. G. F. le Pard (1999) The New Forest Deer Removal Act, 1851, and afterwards. *Hampshire Studies* 54, 75–87.
2. J. Evelyn (1664) *Sylva, or a Discourse of Forest Trees.* John Martyn, London.
3. *Ibid.*, vol. 1 ch. 1.
4. O. Rackham (2006) *Woodlands*, 449. Collins, London.
5. K. Hickman (2015) Second Anglo-Dutch War: Raid on the Medway http://militaryhistory.about.com/od/navalbattles16001800/p/medway.htm. Accessed Sept. 2017.
6. Pepys, Samuel (1633–1703) (n.d.) http://www.epsomandewellhistoryexplorer.org.uk/Pepys.html. Accessed Sept. 2017.

7. Vesey-Fitzgerald (1966) *Portrait of the New Forest*, 93, 96. Robert Hale, London.
8. NFNP (n.d.) www.newforest.hampshire.org.uk/history3.html. Accessed Jan 2014.
9. Fifth Report of the commissioners appointed to enquire into the state and condition of the woods, forests and land revenues of the crown. 22nd July 1789, 22.
10. Tubbs C. R. (2001) *New Forest, the History, Ecology and Conservation*, 85–86. New Forest Ninth Centenary Trust, Fordingbridge; see also Chapter 5.
11. Peterken G. F. (1981) *Woodland Conservation and Management*, 17. Chapman and Hall, London.
12. New Forest Association (n.d.) *A History of the New Forest and its Adjacent Commons.* New Forest Association, Fordingbridge.
13. P. Roberts (2014) pers. comm.
14. N. Fergusson (2003) *Empire*, 44. Penguin, Harmondsworth.
15. J. Ivy (n.d.) http://www.newforestcentre.org.uk/uploads/publications/65.pdf. Accessed Sept 2017.
16. A. Driver and W. Driver (1794) *A General View of the Agriculture of the County of Hants*, 36.
17. *Ibid.*, 36–37.
18. D. J. Stagg (1983) *A Calendar of New Forest Documents: the fifteenth and sixteenth centuries*, xxxi. Hampshire Record Series V, Hampshire County Council, Winchester.
19. D. J. Stagg (1990) Silvicultural inclosures in the New Forest from 1780 to 1850. *Hampshire Studies* 46, 131–43.
20. *Ibid.*
21. *The Fifth Report* 1789 op cit.
22. Maps of the New Forest (n.d.) http://www.newforest.hampshire.org.uk/historic_maps/maps_intro.html. accessed Sept 2017.
23. H. F. Cook (2010) Boom, slump and intervention: changing agricultural landscapes on Romney Marsh, 1790 to 1990. In M. P. Waller, E. Edwards and L. Barber (eds), *Romney Marsh: Persistence and Change in a Coastal Lowland*, 155–83. Romney Marsh Research Trust, Sevenoaks.
24. Stagg (1990) *op. cit.* in note 19.
25. *The Fifth Report* 1789 *op. cit.* p. 20.
26. *Ibid.*, 28.
27. *Ibid.*, 9.
28. *Ibid.*, 7.
29. Chapter 6 and HRO149M89/R4/6137.
30. P. Lewis (1811) *The New Forest*, 28–33. T. Payne, London.
31. *Ibid.*, 205–206.
32. *The Fifth Report* 1789 *op. cit.*, 128–29. Survey notes refer to 1787.
33. *Op. cit.* note 23.
34. History of the Forestry Commission. Forestry Commision. http://www.forestry.gov.uk/forestry/CMON-4UUM6R accessed Oct 2012.
35. D. J. Stagg (1984) *Verderers of the New Forest*, 3. New Forest Association, Fordingbridge.
36. R. Reeves (2013) pers. comm.
37. The Crown Lands Management Summary 2008. https://www.forestry.gov.uk/pdf/eng-new-forest-summary.pdf/$file/eng-new-forest-summary.pdf. Accessed Jan 2017
38. Avon Valley (2012) http://www3.hants.gov.uk/3a_avon_valley.pdf. Accessed Sept 2017.
39. Hampshire Historic Landscape Assessment (1999) http://www3.hants.gov.uk/hcc_historic_landscape_2-2.pdf. Accessed Sept 2017.
40. New Forest Association (n.d.) *A History of the New Forest and its Adjacent Commons.* New Forest Association, Fordingbridge.

41. New Forest Committee (1947) (Baker) Report, 8. cmd 7245 Forestry Commission, HMSO, London.
42. D. J. Stagg (1986) *Commoners of the New Forest*, 13. New Forest Association, Fordingbridge.
43. Le Pard (1999) *op. cit.* in note 1.
44. D. J. Stagg (1992) Silvicultural inclosures in the New Forest from 1850 to 1877. *Hampshire Studies* 48, 143–59.
45. Le Pard (1999) *op. cit.* in note 1.
46. *Ibid.*
47. *Ibid.*
48. Tubbs (2001) *op. cit.* in note 10, 221–22.
49. *Ibid.*, 222.
50. *Ibid.*, 220–21.
51. *Ibid.*, 88.
52. *Ibid.*, 89.
53. New Forest Association (n.d.), *op. cit.* in note 40.
54. Tubbs (2001) *op. cit.* in note 10, chap. 17.
55. J. J. Wise (1883) *The New Forest Its History and Scenery*, 44. Sotheran, London.
56. New Forest Association (n.d.) *op. cit.* in note 40.
57. *Ibid.*
58. Tubbs (2001) *op. cit.* in note 10, 223–24.
59. New Forest Association (n.d.) *op. cit.* in note 40.
60. The National Archives (n.d.) http://www.legislation.gov.uk/ukla/Vict/40-41/121/section/3. Accessed Sept 2017
61. New Forest Committee (1947) *op. cit.* in note 41, 10–11.
62. Heywood Sumner *c.*1930. *op cit.* in note 1.
63. New Forest Association (undated) *op. cit.* in note 40.
64. The History of the Crown Lands (n.d.) http://www.forestry.gov.uk/pdf/eng-new-forest-b2-history.pdf/$FILE/eng-new-forest-b2-history.pdf. Accessed Sept 2017.
65. Cook (2012) *op. cit.* in note 23.
66. A. Passmore (1977) *Verderers of the New Forest: A history of the New Forest 1877–1977*. Pioneer Publications, Beaulieu.
67. Tubbs (2001) *op. cit.* in note 10, 89.
68. *Ibid.*, 90.
69. Stagg (1983) *op. cit.* in note 18, xxxiii.
70. New Forest Committee (1947) *op. cit.* in note 41, 12–13.
71. Tubbs (2001) *op. cit.* in note 10, 90.
72. Stagg (1983) *op. cit.* in note 18, xxxiii.
73. *op. cit.* in note 64
74. Stagg (1983) *op. cit.* in note 18, xxxii.
75. New Forest Commoners (n.d.) http://www.newforest.hampshire.org.uk/today1.html. Accessed Sept 2014.
76. N. Smith (1999) The earthwork remains of enclosure in the New Forest, 34. *Proceedings of the Hampshire Field Club and Archaeological Society* 54, 35; C. R Tubbs and G. W. Dimbleby (1965) Early agriculture in the New Forest. *Advances in Science* 22, 88–97.
77. Cook (2010) *op. cit.* in note 23.
78. New Forest Association (n.d.) *op. cit.* in note 40.
79. Smith (1999) *op. cit.* in note 76.
80. *Ibid.*, 35, 37.
81. Lewis (1811) *op. cit.* in note 30, 65.

82. L. Smith (2004) *Romany Nevi-Wesh: An Informal History of the New Forest Gypsies.* Nova Forest Publishing, Lyndhurst.
83. *Ibid.*, 24.
84. *Ibid.*, 47, 79.
85. *Ibid.*, 81.
86. The Hampshire Gypsies. http://www.southernlife.org.uk/gypsies2.htm. Accessed Oct 2012.
87. Smith (2004) *op. cit.* in note 82, 134.
88. New Forest Association (n.d.) *op. cit.* in note 40.
89. D. J. Stagg (1983) *Snake Catchers of the New Forest.* New Forest Association, Fordingbridge.
90. *Ibid.*, 7.
91. *Ibid.*, 9.
92. D. H. Kerridge (2002) *Nomansland: Its two hundred years of history.* Published in conjunction with the Redlynch and District Local History Society. Wiltshire Community History. http://www.wiltshire.gov.uk/community/getcom.php?id=189.
93. A. P. Baggs, E. Crittall, J. Freeman and J. H. Stevenson (1980) Parishes: Downton. In D. A. Crowley (ed.), *A History of the County of Wiltshire: Volume 11, Downton Hundred; Elstub and Everleigh Hundred*, 19–77. London. British History Online http://www.british-history.ac.uk/vch/wilts/vol11/pp19-77. http://www.british-history.ac.uk/report.aspx?compid=115483. Accessed Sept 2017.
94. Kerridge *op. cit.* in note 92, 11–14.
95. *Ibid.*, 16.
96. *op. cit.* in note 93.
97. P. Roberts (2014) pers. comm.
98. NFNP (2009) Western escarpment file:///C:/Users/Hadrian/Downloads/weforwebfile:///C:/Users/Hadrian/Downloads/weforweb%20(1).pdf and http://www.newforestnpa.gov.uk_data/assets/pdf_file/0006/29229/weforweb.pdf. Accessed Jan 2014.
99. J. James (1994) *East Boldre: A New Forest Squatters Settlement 1700–1900.* http://www.geodata.soton.ac.uk/newforest/public/resources/eastb.html.
100. *Ibid.*
101. M. M. Postan (1972) *The Medieval Economy and Society*, 148. Penguin, Harmondsworth.
102. R. M. Smith (2008) *Social Security as a Developmental Institution? Extending the Solar Case for the Relative Efficacy of Poor Relief Provisions under the English Old Poor Law.* Brooks World Povety Institute, University of Manchester BWPI Working Paper 56.
103. J. Broad (2000) Housing the rural poor in southern England 1650–1850. *Agricultural History Review* 48(2), 51–170.
104. S. Ings (2010) *Shot for a White-faced Deer*, chapter 7. Hobnobb Press, Salisbury.
105. *Ibid.*, chapter 2.
106. *Ibid.*, 199; Cook (2010) *op. cit.* in note 23.

CHAPTER 8

The Search for the Workable (1900–1980)

A recent reviewer[1] quotes John Wise (1883):

> 'But in its wild scenery lies its greatest charm. From every hill-top gleam the blue waters of the English Channel… Nowhere, in extent at least, spread such stretches of heath and moor, golden in the spring with the blaze of ferns, and in the autumn purple with heather, and bronzed with the fading fern. Nowhere in England rise such oak-woods, their boughs rimed with the frostwork of lichens, and dark beech-groves with their floor of red brown leaves, on which the branches weave their own creative warp and woof of light and shade.'[2]

Conservation to the Second World War

This quotation from Wise is more an invitation to visit a place replete with revitalised English historic charm, then (the later nineteenth century) seen as a kind of ecological Sherwood Forest, albeit lacking its own Robin and Marion. This description invokes nothing of an area long valued for any strategic or industrial purpose. Perhaps from a modern perspective it was fortunate that battleships were now made of iron, although forestry supplying other markets (those requiring fast growing softwood) were developing apace. This trend had been evident way back into the nineteenth century, but coniferisation of broadleaved woodland has had few supporters, at least those located outside commercial interests.

Crown ownership and control of the forest lands under forest laws set it aside from mainstream common law, manorial or other jurisdiction. Then the New Forest moved decisively towards 'statism'. Although this had not only ensured revenue for the crown, it (significantly) enabled national interests to be satisfied providing timber for the navy. Since the sixteenth century there emerged a political clash between the Lord Warden of the New Forest (representing the *Ancien Régime*) and what became known as the Office of Woods, representing state interest. Thus was generated the *Divisum Imperium*. Sources of political strife remained in the upper echelons of New Forest governance through to the twentieth century, by then it was manifest not only in terms of direct economic interest clashes between Forestry Commission interests (timber production) and the rights of commoners but also between the Forestry Commission and interests concerned with landscape and biodiversity. Ancient governance had been reformed to the point when it was providing for on-the-ground management in a real and practical sense.

To Victorian writers (but presumably not the Office of Woods) there is no celebration of a 'production landscape' for timber and wood products *per se*; and it is very likely that John Evelyn, a conservative-minded improver of woods like his 'whiggish' near-contemporary Walter Blith (Chapter 6), would see such romanticism as retrogressive, if indeed they understood it at all. The conflict between forest function and amenity would erupt in the twentieth century, making it a suitable place in which to scrutinise the emergence of a 'conservation ethic'. The 1851 *Deer Removal Act* evidently failed, although 'inclosure' increased until the *New Forest Act* of 1877, after which an uneasy accommodation was reached between conflicting interests of timber production and commoners.[3] As an indication, the holly understory regenerated due to reduced grazing pressure. Some thought the interests of 'silviculture' had, indeed, reached an end, yet the latter *Act* remained in force until the *New Forest Act* 1949.[4] But what about the rise of conservation of habitat and landscape?

There arose a perceived pressing need to conserve what was regarded as remaining of the English countryside. In his perceptive account of environmental history in the twentieth century, John Sheail identifies the emergence of a rural economic 'third force' additional to farming and forestry.[5] This provides for 'conscious stewardship of rural landscapes for their amenity and wildlife'; it is linked with opportunity of city and town dwellers to visit the countryside. To be fair, this has its origins in nineteenth century state concerns over human welfare, the third force reflects a 'philanthropic and voluntary response' from those in positions of responsibility and influence.[6] It drove conservation imperatives; and later in the century the statutory planning process was to emerge. A phase of campaigning and voluntary action saw the rise of several non-governmental organisations familiar today. For example, the National Trust was formed in 1895, with an Act of Parliament enabling it to own property passed in 1907.[7] Locally, the Hampshire and Isle of Wight Wildlife Trust was formed after the Second World War.[8]

Concern centred on the expansion of the urban population around the forest. The New Forest Commoners' Defence Association (NFCDA) was formed in 1909 including organisations of the immediately preceding decades with similar objectives.[9] Its role was to represent the commoners where friction arose from animals grazing outside the perambulation and its views were mirrored, if not initiated, by a reinvigorated New Forest Association (NFA) in the 1920s.[10] Because it supported grazing in the open forest, it also had wider landscape impact, for it petitioned the Office of Woods (later the Forestry Commission) to improve drainage in the 1920s. Later, in the 1960s, it supported the fencing and gridding of the New Forest and the establishment of a 40mph (64 kph) blanket speed limit. It continues to champion the rights of grazing and defends the forest from perceived development and recreation threats.

At the dawn of the twentieth century, Britain was a major industrial power, a player on the world stage and prone to look back with longing to a (largely fictionalised) past, the state of mind dubbed 'the English Rural Idyll'. Actually, migration from the countryside, from villages and from towns to large and growing centres was fuelled by poverty, unemployment and lack of opportunity, even if hitherto the Poor Law-based 'social security' had moderated such migration (when compared with other countries).[11] Then, from the 1870s until 1939, English agriculture experienced a protracted depression that was triggered by a series of poor harvests and prolonged by cheap grain imports from North America and Australia.[12] During times of agricultural recession, livestock numbers generally increase in agricultural areas and grazing pressure in the forest also increased after 1900. There was a short respite during the Second World War, when livestock was removed.[13] The poverty of many in the New Forest was no surprise, although a certain shift of resources towards timber production may be furthermore discerned.[14] The very establishment of the Forestry Commission from the Office of Woods reflected a strategic concern over security of timber production and in times of agricultural recession, timber, coppice and forestry provided employment in rural areas.[15]

Symptomatic of the changing values during the inter-war period was concern over unplanned urbanisation that led to an appeal to the counter-industrial and counter urbanisation in the English Rural Idyll. This was decisively followed by a politicisation of countryside conservation manifested in the formation of the Campaign to Protect Rural England (the modern name for the non-governmental organisation 'CPRE') that dates from 1926. CPRE formation is set alongside the ever-growing power through numerical support of the National Trust and increasingly more numerous county Wildlife Trusts, as well as the growing Royal Society for the Protection of Birds. CPRE founders, the Earl of Crawford and Balcarres (politician and art historian), Sir Guy Dawber (architect) and the pioneering town planner, Sir Patrick Abercrombie, represent the cultural elite of the British establishment. Abercrombie could state that 'the thing that is England, is the countryside'. Interestingly, the rise of conservation to 1940 was overwhelmingly a voluntary sector activity. This was to be matched after the Second World War by state intervention.[16]

What may be difficult to comprehend regarding the emergence of the New Forest as a valued landscape, were ensuing battles around the future of what was already appreciated pre-1900 as a national gem. The twentieth century clashes – between timber production and ecological and landscape conservation imperatives – may have produced twentieth century optimism without the perambulation, but pessimism ruled within. This would be especially manifest after the Second World War and would be resolved first by the curtailment of Forestry Commission activities and finally by the establishment of the New Forest National Park Authority (NFNPA). However, the interplay of institutional and stakeholder interests proved far from straightforward, yet the emergent conservation ethic would preserve the New Forest – in its entirety.

During the Second World War, 'national interests' had two impacts on the New Forest. One was the creation of 12 airfields from 1940, with a bombing range at Ashley Walk (near Boscombe) that was controlled by the Armaments Squadron located at Boscome Down, Amesbury, Wiltshire. Here, 5000 acres

(2025 ha) were fenced off and today what look like natural wetlands and ponds are in fact bomb craters.[17] Apparently prototypes for the Bouncing Bomb were tested here. Specific administrative and economic efforts were created to ensure food security at this time,[18] and these saw the Hampshire War Agricultural Executive Committee enclose, crop and re-seed 350 ha of open forest between 1941 and 1952 with the agreement of the verderers, although there was apparently no legal basis for this course of action.[19] Wartime encroachments (bombing ranges, aerodromes, cultivations, sawmills, military trenches, barbed wire, waste dumps, old concrete bases of buildings) were seen as a serious matter detracting from the condition of the forest immediately post-war.[20] These disfigured the landscape and caused hazards.

A new land fit for heroes, 1945–1949?

Second World War hostilities were over by September 1945 and, as with 1918, expectations for a new order were high. The immediate post-war Labour (Attlee) government was to produce what were aimed to be statutory responses to onslaughts on the countryside by both agriculture and urban development. Publication by John Dower of his report, first laid out a need for 'relatively wild country' to be preserved for open air enjoyment, while conserving historic buildings and wildlife and maintaining farming.[21] The *Dower Report* (1945) included the New Forest in the 'Other Amenity Areas not suggested as National Parks' category, although it should be noted this was primarily because Dower felt the New Forest was adequately dealt with by the Forestry Commission, rather than it not meeting the criteria.

However, there was seen to be no need for a New Forest National Park at that time. Dower's report led to that of Sir Arthur Hobhouse, which in turn prepared the legislation for the creation of national parks in England and Wales. The *Hobhouse Report* (1947) identified the New Forest as one of 12 proposed national parks. It took until the present century for the 12 landscapes thus recommended to be formally designated as national parks.[22] Hobhouse described the essential requirements for a national park:

> '…it should have great natural beauty, a high value for open-air recreation and substantial continuous extent. Further, the distribution of selected areas should as far as practicable be such that at least one of them is quickly accessible from each of the main centres of population in England and Wales. Lastly there is merit in variety and with the wide diversity of landscape which is available in England and Wales, it would be wrong to confine the selection of National Parks to the more rugged areas of mountain and moorland, and to exclude other districts which, though of less outstanding grandeur and wildness, have their own distinctive beauty and a high recreational value.'[23]

Hence, the statutory planning process reflected concerns typified by Abercrombie and his associates. Such developments had been triggered not only through voluntary action, but were enshrined at the creation of the modern planning system.[24] After the Second World War, major legislation in the *Town and Country Planning Act* (1947) established a need for planning permission[25] and the *National Parks and Access to the Countryside Act* (1949) established the statutory Nature Conservancy ('Council' was added to the full title when re-constituted in 1973),[26] the forerunner of Natural England (NE was formed in 2006). Nature Reserves became a matter of direct 'national intervention';[27] hence mid-twentieth century solutions were still seen in planning[28] although the dialogue had opened to include a range of heritage interests (landscape, heritage farming and architectural features) as well as providing for open-air recreation.

Once more, the typical British response to emerging governance issues in the New Forest was to set up the 'New Forest Committee' that reported in 1947 as the *Baker Report*.[29] This was very much a planning document of its time, making recommendations that included the creation of adequate shelter for forest labourers, changes to the verderers' constitution, further inclosures for planting and empowerment so the Forestry Commission might temporarily suspend common rights over land for afforestration drains and bridges were to be surveyed and faults remedied, leases provided for playing fields and golf courses, provision for camping, although no longer would aircraft land there. Ironically, it was to be 'declared a Nature Reserve'.[30] The *Report* was laid before Parliament in September 1947 and soon petitions were heard before a select committee of the House of Lords.[31] Most controversial was the enclosure of another 5000 acres (2024 ha) of the hitherto unenclosed forest. Local opposition was largely ignored and the result was the 1949 *New Forest Act* which was to join the legislation of 1877, 1964 and 1970 in dominating post-war governance of the New Forest.

The year 1949 was momentous for countryside conservation across England and Wales, but not for the New Forest. The *National Parks and Access to the Countryside Act* 1949 was to be:

> 'An Act to make provision for National Parks and the establishment of a National Parks Commission; to confer on the Nature Conservancy and local authorities powers for the establishment and maintenance of nature reserves; to make further provision for the recording, creation, maintenance and improvement of public paths and for securing access to open country, and to amend the law relating to rights of way; to confer further powers for preserving and enhancing natural beauty; and for matters connected with the purposes aforesaid.' [16 December 1949].[32]

Within this *Act* was also provision for Sites of Special Scientific Interest (SSSI) that are discussed below, and National Nature Reserves (NNR) that are today designated by Natural England (formerly the Nature Conservancy Council) as key places for wildlife and natural features. The can also reside in public ownership.[33] By the 1950s, there were ten national parks in England and Wales. These are the protected landscapes of the Peak District, Lake District, Snowdonia, Dartmoor, Pembrokeshire, the North York Moors, Yorkshire Dales, Exmoor, Northumberland and the Brecon Beacons.

The New Forest had lost out. This was perhaps an unexpected victory of the 'pro-timber lobby', given the drive for countryside conservation dating from the inter-war period and culminating in the contemporary *National Parks and Access to the Countryside Act* 1949. This was to have significant influence outside the perambulation, at least in 'upland' Britain.

The response to the needs within the New Forest was the *New Forest Act* of 1949. There was, however, acknowledged 'due regard to the existing rights and interests' ... and enigmatically provision for adjusting the forest to modern requirements. While consultation with the verderers by the Forestry Commission was a requirement in setting management prescriptions, and there were (for example) measures to protect the ancient and ornamental woodland, the presumption was otherwise towards timber production. Many of these concerns were addressed in the *New Forest Act* of 1964 (see below), including 'due regard to the interests of amenity', and again in 1970 when the verderers' effective control over recreational facilities, among other measures was realised.[34]

Peter Roberts can state:

> 'Throughout the thirties and forties the Forestry Commission pushed for greater powers to enclose new lands for timber production. They finally achieved their goal with the 1949 New Forest Act, making use of the perceived national need for timber following the war despite the presentations and concerns of the New Forest Association'.[35]

In 1949, however, it is as if the area had effectively been by-passed by the full conservation legislation of the time and it would be decades before the New Forest joined the 'family' of national parks, and together with the Norfolk Broads and the South Downs; the move represents an extension of the national park ethos into lowland Britain (Chapter 9). We may now ask: what of marginalised people within the perambulation?

Misfits

Some were evidently not accommodated in the emerging Brave New World in the first half of the twentieth century. Following his eviction and the hut burning in 1903 (Chapter 7), Harry 'Brusher' Mills had been permitted to erect a new hut on the estate of one Mr Price of New Park. Apparently he earned 1 shilling per snake. Brusher sadly passed away of heart disease on 1 July 1905 at the *Railway Inn* (now named the *Snake Catcher* in his honour) in Brockenhurst where a doctor pronounced him dead. Here he had been a regular figure given to drinking brandy and consuming bread and pickles, a lifestyle largely funded by the Zoological Society of London.[36]

The main tools of this trade were a forked stick and tongs that, following his passing, were inherited by one George Wateridge (1869–1948) who continued to supply snakes to London Zoo. George's problem was that his wife did not appreciate the storage of snakes in a dustbin; but his supply chain problems were partly eased by his 11 children who carried the serpents to the station for dispatch. After 1948, the trade passed to Mr Douglas Bessant, who eventually sought fresh horizons in New Zealand.[37] While this intriguing outcome of a division of labour in the New Forest came to an end (as far as we know) it is interesting to reflect it would not have survived the conservation legislation of the twentieth century. Furthermore, there are no snakes reported from New Zealand.

Following the Second World War, it is especially unfortunate that ethnic minorities could be described as inherently problematic in official documents. The *Baker Report* of 1947, states that 'in the Gypsies we meet a problem of more than local significance'.[38] The passage concerned describes them a group that has 'hardly reached the standard of the Stone Age', while the report also regrets there was no Gypsy representation to the New Forest Committee. It was commented that, using somewhat colonial language, apparently they had 'no headman to control them'. The account suggests a serious loss of traditional Romany ways, in effect their situation may be seen as a form of de-culturation. Until 1925 they camped where they chose, although they were accused of theft and general environmental degradation, including cutting trees and removing underwood. Apparently the conditions within the settlement camps subsequently established was reported as unsanitary.[39] Perhaps the move at that time, and indeed subsequently, was well-intentioned, for one thing 'some have worked on farms or in the Forest and did useful work during the war, their source of livelihood is a matter of speculation'. Settlement presumably might hasten the process of procurement of permanent work and their children might thereby attend school and healthcare provided. The gypsies would then be in a position to catch up economically with the general population by taking more regular employment – jobs in agriculture, horticulture and forestry being available in the area. However, on the basis of local representation, 'The simple solution is to remove all the gypsies as soon as possible to some place at least five miles distant from the perambulation of the Forest'.[40] Here they would be re-housed under the appropriate legislation, for after all, 'we would regard the gypsies as persons of the working class'.[41] The intention evidently sought full integration into the monetised economy.

The Romany community was largely driven out of the forest in the 1960s. Gypsies had long-established traditional camping grounds by the end of the nineteenth century and, by 1927, there were permanent compounds at Blackhamsley, Broomhill, Hardley, Latchmoor, Shave Wood and Thorney Hill, where the deputy surveyor could grant 6-month permissions,[42] however the system was seen by the gypsies themselves as harassment as it did not conform with their expectation of traditional lifestyles.

Redeeming the New Forest?

As a result of the 1949 *New Forest Act*, in effect the New Forest was managed by the Forestry Commission and it has been noted how that caused controversy.[43] Colin Tubbs agreed:

> 'Neither arguments by biologists that it was unnecessary for the perpetuation of the woods (the claimed objective) nor protests that it was illegal and an affront to an unparalleled cultural heritage, immediately prevailed'.[44]

While there have undoubtedly been tensions over the years, the Forestry Commission came to work with the verderers of the New Forest and latterly the New Forest Park Authority to take forward conservation objectives.

The 1949 *Act* was, however, seriously deficient despite increasing the number of verderers from six to ten. An official verderer was nominated by the crown, five elected by persons who occupied not less than one acre (0.4 ha) of land to which common land was attached, with four more representing the Ministry of Agriculture, Forestry Commission, the local planning authority and a countryside conservation organisation, first CPRE, later the Countryside Commission. The qualification for an elective verderer was similar to the electorate and the situation pertains today.

The verderers could now make by-laws and constrain livestock during times of infectious disease, however, drainage, control of coarse herbage/scrub encroachment (a process of dubious ecological value as it would restrict the expansion of woodland) and bridge maintenance became the responsibility of the Forestry Commission. Even worse, the *Act* charged the Forestry Commission with producing plans of common rights attached to each parcel of land, replacing the Register of Common Rights that had defined rights, by reference to tithe map numbers, a process that had become cumbersome. The *Divisum Imperium* was unfortunately recast by the mid-twentieth century,

The post-Second World War paradigm of supporting agricultural production through government investment became the norm. Softwood production for the market was to be the same.[45] Fortunately for the forest dwellers, the extensive reforms of the nineteenth century had given them some sort of voice, and subsequently the *New Forest Act* of 1949 provided for consultation of the re-constituted verderers by the Forestry Commission. The verderers could authorise the Forestry Commission to enclose a further 5000 acres (2025 ha) of open forest[46] but compensation was due to the verderers. The 'verderer's inclosures' were thus created, although seeded grazing strips were offered around these, in part to buffer against urbanisation and in part to keep livestock off the roads. In 1958, the New Forest Commoners' Defence Association, the New Forest Association and local residents resisted the enclosure of 2005 acres (1213 ha) held not in perpetuity, but as 150-year leases.[47]

There were further powers under the *New Forest Act* 1949. In the spirit of the age, the verderers could authorise the Minister of Agriculture to enclose land from the open forest for cultivation and improvement of grazing. Although there were limits placed for fencing at a particular time, eventually the entire heathlands and grasslands could be re-seeded and otherwise 'improved' following the wartime experience.[48] The *Act* also gave the Forestry Commission (with the consent of the verderers) powers to enclose parts of the unenclosed woodlands to ensure regeneration. Felling and replanting could be used, and

Site Name: New Forest SSSI

Status: Site of Special Scientific Interest (SSSI) notified under Section 28 of the Wildlife and Countryside Act 1981
Local Planning Authority: Hampshire County Council, New Forest District Council, Wiltshire County Council, Salisbury District Council, Test Valley Borough Council
National Grid Reference: SU 298081
Ordnance Survey Sheet 1:50,000: 195, 196
1:25,000: SU 10, 11, 20, 21, 30, 31, 40, SZ 29, 39
Area: 28,947.37 (ha) 71,528.95 (ac)
Date Notified (Under 1949 Act):
1959, 1971, 1974 Date of Last Revision: 1979
Date Notified (Under 1981 Act):
7 May 1987 Date of Previous Revision: 1987
Date of Last Revision:
28 February 1996 Date Confirmed: 14 November 1996
Other Information:
The New Forest is classified as a Grade 1 site in OA Nature Conservation Review

TABLE 8.1. Extract from the legal protection for the New Forest SSSI derived from the 1949 legislation.

this was to prove especially deleterious to the wellbeing of deciduous plantation and loss of biodiversity.[49]

For conservation there was one glimmer of hope. The *National Parks and Access to the Countryside Act* 1949[50] has created provision such that it was the: 'Duty of Conservancy to inform local planning authorities of areas of special scientific interest'. SSSIs are today the backbone of UK conservation legislation and are usually on private land. The re-designation of SSSIs and strengthening of powers under the *Wildlife and Countryside Act* of 1981[51] imposed a responsibility on owners and occupiers to manage the land according to the notification. This was deemed necessary largely because previous legislation had proven weak, as pressure on rural land use increased with intensification and development.[52] In 1959 parts of the New Forest were designated SSSI[53] followed by the entire area in 1971, designated in terms of the *National Parks and Access to the Countryside Act* 1949.

Thus, the New Forest is protected under this legislation (see Table 8.1) on account of its habitats (especially lowland heath (13,633 ha); valley mire (1450 ha); and ancient woodland pasture (3692 ha). The New Forest itself is not a National Nature Reserve. The national park, however, does include three NNRs – Langley Wood; Kingston Great Common and the North Solent NNR. It also includes a Ramsar site designation, and under European designations, it is a Special Protection Area and a proposed Special Area of Conservation,[54] something that will be amplified in Chapter 9.

With environmental issues coming to fore, the Forestry Commission's management policies and (particularly) its apparent lack of environmental

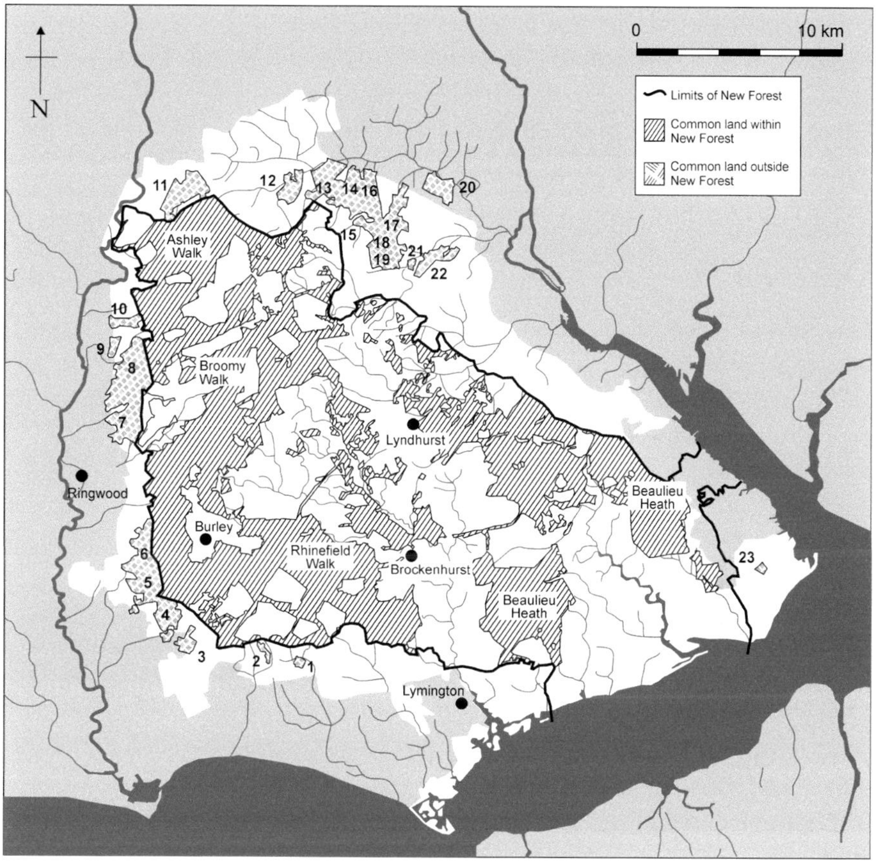

FIGURE 8.1. New Forest Common land. The Commons, located both both inside and outside the New Forest boundary, are: 1. Arnewood; 2. Bashley; 3. Poors; 4. Shirley; 5. Bisterne; 6. Kingston Great; 7. Rockford; 8. Ibsley; 9. Gorley Hill; 10. Hyde; 11. Hale Purlieu; 12. Hamptworth; 13. Landford; 14. Plaitford; 15. Penn; 16. West Wellow; 17. Half Moon; 18 Furzley Hill; 19. Cadnham; 20. Shelly; 21. Newbridge; 22. Copythorne; 23. Badminston.

AFTER HOSKINS AND STAMP 1963, 173

awareness, has caused heavy criticism, notably because of its long-standing promotion of commercial foresty, including the felling of broadleaved woods in inclosures, and there were threats to unenclosed wood pasture, although there were other issues including the management of visitor pressures.[55]

The 1960s started a number of legislative and managerial changes that set the tone for the next half century or so. First considered are the commons that do not form a part of the crown lands, although the historic relationship is self-evident. The term 'adjacent commons' was probably first used by the New Forest Committee.[56] This investigated the management of the forest, and within that report there is a list of these commons – common land contiguous with or near to the New Forest. Acknowledged is the need to maintain grazing, but this is not a very accurate list, because it includes land which had long since ceased to support the exercise of rights. In the later *New Forest Act* of 1964, many such areas, and a certain amount of enclosed land, were brought within partial control of the verderers' court. In the *Act* they are referred to as the 'Added Areas'. The change is important in considering the modern history of the forest.

Adjacent commons may or may not be actually abutting the New Forest as legally defined.[57] Their locations, as of the early 1960s, are shown in Figure 8.1.

The New Forest Association[58] states there are more than 25 such areas, the two additional to the map derived from that of Hoskins and Stamp. Excluding their third and fourth categories, Hightown, Furzeley, North Ripley, a part of Langley Wood (excluding Downton Common) Pound Bottom (ex-Downton Common) and Landford Bog (excluding Landford Common) are not mentioned by these authors, while the New Forest Association does not list Arnewood Common.

Category I Present-day Adjacent Commons
Hyde, Hale Purlieu, West Wellow, Gorley, Plaitford, Ibsley, Penn, Rockford, Furzley, Hightown, Cadnam, Kingston Great and HalfMoon

Category II Former Adjacent Commons
Bisterne, Shirley, North Ripley, Pound Bottom (ex Downton Common), Copythorne, Landford Bog (ex Landford Common), Part Langley Wood (ex Downton Common) and Franchise Wood (probably ex Downton Common).

Category III Minstead Manor Waste and land at The Grove
Minstead Manor Waste is unique in comprising the only major area of common land *within* the 1801 perambulation of the New Forest which is not owned by the Minister of Agriculture.

Category IV Lands with former management but not directly related to the New Forest
Whiteparish Common, Langley Wood (greater part), Loosehanger Woods *etc.*, Roydon Woods (but includes a former part of the crown lands) and Upper Pennington Common)

The lack of clarity of definition perhaps reflects the uncertainty as to where commoners' rights outside the forest actually reside. Furthermore, there is seldom any clear indication on the ground that demonstrates where a common ends and the crown lands begin. The matter of commons is returned to in the next chapter.

A further *New Forest Act* was passed in 1964. This was on account of there being increased accidents involving commoners' animals, and so there was provision for fencing off roads, especially the A31 and A35. A second imperative was the exercising of common rights over the manorial wastes around the northern and western fringes, outside the perambulation.[59] These 'adjacent commons' as well as the open forest could be thus exploited under rights of 'vicinage' due to their proximity[60] and many commoners could avoid marking fees by turning animals out on unregulated commons. Marking fees relate to animals belonging to a commoner with rights that should be branded and turned out upon payment of a marking fee to an agister.[61]

The New Forest Act 1964 thus extended the perambulation to include an extra 1395 acres (565 ha) of adjacent commons, emplaced cattle grids and fenced the forest to constrain animals. The additional commons are Rockford, Hyde and Ibsley Commons on the western edge, Hale Purlieu and Bramshaw Common on the north-east side.[62] Although the *Atlas of Claims to Common Rights* was reinstated and admitted claims to pasture over the additional areas, other rights were not affected. Campsites were permitted on the unenclosed forest and the

FIGURE 8.2. Extract from Milne's map (1791) scale 1:63,6330.[63]

WITH PERMISSION FOM PORTSMOUTH UNIVERSITY

pannage season became flexible. The verderers and Forestry Commission were 'to have regard to the desirability of conserving flora, fauna and geological and physiographical features of special interest'. Evidently the tide was turning on the problematic (some say disastrous) *New Forest Act* 1949. 'Having regard' for conservation was playing catch-up with events outside the perambulation, but it remains curious how the amenity value of the forest was not yet pushed to the fore, despite the prevalence of the motor car by the 1960s.

Historically, manors of both sides of the lower Avon had grazed stock on peripheral areas, but not within the perambulation during the summer.[64] There were strong and defended grazing rights and the relationships of vicinage with peripheral areas was being addressed, for outside the perambulation, the floodplain supplying fattening pasture, and hay, pony economy within the forest, so that for the ecologist, animal production within was supplemented by grazing without the perambulation. By way of illustration, Thomas Milne's map published in 1791 shows linked to Avon valley with east–west drovers' roads (Fig. 8.2), but these closed in 1960s with the perambulation cattle gridded.[65] Was this to be Fortress Forest? The domain of kings had become the fiefdom of the Forestry Commission.

The Forestry Commission was clearly high handed, yet it had begun to consult with the verderers as was required. It is all too easy to characterise a clash of modernity and historic management systems; the latter has been reformed several times. It is a clash of aesthetic and 'production' values, for perceived beauty of the area was already producing its own conflicts as visitor pressure signified by the rise in deaths of grazing animals on roads, meaning that day-trippers to penetrate even the most remote parts of the New Forest. There were worse plans in the offing.

The 1963 working plan virtually to eliminate broadleaved trees from the inclosures was leaked in 1970. As a result, the Minister of Agriculture was called in and issued a temporary ban of broadleaved felling. Unfortunately further damage occurred at this time[66] for the Forestry Commission continued to straighten and deepen watercourses to favour coniferous afforestation over broadleaved. At a crisis meeting in November 1968 in the verderers' court, the deputy surveyor resigned on a point of confidence, while the New Forest Association sought (without success) to suspend the broadleaved felling programme. Taken to its logical extent, the status quo might have reduced the broadleaved area to screening belts around coniferous plantations. The impact on watercourses and wetlands is something only now being remedied (Chapter 9). The commission also assumed powers under the 1964 *Act* to commercially exploit unenclosed pasture woods, generally through thinning. This badly affected the Brinken and Rushpole woods in 1969. By this date, plans for extensive clear-felling emerged.

The formation of the New Forest Consultative Panel by the Forestry Commission in 1970 created a forum for local public opinion and management objectives. While Tubbs was skeptical about its motives,[67] it came to fulfil 'a useful guardianship role and has killed off many potentially damaging ideas before germination'. The Forestry Commission was reined in by a mandate of 1971 that was renewed unaltered in 1982.[68] This mandate declared that the New Forest must be regarded 'as a national heritage priority and priority given to the conservation of its traditional character'. In any event, the unenclosed woodlands were to be conserves, without regard to timber production and the conversion to conifer stands within inclosures was to cease.

The *Commons Registration Act* 1965 was 'An Act to provide for the registration of common land and of town or village greens; to amend the law as to prescriptive claims to rights of common; and for purposes connected therewith.' Defra holds over 12,000 Commons Commissioners' decisions (this was a statutory body abolished in 2010). The *Act* of 1965 required local authorities in England and Wales to establish registers of common land and town or village greens within their areas; recording the extent of the land, the owners of the land and rights of common held over them. Commons Commissioners were appointed to settle disputed entries, and to determine the ownership of unclaimed common land and greens.[69] In the New Forest, few common rights were so far registered under Register of Commons.[70]

Actually, the view from the verderers finds that the New Forest was excluded from the *Act*, causing enquiries to be directed towards them specifically, who were not in a position to answer.[71] Then differences in extent of the forest before and after the revision of the perambulation in 1964 may be clarified by inspection of a definitive map held in the verderers' office. However, there is no definitive register of lands within the forest subject to common rights; the verderers can only provide general guidelines. Enquirers are invited to 'in the final resort, have to rely on their own researches'. There are, however, two atlases concerned with common rights. One concerns rights exercisable over land in the ownership of Defra, or acquired by that ministry, both inside or outside the 1964 boundary. The second deals with only the common of pasture (not the other traditional rights) for certain commons inside or outside the 1964 boundary, but located inside the 1964 boundary, but outside the boundary of 1801. For other rights over this land, interested persons are referred to Dr Tavener's *The Common Lands of Hampshire* but it must be remembered that this book pre-dates both the *New Forest Act* 1964 and the *Commons Registration Act* 1965.

Conclusions

The New Forest represents both a continuation of the silviculture of earlier times but it also reflects the changes in a wider agriculture into the twentieth century as the switch to softwood reflects the end of demand for timber for the navy. The collision of interests emerged as largely between the Forestry Commission planning and operations and a wider landscape, heritage and biodiversity lobby. This conflict is manifest through interests represented by both state agencies and the voluntary sector, including pressure groups such as the NFA and NFCDA, while the interests of the commoners remains a thread from the early medieval period reflecting forest dweller interests. The late arrival of a national park reflects these tensions.

Commoners were, through the reforms of the 1877 *Act*, able to have a formalised voice. Their input is absolutely central to the maintenance of open and wood pasture areas; without the protection of their interests and contribution through grazing animals the New Forest would likely be all forestry, in the fully modern sense, as is the Forest of Dean. The twentieth century is the century of the Forestry Commission, whose support for widespread afforestation was finally reigned in in the 1970s, and who now co-operate in schemes for conservation.

During the Second World War there was a periodic suppression of grazing and the forest was once more brought in to directly serve state interests; military in terms of airfields and bomb ranges, agricultural in terms of (apparently) ill-fated efforts at the production of food crops in the decade after 1940. One suspects that once more, the soils of the New Forest had the last say. Longer-term changes in drainage, however, persisted into the present century as another lasting manifestation of Forestry Commission investment in the area.

Very significant is the rise of both state and voluntary sector conservation initiatives, reflecting the developments of the twentieth century environmental politics. The National Trust and the Hampshire and Isle of Wight Wildlife Trust both have a high profile in the New Forest alongside statutory agencies (Chapter 9). Arguably the activities of the Forestry Commission between the *New Forest Act* 1949, and the rise of the New Forest National Park Authority were mitigated by the presence of the range of agencies (statutory and voluntary) that were concerned with conservation. Efforts to record commoners' rights were clearly less successful than might have been desired, and certainly would not match the surveying and resource auditing linked with forestry and habitat. Thus, between 1900 and 2000 the governance of the New Forest was to change as never before in a single century. The next chapter will deal with the rise of the New Forest National Park in this context.

Notes

1. Past book reviews (n.d.) http://www.newforestcentre.org.uk/pastbooks/#March2009. Accessed Sept 2017.
2. J. R. Wise (1883) *The New Forest: Its History and Scenery*, 44. Sotheran, London.
3. G. F. Peterken (1981) *Woodland Conservation and Management*, 17. Chapman and Hall, London.
4. *New Forest Act* (1949) http://www.legislation.gov.uk/ukpga/Geo6/12-13-14/69.
5. J. Sheail (2002) *An Environmental History of the Twentieth Century*, 10. Palgrave, London.
6. *Ibid.*, 16.
7. The National Trust (n.d.) http://www.nationaltrust.org.uk/main/w-nt_acts_1907–1971.pdf. Accessed Oct 2010.
8. Hampshire and Isle of Wight Wildlife Trust Celebrates Golden Jubilee. http://www.thetraveleditor.com/article/6192/News_Events_Hampshire_Isle_of_Wight_Wildlife_Trust_celebrates_Golden_Jubilee.html.
9. P. Roberts (2014) pers. comm.
10. New Forest Commoners Defence Association. http://www.nfcda.co.uk/. Accessed Oct 2012; P. Roberts (2014) pers. comm.
11. See Chapter 7.
12. J. Thirsk (1997) *Alternative Agriculture: A history*, 149. Oxford University Press, Oxford.
13. Peterken (1981) *op. cit.* in note 3, 17.
14. Thirsk (1997) *op. cit.* in note 12, 165.
15. History of the Forestry Commission (2017) http://www.forestry.gov.uk/forestry/CMON-4UUM6R. Accessed Sept 2017.
16. H. Cook, and A. Inman (2012) The voluntary sector and conservation for England:

achievements, expanding roles and uncertain future. *Journal of Environmental Management* 112, 170–77. http://dx.doi.org/ 10.1016/j.jenvman.2012.07.013.

17. BBC (2012) *A Great British Story*. http://www.bbc.co.uk/programmes/b01jxr9z. Accessed June 2013.
18. H. F. Cook (2010) Boom, slump and intervention: changing agricultural landscapes on Romney Marsh, 1790 to 1990. In M. P. Waller, E. Edwards and L. Barber (eds), *Romney Marsh: Persistence and Change in a Coastal Lowland*, 155–83. Romney Marsh Research Trust, Sevenoaks.
19. C. R. Tubbs (2001) *New Forest, the History, Ecology and Conservation*, 94. New Forest Ninth Centenary Trust, Fordingbridge.
20. New Forest Committee (1947) *The Baker Report*, 44–45. cmd 7245 Forestry Commission London HMSO.
21. 1940 to 2009 *National Parks and Access to the Countryside Act*. http://www.diamondsinthelandscape.org.uk/home/about-us/nationalparkstory.htm. Accessed June 2013.
22. New Forest Association. http://www.newforestassociation.org/history.html.
23. *National Parks and Access to the Countryside Act*. *op. cit.* in note 21.
24. Cook and Inman (2012) *op. cit.* in note 16.
25. P. Brandon (1998) *The South Downs*. Phillimore, Chichester.
26. OPSI (n.d.) *National Parks and Access to the Countryside Act* 1949. http://www.legislation.gov.uk/ukpga/Geo6/12-13-14/97/data.pdf.
27. D. Evans (1992) *A History of Nature Conservation in Britain*, chapter 4. Routledge, London.
28. J. Sheail (2002) *op. cit.* in note 5, 115.
29. *Ibid.*
30. *Ibid.*, 77–84.
31. Tubbs (2001) *op. cit.* in note 19, 91.
32. *National Parks and Access to the Countryside Act (*1949) http://www.legislation.gov.uk/ukpga/Geo6/12-13-14/97.
33. Naturenet. http://www.naturenet.net/status/nnr.html. Accessed June 2013.
34. R. Daponte (2004) Managing Recreation. https://www.forestry.gov.uk/pdf/ManagingRecreation.pdf/$FILE/ManagingRecreation.pdf. Accessed Sept 2017.
35. New Forest Association (2016) http://www.newforestassociation.org/our-history.html. Accessed Sept 2016.
36. D. J. Stagg (1983) *Snake Catchers of the New Forest*. New Forest Association, Fordingbridge.
37. *Ibid.*, 11–13.
38. New Forest Committee (1947) *op. cit.* in note 20, 66.
39. *Ibid.*, 66–67.
40. *Ibid.*
41. *Ibid.*, 103.
42. L. Smith (2004) *Romany Nevi-Wesh: An Informal History of the New Forest Gypsies*, 136. Nova Forest Publishing, Lyndhurst.
43. Clive Chatters (2011) pers. comm.
44. Tubbs (2001) *op. cit.* in note 19, 102.
45. Cook (2010) *op. cit.* in note 18.
46. History of the Crown Lands (n.d.) http://www.forestry.gov.uk/pdf/eng-new-forest-b2-history.pdf/$FILE/eng-new-forest-b2-history.pdf. Accessed Sept 2017.
47. Tubbs (2001) *op. cit.* in note 19, 93.
48. *Ibid.*, 94.

49. *Ibid.*, 222.
50. National Parks and Access to the Countryside Act (1949) http://www.legislation.gov.uk/ukpga/1949/97/pdfs/ukpga_19490097_en.pdf. Accessed Sept 2017.
51. Wildlife and Countryside Act (1981) http://www.legislation.gov.uk/ukpga/1981/69. Accessed Sept 2017
52. 'Naturenet' The History of Conservation Legislation in the UK. http://www.naturenet.net/status/history.html.
53. England's Woods and Forests (2017) https://www.forestry.gov.uk/forestry/infd-6a5kw3. Accessed Sept 2017.
54. *Ibid.*
55. History of the Forestry Commission (2017) http://www.forestry.gov.uk/forestry/cmon-4uum6r. Accessed Sept 2017; Tubbs (2001) *op. cit.* in note 19, 102.
56. New Forest Association (n.d.) *A History of the New Forest and its Adjacent Commons*, New Forest Association, Fordingbridge.
57. W. G. Hoskins and L. D. Stamp (1963) *The Common Lands of England and Wales*, 173. New Naturalist, Collins, London.
58. New Forest Association (n.d.) *op. cit.* in note 56.
59. Tubbs (2001) *op. cit.* in note 19, 94–96.
60. Commoning in the Forest. http://www.newforest.gov.uk/index.cfm?articleid=295 Accessed Oct 2012.
61. Forest Rights (2016) http://www.verderers.org.uk/rights.html. Accessed Sept 2017.
62. Tubbs (2001) *op. cit.* in note 19, 96–97.
63. http://www.geog.port.ac.uk/webmap/hantsmap/hantsmap/milne1/milne1.htm http://www.geog.port.ac.uk/webmap/hantsmap/hantsmap/milne1/mln23.htm
64. R. Reeves (2013) pers. comm.
65. Clive Chatters (2011) pers. comm.
66. Commoning in the Forest *op. cit.* in note 60.
67. Tubbs (2001) *op. cit.* in note 19, 102.
68. *Ibid.*, 222.
69. Commons and Greens (n.d.) http://www.acraew.org.uk/index.php?page=commissioners-decisions. Accessed Sept 2017.
70. Clive Chatters (2011) pers. comm.
71. Forest Rights *op. cit.* in note 61.

CHAPTER 9

The Rise of the National Park (1980–Present)

Recalling changes during 900 years of forest management:

> 'And the lord king has commanded that, when a forester has the lord king's own woods in his charge, if those woods are destroyed and he can by no means show good cause for the destruction of the woods, vengeance shall be taken on the forester's own body and not otherwise.'[1]

For the understatement of the millennium, we may concur the style of forest governance somewhat changed between the twelfth and the twenty-first centuries. More humanely, but perhaps less clear:

> 'The Department for Environment, Food and Rural Affairs (Defra) has commissioned this review of its part in the process of establishing the New Forest National Park Authority (NFNPA). It has done so in order to establish what lessons might be learned. A separate review of the process of designation is planned by the Countryside Agency. The period covered is from the announcement that the Secretary of State was "minded to confirm the designation" of the New Forest on 28th June 2004, up to the time when the permanent Chief Executive took up her post on 11th July 2005. That was the period during which Defra had the practical leadership in the establishment the National Park Authority (NPA).'[2]

New Forest National Park (NFNP)

Set within a somewhat different discourse to medieval monarchs and to the subsequent charters limiting their powers (or guaranteeing the rights of commoners and others against arbitrary authority), the New Forest today falls within modern concepts of a highly valued area. Not only does it constitute a specific range of landscapes and require specific management prescriptions, but there is multi-sectoral involvement within the New Forest. The crown owns much of it (but by no means all), the Forestry Commission manages much of it by proxy, there is admirable support from the voluntary sector (largely the Hampshire and Isle of Wight Wildlife Trust and the National Trust), while there are a range of private concerns, relating to tourism, visitors and agriculture.

In the New Forest, the Hampshire and Isle of Wight Wildlife Trust today works in partnership and manages land within the NFNPA area. Nature reserves within National Park include Roydon Woods, Fletchwood Meadows, Holmsley Gravel Pit, Long Aldermoor, Copythorne Common, Lymington Marshes and Linwood.[3]

The National Trust is only second to the crown as a landowner in the New Forest, with some 2400 ha on five different sites on the western and eastern edges. The properties within the established New Forest boundary are: Hale Purlieu, Bramshaw Commons, Rockford, Ibsley, Hightown Commons and Foxbury Plantation (just outside this boundary, but within the national park).[4] It will be recalled that in 1924, the Royal Forests including the New Forest and the Forest of Dean were transferred to the Forestry Commission.[5]

The Forestry Commission actually manages almost half of the national park area. Within the national park, the Hampshire and Isle of Wight Wildlife Trust is a major landowner, with its two largest reserves, Roydon Woods and Keyhaven and Lymington Marshes, both within the boundary.[6] The National Trust owns and manages 1600 ha (4000 acres) on five different sites, and supports 'commoning', the ancient system of farming that has shaped these commons and is directly involved in management of these areas, including its car parks.

The properties within the established New Forest boundary are:

- Hale Purlieu
- Bramshaw Commons
- Rockford, Ibsley
- Hightown Commons
- Foxbury Plantation

The Foxbury plantation is just outside the historic boundary (but within the national park) and the trust plans to return it to heathland and deciduous woodland following a long period as a plantation. The old network of ponds, ditches and streams will be restored and public access encourage. Otherwise they have cleared out plantations and plan to restore historic landscapes, including those of their common.

The creation of the NFNP occurred in the twenty-first century, yet it legitimately claims its origins in the *National Parks and Access to the Countryside Act* 1949; this provided the framework for the creation of national parks and Areas of Outstanding Natural Beauty. While it was to be over half a century before the New Forest joined the 'national park family' the *New Forest Act* of the same year saw an adjustment of the New Forest perambulation with conservation in mind and there was the establishment of a new Verderers' Court.[7]

Yet, effectively, a significant proportion of the New Forest was managed by the Forestry Commission and that caused tensions. Specifically, the senior managers of the Forestry Commission had a role to promote their institutional priorities rather than champion the interests of the whole forest.[8]

For context, between 1951 and 1957 ten National Parks were designated in England and Wales, followed by the Broads in 1989 and then the New Forest in 2005. Subsequently the South Downs National Park became fully operational in 2011. The break of over 40 years in national park creation not only separates the times of creation of upland and lowland national parks in England but also incorporates the period of massive state intervention in British agriculture. While this point is highly relevant to the South Downs and the Broads, due to egregious arable agricultural development since 1940, it is not so much the case for the New Forest, which has experienced relatively little by way of investment in modern production agriculture, despite moves in that direction during and after the Second World War.

The *zeitgeist* manifest by the 1990s still favoured the creation of national parks by the state, despite 15 years or more of neo-liberal economic reform in the UK. Evidently, government looked to become ever more inclusive of direct stakeholder interests to include local communities. The 'Third Force' (Chapter 8), that is the voluntary sector in countryside conservation, was incorporated as the National Trust and the Wildlife Trusts within the Forest[9] alongside moves to strengthen local democracy.

The *Environment Act* 1995 revised the original legislation and set out two statutory purposes for national parks in England and Wales:[10]

- Conserve and enhance the natural beauty, wildlife and cultural heritage
- Promote opportunities for the understanding and enjoyment of the special qualities of national parks by the public

When national parks carry out these purposes they also have the duty to:

- Seek to foster the economic and social well-being of local communities within the national parks

All the above would be easily applied in the New Forest.

Of the 13 national parks in England and Wales, the New Forest (area *c.*570 km^2) is the second smallest whilst the Peak District is the fifth largest at 1,437 km^2. Yet, in many ways the New Forest is a lowland counterpart for the long-established Peak District National Park. Both are excessively visited, and both are located in a populous part of the country, being surrounded by conurbations. This consideration was arguably the single greatest change in the UK's countryside management, ensuring not only the conservation of whole landscapes, but enabling their management and conservation such that millions of urban dwellers could enjoy the countryside.

The combination of economic sectors and imperatives of access is recognised as a 'pluralist' approach (incorporating private, state and voluntary responses). It is also the outcome of the post-war development of the planning process.[11] Historic landscapes and 'heritage' farming are to be preserved. Incorporation in the national parks is designated under the *National Parks and Access to the Countryside Act* 1949 as amended by the *Environment Act* 1995. The New Forest was the first national park to be designated since the 1995 *Act*, and it allowed for the creation of free-standing National Park Authorities.[12] The *Environment Act* 1995 also confirms that all NPAs will be the sole local planning authorities for their administrative areas – a major development and based on over 40 years of experience where the alternative (of having constituent local authorities retain planning powers) proved ineffective.

Boundaries again

By the mid-noughties, the boundaries defining the New Forest varied by purpose, leading to many apparent anomalies; in short there are various boundaries for, and ways of referring, to the New Forest which could lead to confusion.[13] These are summarised below:

- New Forest District – the area administered by New Forest District Council. It includes the majority of the New Forest National Park
- New Forest National Park – the area designated as national park in March 2005, it includes land outside New Forest District in the former Salisbury District (now Wiltshire unitary) and Test Valley Borough
- New Forest Heritage Area – the area formerly defined through local plans that had national park status for planning purposes. It became defunct on the designation of the national park. Most of the area has been incorporated into the national park
- New Forest Perambulation – the area where the verderers' byelaws apply to unenclosed land, principally the core area of the forest. The perambulation has no significance in planning and we may add
- Designation of the New Forest SSSI under the *Wildlife and Countryside Act* (Chapter 8)

On the NFNPA there is a legacy for county councils. For both Wiltshire Council and Hampshire County Council are active partners working within the national park and are represented by seven members (out of 22) on the National Park Authority.

Figure 9.1 gives an idea of certain 'protected areas' within the NFNP and the NF District Boundary and also the Ramsar (wetland), Special Protection Areas and the Special Area of Conservation in order to demonstrate not only the importance of the New Forest today, but also its problems of definition at a political level. The draft Designation Order proposed a much larger boundary for the national park, including land around the River Blackwater in the Test Valley, the towns of Lymington and Ringwood, and Dibden Bay, as well as parts of the Avon Valley. The lower Avon valley is excluded from the NFNPA, but originally the plan was to include this too.

The New Forest District outside the national park also contains substantial areas of nature conservation designation, for example the rivers Avon and Test are both Sites of Special Scientific Interest (SSSI) and the river Avon and lower Test Valley are included in Special Areas of Conservation. Included are Blashford Lakes; north of Ringwood are SSSIs, SPAs and Ramsar sites. The majority of the waterside coastal marshes and mudflats are designated as SSSIs, set within an SPA and a Ramsar site. For example, there is the North Solent National Nature Reserve (NNR)[14] 'within the NFNP, the North Solent NP is a large coastal reserve, where ancient oak woods meet estuaries and salt marsh to create a diverse and rich mix of habitats and wildlife'.

In addition to the Sites of Scientific Interest (SSSI) that have their origins in the *National Parks and Access to the Countryside Act* 1949 with re-notification in

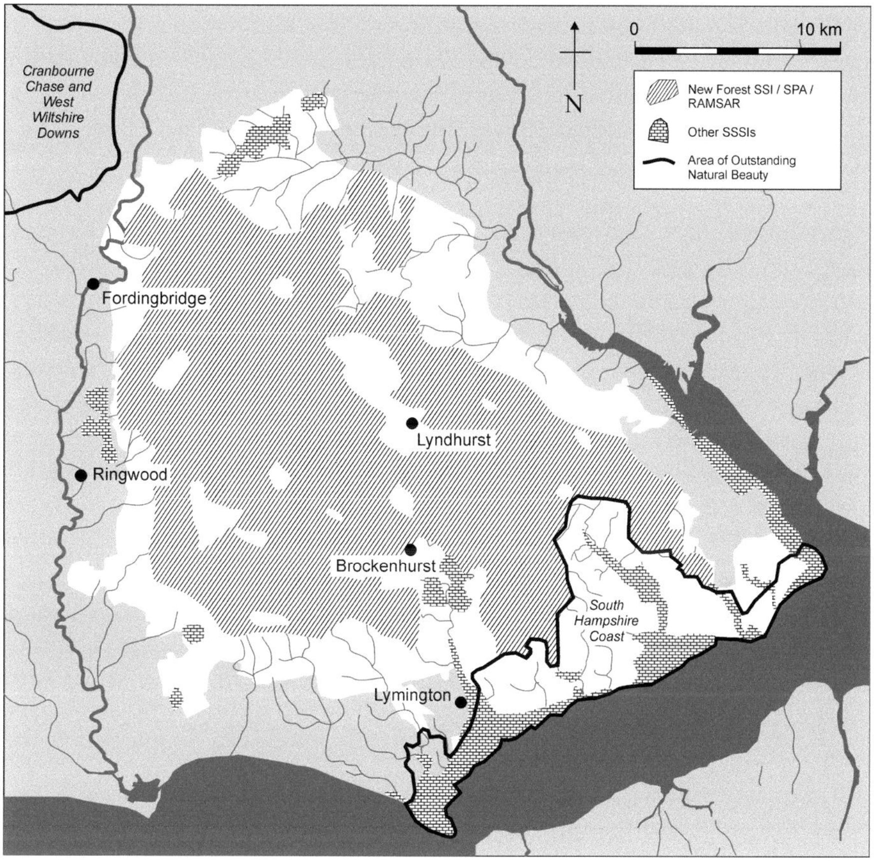

FIGURE 9.1. Protected areas in the New Forest.

WITH PERMISSION OF SOUTHAMPTON UNIVERSITY: HTTP://WWW.GEODATA.SOTON.AC.UK/NEWFOREST/PUBLIC/RESOURCES/STRATEGY.HTML

1981, there are also (local) Sites of Importance for Nature Conservation (SINC) and County Wildlife Sites recognised by the NFNPA.

Neither should the European and international dimensions be overlooked. Special Protection Areas (SPAs) are designated due to their international importance for birds in line with EU legislation. The main New Forest SSSI is also an SPA, because of rare and vulnerable bird habitats and include the honey buzzard, nightjar, woodlark and Dartford warbler.[15] Special Areas of Conservation (SACs) are designated under the European Commission's Habitats Directive. Within the national park there are several sites of SAC including coastal/maritime locations. The New Forest SAC encompasses around 29,300 ha including most of the unenclosed forest and inclosures together with Langley Wood, Whiteparish Common, Landford Heath and Loosehangar Copse and Meadows in the north, and Royden Woods in the south. The Solent maritime SAC extends for 11,325 ha and comprises the Solent coastline and maritime habitats to the mean high water mark, including estuaries of the Beaulieu Rivers and Southampton Water. The River Avon SAC (450 ha) comprises the river and river valley from Breamore south to Christchurch.

Ramsar sites are international designations dating from 1971, denoting wetlands of international importance. This level of protection is also given to

SACs and SPAs so that, if planning permission is sought, the same stringent procedures need to be adhered. The main New Forest SSSI is a Ramsar site, because of the rare plant and invertebrate species associated with its wetlands. The Solent and Southampton Water is another important Ramsar site within the national park.

The national park has one outstanding minerals site to be completed (at Badminston) and no new minerals sites are proposed. Pressure for development and from the sand and gravel extraction interests effectively excluded the western side of the lower Avon valley; the area also contains some agricultural land. There is also one large scale active landfill site within the national park at Pound Bottom, which was originally granted planning permission by Wiltshire County Council prior to the creation of the national park. Of course critics may legitimately argue that designation of the NFNP boundary imparts outward pressure for development of sand and gravel, and indeed for subsequent landfill.

Even land-use consultants can wax lyrical:

> 'The NFNP has the largest area of "unsown" vegetation in lowland England, the largest area of depressions on peat substrates and the largest area of mature, semi-natural beech woodland in England. It is also the largest area of lowland heath in Western Europe and the most extensive area of active wood pasture with old oak and beech in north-west Europe. It contains about 90 clearly defined valley mires or bogs, within 20 different valley systems, with more of this habitat in the New Forest than the rest of Britain and western Europe combined. The open heathland, mire and pasture woodland of the New Forest are unique at this scale and in this combination. The Forest also contains a large number of older trees which support a wide range of species including insects, birds, bats, mosses, lichens and fungi.'[16]

Critics say the national park boundary was drawn by consultants who saw it through, but lacked in-depth local knowledge, and it is said that only the objectors were heard. The sand and gravel industry interests also expressed their views on boundaries. They did, however, find 'a long legacy of environmental and recreational management by established bodies.' This includes the historic system of verderers and agisters, reformed in the nineteenth century, but going since before Henry II. Today, the Court of Verderers manages the traditional activity of communing, whereby some property owners are entitled to let their ponies, donkeys, cattle, pigs or sheep roam.

There was a problem in terms of defining a 'new perambulation', or more accurately deciding what was within and what was without the new national park. Figure 9.2 shows the finally agreed national park boundary.[17] In drawing the boundary, allegedly only the objectors were listened to and some of the historic perambulation was left without the national park. Although Dibden Bay was originally proposed for inclusion within the New Forest National Park, the final designation in 2005 excluded it, following representations from the landowner (Associated British Ports). Ultimately, it was a central government decision what land was included within the national park, for the NFNPA has, of itself, no power to amend the national park boundary.

FIGURE 9.2. The National Park boundary.

REPRODUCED BY PERMISSION: HTTP://1.BP.BLOGSPOT.COM/-3GSCSIY2XBU/TLKC9IIHP6I/AAAAAAAAAWM/QLKAJRE3RHE/S1600/NEW-FOREST-MAP.GIF

It has been noted how the original plan was to include much of the lower Avon valley (floodplain) and also, in two instances resulted in a park and a power station being excluded from the New Forest National Park. Despite this being a scenic and historic landscape in its own right, it provides context for the New Forest. The first related to the inclusion of Hinton Admiral Park and a challenge to the new Forest Order was made by Meyrick Estate Management Ltd, the second was a challenge from RWE NPower and related to the Fawley Power Station plc; this was settled out of court with the power station area excluded. The challenge from Meyrick Estate Management Ltd was upheld by the High Court. The Court of Appeal found in favour of the first appeal, the judgement included parkland different from that of the forest excluding Hinton Admiral Park from the NFNPA area.[18]

Modern commoners

The situation of common land is covered in Chapter 8 and illustrated in Figure 8.1. A Right of Common is the authority for the occupier of a plot of land to take specific material or products from somebody else's land. Common rights are attached to specific plots, and may be purchased or sold as a property changes hands. It is generally believed that possession of rights today has no significant effect on property value.

Today, the principal product is grazing and the owner of the land is the crown. Land with Common Rights may be outside the perambulation, with many holdings in villages on the periphery of the forest.[19]

In the New Forest, rights are generally attached to a particular property. Historically, estovers (fuel cutting) continued to be exploited and there was conflict between the needs of local people, and that of the timber plantation. Today, there are around 500 practising commoners and some 7000 animals in the forest each year.[20]

The exercise of common rights is seen by many as the only efficient (and cost-effective) way of managing such an extensive area of lowland heath. The administrative body designed to control the exercise of rights is the Court of Verderers of the New Forest, and this is largely the product of a series of post-Ssecond World War Acts of Parliament. Verderers' figures show there were 446 practising commoners in 1998 but some of these operated on private commons adjoining the open forest. Once commoners were almost exclusively members of old, established families, their number now includes a number in 'incomers' who are interested in customs and hence keep animals. There are perhaps 7000–8000 head of domestic stock, this high number attributed to problems of disposing of ponies (for which there is no demand) and also a large numbers of cattle encouraged by recent past high subsidy levels.[21] The grazing is regulated by the Verderers' Court (the verderers being elected by the commoners) and there is an electoral register. The comprehensive New Forest Commoning Review (2007)[22] identified, among other imperatives, the lack of affordable housing for commoners and the need to protect back up grazing land as perhaps the two biggest issues facing commoning in the twenty-first century. Therefore not only are there economic problems in maintaining grazing, but also there are practical problems from visitor pressure including motorists, walkers, mountain bikers and dogs.

Agri-environment payments

Governmental intervention in agricultural and woodland management provides for a number of options. Similar arrangements are to be found throughout the European Union and beyond. Farmers and others concerned with managing heritage landscapes may be paid what amounts to (a) subsidy for their produce to supplement their income, manage the supply of agricultural commodities or ensure security of food supply (b) receive payment that is not strictly a subsidy (although it will help business income) given for environmental services rendered. The latter case now applies in England and 'subsidy' payment is now 'de-coupled' because agri-environmental payment is not linked to livestock numbers, sale or crop production, but to agri-environmental benefits to accrue for managing a particular land holding is a 'sustainable' manner.

There is a particular and inherent problem with marginal land, for what may be rich ecologically is 'marginal' in the economic sense. Such areas may not command a high price on any open land market, or command high rental value on account of it producing poor returns on a purely profit and loss basis. Indeed, many of the 'traditional' commoners who do not have other sources of income are living, in micro-economic terms, somewhere close to subsistence level.[23] With this in mind, there is a purely economic problem of maintaining the historic landscape, especially in terms of keeping up grazing pressures and preventing scrubbing over of the land surface.

Modern environmental payments under 'Environmental Stewardship'[24] for England include payments for hedgerow management, managing permanent grassland, managing ditches or emplacing buffer strips. There is a provision for conversion to organic agriculture, managing upland areas and 'Higher Level Stewardship' pays for more complex types of management and agreements that are tailored to local circumstances, including historic landscapes and enrolment is for ten years to give some stability. Single payments also are available under management agreement for Sites of Special Scientific Interest in England.

In the New Forest, Higher Level Stewardship (HLS) Scheme and the Verderers' Grazing Scheme[25] have replaced, and improved, payments based in the earlier (and in some ways similar) Countryside Stewardship Scheme (Table 9.1). For example:

> 'In addition to direct payments to commoners for depasturing stock, which is so essential to the ecology of the Forest, the Scheme is now able to fund a range of projects to sustain commoning on the Forest, now and into the future. These include the New Forest pony 'Bloodline Scheme' which is intended to re-introduce selected

TABLE 9.1. Eligibility criteria for The Verderers' Grazing Scheme (see text). There are further requirements that relate to animal welfare, timing of depasturing, farm standards *etc.*

Eligibility. To be eligible for the Scheme a commoner must:

1.1 Hold common rights for the animals that they enter in the scheme.
1.2 Actively depasture all their animals that are entered in the scheme, for the full qualifying periods.
1.3 Pay Marking Fees for all their animals that are depastured.
1.4 Enter all depastured animals into the Scheme, both those on the Crown Lands and those on the adjacent commons.
1.5 Comply where they apply with the Verderers' byelaws, the *New Forest* Acts, the Forestry Commission byelaws, National Trust byelaws, the 1964 Commons agreement, and the terms and conditions of the Scheme, at all times.
1.6 Meet the Verderers' standards for animal welfare and any additional welfare requirements introduced by law or good agricultural practice.
1.7 Own all the animals that he or she enters in the Scheme and provide proof of ownership to the Scheme Manager on request.
1.8 Have a valid Equine or Bovine Passport, or an entry in the Verderers' List, for all of their ponies and/or cattle that are depastured – regardless of whether or not they are entered in the Scheme.
1.9 Comply with all directives issued by or on behalf of the Verderers.
1.10 Maintain reasonable commoning standards and practices at all times (as determined by the verderers).
1.11 Not encroach on the Crown land or other common land.

> bloodlines into the Forest; the 'Stallion Scheme' which manages the selection and number of stallions which run on the Forest each year; and a newly introduced 'Pony Welfare Programme' which encourages commoners to replace older ponies with young stock, avoiding the inevitable welfare problems encountered by older ponies on the Forest'.[26]

HLS payments have been allocated to the New Forest amounted to some £16 million in 2010 over ten years, the largest single payment in Europe and recognising its international importance.[27] Significant payments have gone to other land owners in the New Forest including private estates, other landowners, the Wildlife Trust (for reserves) and County Councils.

Who needs another layer of bureaucracy anyway?

While words like 'remote', 'beautiful' and even occasionally 'unspoilt' may be applied to certain of Britain's national parks; this must not obscure two key points: England and Wales contains national park landscapes that are the consequence of human activity (generally agriculture or woodland management), and this human activity since at least the mid-twentieth century has included ever growing numbers of visitors. For comparison, the relatively small Peak District (area 1437 km^2, population 38,000) is ringed with large towns and cities including Sheffield, Manchester, Leeds, Stoke-on-Trent, Derby and Nottingham, all of which within relatively easy reach, and therefore receives around 8.4 million visitors per year.[28] Consequently the Peak District suffers badly from visitor pressures, including footpath erosion.

The New Forest (with an area of only *c.*570 km^2) is easily accessible from Portsmouth, Bournemouth and Poole, Southampton and Salisbury and accessible to visitors from further away including the London conurbation. With a resident population around 34,400 and a population density of 60.4 persons per km^2 (second only to the South Downs NP), the number of visitors per year is astounding, perhaps 20 million.[29] Actually, one reason proffered for the establishment of the South Downs NP was the number of local authorities; the New Forest on the other hand is largely within the New Forest District Council, and there are the Verderers' Courts who are dedicated to maintaining fairly the traditional ways.[30] However, are governance issues *otherwise* so complicated as to require a new, dedicated body? Visitor pressure alone, while good for business, is eye-wateringly great in the forest. There are many well-to-do residents within the New Forest, contrasting not only with the past, but also representing powerful resident and economic interest groups. Hence it is an exemplar of not only the imperative to conserve habitat, biodiversity and landscape but also the very human need of community inclusion.

Crown privileges were curbed by *New Forest Act* of 1877, leaving a reformed but nonetheless ancient form of governance to be seen in the Verderers' Court at Lyndhurst and, like the Forest of Dean, no legal disafforestation occurred. There is sense in modern notions of the 'vert' and 'venison' in conservation (but including the famous ponies) being retained. The verderers consist of ten officials: an official verderer, another elected by the Forestry Commission, five elected members and a further three appointed by Defra, Natural England and the National Park.[31] In 2011, the court met monthly. The five agisters are employed by the verderers and have specific functions, mostly related to watching over livestock and their compounds. In a sense, the medieval and Tudor roles have been collapsed into 15 officials, however critics (of the national park) have claimed it had worked well enough to date.

A 1991 National Parks Review Panel Report (*Edwards Committee Report*[32]), endorsed the view that the New Forest is a prime candidate for national park status, noting that a 'tailor made constitution' was required and comprised an informal grouping of the verderers, Nature Conservancy Council and local authorities (that is no Whitehall or other formal support was at this stage involved). It proposed that the New Forest needed a 'tailor made' national park. The problem was defining what is needed. The Countryside Commission (1992) not only listed the listed the New Forest among protected Areas as The New Forest Heritage Area; it could roundly assert:

> 'The New Forest Heritage Area should be recognised at Government level as requiring special protection, being of the highest national and international importance and of equal status with the National Parks and the Broads'.[33]

Next, in 1993, the New Forest was designated a Wetland of International Importance under the Ramsar Convention, and also a Special Area of Conservation (SAC) under the EC Habitat's Directive for conservation of particular species (honey buzzard, Montagu's harrier, kingfisher, woodlark, nightjar and Dartford warbler.[34]

Such developments were confirmed in 1994, by virtue of a statement from the government, the New Forest Heritage Area was given comparable planning protection policies as existing national parks, following public consultation. In the same year, the New Forest Association produced 'An Agenda for the Forest's Future', setting out the association's policies and priorities. Two years later, 'A Strategy for the New Forest' was produced by the New Forest Committee and this recognised the European importance of the area.[35]

In 1999 John Prescott, then deputy Prime Minister, announced the government's intention to designate the New Forest as a national park; in October of that year the Countryside Commission commenced work on identifying a boundary. However, seen by some as a party political issue, there was actually support from across the political spectrum.[36]

In 2001, the Forestry Commission produced its management plan for the crown lands of the New Forest 2001–2006 and 'Forest Friendly Farming' was set up by the New Forest Committee in order to develop support for farming, for commoning and also woodland management. In the following year, the designation order for the New Forest National Park was published under the *National Parks and Access to the Countryside Act* 1949. Then, in 2003, the public inquiry into the designation concluded and the New Forest Trust, which seeks to secure the future of the forest for those who live and work in it, was established. The *Parliament Act* was invoked in 2004 to push through the *Hunting Act*, which banned hunting with hounds. Finally, the New Forest Hounds, formed in 1781, has continued as a trail hunt.[37]

With the policy instruments and widespread, if not universal support for its mission, the NFNPA was established 1 March 2005. This was originally chaired by Dr Ted Johnson, who handed over the chair to Clive Chatters, a seasoned conservationist who works for the Hampshire and Isle of Wight Wildlife Trust.

Evolving governance and its dissenters

The answer to the question posed in the heading of the last section is rhetorical: 'Perhaps for the first time, the NFNPA there was an agency that could champion the whole forest'.[38]

This is something that has to be reflected in governance arrangements. The members of the NFNPA are the people with overall responsibility for making decisions. They are responsible for setting policies and priorities ensuring efficient, and effective, use of resources and that money. It is their job to represent the interests of the national park and to balance out any conflicting pressures. The outcome is a NFNPA of 22 members, these being:[39]

- Twelve appointed by the county, district, and borough councils with land within the national park. They provide local knowledge and expertise, without representing only their own local authority. Five come from Hampshire County Council, four from New Forest District Council, one from Test Valley Borough Council and two from the newly formed Wiltshire County Council.
- Six appointed by the Secretary of State for Environment, Food and Rural Affairs. They bring key skills, knowledge and experience relevant to the work of the NFNPA, with a particular interest in the New Forest and a wider national viewpoint.
- Four, appointed to represent the wider national park view, not just the interest of their own parish. They ensure the truly local concerns of those who live or work in the New Forest are represented.

The resolution at the time of writing finds the verderers working in partnership with the NFNPA and the Forestry Commission.[40] Evidently this is going some way to meeting the governance objection that the 'traditional' means of regulation are discrete from those of the modern.

Yet the National Park Governance Review was initiated by the Coalition Government in late 2010 and hence represents central government action. By mid-2014 they had placed proposed amendments to the make-up of the NFNPA's membership on the back burner, due to cost and lack of public interest.[41]

In terms of outcome nonetheless: 'The Government wishes to retain an independent authority, as currently exists, for each of the national parks and the Broads. It intends that these authorities ("the NPAs") should continue to be the local planning authority for their areas'. They were to:

- look for ways in which the governance of the NPAs can be made more effective;
- look for ways in which the NPAs can be more responsive to the concerns of their local communities (whilst still operating within the existing statutory purposes and the Spending Review 2010 budgets); and
- consider the extent to which different arrangements are appropriate for different NPAs.[42]

At the conclusion of the formative discussions, the members agreed a number of recommended changes to the governance arrangements of the Authority to improve transparency and increase local accountability, including:

- Ensuring that the criteria for the appointment of the 12 local authority members are made more transparent.
- Removing the role of the Secretary of State in formally appointing the four Parish Council members.
- Recommending that the Secretary of State consults closely with the National Park Authority, the Verderers of the New Forest and the Chair of the New Forest Consultative Panel in selecting the 'national' appointees.

It was recommended that, apart from such changes, the composition of the membership (local authority members, parish council members and the Secretary of State 'national appointees') should be retained. The size of the membership should remain at 22 to ensure there are sufficient resources to engage with local communities.[43] However, it is instructive to see, in the light of the developing NFNPA, how the chance for review was received in certain quarters. There are several recorded objections from the governance consultations.[44] Selected examples illustrate some key views.

One local resident stated that 'The New Forest NPA should be closed down and finished off'. And that 'Defra and Natural England should be radically reduced' [*sic*]. No further information in support of these contentions has been forthcoming. Others sought to improve governance in more reasoned manner. The Hampshire Association of Local Councils, while broadly supportive, expressed a view that 'Putting a restriction that any review must stay within the "existing statutory purposes" reinforces current problems relating to governance, public apathy and confusion'. 'A four tier local government structure is neither cost nor delivery effective'. A tentative suggestion might be for unitary area. Ringwood Town council similarly were concerned about the unelected nature of an NPA. For the NPA to be more locally accountable, the role of the Secretary of State should be reduced.

Community membership from parish councils and third sector organisations are vital for 'bottom-up' governance to occur.[45] Another individual expressed the view that Parish Council members should be elected by residents and not simply by the Parish Council. Someone else commented that, as a resident and a commoner living in the national park, the verderers and the Forestry Commission are critical in protecting and managing the forest. They should have guaranteed seats on the NFNPA on account of their knowledge. It was commented that the second function NPAs have is as the planning authority.

As a non-elected body this is not acceptable and should come through an elected body representing local opinion as well as national needs. A further comment added that: 'to achieve Big Society benefits, the impetus for NPA membership must spring from empowering local people not by central government election'.

Modern Tory pre-occupations against statism, and pro-voluntary action are linked in a wider political agenda favouring 'localism'. Hence, there are elements not only of the fears of 'them' versus the citizen, including attacks on bureaucracy as 'unaccountable power', but a call for integration of the traditional system of governance and a literal call for realisation of the Big Society (something that has now largely lost currency) are consistent with such a viewpoint. Subsequently, the failed policy of forest privatisation, the silence of central government around the Big Society now looks like a rather ignominious retreat, however the *Localism Act* 2011 remains[46] and it may be summarised as:

- new freedoms and flexibilities for local government
- new rights and powers for communities and individuals
- reform to make the planning system more democratic and more effective
- reform to ensure that decisions about housing are taken locally

Furthermore, such would have repercussions for the NFNPA as a planning authority, and there is an arguably welcome role for communities, local government and (one presumes) the voluntary sector. Such that a resident[47] felt moved to comment:

> 'The Government should restore democracy for the governance of the Forest. The right to a democratically elected representative on the planning authority was removed by the establishment of the Park. We were not consulted and our local councillors never advised us of the implications.'

The funding of the NFNPA will be a feature of its success or otherwise, and critics of present policy will inevitably see the 'virtue' of local empowerment that nonetheless may mask public spending cuts aimed to reducing the size of central government expenditure in the long-term.

Of course, while localism is appealing to many political persuasions, there runs the risk, in the complicated, 'multi-level governance' ranging from state agencies down to parish councils (and the verderers' courts) that issues that need to be addressed at a regional, even national level, are side-lined (this ranges from nationally enforced policy and planning guidelines and imperatives such as access and traffic problems) leaving power in the hands of local oligarchies. The hope is that the correct balance can be achieved between landscape and ecological conservation and provision of local livelihoods.

Economic and governance challenges

The NFNPA, employing around 65 staff, is still seen locally as very new idea, and like all modern national park authorities, it is the statutory local planning authority, a status that conveys real power, as is required by the *Environment Act* 1995. It presents an overall corporate plan, it should have a guaranteed income and although this is small, it is less than most wildlife trusts. Sadly the NFNPA is also vulnerable to public expenditure cuts.

Overall, as a national park, the New Forest is a communal resource, free at point of delivery. The presence of visitors to the New Forest is perhaps the single greatest challenge to its preservation. There are 4 × 4s, motor bikes, horses (and other grazers), cyclists, dogs off lead and walkers that impact not only on each other, but on footpath integrity and affect the vegetation and ecology, ground-nesting birds being a prime example. With open access, the NFNP faces problems of congestion; ultimately damage or depletion will deprive other users of the amenity – it becomes a 'subtractable resource' without suitable care. There are also problems of equity, for example measures aimed to control dogs belonging to residents, although the issue for dogs of visitors may need addressing. The political challenge is to balance the needs of all users.

This can take the form of 'wear and tear' due to visitor pressure, or developments that may be regarded as transforming the landscape and implicitly affecting, amenity, ecology, hydrology *etc.*). One early definition (1970) of carrying capacity by the Countryside Commission was: 'the level of recreation use an area can sustain without an unacceptable degree of deterioration of the character and quality of the resource or the recreation experience'.

This was followed by an identification of four types of recreational carrying capacity: physical, economic, ecological and social carrying capacity.[48] Major development proposals should be demonstrated to be in the public interest before being allowed to proceed. Consideration of such applications should therefore include an assessment of:

- The need for the development, including in terms of any national considerations, And the impact of permitting it, or refusing it, upon the local economy;
- the cost of, and scope for, developing elsewhere outside the designated area, or Meeting the need for it in some other way; and
- Any detrimental effect on the environment, the landscape and recreational opportunities, and the extent to which that could be moderated.

In 'Sustainable Development in Rural Areas', formerly *Planning Policy Guidance (PPG)* 7, sometimes called the Silkin Tests[49] applies *inter alia* to minerals. In general, approved development must be development 'in the national interest'; specifically there must be no alternative to development in a national park and development should minimise impact on the local environment. In the New Forest, sand and gravel extraction remained into the 1980s. *PPG*7 (and its successor *Planning Policy Statement (PPS)* 7) have both been formally superseded by the Government's National Planning Policy Framework (NPPF), published March 2012. However, the Framework still essentially retains the 'Silkin Test' in paragraph 116.

The only remaining mineral extraction issue affecting the national park involved plans for gravel extraction at North Gorley,[50] something that remained controversial locally, but that has ceased today. Today, it helps that the verderers are effectively a kind of 'common commissioners' in the New Forest; that is they are fully incorporated into the new governance with their role supported and recognised. The need for a 'whole forest' champion has been noted. Perhaps it is a tribute to the late Colin Tubbs that a NFNPA is in place and will be able to present the New Forest to the wider world. However, urban growth of south Hampshire need to be accommodated as it affects visitor pressure and the NFNPA's strategic and developmental role must involve liaison with Whitehall.

A wide range of occupations are present among forest dwellers. Old families are established as commoners and working in forestry and agriculture. Modern industry includes the extensive oil refinery at Fawley. Traditional commoners are concerned that the grazing economy could collapse, and because the landscape relies upon grazing more than any other single factor, maintenance of this is central with the number of livestock carefully regulated; however at the time of writing, the number of branding of animals seems fairly stable. The development of new markets for produce is always welcome.

The responses to consultation noted above reflects a strong libertarian outlook, perhaps redolent of a sense of independence inherited from a complicated 'forest economy' of the past, yet ironically with upwards of 34,000 residents it is effectively an urban economy reflecting a predominantly a dormitory function with out-migration, especially to Bournemouth and Southampton. On a daily basis, there is an influx of poorer service sector workers, as part of the amenity-based service economy is inevitably strong, but not limited to traditional system, as there a whole range of whole range of service activities. Thus there is room for further clashes, for example how is localism to link to commoners' agenda? Otherwise, like the rest of southern England, care homes, hospitality, retired people, commuters, and of course recreation of various kinds will continue to dominate the economy and society of the New Forest but without regard for economic integration and impact in a fragile area.

For example, commoners' rights are bought and sold and linked to individual houses meaning there is a property qualification to graze. The purchase price of cottages is way beyond the purchasing power of many. Yet, only a small proportion (no more than 3%) of 'quaint' or otherwise prestige properties remain in part-time occupation or as holiday lets. And while the crown owns the land there are around 50 other landowners present. The price of agricultural land within the perambulation seems fairly constant. To tackle housing shortages, the controversial Homes for Hope, may provide a means of providing cheap housing, although there are emerging fears about where the new homes are located, with CPRE already expressing its concern.[51]

The Crown Estate is a property portfolio owned by the Crown, although it is managed by the Crown Estate Commissioners on a commercial basis and cannot be regarded as the private property of the monarch since Edmund Burke's reforms of 1760. It is accountable to Parliament and surplus revenue thus generated is payable to the treasury, that is after the cost of running the estate itself and paying for the monarchy.[52] By a slight of constitutional hand that maybe deflects criticism from English republicans, it is actually a 'statutory corporation'; it is also one of the largest property owners in the United Kingdom, with a portfolio worth £7 billion in 2011. Among it is the New Forest. Nonetheless, historically, it is state interests that dominate, as witnessed by the Forestry Commission, and before that the Office of Woods, managing the crown lands in the New Forest on the crown's behalf. Yet, ramifications on the proposed 'privatisation' as it may affect the New Forest continued well into 2011 in what may not have been a well thought-through agenda for privatising crown land.[53]

With the agreement of most stakeholders, the NFNPA appears in a political sense to improve local democracy in its actions, in response to local concerns over the powers that are invested in this latecomer. The Authority's members gave detailed consideration to all of the consultation responses and debated at length both the issues contained therein and various proposals and ideas suggested by members at the meeting.

New governance arrangements permit new partnerships, and these potentially embrace not only nationally important state agencies, the voluntary sector but also the engagement of communities. A significant landscape and ecological project within the forest relates to the LIFE III hydrological restorations[54] including a Special Conservation area (SAC). The heathland/grassland/mire mosaic is the largest single unit of similar habitat remaining in lowland England, totalling 14,800 ha and is, in its complexity, unique in Europe. In addition there is over 4000 ha of pasture woodland, the largest remaining woodland of its type in Western Europe. There are rare habitats such as alder woodlands on floodplains and bog woodlands that survive within relatively pristine and unpolluted catchments.

New partnerships in hydrological projects? A case example

LIFE III commissioned surveys of the hydrology, geomorphology, topography, fish and aquatic insects were carried out along sections of the Lymington River by the Environment Agency (EA): to inform the partners of the state of the river before restoration; to aid the preparation of work plans and identify priority areas for river restoration. Additionally, the Forestry Commission (FC) mapped out the areas of priority wetland habitat to be restored. These were riverine and bog woodland, mires and wet grassland (also known locally as 'lawns'). Bog woodland is an increasingly rare habitat that is to be found on peat and where the ground flora is significant as well as the deciduous trees, especially birch. Restoration along streams has included the removal of conifers, such as also along Dockens Water.

There are six water catchments in the New Forest: Avon Water (flowing south-eastwards towards Lymington), the Lymington River (adjacent to this also flowing south-east), Beaulieu River (again adjacent to Lymington River and also flowing south-east), Bartley Water (flowing eastwards), the Cadnam River (in the north) and the Hampshire Avon tributaries (along the west side). Problems identified include weakly integrated management of the habitats in water basins, a lack of awareness of the significance of certain New Forest habitats, damage to the hydrological system including bogs by drainage and watercourse straightening, and native and non-native invasive species requiring management or eradication. The main objective is to establish long term sustainability of habitats through the development of integrated management of the main water basins. In this is regeneration of priority habitats.

The 'Sustainable Wetland Restoration in the New Forest' project builds on the success of the earlier New Forest LIFE II project that ran between 1997 and 2001, it was designed to implement innovative techniques for natural river channel and mire restoration, although resistance to the reversal of historical drainage was disappointing[55] and there was much success in restoration of woodland and heathland habitats, with financial incentives for horse grazing. LIFE III aimed to develop a better understanding of the hydrological networks that support these habitats and establish their long-term sustainability through the development of integrated management for the main New Forest water basins. A major requirement is to preserve mires and high water table tables, as well as restore natural watercourses. LIFE III is a project partnership (Natural England, Environment Agency, Royal Society for the Protection of Birds, Forestry Commission, National Trust and Hampshire County Council) that is funded by the European Commission and ran between 2002 and 2006. This has been judged successful over considerable areas of the New Forest as it restored vulnerable habitats and encouraged wildlife.

Between 2003 and 2006, 10 km of rivers were restored, mainly on the upper Lymington River, specifically the Black Water and Highland Water. Old meanders were reconnected using clay plugs to block off straightened channels, and river bed levels raised to reverse past overdeepening and headward erosion (Fig. 9.3). Also, wood debris dams reduce flow rates and encourage seasonal flooding. This is a pioneer project in the forest, and is of country-wide significance.

All-in-all, LIFE III has restored a total of:

- 261 ha of riverine woodland
- 18 ha of bog woodland
- 141 ha of wet grassland
- 184 ha of valley mires and
- 10 km of rivers

A Water Basin Management Forum was established to help advise and guide the production of integrated project work plans, in co-operation with a wide range of landowners and managers, technical experts and local interest groups. It aims to facilitate a more integrated planning and management of catchments within the Project and to assist the partners in delivery of the Project. Looking to the future, this new body will have consultation, information gathering, awareness raising within the wider community, including participation.

FIGURE 9.3. Wetland and restored river section near to Brockenhurst. River restoration projects aim to restore wetland areas and meandering river sections.

PHOTO: AUTHOR

Conclusions

The NFNP has come at a good time because of a need to manage the area 'holistically'. While we may presume the boundary of the New Forest reflects current pre-occupations around economic development and conservation, and because the boundary of the New Forest National Park was established following a detailed public enquiry, it is highly unlikely the government will review it again in the short term. There remain environmental challenges, from visitor pressure, from restoration of the hydrology of the New Forest to a pre-Forestry Commission drainage condition, and the removal of conifers in favour of broadleaved woodland.

To give a voice for the entire forest is essential and it also emerges at a time when 'localism' and community engagement is high on the political agenda and across the board. Community participation, something anathema to environmental governance until the closing decades of the last century, will need to be realised through the involvement of local government, voluntary sector action and those representing recreation interests.

There are some real signs of cooperation within the National Park. Different stakeholders, including the commoners, agisters, verders and hopefully the

Forestry Commission are converging in their objectives. The New Forest Association now promotes itself as the Friends of the New Forest:

> 'For 150 years we have been dedicated to ensuring the long-term protection of the special qualities of the Forest, including its flora, fauna and cultural heritage.'[56]

There is also the 'urban economy'. This, it might be argued, is by far the largest consideration, even if perceived impact does not always relate so romantically (and practically) with the ecology and landscape. It may be that in governance terms, the strong tradition of local independence will actually provide the momentum for responsible management with the NFNPA providing the ways, means and lubrication in the process. One can hope that the days of major marginalised communities is receding, yet there remains resentment about high house prices, only affordable for 'incomers' in the main. If the complexity of legislation, boundary definitions for conservation designations, fears of a new *Divisum Imperium* (this time between the verderers' system and the NFNPA) seem complicated, it would merely reflect the *realpolitik*.

The present position is that we value the New Forest for being a largely medieval landscape, for its range of valuable habits and for its recreations and amenity values. Production agriculture was never destined to be a success over much of the area, because it was selected (one presumes) as a playground for the King and his retinue, where manorial returns were poor. The irony of history is that the Crown Estate is a close thing to nationalised land, and recent efforts to privatise woodlands fell foul of media and public opinion. This governmental debacle almost certainly leaves the forest as a common property resource, no longer for hunting, nor intensive timber production, but for visitor appreciation. Time will tell. But the portents for the NFNP look good.

Notes

1. The quote recalls Article Eight of the *Assize of the Forest* (Chapter 4).
2. Defra (2005) *Establishment of the New Forest National Park Authority.* http://archive.defra.gov.uk/rural/documents/national-parks/south-downs/estab-newforest-npa.pdf.
3. Hampshire and Isle of Wight Wildlife Trust http://www.hiwwt.org.uk/ accessed Sept 2017
4. National Trust helps to shape New Forest's future http://www.lymington.org/features/nationaltrust.html. Accessed Sept 2013.
5. Cultural History of the New forest (2017) https://www.forestry.gov.uk/forestry/INFD-6A4KPD. Accesssed Sept 2017; Hands off our Forests (2011) http://www.handsoffourforest.org/documents/submissionlight.pdf. Accessed Sept 2017.
6. http://www.hwt.org.uk/pages/the-wildlife-trust-in-the-forest.html. Accessed Nov 2012.
7. NFNPA (n.d.) *60 years in the New Forest.* http://www.newforestnpa.gov.uk/about-us/links/national-parks/diamonds-in-the-landscape/60-anniversary-timeline.
8. Clive Chatters (2011) pers. comm.
9. H. Cook and A. Inman (2012) The voluntary sector and conservation for England: achievements, expanding roles and uncertain future. *Journal of Environmental Management* 112, 170–77.

10. The aims and purpose of National Parks. http://www.nationalparks.gov.uk/learningabout/whatisanationalpark/aimsandpurposesofnationalparks.htm. Accessed Sept 2017.
11. J. Sheail (2002) *An Environmental History of the Twentieth Century*, 115. Palgrave, London.
12. Defra (1995) *op. cit.* in note 2.
13. New Forest District Council (2006) http://www.newforestnpa.gov.uk/__data/assets/pdf_file/0003/27345/sustainability_scoping_report.pdf. Accessed Sept 2017.
14. The North Solent NNR Sept 2017
15. NFNP (2007) http://www.newforestnpa.gov.uk/__data/assets/pdf_file/0004/26653/conservation1-forweb.pdf. Accessed June 2013.
16. New Forest District Council (2006) *op. cit.* in note 13.
17. The New Forest National Park Map (n.d.) http://mappery.com/The-New-Forest-National-Park-Map. Accessed Sept 2017.
18. Royal Courts of Justice (2005) http://webarchive.nationalarchives.gov.uk/20130403042325/http://archive.defra.gov.uk/rural/documents/national-parks/np-meyrick-judgement.pdf. Accessed Sept 2017.
19. Common Rights (2007) http://www.newforest.hampshire.org.uk/today1.html.
20. New Forest Commoners Defence Association (n.d.) http://www.nfcda.co.uk/ accessed Oct 2012.
21. New Forest Association (n.d.) *A History of the New Forest and its Adjacent Commons.* New Forest Association, Fordingbridge.
22. New forest Commoning review (2007) http://www.dartmoor-npa.gov.uk/__data/assets/pdf_file/0005/4874/recommendationsreduced.pdf.
23. K. Stearne (2013) pers. comm.
24. Environmental Stewardship (2015) http://www.naturalengland.org.uk/ourwork/farming/funding/es/default.aspx. Accessed Sept 2013.
25. Higher Level Stewardship Scheme (2017) http://www.hlsnewforest.org.uk/. Accessed Sept 2017.
26. Verderers' Grazing scheme (2016) http://www.verderers.org.uk/css.html. Accessed Sept 2017.
27. Higher Level Stewardship (n.d.) http://www.newforestnpa.gov.uk/info/20094/commoning/179/higher_level_stewardship. Accessed Sept 2017.
28. National Parks Facts and Figures (2017) http://www.nationalparks.gov.uk/press/factsandfigures.htm. Accessed Sept 2017.
29. New Forest LIFE (2003) http://www.newforestlife.org.uk/. Accessed Sept 2017.
30. Kathy Stearne (2013) pers. comm.
31. Verderers' Court (2002) http://www.verderers.org.uk/court.html. Accessed Sept 2017.
32. R. Edwards (1991) *Fit for the Future*, Countryside Commission, Cheltenham.
33. Protected Landscapes in the UK (1992) Countryside Commission, Cheltenham http://www.archive.org/details/protectedlandsca92ukco. Accessed Sept 2017.
34. NFNPA (n.d.) *op. cit.* in note 7.
35. *Ibid.* and NFNPA (2005) http://www.legislation.gov.uk/uksi/2005/421/pdfs/uksiem_20050421_en.pdf. Accessed Sept 2017.
36. Clive Chatters (2011) pers. comm.
37. NFNPA (n.d.) *op. cit.* in note 7.
38. Clive Chatters (2011) pers. comm.
39. NFNPA (2017) http://www.newforestnpa.gov.uk/info/20012/our_people/79/members. Accessed Sept 2017.
40. New Forest Grazing Scheme (2012) http://www.verderers.org.uk/css.html.

41. Review of National Park governance: implementation update (2013). https://www.gov.uk/government/publications/review-of-national-park-governance-implementation-update. Accessed Sept 2017.
42. Defra (2010) *Consulatation on the National Parks and the Broads.* http://webarchive.nationalarchives.gov.uk/20121205132440/http://archive.defra.gov.uk/corporate/consult/nationalpark-governance/101109-nationalpark-governance-condoc.pdf. Accessed Sept 2017.
43. New Forest National Park (2011) Meeting 10 February 2011 http://www.newforestnpa.gov.uk/_data/assets/pdf_file/0003/76125/nfnpa_368_11_governance_review-2.pdf. Accessed Sept 2012.
44. *Ibid.*
45. *Ibid.*
46. *A Plain English Guide to the Localism Bill – Update* (2011) http://www.communities.gov.uk/publications/localgovernment/localismplainenglishguide. Accessed June 2013.
47. NFNP (2011) *op. cit.* in note 43.
48. Countryside Agency (2005) *Promoting Outdoor Activities in the English National Parks.* Countryside Agency, Cheltenham.
49. National Park Management Plans Guidance (2007) http://www.pembrokeshirecoast.org.uk/files/files/Conservation/Conservation%20publications/National%20parks%20final%20English.PDF CCC 248. Accessed June 2013.
50. Hampshire Minerals Plan (2008) http://www3.hants.gov.uk/eliminated_sites_reportv1.pdf. Accessed June 2013.
51. *Daily Echo* (2012) http://www.bournemouthecho.co.uk/news/opinion/9374646.New_homes_with_new_hope/.
52. Crown Estate (2017) https://www.thecrownestate.co.uk/who-we-are/. Accesssed Sept 2017.
53. NFNPA (2011) http://www.newforestnpa.gov.uk/__data/assets/pdf_file/0009/126666/NPA-response-to-Forestry-Panels-Call-for-Views.pdf. Accessed Sept 2017.
54. LIFE III (2003) http://www.newforestlife.org.uk/life3/life3index.htm. Accessed Sept 2017.
55. T. Holzer and M. Elliott (2010) The Contribution of the LIFE II and III Projects to Wetland Conservation in the New Forest. In A. C. Newton (ed.), *Biodiversity in the New Forest*, 199–201. Pices Publications, Newbury.
56. Friends of the New Forest/New Forest Association. newforestassociation.org. Accessed Sept 2017.

Bibliography

Allen, M. J. (1996) Landscape and Land-use: priorities in Hampshire, 500,000 BC to AD 1500. In D. A. Hinton and M. Hughes (eds), *Archaeology in Hampshire: a framework for the future*, 55–70. Hampshire County Council, Winchester.

Allen, M. J. (2000) Soils, pollen and a lot of snails. In M. Green, *A Landscape Revealed. 10,000 Years on a Chalkland Farm*. Tempus, Stroud.

Baker, C. A. (2001) *The Companion to British History* (2nd edn). Routledge, London.

Baker, C. A., Moxey, P. A. and Oxford, P. M. (1978) Woodland continuity and change in Epping Forest. *Field Studies* 4, 645–69.

Barber, K. E. (1975) Vegetation history of the New Forest: a preliminary note. *Proceedings of the Hampshire Field Club and Archaeological Society* 30, 5–8.

Barber, K. E. (1981) Pollen analytical palaeoecology in Hampshire: problems and potential. In S. Shennan and T. Schadla-Hall (eds), *The Archaeology of Hampshire*, 91–94. Hampshire Field Club and Archaeological Society Monograph 1, Winchester.

Barton, C. M., Hopson, P. M., Newell, A. J. and Royse, K. R. (2003) *Geology of the Ringwood District and Geological Sheet* 314. British Geological Survey, Keyworth.

Barton, N. S. Ford, S. Collcutt, J. Crowther, R. Macphail, E. Rhodes and A. van Gijn (2009) A Final Upper Palaeolithic site at Nea Farm, Somerley, Hampshire (England) and some reflections on the occupation of Britain in the Late Glacial Interstadial. *Quartär* 56, 7–35.

Baskerville, M. (2009) The use of land at Buckholt, a Hampshire Royal Forest from 1200–1900. *Proceedings of the Hampshire Field Club and Archaeological Society* 64, 200–22.

Bathe, G. (2013) Of Commoners and Kings. In: Rotherham, I. (ed.) *Cultural Severance and the Environment. Environmental History* vol 2. Springer, Dordrecht, 177–190. DOI https://doi.org/10.1007/978-94-007-6159-9_12.

Baxter, S. (2011) Lordship and labour. In J. Crick and E van Houts (eds), *A Social History of England 900–1200*, 98–114. Cambridge University Press, Cambridge.

Blith, W. (1649/1652) *The English Improver Improved, or the Survey of Husbandry Surveyed* (2nd edn). Printed for John Wright, London.

Bond, J. (1994) Forests, chases, warrens and parks in medieval Wessex. In M. Ashton and C. Lewis (eds), *The Medieval Landscape of Wessex*, 116, 130. Oxbow Monograph 6, Oxbow Books, Oxford.

Brandon, P. (1998) *The South Downs*. Phillimore, Chichester.

Broad, J. (2000) Housing the rural poor in southern England 1650–1850. *Agricultural History Review* 48(2), 151–70.

Brown, R. A., Colvin, H. M. and Taylor, A. J. (1963) *History of the King's Works* Vol. I. HMSO, London.

Buckley, G. P. (ed.) (1992) the Ecology and management of coppice woodland. Chapman and Hall, London 336pp.

Chatters, C. and Read, M. (2006) *The New Forest National Park*. Halscrow, Tiverton.

Clark, M. J. and Barber, K. E. (1987) *Mire Development from the Devensian Late-glacial to Present at Church Moor Hampshire*, 22–32. Wessex and the Isle of Wight Field Guide, Quaternary Research Association, Cambridge.

Clarke, A (2003) The Roman road on the eastern fringe of the New Forest, from Shorn Hill to Lepe. *Proceedings of the Hampshire Field Club and Archaeological Society* 58, 33–58.

Cobb, D. (1974) Forest trees and ships. *Proceedings of the Hampshire Field Club and Archaeological Society*, New Forest Section Report 13, 28–29.

Colebourne, P. (1983) *Ancient Woodland*. Hampshire's Countryside Heritage 2, Hampshire County Council, Winchester.

Coles, S. (2004) Three Bronze Age barrows at Mockbeggar Lane, Ibsley, Hampshire. *Proceedings of the Hampshire Field Club and Archaeological Society* 59, 31–64.

Cook, H. F. (1994) Field-scale water management in Southern England to AD 1900. *Landscape History* 16, 53–66.

Cook, H. F. (2001) Boom, slump and intervention: changing agricultural landscapes on Romney Marsh, 790 to 990. In M. P. Waller, E. Edwards and

L. Barber (eds), *Romney Marsh: Persistence and Change in a Coastal Lowland*, 55–83. Romney Marsh Research Trust, Sevenoaks.

Cook, H. F. (2008a) Evolution of a floodplain landscape: A case study of the Harnham Water Meadows at Salisbury England. *Landscapes* 9(1), 50–73.

Cook, H. F. (2008b) A tale of two catchments: water management and quality in the Wandle and Tillingbourne, 1600 to 1990. *Southern History* 2008, 78–103.

Cook, H. and Inman, A. (2012) The voluntary sector and conservation for England: achievements, expanding roles and uncertain future. *Journal of Environmental Management* 112, 170–77.

Countryside Agency (2005) *Promoting Outdoor Activities in the English National Parks*. Countryside Agency, Cheltenham.

Cunliffe, B. W. (1978) *Hengistbury Head*. Paul Elek, London.

Cunliffe, B. W. (1993) *Wessex to AD 1000*, 5–35. Longmans, London.

Deakin, R. (2008) *Wildwood: a journey through trees*. Penguin ebooks, London.

De Crespigny, R. C. and Hutchinson, H. G. (1899) *The New Forest, its Traditions, Inhabitants and Customs*. John Murray, London.

Driver, A. and Driver, W. (1794) *A General View of the Agriculture of the County of Hants*. Board of Agriculture, London.

Edwards, R. (1991) *Fit for the Future*. Countryside Commission, Cheltenham.

Evans, D. (1992) *A History of Nature Conservation in Britain*. Routledge, London.

Evelyn, J. (1664) *Sylva, or a Discourse of Forest Trees*. John Martyn, London.

Fergusson, N. (2003) *Empire*, 44. Penguin, Harmondsworth.

Findlay, D. C., Colborne, G. J. N., Cope, D. W., Harrod, T. R., Hogan, D. V. and Staines, S. J. (1984) *Soils and their Use in South West England*. Soil Survey of England and Wales, Harpenden.

Fontana, D. J. L. (2000) Survey of wooden structures around the harbour shoreline. In M. J. Allen and J. Gardiner (eds), *Our Changing Coast: a survey of the intertidal archaeology of Langstone Harbour, Hampshire*, 74–80. Council for British Archaeology Research Report 124, York.

Grant, M. J. (2005) The palaeoecology of human impact in the New Forest. Unpublished PhD Thesis, University of Southampton.

Grant, M. J. and Edwards, M. E. (2008) Conserving idealized landscapes: past history, public perception and future management in the New Forest (UK). *Vegetation History and Archaeobot*any 17, 551–62.

Green, M. (2000) *A Landscape Revealed. 10,000 Years on a Chalkland Farm*, 26. Tempus, Stroud.

Hanson, R. W. (ed.) (1992) *Epping Forest – Through the Eye of the Naturalist*. Essex Naturalist 11. Essex Field Club.

Hardy, T. (1872) *Under the Greenwood Tree*. Tinsley Bros, London.

Harvey, P. D. A. (1979) Forest Laws. In D. J. Stagg (ed.), *A Calendar of New Forest. 94 New Forest Documents AD 1244–AD 1334*, ix. Hampshire Record Series III, Hampshire County Council, Winchester.

Heywood Sumner (*c.*1930) Article later published (ed. G. F. le Pard 1999). The New Forest Deer Removal Act, 1851, and afterwards. *Hampshire Studies* 54, 75–87.

Hill, C. (1972) *The World Turned Upside Downside*. Penguin Books, London.

Hinde, T. (ed.) (1985) *The Domesday Book*. Guild Publishing, London.

Hodson, F. and West, I. M. (1972) The Holocene deposits of Fawley, Hampshire and the development of Southampton Water. *Proceedings of the Geologists' Association* 83, 421–44.

Holzer, T. and Elliott, M. (2010) The Contribution of the LIFE II and III Projects to Wetland Conservation in the New Forest. In A. C. Newton (ed.), *Biodiversity in the New Forest*, 199–201. Pisces publications, Newbury.

Hoskins, W. G. and Stamp, L. D. (1963) *The Common Lands of England and Wales*. New Naturalist, Collins, London.

Hudson, J. (1996) *The Formation of the English Common Law*, 16–20. Longmans, London.

Hurle, P. (2007) *The Forest and Chase of Malvern*. Philimore, London.

Ings, S. (2010) *Shot for a White-faced Deer*. Hobnob Press, Salisbury.

Jacobi, R. (1978) The Mesolithic of Sussex. In P. Drewett (ed.), *The Archaeology of Sussex to AD 1500*, 15–22. Council for British Archaeology Research Report 29, London.

James, T. B. and Gerrard, C. (2007) *Clarendon, Landscape of Kings*. Windgather Press, Macclesfield.

Jarvis, M. J., Allen, R. H., Fordham, S. J., Hazleden, J., Moffat, A. J. and Sturdy, R. G. (1984) *Soils and Their Use in Eastern England*. Soil Survey of England and Wales Bulletin 15. Soil Survey, Harpenden.

Jones, D. K. C. (1981) *The Geomorphology of the British Isles, Southeast and Southern England.* Methuen, London.

Keen, D. H. (1980) The environment of deposition of the south Hampshire Plateau Gravels. *Proceedings of the Hampshire Field Club and Archaeological Society* 36, 15–24.

Kerridge, E. (1967) *The Agricultural Revolution.* Allen & Unwin, London.

Kirby, K. J. (2004) A model of a natural wooded landscape in Britain as influenced by large herbivore activity. *Forestry* 77, 405–20.

Lambdin, L. C. and Lambdin, R. (eds) (1999) *Chaucer's Pilgrims: an historical guide to the Pilgrims in the Canterbury Tales.* Praeger Publishers, Santa Barbara.

Lawton, J. H., Brotherton, P. N. M., Brown, V. K., Elphick, C., Fitter, A. H., Forshaw, J., Haddow, R. W., Hilborne, S., Leafe, R. N., Mace, G. M., Southgate, M. P., Sutherland, W. J., Tew, T. E., Varley, J. and Wynne, G. R. (2010) *Making Space for Nature: a review of England's wildlife sites and ecological network.* Report to Defra. Available at http://webarchive.nationalarchives.gov.uk/20130402170324/http://archive.defra.gov.uk/environment/biodiversity/documents/201009space-for-nature.pdf. Accessed Sept 2017.

Lewis, P. (1811) *The New Forest.* T. Payne, London.

Liddiard, R. (2003) The deer parks of Domesday Book. *Landscapes* 4(1), 4–23.

Light, A. and Ponting, G. (2001) *The History of Fordingbridge.* Charlewood Press, Fordingbridge.

Manwood, J (1665) A Treatise of the Laws of the Forest. London Company of Stationers

McKay, I. (ed.) (2010) *A New Forest Reader: A Companion Guide to the New Forest, its History and Landscape.* Hatchet Green, Southampton.

M. McQuade and L. O'Donnell (2007) Late Mesolithic fish-traps from the Liffey Estuary, Dublin, Ireland, *Antiquity* 81, 569. http://connection.ebscohost.com/c/articles/27172733/late-mesolithic-fish-traps-from-liffey-estuary-dublin-ireland.

Mew, K. A. (1997) Through a Glass Darkly: the biography of a Domesday landscape, 97. Unpublished PhD thesis, University of Reading.

Midmer, R. (1979) *English Medieval Monasteries.* Hineman, London.

Miles, D. (2005) *The Tribes of Britain.* Phoenix, London.

Nash, R. F. (2001) *Wilderness and the American Mind.* Yale University Press, New Haven.

Netzloff, M. (ed.) (2010) *John Norden's A Surveyor's Dialogue 1618: a critical edition.* Ashgate, Farmham.

Neville Havins, P. J. (1976) *The Forests of England.* Robert Hale, London.

Newton, A. (ed.) (2010) *Biodiversity in the New Forest.* Pisces publications, Newbury.

New Forest Association (n.d.) *A History of the New Forest and its Adjacent Commons*, New Forest Association, Fordingbridge.

New Forest Committee (1947) *The Baker Report*, 44–45. cmd 7245 Forestry Commission London HMSO.

Nicholson, A. (2008) *The Earls of Paradise.* HarperCollins, London.

Papworth, M. (2011) *In Search of the Durotriges*, 22–26. History Press, Stroud.

Passmore, A. (1977) *Verderers of the New Forest: A history of the New Forest 1877–1977.* Pioneer Publications, Beaulieu.

Passmore, A. H. and Fortescue, K. (1989) Excavations at Dark Hat August 1988. *Proceedings of the Hampshire Field Club and Archaeolological Society,* New Forest Section 24, 14–19.

Pierre, J. and Peters, B. G. (2000) *Governance, Politics and the State.* Macmillan, Basingstoke.

Peterken, G. F. (1981) *Woodland Conservation and Management.* Chapman and Hall, London.

Peterken, G. F. (1998) *Woodland Conservation and Management*, 7. Chapman and Hall, London.

Pettit, P. A. J. (1968) *The Royal Forests of Northamptonshire: A study of their Economy 1558–1714.* Northampton Record Society, Northumberland Press, Gateshead.

Postan, M. M. (1966) *The Cambridge Economic History of Europe* I, 183. Cambridge University Press, Cambridge.

Postan, M. M. (1972) *The Medieval Economy and Society.* Penguin Books, London.

Powell, A. B. (2009) 2000 years of salt-making at Lymington, Hampshire. *Proceedings of the Hampshire Field Club and Archaeological Society* 64, 9–40.

Preston, E. and Wallis, S. (2006) *The Forest of Bere.* Devon Books, Devon Books, Halsgrove, Wellington.

Rackham, O. (1986) *The History of the Countryside.* Dent, London.

Rackham, O. (2006) *Woodlands.* Collins, London.

Reeves, R. (2007) *Preservation and Decay. New Forest Documents 1565–1624*, xl. New Forest Record Series V. New Forest Ninth Centenary Trust, Fordingbridge.

Reeves, R. (2008) *To Enquire and Conspire, New Forest Documents 1533–1615*, xxxviii. New Forest Record Series V, New Forest Ninth Centenary Trust, Fordingbridge.

Reeves, R. P. (2010) The administration of large holdings in the New Forest 1130–*c*.1430. Unpublished MA thesis, University of Winchester.

Roberts, P. (2001) Elizabethan conservators of the New Forest, *Hampshire Studies* 56, 246–53.

Roberts, P. (2002) *Minstead: life in a New Forest community*, 84–85. Nova Foresta Publishing, Lyndhurst.

Rook, T. (2002) *Roman Baths in Britain*. Shire Archaeology, Princes Risboro'.

Rose, F. (1953) A survey of the ecology of the British lowland bogs. *Proceedings of the Linnean Society of London* 164, 186–211.

Sheail, J. (2002) *An Environmental History of the Twentieth Century*. Palgrave, London.

Smith, L. (2004) *Romany Nevi-Wesh: An Informal History of the New Forest Gypsies*. Nova Foresta Publishing, Lyndhurst.

Smith, N. (1999) The earthwork remains of enclosure in the New Forest. *Proceedings of the Hampshire Field Club and Archaeological Society* 54, 1–56.

Smith, R. M. (2008) *Social Security as a Developmental Institution? Extending the Solar Case for the Relative Efficacy of Poor Relief Provisions under the English Old Poor Law*. Brooks World Povety Institute, University of Manchester BWPI Working Paper 56.

Stagg, D. J. (1974a) The New Forest in Domesday Book. *Proceedings of the Hampshire Field Club and Archaeological Society*, New Forest Section 13, 20–24.

Stagg, D. J. (1974b) A perambulation of the New Forest 1217–1218. *Proceedings of the Hampshire Field Club and Archaeological Society*, New Forest Section 13, 26–27.

Stagg, D. J. (1974c) The *Orders and Rules of the New Forest* AD 1537. *Proceedings of the Hampshire Field Club and Archaeological Society*, New Forest Section Report 13, 33–38.

Stagg, D. J. (1979) *A Calendar of New Forest Documents AD 1244–1334*. Hampshire Record Series III, Hampshire County Council, Winchester.

Stagg, D. J. (1983a) *A Calendar of New Forest Documents: the Fifteenth to Seventeenth Centuries*, xvi. Hampshire Record Series V, Hampshire County Council, Winchester.

Stagg, D. J. (1983b) *Snake Catchers of the New Forest*. New Forest Association, Stockbridge.

Stagg, D. J. (1984a) *Verderers of the New Forest*, 2. New Forest Association, Stockbridge.

Stagg, D. J. (1984b) *Verders of the New Forest* 3. New Forest Association, Stockbridge.

Stagg, D. J. (1986) *Commoners of the New Forest* 3, 5–6. New Forest Association, Stockbridge.

Stagg, D. J. (1989) Silviculture inclosure in the New Forest to 1780. *Proceedings of the Hampshire Field Club and Archaeological Society* 45, 135–45.

Stagg, D. J. (1990) Silvicultural inclosures in the New Forest from 780 to 850. *Hampshire Studies* 46, 3–143.

Stagg, D. J. (1992) Silvicultural inclosures in the New Forest from 1850 to 1877. *Hampshire Studies* 48, 143–59.

Story, J. (2003) *Carolingian Connections: Anglo-Saxon England and Caroligian Francia 750–850*. Ashgate, Farnham.

Szabó, P. (2009) Open woodland in Europe in the Mesolithic and in the Middle Ages: can there be a connection? *Forest Ecology and Management* 257, 2327–30.

Thirsk, J. (1997) *Alternative Agriculture*. Oxford University Press, Oxford.

Tubbs, C. (2001) *New Forest, the History, Ecology and Conservation*. New Forest Ninth Centenary Trust, Fordingbridge.

Tubbs, C. R. and Dimbleby, G. W. (1965) Early agriculture in the New Forest. *Advances in Science* 22, 88–97.

Tuckfield, G. C. (1986). A study of dells in the New Forest, Hampshire, *England Earth Surface Processes and Landforms* 11, 23–40.

Vallance, E. (2009) *A Radical History of Britain*, 172–202. Abacus, London.

Vera, F. W. M. (2000) *Grazing Ecology and Forest History*. CABI, Wallingford.

Vesey-Fitzgerald, B. S. (1966) *Portrait of the New Forest*. Robert Hale, London.

Victoria County History, Hampshire and the Isle of Wight 2. HMSO, London.

Vinogradoff, P. (1924) Feudalism. In J. B. Barry, J. R. Tanner, C. W. Previte-Orton and Z. N. Brooke (eds), *Cambridge Medieval History* Vol 3, 458–84. Cambridge University Press, Cambridge.

Wilson, R. C. L., Drury, S. A. and Chapman, J. L. (2000) *The Great Ice Age*. Routledge, London.

Wise, J. (1883) *The New Forest, its History and Scenery*. Southeran, London.

Yates, E. M. (1985) *The Landscape of the New Forest in Medieval Times*. Dept of Geography, Kings College London.

Yorke, B. (1995) *Wessex in the Early Middle Ages*, 11. Leicester University Press, Leicester.

Young, C. R. (1979) *The Royal Forests of Medieval England*. University of Pennsylvania Press, Pennsylvania.

Index

See also Glossary of Historic Terms, pp. xiii–xxii.
Italicised page numbers refer to illustrations.